W9-CFO-326

THE ASSOCIATIVE ECONOMY

The Associative Economy

Insights beyond the Welfare State and into Post-Capitalism

Franco Archibugi
Professor in the Postgraduate School of Public Administration
Prime Minister's Office
Rome, Italy

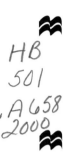

First published in Great Britain 2000 by
MACMILLAN PRESS LTD
Houndmills, Basingstoke, Hampshire RG21 6XS and London
Companies and representatives throughout the world

A catalogue record for this book is available from the British Library.

ISBN 0–333–75132–9

First published in the United States of America 2000 by
ST. MARTIN'S PRESS, INC.,
Scholarly and Reference Division,
175 Fifth Avenue, New York, N.Y. 10010

ISBN 0–312–22380–3

Library of Congress Cataloging-in-Publication Data
Archibugi, Franco.
The associative economy : insights beyond the welfare state and
into post-capitalism / Franco Archibugi.
p.   cm.
Includes bibliographical references and index.
ISBN 0–312–22380–3 (cloth : alk. paper)
1. Capitalism.   2. Welfare state.   3. Social change.
4. Production (Economic theory)   I. Title.
HB501.A658   1999
330.1—dc21   99–32866
                                                          CIP

This book is printed on paper suitable for recycling and made from fully managed and
sustained forest sources.

10   9   8   7   6   5   4   3   2   1
09   08   07   06   05   04   03   02   01   00

Printed and bound in Great Britain by
Antony Rowe Ltd, Chippenham, Wiltshire

Contents

List of Tables and Figures

Tables

Figure

Preface

Gunnar Myrdal back in 1960 published (following a series of lectures held at Yale University in 1958) a 'little book', which he entitled *Beyond the Welfare State: Economic Planning in the Welfare States and its International Implications*.[1]

Almost forty years separate us from this work, and yet I feel I can still recommend its reading, because of its continuing topicality. In it, to be brief, the 'crisis' of the Welfare State was *predicted* in 'rich and progressive Western countries', unless the development of these countries was accompanied by the development of economic planning methods and integrated on an international scale.

This fundamental contribution by Myrdal has been almost ignored in the course of the wider debate which has taken place (in particular in the last two decades) on the 'crisis' and 'future' of the Welfare State.[2]

This book does not intend to be other than a revisitation of the basic thesis of Myrdal, in the light of the further present development of the rich and progressive Western societies, and of the advancing crisis of the Welfare State. It is my opinion that the current debate on the crisis and future of the Welfare State and the possibilities of 'resolving' this crisis does not grasp any of the essential aspects of the changes which have intervened in the economy and in the structure of Western societies, and that this debate has not produced yet a clear vision (of Myrdal's type) of the appropriate routes which would need to be followed by governments of all types – whether left or right wing – in order to face the real needs for adaptation to the changes *in fieri*: starting from the introduction of techniques and procedures of decision-making at the various levels of political and public responsibility. These techniques and procedures I and others continue to call – as did Myrdal in his time – economic and social planning.[3]

The current debate, on the other hand, although not devoid of interesting aspects here and there, seems instead obsessively paralyzed with various arguments and versions, by the *vexata quaestio* of the limits and failures, either of the 'market' or of the 'state', or of the non-market or non-state, i.e., a continued rigmarole in favour of or against public intervention, and how 'mixed' the private and public economy should be. And this occurs without taking into consideration the substantial or 'real' objectives to be achieved; and how they should be achieved and through which suitable instruments and inevitable alternative choices (called 'Public Policies') by public decision-makers or institutions.

Myrdal's basic thesis, therefore, pervades the whole development of this book.

The arguments developed here are based on a report[4] prepared for the European Commission, in the framework of a task force of the European University Institute at Florence, coordinated by Stuart Holland, and commissioned by Jacques Delors, suggesting ways of applying the objectives of the Union for 'the strengthening of social and economic cohesion in the Union itself'. But the more distant basis for the arguments is found in Myrdal's approach, and in its continuing perfected application – on my part – in a series of circumstances in which the analysis starts from different points of view.[5]

Thus, as a first point of view, the crisis of the Welfare State is seen as a *crisis of social integration*; for even though its intention was to accomplish just such a social integration, on the contrary, the various forms of social protection seem paradoxically to 'segregate' even more the 'protected categories' of the elderly, women, the young, the unemployed, the new immigrants, rather than integrate them socially. From this has arisen – in the first introductory chapter – a first brief examination of the fields of intervention aimed at their integration.

A second point of view is that the Welfare State is in crisis because of the *structural changes* in the capitalist economy during the second half of this century, founded essentially on the basic changes in the final demand of the citizens. It is from this point of view that the analysis of these changes begin.

Thus, closely linked to the previous point of view (of which it constitutes a corollary), a view of a Welfare State highly dependent on changes in production structures and in the labour market, which are determined by the advent of a 'tertiary' or 'service' society (or whatever name it may be given), is developed.

Such an analysis cannot help but lead to the feasible and tendentious routes for the rational correction of the past errors of the Welfare State by:

- the recommendation of general strategies aimed at overcoming, in particular, the role and significance of economic planning;
- the design of a new employment and production model, which I have called the 'associative economy', but which has had many other designations ('third sector', 'social economy', 'independent' sector, 'non-profit' sector, the 'non-mercantile' private sector, etc.);
- finally the discussion of the set of measures of economic policy and involvement of the social partners (trade unions, employers, consumer associations, profit and non-profit organizations) through collective bargaining, in designing the new employment and production model, and societal model.

In this book I have moved, along Myrdal's lines, towards the conviction and realization that the Welfare State cannot have any autonomous future *if separated from the planning process* that is indispensable to its rational management, and unless it is accompanied by a process of domestic and international social integration. From these objective conditions of the

Welfare State, we have so far had, in this second half of the century, only very poor results.

Nobody would dare to deny that the successes obtained by the Welfare States are remarkable: but it would be a big mistake to ignore the disorder, incongruence, and latent risks which would still exist in advanced industrial societies if they are not able to '*socialize*' their successes, take steps towards a *reduction of poverty, and a redistribution of employment and income opportunities*, not only within each society, but in relation to the growth of the entire population of the world, with a *shortening of the distances* and a *substantial economic integration on a planetary scale.* Exactly as Myrdal indicated forty years ago.

With this book I hope to give an updated contribution to the reading of the situation, inspired by Myrdal's approach, to analyze some action proposals from those in government, trade unions and politics. The reflections which it contains – inspired by the three points of view evoked above – hinge on three essential points:

– On what conditions and in which forms can we pass from the model of 'social protection' to that of better 'social integration' (while moving from the Welfare State to a Welfare Society)? (Introductory chapter)
– What are the factors of structural change that strongly condition the ways of the transition to the Welfare Society (while moving from a 'capitalist' to a 'post-capitalist' or 'associative' economy)? (Part I)
– What are the institutional characteristics to be assumed by this Welfare Society, in order to be managed with greater information and planned control of its development? (Part II)

On the other hand, I have neglected deliberately in this book (as being outside its essential scope) the more technical and operational issues concerning *socio-economic planning*. In spite of that, it is evoked here many times (especially in Part II) as an indispensable tool for managing a better social integration and generally for a better societal governance.

These specific and technical issues concerning socio-economic and territorial planning – the field where I spent most of my time as scholar and teacher – have also been the subject of several other works of mine, already published or forthcoming.[6]

FRANCO ARCHIBUGI

Acknowledgements

The debts accumulated towards institutions, colleagues and friends in the preparation of this work are many.

Since the book represents an outcome of many years of intellectual application to the subject and numerous essays published on many occasions, I am grateful to the following commissioning institutions for allowing me to revive the contents of such essays: the OECD for the essays on *structural change and employment growth*, and the European Commission for the use of passages from two Reports prepared for it: the first on the *strengthening of social cohesion in Europe*; the second (in cooperation with Mathias Koenig-Archibugi) on perspective on the relationship between the *Third Sector Emergency and Trade Unions*.

For some of the analysis in the book I have used the findings of several research projects by the Planning Studies Centre (the research centre that I have directed since 1963), projects funded by the (Italian) National Research Council.

Among the people who have helped me with the English edition of this text, I should mention those who assisted me with a difficult translation: Neil Campbell, Andrew and Virginia Krumholz, Leslie Emslie, Douglas Ewert, and, lastly, Keith Povey, the copy-editor. I am not at all sure that the English reader will find the translation comfortable, as it is a result of a difficult trade-off between good English expression and my way of reasoning. Thus, I am extremely grateful to those who have helped me in this translation.

In a final revision of the text, the comments of Mathias Koenig-Archibugi, my son, and of Giorgio Ruffolo, a friend, have been particularly useful and welcomed. To the former, I am also in debt for his contribution in the drafting of Chapter 12, which was drawn, as stated above, from a report to the European Commission. To Giorgio Ruffolo, I am in debt for steady attention and a continuous, involving dialogue, over many years, on the subject-matter of this book. It is appropriate, therefore, that I dedicate to him this work, as a testimonial to that *concordia discors* which was bound us for a good deal of our past.

How not to mention – lastly – the person with whom I have implemented, on a personal level, that 'associative life' which has allowed me to achieve most of my research and study activities? Her name is Fulvia.

FRANCO ARCHIBUGI

Chapter Sources

This work is a summary and reorganization of some decades of reflection on contemporary industrial society and its development. In this effort of reorganization, I have utilized again materials that have already appeared in several conference contributions, reports, and papers, both unpublished and published, most of which are in episodic form and difficult to find.

I owe to the reader a list of these papers and publications, with reference to the chapters of this book.

1. Chapter 1 contains ideas and arguments presented in a contribution to a Seminar of the Italian Gerontological Society (Florence, 10–12 October 1975), published in the Italian review *Economia e Lavoro* (January–March 1976) under the title 'The Social Integration of Marginalized People between Past and Future' (Archibugi, 1976). The bibliographical references are updated, but I do not find obsolete the core of the question posed, to such an extent that put it introduces the whole work presented here.

2. Chapters 2, 3, 4, and 5 present, in a strongly revised form, ideas that get their initial form in a report I wrote in December 1982 as Consultant to OECD (which was preparing an Inter-Governmental Conference on the topic 'Structural Change and Employment Development', then considered 'pivotal' and which remained so to the present day). This report was titled 'Structural Change in the Production Process: Its Implication for the Labour Policies', and remained unpublished (it circulated inside the OECD).

3. Chapters 6, 7, 8 develop further my contribution to the OECD Conference just mentioned, as finally it took place two years later. The contribution was titled 'The Possibilities for Employment Creation in the Third Sector', and was published by OECD in an abridged version in *Structural Change and Employment Growth* (OECD, Paris, 1985).

4. Chapters 9, 10, 11 re-elaborate texts already included in a document prepared on request for a 'Programmatic Conference' of the Italian Socialist Party (Rimini, 31 March–4 April 1982), in the Report to the just mentioned OECD Conference, and in an article published in the review of the Italian Trade Union Confederation CGIL, *Rassegna sindacale*, no. 113, March–April 1985.

5. Chapter 12 is also an expansion of the arguments presented in the mentioned OECD Conference. The material was partially used in a Report, written with the collaboration of Mathias Koenig-Archibugi,

xvii

committed by the European Commission (*Industrial Relations and the Social Economy: Forms and Methods of Negotiated De-statalization of the Social Welfare Systems in the European Union*, Brussels 1995), as well as in a contribution – again with M. Koenig-Archibugi – to a Seminar (Brussels, 5–6 December 1996) organized by the Members of the European Parliament belonging to the 'Ulivo' coalition. The contribution's title was 'Third System and Post-Capitalist Society'.

6. *Chapter 13* is the re-elaboration of a contribution, titled 'Ends and Means: New Policy Instruments for Social Development', presented to an international conference of the 'Forum for International Political and Social Economy' held in Paris (4–6 November 1982), and published in *Out of Crisis: A Prospect for European Recovery*, edited by Stuart Holland (Nottingham: Spokesman, 1983). There I summarize, in a more schematic and operative form, the conclusions of the analyses presented in my writings cited so far. Part of the material of Chapters 9, 10, and 12 was already presented in a paper ('Beyond the Welfare State: Planning for a Welfare Society') for a seminar of Roskilde University (DK), held 5–6 May 1994, on 'Comparative Welfare Systems', then published in *Comparative Welfare Systems*, edited by Bent Greve (London: Macmillan, 1996).

Introduction

1 From Social Protection to Social Integration: A Glance at the Major Social Issues in the Advanced Countries

The purpose of this introductory chapter is to pose the problems of the evolving relationship between *social protection* and *social integration*, which deserves to be considered as the 'critical point' of the crisis of the experience of the Welfare State, as commonly debated today. This evolving relationship is considered as a starting point for all our analysis into the 'future' of the Welfare State at the conclusion of this century.

Since the critical point of the evolving relationship between social protection and integration is that in which their tendential *convergence* is inverted into a tendential *divergence*, in this introductory chapter we will make a rapid *excursus* into the more evident challenges of this divergence, and into the main policy issues through which the tendential divorce between social protection and social integration could be prevented and avoided. A more careful examination of the structural features of the divergence, and of the policies to avoid it and/or manage it in the best way, is entrusted to the subsequent chapters, which are collected in two parts: the first concerning *the analysis of socio-economic structural change*, and the second concerning the *analysis of the management policies* of the said change.

1 SOCIAL 'PROTECTION' AND SOCIAL 'INTEGRATION'

In the industrialized countries, we have lived from the beginning of this century with the political and social experience of protection of the 'least favoured' or 'marginalized' sections of society.

'Social Security', the principal goal of a large part of this century's political struggles (a protection that would last 'from the cradle to the grave', as enunciated by the standard-bearer of social welfare, Great Britain), has consisted, for the most part, in the economic protection of less favoured or

1

marginalized people, the elderly, women, the young, the unemployed, etc., by means of an increasingly extended system of public services and performances, physical and monetary.[1]

Despite the political and historical weight that the problem of marginalization has had in the evolution of our industrial societies this century, we might wonder now whether the direction followed has borne fruit, or whether certain incorrect approaches to the problem have hindered a fuller realization of the goals of more advanced social integration.

1.1 Social Protection versus Social Integration?

We are becoming more and more aware, in fact, that the *social protection* (for which many of us fought and are still fighting), seen in the light of the need for 'social integration', has provoked and is provoking a type of *segregation of the socially protected* and – given the ever greater number of categories of those who are in some way 'protected' (including even the young who are protected in their 'right' to study) – is thus leading to a type of *social disintegration*, the opposite result of what any social (or 'welfare'[2]) policy has assumed as an objective.

If this is the case, it is also legitimate to wonder what expedients there are for preventing the process of social segregation which is implied by the achievement of these objectives, granting the historical objectives to consolidate and improve the level of social security.

It is to this limited field of considerations that this book is devoted. The subject, far from obsolete, must be considered the heart of the matter, to the point that it deserves to be viewed as the introduction to all this work here presented and dedicated to the recovery of the Welfare State and its transition to a (commonly defined) *welfare society*. The theme of social marginalization could be the *critical point* in the relationship between social protection and social integration; the latter could be the crucial point in the passage from a conservative to a progressive society, that is to say – as I see it – the passage from an authoritarian and paternalist society to a truly free society.[3] In this general statement, I deliberately leave aside the very old problem of overcoming the 'capitalist' system and its substitution with other 'systems'. This would involve a more complex defining of concepts and words, beyond the aims of this book.[4] This book, therefore, deals with the problem of the (so-called) modern social gain, in particular those of the countries of the Welfare State, in light of the ethical-political postulate of greater social integration.[5]

But a reconsideration of the Welfare State from this viewpoint is in particular motivated by the impression that the characteristics of modern industrial society, in which the Welfare State is solidly installed, have undergone such a profound change that the actual bases of an efficient management of the Welfare State are also changed radically.

It is thus to the critical analysis of the change that we must refer in order to deduce its implications for the future management of the Welfare State.

1.2 The Welfare State and Social Integration

Turning again to the initial question (*'Has social protection in contemporary society ensured, or will it be able to ensure, adequate social integration?'*), in this first chapter we will limit ourselves to developing, by way of introduction, some main critical points of a deficient social integration in the societies of the Welfare State.

Obviously, the reconstruction of the Welfare State in its historical achievements is taking place in a situation in which it has already successfully carried out its original function of the fight against poverty. In fact, *ubi major minor cessat*, where there is acute poverty, 'protectionism' is a priority need.

But from a certain level of well-being and a certain achieved level of social protection upwards, it is only right that we ask ourselves whether, with respect to the real *social integration* (which technology and the vast productive capacity of post-industrial society would permit), this protectionism is not a sort of *social paternalism*, having, as an initial and immediate result, the isolation of the protected, and their weakening as a participatory force in the social dialectic.

Who are the 'protected'? Obviously they consist of all the 'non-active' categories: *women, the young, the elderly, the unemployed, the handicapped and (in increasing numbers) the immigrants*.

These non-active groups are growing in proportion to the development of industrialized society. In fact, with total increases in labour earnings and state provision (albeit in an always less than satisfactory way) for their minimum needs, their need to work diminishes. Since the basic needs are met, for them the marginal utility of an income gained against work (and moreover not chosen work) decreases strongly. In short, the object of reflection is the following: that with the removal of the 'non-active' from the production process (as much as it may seem – with regard to previous situations – a victory for the system) some serious breaks in behaviour and cohesion are created between the active and the non-active. Therefore, what we have called 'social disintegration' may occur.

By integration I clearly mean (to the extent that words express concepts) any effective opposite to segregation, separation or marginalization. An excessive protection by categories leads in fact – if there are not intervention priorities commonly accepted, at least in the intentions – to a consolidation of the difference among categories and classes. It becomes, by itself, producer of separation between 'beneficiaries' and 'benefactors', protected and unprotected, with consequences contrary to the aims pursued.

1.3   Social Integration from Industrial to Post-Industrial Society

Industrialization, as we know, has created our present well-being. I wonder whether our generation or future ones will ever really 'understand' the advantages that industrialization has offered us, in the form of a liberation from profoundly harder living and working conditions, not having ever really experienced these conditions for ourselves. The inhabitants of developing countries, or at least those from countries which are still behind in the industrialization process, are well aware of this, and will not listen to reason when they defend their firm aspiration to the 'model' of a modern industrial society, of which we acutely feel the disadvantages, damage and obsolescence.[6]

However, every generation has to play its historic role. Ours is that of looking to the future, not to the past: before us we already have post-industrial society.[7] Looking at this, we might well say that we must already know how to see and appreciate the regressive aspects of a regime of 'social protection', which for our grandparents and parents represented an undoubted victory, but which today is showing signs of obsolescence with respect to the model of society to which we are aspiring *today*. In many aspects and in many social sectors the model even sought by our forefathers is a long way from being reached.

We must bear in mind that in this case a classic recurrent dilemma is reproduced when we deal with '*dualistic*' countries, countries that are essentially at a *midway* point: in which the damage co-exists between underdevelopment that has not yet brought the advantages of a modern post-industrial society to full fruit, and the damage of which we are becoming more and more aware that is typical of what we could define as the 'maturity' of industrialization. One might wonder whether it is necessary to pass through the standard phases of social progress, which, however, produce *other* problems that cannot be ignored, or whether it is possible to aspire to some sort of *historic leap*.

Certainly it is well known that for the countries in a medium stage of the transition into post-industrial society (I think especially of Italy) historic leaps are psychologically difficult and politically expensive: but not impossible. In this case it is a question of identifying, with precision, their operational *feasibility*; nevertheless without retreating before evolutionary perspectives only because the degree of backwardness of the system is such that the capacity to realize certain intentions is rather distant in time. Nor because, inversely, it allows us to follow certain easy models of systems already initiated elsewhere, when in reality we know that they too, though having benefited from favourable historic circumstances, have, for the modern conscience, already been superseded.

1.4 From the Present Shortcomings to a New Type of Social Integration

The latter is certainly the case with the system of social protection for all Western advanced countries. There is still a long way to go before realizing this in a satisfactory way and already we feel we must adapt it to new needs and new problems, that will tangibly alter its character.[8]

Here a type of political judgement comes into play which is often used in comparing 'American' society to 'European' society. There is a tendency to see American society as backward, with regard to social protection systems, for the level (undoubtedly lower) of guaranteed and legal protection.

But if we look at European systems from the point of view of the collective or communitarian participation in management of social protection services, and to their absolute level of extension and efficiency, I believe that this claimed 'superiority' is modified considerably.[9]

The basic instrument for the protection of the marginalized is a regime of social security that is adequate and generalized and which ensures in any situation and at any age a certain guaranteed level of income. We know now that such a regime today is neither adequate nor generalized: there are levels of social services that are completely below the acceptable minimum; and there are entire categories of the marginalized (the elderly, the young, the unemployed, the immigrants) who still do not enjoy the providence of the social security system.[10]

It is a common opinion that the possibilities of extending such a regime of security depend on the productive income capacity of the economic system. In effect, in systems with a higher level of income per capita, the social security regime is better. But now even in these systems the problem is not posed in terms of the satisfaction of the income levels of the marginalized, which tend to be progressively unbalanced with respect to those of the 'active' categories.

The trend that is strongly emerging is towards overcoming the concept of protection, in order to attain that of the acquisition of a *guarantee of basic income* for all social categories. However, the very definition of 'basic' means that this guarantee is activated only for a few: the most needy (with the accompanying question of how to define and conceive them).

Thus there is a trend towards a sort of *de-institutionalization* of social security, with the nature and forms that will be briefly outlined.

2   THE CONTEXTUAL CHALLENGES

2.1   The Relationship between the Active and Non-Active Population: A Mystification

We will start from the classic consideration of the progressive 'ageing' of the population, understood obviously not as an *absolute* increase in the elderly (over sixty), but as the *relative* increase with respect to the total population, or even only to the 'active' population. Such ageing is a phenomenon common – albeit with different characteristics – to all industrialized societies. The fall in the birth rate and the increase in life span from birth, are the most well-known causes.[11]

Such a phenomenon, joined with that of the progressive enlargement of the social transfer of income in favour of the marginalized in all countries, has led to an ever more important proportional absorption of national income in favour of the marginalized and this has not failed to arouse worries and alarm amongst 'right-minded' people. The mental scheme has been constructed of the relationship between *active* people, 'producers of income', and *non-active* people, 'consumers of income'. The fact that consumers of income, who make no contribution to its formation, are increasing with respect to those who, while consuming, also participate however in its formation, would seem to present a grave danger for an effective income distribution; and, moreover, a serious injustice loaded with economic consequences. There are numerous opinions on this point, but we will limit ourselves to a few remarks.

In the first place, one asks oneself with what validity workers may rightly call themselves the *title holders* of all the value of productive flow *pro tempore* of goods and services to which they are assigned. This production that certainly would not be achieved without their contribution, is likewise the result of a set of 'factors' in which capital, the technical-social setting and know-how are not less important than the directly attached workers. It is, in fact, *society as a whole* that is the actual productive matrix of that flow, and the productivity or efficiency of labour applied to it is no less than the result of a complex of technical and human capital on which the 'social' work 'precourse', whether incorporated or not, can have the same rights as that 'in course'.

Was it not society itself, at the time in which the pensioners of today were still active and engaged to the productive flow of the past, that decided in one way or another to set aside parts of that flow in order to accumulate the necessary productive means for the active of today to maintain and increase the product of their work? (This they did without considering for the moment whether these shares came from direct contributions on the income of that work, or on the income of society as a whole.)

Who can say – if we wish to be the accountants of the social debit and credit – who has more right to claim credit for the benefits of the marginal capital–product relationship: the workers of yesterday (now retired) who permitted, with the process of accumulation of which they suffered the burdens, the level of present production; or the workers of today who have had no effect on such a relationship (but perhaps will have on that of the future)?

But society, as a whole, *must* care about future generations: for example, by not spoiling in a thoughtless way natural resources, or by investing in research and development, or by taking an interest in producing educational services for the young (other 'non-active' people, other 'pure consumers'). For the same reasons it cannot distance itself from the task of redistributing its own economic resources, according to *pre-established plans* and collective preferences, independent from the ex post consideration of the rewards that the active receive in comparison with the 'non-active'. The decision of income allocation between active and non-active must be based, ex ante, on the priority choices of society, and in an explicit way by planning procedures.[12]

In a community managed according to criteria of rationality and equity, both the incomes of the 'active' – negotiated in the market, but subject as well to interference of a more and more advanced 'social income policy' – and the incomes of the 'non-active' should be regulated by overall evaluations. These evaluations should be linked to a thorough, systematically defined and explicit social policy, and not be at the mercy of the random adjustments of the so-called 'market'.[13]

These are briefly the reasons why any generic considerations on the *burden* of the non-active population on the active one seem completely vacuous rather than just vague. Mystifying, rather.[14]

2.2   The Impact of the Technological Revolution

If the active/non-active relationship does not seem in itself a good starting point for the evaluation of a policy of social redistribution of income, we must at the same time recognize that it is instead the result of the type of organization of our industrial societies – which have been defined as those of 'mature capitalism' (or of the 'third age').[15] We will return to the significance and importance of this concept in the following chapters 2 and 3, when we will relate it to the totality of structural changes in the economy, which are at the basis of the crisis and evolution of the Welfare State.

The operational system of this society is incapable, in fact, of ensuring an adequate redistribution of the 'activity load' which is the consequence of rapid technological change, in the single productive processes, which liberates a great quantity of work input.

The automation and cybernetics that are being increasingly applied to the production processes are creating an ever greater structural unemployment, which is tending also to transfer – because of the international concentration of industrial activities – from country to country.[16] In the presence also of the tendential creation of new activities of the tertiary type with high work intensity (treated more extensively in the following chapters), the effect of technological production and of the subsequent high productivity is the reduction in participation of the categories that are most marginal to the productive process itself, a phenomenon that is seen in all industrial societies of the capitalist type, without exclusion.

In reality the system could realize also an important *redistribution of employment* to the advantage of the marginal or marginalized categories. This could be realized together with the imperfect redistribution of income due to the different sectorial development of technologies. A redistribution of employment would produce an enormous potentiality for growth, freeing the mature industrial societies from the spectre of stagnation, and, at the same time, would rebalance the social weight of the various categories with a socially *integrating* effect.

The experience which we have had (relative to the impact of the current technological revolution) is rather that of an incapacity of today's industrial systems to reabsorb structural unemployment by means of a wider participation in work or 'labour sharing'. Also the increases in the sectorial income capacity (produced by the very intense increase in productivity) have not managed to transfer themselves – given the rigidity of the market and the absence of income controls – to the advantage of the whole population, whether active or not. Indeed this near absolute rigidity of the markets, which impedes in practice any lowering of prices, has presented us with an increasingly serious situation of permanent structural inflation. The deflationary control of inflation, realized only with monetary instruments, does nothing but increase the rigidity of the market system and brake the expansion towards new activities which stimulate new employment.

On the other hand, inflation and the monetary 'veil' seem to be the only (albeit distorted and very paradoxical[17]) tools for transferring onto relative prices the general increases in productivity and for keeping alive a global demand that can ensure a minimum rhythm of expansion. If this inflationary euphoria (or drug) is taken away, one falls immediately into depression. Thus in the present mechanism we are obliged to accept an increase in the inequality that sectorial income formation and inflation produce, only in order to avoid crisis.[18]

Thus the increase of the non-active over the active, and the incapacity of a policy of activity redistribution, are aspects that are inherent to the functioning of the system. The system, despite being thought of as self-regulating or automatic, is in reality no longer so; but it has not been *substituted* by a new type of management, i.e., by a form of social and economic planning (the *invisible hand* no longer works, but has not been replaced by the *visible* one).

The consumerist 'welfare' in mature capitalism, which guarantees a minimum of growth and survival of activities, also by means of that type of social protectionism that was keen to introduce it, is therefore being paid for necessarily in terms of an *increase of the inactivity* of ever wider groups of the population and in terms of persistence of pockets of relative poverty and difficulty, that we have not managed to absorb, even in 'rich' countries, through the described rhythm of expansion.

2.3 Poverty and Marginalization

Poverty and malaise, in fact, are two phenomena which are often joined, but sometimes detached. In the Welfare States, the phenomenon of detachment is becoming increasingly widespread, in that it is possible to be socially marginalized while being at the same time protected from poverty.[19]

Certainly, in the first place there is the combined phenomenon of poverty and marginalization, particularly for the elderly. The poverty of the elderly is by now the most recognized and diffused form of poverty. All social surveys on poverty show – despite historic structural differences in the various countries where they are carried out – that the most frequent co-variable of poverty is old age. Obviously in the world there are the poor and the Poor, the lucky and the not so lucky. But it seems that in both groups of poverty the elderly prevail proportionately.[20]

But marginalization is also developing in forms which are independent from poverty, as we commonly understand it. Also in the cases in which the pension regime has managed in some way to flatten the curve of poverty distribution (in Northern European countries in particular) marginalization has not stopped having an effect on welfare.[21]

Even beyond the area of poverty proper,[22] the growing ratio of the non-active over the active which is inherent to the mechanism of the system, gives us as a result a society that is more and more disintegrated in the system of interpersonal relations. The young at school, women in the home, the elderly in retirement (in the home, if not in rest-homes or in hospitals) and the male adults in the factory, the office, or in the squares 'of unemployment' are examples.

And they are all deeply isolated and dissatisfied. The work place and the activity no longer seem to be the 'places' of *social integration*.

The *young* feel marginalized, excluded from the social complex, isolated in the ghetto of an ever lengthening educational process, which is becoming more and more an end in itself, and which is tending, given the objective elimination of work input in the productive process, to become a sort of 'parking area'. And the above is developing despite the fact that more important 'social investment' in schools and the better conditions of 'sons of the family' is probably allowing the young to absorb the relatively most important part of the benefits of the social *dividend*. But the psychological factor of marginalization makes them impatient, and unaware that they are probably the major 'real' beneficiaries of the actual production process.

Non-active *women* equally, apart from a few exceptions, are more and more frustrated, willingly or unwillingly, with their condition, and are, as a consequence, at the base of all degenerative forms of superfluous and neurotic consumerism. In some countries female activity is managing to go up, but at a much slower rate than that which was necessary in order to compensate for the annually growing female 'rate of frustration'.[23] In other more backward countries, like Italy, that growth of activity is even going down. The sense of marginalization among women at work, as at home, is chronic.[24]

Adult men, that is those who bring home the income, who are more and more dully concentrated on the production of this income, do not have the time – which they could have, on the other hand, with the improvement of the productivity of the system – to keep themselves up-to-date on the professional and 'cultural' developments characterized, as it happens, by the hegemonic presence of idle youth. The adults, too, are suffering the frustration of this state of cultural 'inferiority', towards the more 'cultured', 'prepared' and 'know-it-all' young. They feel, in their own way, marginalized as well from that social context for which they have the conviction of providing the supporting structure. They find themselves thus frustrated and unprepared, and ever nearer to crossing the threshold of retirement, which becomes a 'psychological retirement', even before a real one.[25]

The *elderly*, finally, having actually crossed this threshold feel further marginalized, in the most dramatic of ways, without even the psychological resource of a future that is physiologically expansive, and are often estranged from social processes, whether of work, culture or recreation. And this despite the fact that the pension regime and health assistance have grown to levels of protection never before known.[26]

There is also the growing *immigrant population* in the industrialized countries, whose marginalization is, so to speak, 'official'. And in this quality, it is largely accepted as inherent to their escape and liberation from the underdevelopment of their countries of origin.[27]

3   THE POSSIBLE PERSPECTIVE ISSUES

3.1   The De-institutionalization of Social Roles

Social marginalization, therefore, is born from growing inactivity. Inactivity is born from the incapacity of the system to automatically redistribute jobs. It is the crystallization of the processes of social protectionism that has, as mentioned, institutionalized the social *roles* of large numbers of citizens (the young, women, elderly, working adults, migrated people) without relation to professional skill, and carries out a function of cause and effect with the growing inactivity.

Nobody could deny that the tendency in recent decades has been towards greater protection of the marginal categories: more schools and more scholarization for the young, more money and more recognition for maternity and housework, more pensions and health care for the retirement and care of the elderly.

We have *institutionalized* protection with the amount of means supplied for 'Education Services', 'Maternity and Child-Care Services', 'Retirement and Health Services', and the other 'allowance' service (unemployment, invalidity, and so on): that is, with the services of the Welfare State.

We would ask anyone prepared to complain about the deplorable condition of the current Welfare State: 'When were there ever better services and less marginalization in the recent and past history of our industrial society?'

What we wish to emphasize here is that, with the expansion and improvement of social services we have not realized that the current condition of the young, women, the elderly, and so on, was not 'organic' ('natural'), but almost the by-product of a rigid market situation and of the control of occupational situations. If we had had a policy of redistribution of work activities, we would have easily obtained *social integration of working groups* and, therefore, greater effective and meaningful protection.

Thus new stimuli towards a policy of greater social integration should pass through a process of *de-institutionalization* of roles and, therefore, of the services sanctioned for these roles. We will try to be even more explicit (if also a bit 'extreme'), sketching here a sort of policy guideline.

Do the *young* have the 'role' of educating themselves? Yes, but also the role of working and enjoying themselves, for which the education service must not only serve the young but also – to the same extent – women, adults and the elderly.

Is a *woman's* role to have children? This is probably inevitable, but she also has the role of educating herself, working and having enjoyment. Therefore the maternity and child care services must above all help to lighten the role of the mother and integrate it with social or associative functions (for which she may not be so prepared, avoiding harmful effects on the sociality of the child and the future adult).

Do the *elderly* have the role of retirement, looking after themselves, and amusing themselves? They also have the role of working and educating themselves like everybody else, for which the retirement and health services must be organized in such a way as to stimulate and not to discourage the incentive to work and study of the elderly.

Does the *adult* have the role of work? Yes, and also the role of educating, resting and amusing himself or herself *to the same extent* as any other person. Therefore, the work services must not only create work opportunities for the adult, but opportunities that are reduced in time and intensity (part-time) with a sensible redistribution of working times and type of work.

If these are therefore the stimuli to produce a new trend, it will be obviously necessary (given the resources constraints) to 'dose' the efforts to be applied in every direction, according to a scheme of preferences that can emerge only when we have, in an efficient system of socio-economic planning, the essential framework of the costs and benefits of all the situations, of all the pluses and minuses of any measure.

But it is important likewise not to push beyond the protection system in directions that distance rather than bring closer the objective of *social integration* and of the redistribution of jobs. It will also be necessary to bend and make functional to this aim the social institutions of social protection.

Here we will briefly discuss, by way of introduction, only some issues of a rational response to the stimuli emerging towards greater social integration, leaving to the following analysis the task of delving more deeply into causes (Part I) and remedies (Part II). Here we will only mention the cases of de-institutionalization of schools and 'continuing education'; the reduction of working time; and guaranteed income. We will also mention that each of these innovative tendencies in the welfare systems have one condition to be progressively implemented: that they are implemented under the control of a system which implies their technical feasibility and consistency with resources (or economic consistency), and which assures that it is the result of appropriate trade-offs between decision-makers, in a decision system which is as 'democratic' and 'participatory' as possible.[28]

3.2   De-scholarization and 'Permanent Education'

There is no doubt that the objective conditions for this process of de-institutionalization of roles exist. In fact, as said, they are the same conditions – inherent in the technological process – that have led, *for want of adequate social planning*, to the recrudescence of inactivity over activity, and have consequently strengthened 'protectionism', the institutionalization of roles and finally of social marginalization.

Above all, it is commonly recognized that the educational process without training on the job is becoming sterile. In no professional discipline or skill does the rapid and furious change in knowledge allow us to make do with a *corpus* of doctrines that is only studied and learned, without practice (i.e. application and work) changing permanently its content and nature. This obsolescence of the school and of the processes of pure learning have as an obvious (but not inappropriate) response, absenteeism and the refusal of the young towards learning of the traditional type. From the old, and never seriously applied, schemes of the 'active' school or of 'apprenticeship school' for the lower levels, we are moving gradually closer to conceiving, and applying, generally study not only *as* work, but as the complement – in an opportune and mixed form – of a process of productive work.[29] Even academic studies are today re-evaluating the spirit of the workshop, or of the classic 'school'.[30]

Probably in the long run, schools will be increasingly abandoned as autonomous centres, and will become factories, workshops, and offices. Apprenticeship will be a regenerated and modernized form of 'on the job' education.

On the other hand, schools will go back to being the permanent centres of updating for all the population, including adults, women, and the elderly.

Why should 'permanent education' (i.e. continuing education 'for adults') be different from the non-permanent type for the young, when – and all parents know this – the daily content of teaching for the children does not constitute a repetition of the contents of the same learning of the parents?

What parent today would not wish to constitute *ex novo* the cultural learning heritage of which the children are the present beneficiaries and who, in all honesty, would consider it superfluous for him or herself?

On what basis of criteria could one sanction that children have a greater need, right or duty than the parents with regard to this learning? Why on earth should the children enjoy this benefit exclusively for themselves, when the personal *results* of that learning would probably be much higher for the adults? (And for the children the results would most certainly be better if they went out to work to earn a living.) Who could claim for certain that the much vaunted *'right' to study* (that is felt by the young as a 'duty' towards study) is something that ceases at a certain age, and that the much vaunted *'right' to work* (which is 'felt' by adults as a 'duty' to work, as something which they would be better off without) should begin only from a certain age, which is today becoming absurdly higher and higher? And as for retirement, why on earth must the *right to rest* (which is 'felt' by the elderly like a 'duty' which they would often prefer to do without) be a prerogative only of the so-called 'third age'?

Why therefore do we not begin to free ourselves from such obsolete mental 'schemes' and look at such things as the use of resources, distribution of employment, and work length, on the basis of *objective criteria* that express the free *options* both of individuals and of society as a whole, rendered opportunely 'compatible'?

3.3 Cutting Down Working Time

The dominant work processes do nothing but facilitate this reshuffling.

The reduction of average working time may well be more or less a victory of trade unions over the individual entrepreneur. But it has become a *need for the system overall* to respond to the needs of the reduction of work input in the transformation of productive processes.

We complain, particularly in 'dualistic' countries, about a certain growing unproductive work in tertiary activities, and we would want everybody to work in industry, because here one obtains a *high 'added value'*.[31] But why? Does one not have an impression, on the contrary, that industry has exhausted its mass production services and has to perform acrobatic feats in order to create a market of artificial and useless consumption, whatever the 'added value' that, given price controls and very high technical productivity, we manage to obtain? And does not one have the impression, on the other hand, that services of inestimable value, albeit not in the sector of the services that can be acquired on the 'market', could be carried out in the tertiary sector, if appropriate forms of part-time organization were introduced?[32]

Are we sure it is possible to evaluate this new and different type of *added value*? And if not (as yet), are we sure that we should prefer activities with a high conventional added value to those with little or no added value of the tertiary sector? In other terms, are we sure that the preference for high added value without substantive indications – as an end in itself – is the right way to create better economic welfare? (We shall return to this point in analytic terms in Chapter 4 and in propositive terms in Chapter 12.)

The 'tertiarization' that is implemented in post-industrial society is but a response to a certain saturation of the demand for industrial goods and to the almost complete automation of the processes inherent to these goods (this point will be illuminated in Chapter 4). It is also counter-productive to think still of retracing the phases of the same industrialization in order to artificially develop a demand that is lacking, and which leaves disorganized a growing sector of demand (that of services), the entrepreneurship of which is in the hands of the state.

The proportional decline of industrial employment can and must be accompanied by the decline of the average working time.[33] In all fields, including that of industry itself, employment favourable to the young, women and the elderly is increasing disproportionately. What should be applied is an organizational method that tends to place in the productive processes the new part-time contingents, without creating enormous upsets in the structure of individual and family incomes.[34]

3.4 Towards Guaranteed Income

For some time, *guaranteed income* has been seen as the *correct* response to give to the now unbalanced advance of personal income capacity with work productivity. Unemployment produced by the cybernetic and post-industrial society will slow-up development if a process of redistribution of wealth is not implemented which will guarantee overall demand.[35]

Certainly we also recognized before in the text the objective separation between productivity and performance, and the necessity therefore to go beyond these schemes, as if the protagonists of 'productivity' were only the 'active' and not society as a whole (see above, Section 2.1).

Nevertheless, the policy of guaranteed income by itself risks transforming itself in a further element of social 'protectionism', if it is not accompanied by a policy of social redistribution of work and other roles. From the strict point of view of retirement, the introduction of a system of guaranteed income for all constitutes nevertheless an important step towards 'de-institutionaliza-tion'. In fact it would represent the desired suppression of retirement. The elderly would have thus a *right* to their income not *as* the elderly, with the role, as such, of rest and non-work, but as citizens with the best prerequisites to enjoy guaranteed income. It would be almost like what happens with the national health services which cover the needs of citizens as the circum-stances arise, and are not exclusively for the elderly, even if they are its most numerous users.

The introduction of any system of 'guaranteed income' would make some sense in an administration that aims at social integration only if accompanied by a policy of redistribution of jobs and working time and of the policy of adaptation connected to it.[36]

4 EMPLOYMENT AND ACTIVITIES PLANNING OR THE CRISIS OF THE WELFARE SYSTEM

The need to 'defend' the situation that has been achieved, and the need for a minimum amount of protection and well-being for those who have not yet reached this minimum, constitute a brake not only on the implementation, but also on the very understanding of the policies outlined.

It is only with an *overall strategy* that we will be able to 'govern', measure actions and calibrate objectives in an optimum way, according to procedures that have a name: *integrated planning*.[37]

It is only by means of a process of integrated planning and not with 'sectorial policies' in favour of this or that social category, or category of social needs, that one can hope to overcome the contradictions of an ex-tremely unbalanced development. The adoption of a 'new way of managing' begins from a precise quantification of the present situation and arrives at a policy-oriented future quantification founded on overall projections and on options to be negotiated and chosen, with procedures and determined requests, on the basis of alternative overall 'scenarios'.[38]

In the field that interests us here, one cannot adopt a policy aware of the marginalized and of social security unless on the basis of a precise evaluation of the quantitative development of the problem in the medium and long period: the input and output in the categories that are marginalized or potentially marginal (the elderly, the young, women, etc.) for each of the years in prospect and precise conditions of education, work and behaviour of the contingents in question.[39] Only in this way can one predict well in advance such social policies that are necessarily differentiated by sex and age group for these classes that today do not find themselves being influenced by a desired and rational policy of capacity recycling, and those classes, on the other hand, that could be influenced. In fact, the point of a policy for the marginalized and for social integration will be that of ensuring for integration the maximum *flexibility*. At the same time – with opportune calculations – it will have the objective of planning for readaptation of all possible recycling which could be realized in the various productive sectors on the basis of a controlled reduction of working time and a revision of tasks.[40]

Little is still said about policies for the readaptation of workers to new activities – policies which would become more propitious, for instance, to elderly work.[41] Yet if in some countries relevant discussion and experience is much more advanced,[42] I still emphasize the conviction that such policies will have a satisfying operational result only if linked and integrated to a project and policy-oriented evaluation of the entire labour market. The results will also depend on the fixing of targets and indicative goals on the basis of which to excogitate the policies of intervention.

This is not the occasion to dwell on employment planning as a sub-system of a process of integrated planning.[43] Here it is useful to emphatically confirm that the redistribution of activity and income and the full social utilization of the expansion of productive forces and technology, can only be obtained by means of an ordered and integrated process of social planning which substitutes the market mechanisms which no longer function.[44]

5 SUMMARIZING THE TRANSITION TOWARDS SOCIAL INTEGRATION AND PLANNING

To summarize, we have wished to develop in this chapter a rapid overview of all problems of social protection, highlighting the tendencies and advances towards a long-term evolution, oriented towards the implementation of a more advanced social integration. This integration encompasses all the social groups and roles of the population: especially the non-active, marginalized groups, such as the elderly, women and the young; but also the active, apparently non-marginalized, who, for multiple reasons (not excluding their reduction to a numeric minority) show signs of a kind of marginalization (for instance, from access to some 'social' consumption like culture, free time, or recreation).

These advances will lead to a sort of *de-institutionalization* of the regimes of protection (i.e. of the Welfare State).

This de-institutionalization process of the Welfare State, favourable to the passing from social protection to greater social integration, will probably be favoured by objective circumstances such as:

– the development of *work technologies*, that will greatly reduce the input of physical work, and permit greater use of workers that are today marginalized: women and the elderly;
– the growing *tertiarization* of the economy that will create a strong additional demand for social services, suitable for the application of marginalized workers left in the inactivity;
– the development of *permanent education* that will make access possible to non-work educational activities on the part of adult workers, and will have two direct effects on the work of women and the elderly: it will free new *part-time jobs* especially for the woman, on the one hand, and allow today's adult workers, who will be the elderly of tomorrow, to recycle themselves and adapt themselves easily to new working activities;
– the objective *reduction of average working time*, which, rather than automatic, will be the consequence of appropriate 'active' policies for employment and mobility;
– the progressive introduction of the concept and practices relating the 'guaranteed income'.

Nevertheless, it will be necessary to put into being new methods of economic management and a serious activity of *integrated, social and economic planning*, in order that these favourable circumstances play a role in the rational expansion of the work of the marginalized and their recovery in the integrated process of social production.

Without this substantial overturning of the approaches to economic management, the factors of resistance and the risks that may ensue from uncoordinated measures (including the type indicated above) will act as brakes and factors for conservation. The objective evolutionary conditions of 'social protectionism', irreversible in themselves, will place in crisis, with grave dangers for its stability, the *welfare system itself*, yet will not allow for likewise feasible configuration of a serious policy of remedies.[45]

It is only through the ability to set up a new economic regime of social planning that the present contradictions and dominant ambivalence in social protection policies may have an efficient outcome, with the implementation of a real policy of social integration. I continue to believe that this is the main – and essential – goal of any social (or societal or socialist, as preferred) policy.

It is to the design of this new socio-economic regime, or 'planning society', that this book is devoted. From now, however, we would like to refer this book to an opening vision or 'philosophy' of planning, that come from sources, documents and statements belonging to two American federal official entities:

1. The first is *The Congressional Institute*, an independent body[46] presently heavily engaged in consultancy with the Congress for the implementation of the 'General Performance and Result Act' (GPRA) voted in 1993. The GPRA is an epoch-making act which has primed in the Federal administration of that country a real 'revolution' in the practices of public management, introducing strategic planning – as an amendment of the United States Code – in all federal agencies (with demonstration effect in all state and local governmental agencies). We will examine this act in Chapter 13.
2. The second is the *Advisory Committee on National Growth Policy Processes*, created jointly by the US Congress and President[47] in 1976 (under Carter's Presidency), which suggested a reform of the *decision system at national level* through the introduction of a socio-economic planning system, reform whose implementation has been missed completely in more recent years, but that is presently becoming more and more topical, especially in connection with GPRA implementation.

We will draw from the above mentioned sources only a few passages of the most meaningful and general, in which is outlined a vision which inspires also my planning conception. When we analyze the management problems of societal change (in Part II) we define some issues of socio-economic planning. (Any more specific dealing of such matter will be outside the goals of this book.)

In the Congressional Institute's document (1997) their 'planning vision' is expressed as follows:

> America needs a plan. With the twenty-first century quickly approaching, America finds itself at a historic crossroad...The strategic plan...must be visionary in its focus, transformational in its thinking, and comprehensive in its consideration of issues. At the end of our efforts, we will have a Strategic Plan that describes a new 21st century governance paradigm and offers specific, concrete, and creative recommendations to our nation's leaders.

This vision of strategic planning does not only concern the government's role or that of the government institutions or agencies. It is explicity directed to society as a whole, society that in the Congressional Institute vision is constituted by three general 'sectors': 'public', 'private' and 'social'.[48] These sectors correspond to the 'government sectors', 'private business', and the 'non-profit associations or organizations', which presently are growing to an enormous degree. This is fitting to the analysis of societal change that we will develop especially in Chapters 11 and 12.

The final Report of the Advisory Committee on National Growth Policy Processes (1976) states (pp. 12–13):

It was to recommend improvements in mechanism, in techniques, in methods that our governmental institutions might employ in dealing with our nation's problems, so that conceivably America might enjoy more balanced growth and development.

In complying with our Congressional mandate...we found that our Federal policy-making suffers particularly from two deficiencies:

(1) a lack of coordinated policy, evidenced by the tendency for our nation to tackle problems piecemeal with frequently disappointing or partly counterproductive results, and

(2) a lack of foresight, causing our nation to react to problems after they become acute, instead of averting them or mitigating them.

In proposing techniques to improve our nation's performance...the Committee does not advocate a planned society. We urge that America become a planning society. In the long run, we believe that intelligent planning will actually reduce burdensome governmental intervention in matters affecting the private sector. Much governmental interference in the economy now consists of ad hoc reactions to situations which have become acute because they had been ignored until they become intolerable. With the benefit of foresight, the Committee expects that any necessary government intervention will be more considered, more timely, and less heavy-handed...

...Programs must be subject to continous 'course correction'. Planning should be a process of continuous readjustment:

– we need means of measuring performance. Evaluation is difficult, but it must not for that reason be abandoned;

– we need feedback – 'return information' – from the level at which the program is administered;

– we need multiple evaluation centers, including some in the private sector, since some question always attaches to an agency or an administration that is evaluating its own performance. Congress and the private sector have significant roles to play here.

6   BRIEF SCHEME INDICATING HOW THE SUBJECT WILL BE TREATED, OR SCHEDULE OF THIS BOOK

This first chapter has, as said, the characteristic of an introductory overview of the entire question. The following chapters will all be developed as the analytical examination of this programme. This examination is articulated in two parts, which concern:

1. the first, a critical analysis of *the bases of the structural and social change*;
2. the second, a critical analysis of *the management problems of the social change*.

Among the bases of the change (Part I), the following rational scheme has been followed:

–   First we analyze the structural and social changes in general and the different approaches (technological, economic, historic-institutional, sociological) pursued (Chapter 2).
–   Furthermore, we assess the substantive convergence of the approaches and evaluate its operational implications (Chapter 3).
–   Then an attempt is made to connect the structural factors of the change with the effects of mass production and its connection and adaptation with the structure of consumption; and thus identifying the passage from the phase of industrialization to that of tertiarization (Chapter 4).
–   Following this, we proceed to a critical analysis of the changes in production structures (Chapter 5).
–   Then, analogously, we critically analyze the changes in the behaviour of the labour market: labour supply and demand, and structural implications for employment (Chapter 6).
–   We then re-examine the structural and social changes, with a comparison of the characteristics of the two ideal-typical models of society: 'service society' versus 'industrial society' (Chapter 7).
–   We proceed to a specific analysis of the two models of society from the point of view of the process of labour and income distribution (which becomes a crucial problem for the management policies of the 'service society') (Chapter 8).
–   Finally, the part concerned with analysis of changes is concluded with a comparison of the structural changes with the specific role of the state: in particular its expansion and decline (Chapter 9).

In Part II, as mentioned, the managerial problems of the change have been critically analyzed. And in particular:

- The new operational conditions of the change have been designed, firstly analyzing the indispensable management of the redistribution: 'from the invisible hand to the visible hand'; and the operational conditions which represent the overcoming of the traditional social state and its 'crisis' factors (Chapter 10).
- Second, a more specific evaluation of (a) the modalities of introduction of suitable processes of economic and social planning; (b) its implicit corollaries of social bargaining; in a general context of (c) entrepreneurship crisis and emergence of the 'third sector' of the economy (or non-profit economy); furthermore, (d) convergence of all these transformations in characterizing a 'post-capitalist' stage of the economy (Chapter 11).
- Then we treat in greater depth and detail characters, forms, promotional and managerial modalities, experience, and contradictions of the emerging 'third sector' of the economy, or 'associative economy', and its significance for institutional change of the economic system: as a passage from 'social protection to social integration' and from the 'Welfare State to the Welfare Society' (Chapter 12).
- Finally, we conclude with a catalogue of the main policies and instruments available for a management strategy of the above mentioned structural and social change (Chapter 13).

Part I
Critical Analysis of the
Social Change

2 Structural Change: A Reappraisal of the Various Approaches

In the preceding introductory chapter, the evolution and, for some, the 'crisis' of the systems of social protection (which we call the 'Welfare State'), and the evolution towards greater social integration, have been placed in relation to the structural changes of the contemporary economy. However, the reference to such changes was very general.

Part I of this book is devoted to a more specific examination of these changes.

In this chapter, after some explanation of what I mean by 'structural change' of the contemporary economy (with the aim to better discuss later the connections with the already described relation of social protection/integration), I will try to recall the different approaches to the structural change, as put forward by the most insightful scholars in this field. This renewed exploration of the roots of the historical debate on the structural change, I believe will be useful for two purposes:

1. to remind us that our theme is not at all new, and to find its frame in a wider production of ideas already 'decanted';
2. to testify – at the same time – that my 'addition' to the debate takes these ideas for granted, while going a little further.

In other terms, it is useful to make clear to what extent we will take account of the roots, and to what extent we do not wish to take account of them.

This reappraisal of the structural change is far from being exhaustive. It is, on the contrary, strongly selective. It is focused on a selection of authors considered by me as highly significant for every approach studied. My intention is not to offer a survey[1] of the approaches, but only to recall, as a basis of our own analysis, some viewpoints borrowed by the past, the most valuable as possible.

1 WHAT IS MEANT BY 'STRUCTURAL CHANGE' IN THE CONTEMPORARY ECONOMY?

Let us say first that by 'structural change' in the contemporary economy we are here referring to those changes which in advanced Western and industrial societies began in the second half of this century, and which, after a long series of developments, crises, or cyclical movements (or, more or less extended, waves), gave rise to a type of 'new' society, described by many and taken for granted by everyone, which has been named in various ways: *post-industrial society*; *service* or *tertiary society*; the *information society*; *late-capitalist* or *post-capitalist society*, etc.[2]

Such denominations reflect the different ways in which the analysis of change has been formulated and carried out: for example, whether the changes have been seen from the point of view of *technological inventions and innovations*, or from that of the *movement* of the most used *economic variables* (production, overall product, investments, productivity, exchange, income and consumption, etc.), or from the point of view of the respective role of the *economic institutions* (like the State, large industries, small industries, property holding, etc.), or finally from that of some social structures or attitudes (motivation for enterprise, work, consumption, life styles, class relations, etc.).

Analyses have not been lacking, starting from the assumption (based more or less on theoretical reasoning or on empirical observations or data) that the relationship between the various phenomena mentioned above should highlight the priority or causal factor of one over others (technology, economic development, institutions, social structure).[3] But there have also been analyses which, without starting from any presupposition, have tried and sought to extract the causal relation and function, from the analysis itself of the change being examined.

We will see, case by case, some of these approaches and analyses. But first an approximate, general reference to the question of 'periodization' of the evolution of industrial society will help us to clarify the problems of the most recent change, that which is still under way, which interests us most of all.

The structural changes in the economy have been (and will probably continue to be) observed and described from many points of view,[4] and at the risk of excessively simplifying the complexity of the problems underlying all these various points of view, I am inclined, following convention, to group them in four main categories:

1. the point of view that looks at *dominant technologies* (which we could call, in brief, 'technological') and underlines their decisive role;
2. the point of view which looks at the movement of more significant economic phenomena, such as *economic cycles* or '*long waves*' (which we could call, in brief, 'economic');
3. the view which highlights as a determining factor the *institutional forms of production* (which we could call 'historical' or 'institutionalist');
4. and, finally, the view which describes and interprets the development in terms of *social forms of behaviour* (which we could call 'sociological').

We will make some reference to these various approaches, pointing out immediately that, notwithstanding the differences between the four categories (and perhaps because of the complexities, multiple variants, dissent and uncertainty present within each approach), for the purposes of our analysis of the change, a great *convergence* is produced from the periodization and also analytic point of view.[5]

2 THE TECHNOLOGICAL APPROACH

2.1 The Historians of Technology

The technological approach, practised obviously by the historians of technology and scientific development,[6] and also much followed by economic historians and historians in general, tends to identify in any significant 'invention', and in whatever application to production, an important phase of economic evolution. Thus was born, for example, the notion of the 'industrial revolution'[7] applied to the radical technological innovations which were produced in particular in England in the eighteenth century.[8]

But, following consolidation of this notion (not without disputes between the historians concerned with the most detailed descriptions of events, and led thus to see events as slow evolution without too many sudden jumps[9]), there have been applications of that notion to later periods of more or less technological innovations, such as that of *electrical energy* or industrial *chemistry*, the *car*, configuring thus a 'second' and 'third' (and perhaps others as well) *industrial revolution*.[10]

Thus in the first category of approach are the same historians (which we already mentioned) that have illustrated the technological events of the first industrial revolution, without posing to themselves big historiographical questions on the general factors that determined them.[11]

A recent interesting historical periodization (also linked to a 'technological' approach) is the one proposed by Drucker, who sees the 'first' industrial revolution (or first phase of the industrial revolution) starting around 1750 and lasting until 1850–80, as a revolution in the meaning of (and way of using) knowledge. While neither capitalism nor technological innovations were something new,[12] the rapidity of diffusion, moreover across different cultures, places and classes, transformed 'capitalism into Capitalism', i.e. a system. Similarly it has turned technological advance into an 'Industrial Revolution':

This transformation was driven by a radical change in the meaning of knowledge. In both West and East knowledge had always been seen as applying to being. Almost overnight, it came to be applied to doing. It became a resource and a utility. Knowledge had always been a private good. Almost overnight it became a public good.

For a hundred years – in the first phase – knowledge was applied to tools, processes, products. This created the Industrial Revolution. But it also created what Marx called 'alienation' and new classes and class war, and with it Communism. In its second phase, beginning around 1880 and culminating around World War II, knowledge in its new meaning came to be applied to work. This ushered in the Productivity Revolution which in 75 years converted the proletarian into a middle-class bourgeois with near-upper-class income. The productivity Revolution thus defeated class war and Communism. The last phase began after World War II. Knowledge is being applied to knowledge itself. This is the Management Revolution. Knowledge is now fast becoming the one factor of production, sidelining both capital and labour. It may be premature (and certainly would be presumptuous) to call ours a 'knowledge society' – so far we only have a knowledge economy. But our society is surely 'post-capitalist'.[13]

This version of Drucker can be considered the most contemporary and modern among those of the 'technological approach'. Technology is seen as an effectuation of knowledge, knowledge as an effectuation of the rational approach or spirit, and the rational approach as the capacity to control the world (at least on its controllable side) and to determine human events.

Yet it should be acknowledged that the most serious technological approach (the one which starts from the analysis of the social-economic impact of technical and scientific inventions and of technological innovation, attributing to this a 'determining' function, or decisive role, on the changes of the economy and society) is represented, even better than by technologists or historians of technologies, by economists. But it is a matter for unorthodox economists, largely contesting the usual paradigms of economic analysis. Let us follow their path briefly. Their problem arises on the way to considering whether technological progress is the subject or not of economic analyis, whether or not it is its business.

2.2 Technology: Is it Exogenous or Endogenous to Economic Progress?

This 'technological' approach, however, developed later as a response to the attempt by economists to find the 'economic causes' of change, without including the technological factor, considered as exogenously 'given' (as the natural and geographical factors) and without any attempt to 'explain' it; or, as in the most clamorous case – Schumpeter's – as an overly simplistic claim by economists[14] of defining 'endogeneously' the change (both structural and technological), i.e. assuming it dependent above all on economic factors or variables, such as the development of demand, of income, of population (itself a source of demand), of market structure, and so on.

From this starting point a series of studies has developed, aiming at discovering to what extent technological development is a 'factor' or 'cause' (instead of 'effect') of other social and economic variables; how it is an independent and 'exogenous' variable of overall social-economic development. This has produced many 'visions' of the relations between technology and economic development which, while deserving to belong (beginning with Schumpeter's) to the category of 'technological approach', are perhaps better recalled within the more extended debate, the economic interpretation of development and change, which, after I have drawn rapidly the threads of reasoning of the other category of approach, I call 'economic'.[15]

Examination of the numerous phenomena of technological innovation, and their relations (of cause? or effect?) with scientific discoveries,[16] on the one hand, and with the wider historic-economic ones, on the other (population trends, price trends, times of depression and expansion for the demand of goods and services, etc.), has pushed towards more sophisticated historical analyses.[17]

3 THE ECONOMIC APPROACH

In the beginning, there was speculation as to whether there was, beyond any more or less accidental 'external' historical factors, some natural occurrence and reoccurrence as well in the evolution of economic events. Moreover, one wished to see whether this cyclical movement was characteristic of capitalist society, with which the era of rapid industrialization was marked, and something inherent in the accumulation of capital, so intimately correlated with the introduction of new production techniques.

3.1 The Internal Dynamic of Economic Progress

Regarding the subject of structural change, analyses have thus been developed which we would define as the 'economic approach', aimed at theorizing a sort of 'dynamic' of the change or an economic law, to explain the change itself within 'internal laws' of movement.

Through the 'economic' approach, there is a tendency to look for a sort of *auto-sustainability* of development, and an attempt has been made to 'endogenize' the phenomenon itself of technological innovation. The economists, in short, doubted the legitimacy of introducing technological innovation as an 'external' factor (and thus largely exogenous) of the historical and economic development.

This new approach showed itself first by examining the movement of economy across time in its dynamics. Economic history, economic statistics and economic theory joined for a common effort. Firstly, the historical series of these supposed variables which significantly indicate economic progress (prices, productions, etc.) are recorded; and it has been observed that such progress was dominated by a 'major' trend of this series of a cyclical type which started the study of internal laws. This work led, as we know, to asserting a reality (and a connected problem): the existence of a cyclical trend of the entire economy and of long waves. Then an attempt was made to give an explanation of this trend, to build a 'theory of major cycles'.[18]

Pareto (who was among the first, albeit little recognized,[19] treatise writers of the medium and long-term cycles) first constructed (1913, 1917) his own statistical surveys, classifying, exactly like Kondratief some years later, the waves in three types of cycles: 'long term', 'medium term', and 'short term'.[20] Later, he too put forward a theory: 'In the periods of economic stagnation the quantity of available savings increases, and so the following period is prepared for a rapid increase in economic prosperity in which the quantity of available savings decreases and a new period of stagnation is prepared, and so on indefinitely' (Pareto, 1916).[21]

More recently, the theme has been taken up again and amplified with extensive use of empirical and statistical, technically sophisticated studies,[22] but the basic questions have not altered; they have still remained:

1. Is the evolution of the economy revealed through 'long waves' of prosperity and recession? And how are these long waves related to the successive development stages of the economy itself?
2. If these long waves exist, how can they be explained? What are the factors determining them, intrinsically to the working of the same economic system?

However, the answers, compared to Pareto's rather simple one, do not seem today to be much more certain than yesterday. On the other hand, the result seems to reach the conclusion, despite the diversity of the answers, that:

1. Yes, major cycles and long waves exist, but they cannot be determined chronologically nor defined historically.[23] (Never mind predetermined or forecast!)
2. The endogenous factors, such as that put forward by Pareto, are intertwined with such a great number of other exogenous factors (wars, revolutions, immigrations, scientific discoveries, demographic factors, etc.) that they escape any satisfactory explanation, other than a 'historical' one, which by its very nature is incompatible with any assumption of 'periodicity', and also with any simplification in a model (which is, moreover, based only on 'economic' type variables).

But, as said, to the conventional economic approach, to the explanation to the structural changes (or major changes, i.e.: those which are not short-term or conjunctural), the Schumpeterian objections had been counterpointed.

3.2 The Schumpeterian Objection

The Schumpeterian objection is deep-rooted: it originates from the debate about Capitalism at the end of the last century and on the conditions to guarantee a balanced development of the economy. Schumpeter's *Theory of Economic Development* (written in the first years of the century),[24] argued that there could be a relationship between the structural, or major changes ('true' economic development), and the conditions of equilibrium. These conditions can exert their influence, according to Schumpeter, within the economic mechanism (described properly by conventional economics), which is expressed mainly by equilibirium/dis-equilibrium through a set of variables: demand/supply; investment/consumption; labour/capital; cost/return; etc. Schumpeter calls it the *'circular flow of the economy'*[25] where there are production crises at short terms, relaunches, adjustments at margin, by consumers, producers, workers, capitalists and also of the State in connection to its fiscal withdrawal/expenditures relationship.

According to Schumpeter, all these have nothing to do with the economic development or change. Both of these are determined outside those systemic relations oriented to the equilibrium that he defined as 'static'. The *'fundamental phenomena of development'*[26] do not follow the rules of economic statics, that of *'circular flow of the economy'*. This flow has its basis in a dynamics of which the causal principle must be sought elsewhere. As we know, according to Schumpeter, it must be sought in the 'innovation', which eludes economic rules; but which for him always provides an economic explanation of change.

From this ambiguity derives my location of Schumpeter mid-way between the 'technological approach' and the 'economic approach'.

In fact, Schumpeter, in search of the 'fundamental phenomenon of economic development' (more precisely, the determinant factor of historical social change, beyond the mere 'equilibrium' between economic phenomenon, which he defined as flows – 'circular flows', 'comparable to the circulation of the blood in the animal organism', that have been enlightened by traditional economic theory), goes away from the 'economic explanation' that he claims to always provide.

For Schumpeter, that basic phenomenon and determinant factors are the 'new combinations of the means of production', activated by these subjects, who only if they are actors of such combinations (as *'innovators'*) deserve the title of 'entrepreneur' (*Unternehmer*). While others who do not create any new combinations do not deserve the title of entrepreneur, but only that of businessman or speculators.[27]

But these new combinations of the production means are not produced, according to Schumpeter, within the phenomena of economic equilibrium; therefore they are not 'explained' by economic analysis. We can follow him through his own words:

> The [economic] theory describes economic life from the standpoint of the economic system's tendency toward an equilibrium position, which tendency gives us the means of determining prices and quantities of goods, and may be described as an adaptation of the data existing at any time[28] ... The position of the ideal state of equilbrium in the economic system, never attained, continually 'striven after' (of course not consciously), changes, because the data change. And theory is not weaponless in the face of these changes in data. It is constructed so as to be able to deal with the consequences of such changes ... If the change occurs in the non-social data (natural conditions) or in non-economic social data (here belong the effects of war, changes in commercial, social or economic policy) or in consumers' tastes, then to this extent fundamental overhaul of the theoretical tools seems to be required. These tools only fail ... where economic life itself changes its own data by fits and starts...Continuous changes, which may in time, by continual adaptation through innumerable small steps, make a great department store out of a small retail business, come under the 'static' analysis. But 'static' analysis is not only unable to predict the consequences of discontinuous changes in the traditional way of doing things; it can neither explain the occurrence of such productive revolutions nor the phenomena which accompany them. It can only investigate the new equilibrum position after the changes have occurred. It is just the occurrence of the 'revolutionary' changes that is our problem, the problem of economic development in a very narrow and formal sense ...
>
> By 'development', therefore, we shall understand only his changes in economic life, as are not forced upon it *from without* but arise by its own initiative, *from within*. Should it turn out that there are non changes arising in the economic spheres itself, and that the phenomenon that we call economic development is in practice simply founded upon the fact that the data change and that the economy continously adapts itself to them, then we should say that there is no economic development. By this we should mean that economic development is not a phenomenon to be explained economically, but that the economy, in itself without development, is dragged along by the *changes in the surrounding world*, that the causes and hence the explanation of the development must be sought *outside* the group of facts which are described by economic theory ...

Nor will the mere growth of the economy, as shown by the growth of population and wealth, be designated here as a process of development. For it calls forth no qualitatively new phenomena, but only processes of adaptation of the same kind as the changes in the natural data. Since we wish to direct our attention to other phenomena, we shall regard such increases as changes in data...

And – in a Note:

we do this because these changes are small per annum and therefore do not stand in the way of the applicability of the 'static' method. Nevertheless their appearance is frequently a *condition* of development in our sense. But even though they often *make the latter possible*, yet they do not *create it out themselves*. (Emphasis by Schumpeter only in the German edition)

And in the text, he continues:

Development in our sense is a distinct phenomenon, entirely foreign to what may be observed in the circular flow or in tendency towards equilibrium. It is spontaneous and discontinous change in the channels of the flow [about which he considers engaged – as seen – all traditional economics], disturbance of equilibrium, which forever alter and displaces the equilibrium state previously existing.
(Schumpeter, *Theory of Economic Development*, English edn 1961, pp. 62–4)

And the German edition also included:

Our theory of the development is none other than the treatment of this phenomenon and of the processes in it.[29]

This is quite similar to what we mean in this book by 'structural change', which we will try to investigate. In these few passages I think that the intrinsic ambiguity of the Schumpeterian paradigm is defined very clearly: from one side are researched the *extra* economic factors of the economic development, and from the other side are researched the factors (or more simply, the conditions) which explain the economic development from its *interior*, yet do not respond to the variability of the *external* data as the traditional economic theory seems to do.[30]

In sum, from a certain point of view, the Schumpeterian theory of development provides itself as an economic theory which 'endogenized' the technological change; that theory, in other words, which tries to define the basic phenomenon or factor of the development itself. Curiously, he located such a factor *outside* the economic phenomena usually considered; i.e. population, income, consumers, and also cultural factors, scientific knowledge and inventions (since that, as well known, Schumpeter made a firm distinction between invention and innovation in the technological development process).

But Schumpeter insists on considering as 'data' (therefore exogenous elements in his system of logical relations; i.e. natural data, population, wealth, state of knowledge and state of art, etc.) all possible external factors, and the changes concerning them as 'conditions' which often make the change possible but do not 'produce' it. In this way he goes in to the research, this time, of an *internal* factor. In a famous note, added to the 2nd English edition (1934), he stated:

> In the first edition of this book, I called it 'dynamics'. But it is preferable to avoid this expression here, since it so easily leads us astray because of the associations which attach themselves to its various meanings. Better, then, to say simply what we mean: economic life changes; it changes partly because of changes in data, to which it tends to adapt itself. But this is not the only kind of economic change; there is another which is not accounted for by influence on the data from without, but which arises *from within* the system, and this kind of change is the cause of so many important economic phenomena that it seems worthwhile to build a theory for it, and, in order to do so, to isolate it from all the other factors of change.
>
> The author begs to add another more exact definition, which he is in the habit of using: what we are about to consider is that kind of change arising *from within* the system which so displaces its equilibrium point that the new one cannot be reached from the old one by infinitesimal steps. Add successively as many mail coaches as you please, you will never get a railway thereby.
>
> (Schumpeter, *Theory of Economic Development*, English edn 1961, p. 164)

The Schumpeterian *internal* factor of economic development is therefore the 'introduction of new combinations' (of productive factors).[31] The five canonical cases with which Schumpeter has articulated and ordered that introduction are well known and still very valid:

1. Production of new goods, that is goods still not familiar to the circle of the consumer, or of a new quality of goods.
2. Introduction of a new method of production, that has not yet been experimented in the branch of the industry concerned, which does not need at all to be based on a new scientific discovery, and which can consist also in a new way of dealing commercially with a commodity.

3. Opening of a new market, that is a market in which a particular branch of the industry of a certain country has not penetrated, whether this market already existed or not.
4. Conquest of a new source of supply of a basic material or of semi-processed material from a source already existing or necessarily created anew.
5. Implementation of a reorganization of any kind of industry as well as the creation of a monopoly (for instance, through the institution of a trust) or its destruction.

We will refer to the above five taxonomic cases as follows: (1) New goods; (2) New processes; (3) New market; (4) New basic material; (5) New organization.

But who activates these factors of development, named innovations? And why are they activated? Who researches the new goods, the new processes, the new markets, the new basic materials, the new organization, in order to innovate the production and the distribution of goods and services? And what is his or her motivation?

Here, Schumpeter embarks upon an analysis with which he is tormented for his entire life (and with him, equally tormented, a dozen serious scholars of the development).

The answer at first view seems clear: the person is, of course, the entrepreneur who acts as 'innovator'; but not all entrepreneurs are able to be as such. Here enters into the game the specification of the entrepreneur-innovator, or the 'true' entrepreneur (according to Schumpeter).

Neither the enterprise property, nor the assumption of risk[32] are sufficient to connote the entrepreneur-innovator. Schumpeter states:

> everyone is an entrepreneur only when he actually 'carries out new combinations', and loses that character as soon as he has built his business, when he settles down to running it as other people run their business. This is the rule, of course, and hence it is just as rare for anyone always to remain an entrepreneur throughout the decades of his active life as it is for a businessman never to have a moment in which he is an entrepreneur, to however modest a degree. (ibid. p. 78)

For these reasons also, according to Schumpeter, there are not the conditions for entrepreneurs to acquire a 'class position'.[33]

Therefore, it would be right to state that with the Schumpeterian theory of economic development, whilst the traditional theory is accused of 'exogenizing' the technological phenomenon assuming it as a 'datum' of the economic phenomenon, in reality technology is placed as an external factor, or engine (therefore, truly exogenous) in regard to the development, when it is not explained economically and it becomes the motor variable of the economic progress.[34]

In conclusion, Schumpeter's effort to place innovation among the 'endogenous' factors of the development is one he repeats.[35] The validity of this effort however depends on the success which he achieves in giving an economic explanation to innovation; but an economic explanation different from that which would have made him fall again into the logic of the economic equilibrium he claimed to be outside of. (Otherwise, he could have risked being ridiculed by the traditional and conventional economists to whom he was an opponent, with the metaphor of the trial of the Baron of Münchausen, who pretended to have pulled himself out of the river by his own hair).

And so, did Schumpeter succeed? Was he able to tell us, 'from where comes innovation'? Or at least, what is the process that leads to innovation? (Other than telling us, and this he did very well, that innovation is the first factor of the change, major, strong, radical, internal, of the economic system that we wish to describe.)

This is the obsessive thinking of many scholars who have studied Schumpeter's theme of innovation.[36] And, in my opinion, the obsessive thinking of Schumpeter himself in trialling the endogenization of innovation, in the study of economic cycles, was unique too in allowing a logical way out of the claim to remain within economic analysis and to modify the theory of economic development.

As we have already said, Schumpeter, and after him a dozen scholars of innovation, characterize innovation as a new 'combination of factors'. But instead of giving an answer as to where it comes from, they only say what it is.[37]

We have already also said that the Schumpeterian innovation can be described in several forms (new goods, new methods, new markets, etc.). But what is the paste that holds together all of these new forms of the 'combination of the productive factors' in the direction that would not be an ordinary administration of the existing system, or of the 'given' system that according to Schumpeter is the field not contested of traditional economic theory, that of the circular flow or economic statics? For Schumpeter this paste is the enterprise or the entrepreneur without whom no innovation is generated.

Therefore, summarizing, the logical simplified sequence of Schumpeter can be expressed as follows: economic development (the true one) is generated by innovations (the true ones); the innovations (the true ones) are generated by the enterprise and entrepreneur (the true one).

But from whom and from what are the enterprise and entrepreneur (the true ones) generated?

If the theory must remain endogenous, we have to answer the above question in some way with an answer that we could define as 'economic'.

But, since neither Schumpeter nor his numerous followers have been able to provide an answer on the last link of the chain, we think that the Schumpeterian approach and, more generally, the students of economics of technological change, especially those of economics of invention, are unable to build an *economic* theory of change. This is why we will continue to classify them among the 'technological approaches' rather than among the 'economic' ones.

3.3 The Rostow Objections to the Theories of Economic Development

The economic approach, however, has long since given a more sure response, not so much with regard to the 'factors determining' economic development[38] as to its indicators.

And from this point of view we may take as representative of this type of analysis (which for more than three decades has accompanied all the debate on development) the well-known scheme by Rostow of the *'stages'* of economic growth.[39]

His analysis distances itself to such an extent from an economic 'explanation' of growth, that if it was not for its pertinacious decision (which we will discuss below) to define his position as that of a 'dynamic disaggregate theory of production', and the fact that it does not uphold (for example, against Hirschman's praise of 'unbalanced growth') the theory of a 'dynamic balanced growth',[40] it would be better classified among the non-economic approaches, between perhaps the 'technological' ones and the 'historical-institutional' ones. In fact, overall, Rostow's approach is mainly descriptive rather than 'explanatory'.

As is known, Rostow's contribution to our problem of structural change and more generally to the theory of development, is that of the classification of this development in a certain number of stages (Rostow, 1960, Chapter 2), which we limit ourselves here to listing:

1. *'Traditional society'*: 'limited productive functions, founded on pre-Newtonian science and technology'.
2. *'The preliminary conditions for take-off'*: historically determined – in the original industrial revolution countries – 'when the intuitions of modern science began to be translated into new productive functions, both in agriculture and in industry'; nevertheless, 'in the most frequent case of modern history the stage of the preliminary conditions has not arisen endogenously, but has derived from some external intrusion from more advanced societies'.
3. The *'take-off'*: the *'great watershed'* of life in modern societies. The take-off, for Rostow, is the interval in which the old delays and resistance against decisive growth are definitively overcome; in Great Britain and in

the wealthy parts of the world populated mainly by Anglo-Saxons (United States, Canada, etc.) the most direct stimulus to take-off was above all, but not entirely, of a technical nature.[41] More generally, in the other cases, 'the take-off awaited not only the build-up of social overhead capital and a surge of technological development in industry and agriculture', but also the ascent to power of a group prepared to consider modernization of the economy as a serious, primary political need.

4. *'The passage to maturity'*: After the 'take-off' follows a long interval of sustained progress, which is albeit subject to fluctuations whilst the economy, now in regular development, tends to extend modern technology to all fronts of its activity. And: 'formally, we can define maturity as the stage at which an economy demonstrates the capacity to move beyond the original industries which powered its take-off and to absorb and apply efficiently over a very wide range of its resources, if not the whole range the most advanced fruits of (then) modern technology'. Apart from his descriptive taxonomy, Rostow makes some cognitive conclusions: 'historically, it would appear that something like sixty years was required to move a society from the beginning of take-off to maturity... but, clearly, no dogmatism is justified by the exact length of the interval from take-off and maturity'.[42]

5. *'The period of high mass-consumption'*, in which the lead-sectors turn to consumer durables and services, a stage from which Americans are now [1960] beginning to come out of, whose not completely limpid pleasures Western Europe and Japan are beginning to enjoy, and with which Soviet society is engaged in a difficult courtship.

When societies reached maturity, in the 20th century, two events occurred: pro capita real income rose to such an extent that many people found a buying power that transcended the need for food, housing and clothing; and the structure of the labour force has changed in such a way as to increase not only the proportion of urban population in relation to overall population, but also the proportion of the population employed in services and factories, who are aware and keen to obtain the consumer fruits offered by an economy that has arrived at maturity. In addition society has begun to no longer consider the further extension of modern technology as a predominant objective. It is in this stage that is subsequent to maturity, for example, that by means of the political process Western societies have chosen to allocate greater resources to well-being and to social security. The rise of the welfare state is one of the manifestations of a society that is passing beyond technical maturity.

Rostow's scheme of growth, like other more sophisticated theorems of the economics of development (such as those, which come to mind, of Kuznets,[43]

Rosenstein-Rodan[44] or Chenery[45]), have offered the possibility of linking analyses concerning the economic problems of some countries (from those of Western countries bringing up the rear to those of all the third-world countries and Eastern Europe) with some indicators of growth and some gradients connected to it, such as to suggest surer answers on the validity of some policies. In other words it has permitted a classification not only of the 'stages' of growth, but also of the policies that are most suitable to each of them.[46] But he has certainly not supplied any 'theory' of economic growth, in the conventional sense.[47]

Nevertheless, Rostow himself does not shrink from formulating some sort of 'theory'.[48] For example, in another work he states:

> I believe it is possible to bring within the structure of a dynamic, disaggregated theory the forces making for population change, as well as the generation of scientific knowledge and invention, and the process of innovation. It is then possible to conceive of a dynamic equilibrium path for a peaceful, closed economy and all its sectors. Those overall and sectoral optimum paths imply that investment resources are allocated to the sectors without error or lag, taking into account changes in technology as well as demand. We can thus formulate abstractly a disaggregated, moving rather than static, equilibrium. In fact, of course, the economies we study were not closed; they were often at war or affected by war; and investment was subject to systematic errors and lags. Moreover, the coming of new technologies and the opening of new sources of food and raw-materials supply often took the form of large, discontinuous changes in the economy and its structure. And, even in the most capitalist of societies the economic role of government was significant. What we observe, then, are dynamic, interacting national economies, trying rather clumsily to approximate optimum sectoral equilibrium paths, tending successively to undershoot and overshoot those paths.   (Rostow, 1978, pp. xi–xli)

In brief, he underlines the importance given by himself to the concept of a 'dynamic disaggregate optimum pattern of growth', from which deviations may be evaluated.[49]

But what does Rostow's historical-economic approach give us for an exploration of a possible transformation of contemporary society, and the identification of a possible future stage? The problem could be posed in these terms: does the ordering of historical growth, from 'traditional society' to 'modern society' in five stages, help us in some way, or does it suggest something of the next stage, the sixth, which we obviously cannot yet name, but which should come after that which Rostow has called the stage of *'high mass consumption'*?

The problem is not absent in Rostow's work. In 1960, in his well-known exposition of the stages, he confronts, albeit fleetingly in two paragraphs (in chapters 2 and 6), the theme: 'beyond the great consumption stage', and he states: 'beyond, it is impossible to predict, except perhaps to observe that the Americans has behaved in the past decade [we are in 1960] as if diminishing relative marginal utility sets in for durable consumers' goods; and they have chosen, at the margin, larger families' (it was the time of the American baby boom). He calls it the 'Buddenbrooks' dynamics' (referring to the three generations of Germans in the famous novel by Thomas Mann): 'the Americans have behaved as if, having been born into a system that provided economic security and high mass consumption, they placed a lower valuation on acquiring additional increments of real income in the conventional form as opposed to the advantages and values of an enlarged family' (pp. 11–12). And tracing again the route of modernization he repeats that after the period of transition ('when the pre-conditions for take-off are created, generally in response to the intrusion of foreign power converging with certain domestic forces making for modernization'[50]), after the actual take-off, and after the advent of maturity, 'generally taking up the life of about two further generations', there is – (as before) 'if the rise of income has matched the spread of technological virtuosity – the diversion of the fully mature economy, to the provision of durable consumer goods and services (as well as the welfare state), for its increasingly urban and then sub-urban population.' And he concludes: 'Beyond lies the question of whether, or not, secular spiritual stagnation will arise, and, if this does, how man might fend it off' (p. 12). (Rostow, 1960, pp. 10–12)

In chapter 6, intended to outline the features of the mass consumption period, his effort at searching for something 'beyond' does not go further than certain unsure allusion to the 'boredom' of a society without problems, and does not try to examine from within this consumer society the structural transformations that could lead to the birth of new and no-less-acute problems.

But if this did not take place in Rostow's work in the 1960s, nor did it take place subsequently in his written works – in the wake of his successfully proposed periodization – when some new events in the last thirty years, and the many works intervening in order to interpret the further lines of development, could suggest some new commentary.[51] For this reason, we are induced to conclude, even with hindsight, that Rostow's classification, albeit very useful for a critical reading of the growth situations of single societies, in the context of an overall line of growth, and for linking to this reading many evaluations and suggestions for policies, has not however created the stimulus to understand more the nature and meaning of contemporary structural changes, and their socio-economic implications (as is, for example, the intention of this work, and that of many others produced in the meantime).

To conclude this long digression on the 'Rostowian' approach, (or 'economic', or whatever) we can say that Rostow's position, in his last works as well (1990), is certainly, rightly and progressively anchored to a critique of the 'conventional' economic position,[52] and it is also based on a meta-economic vision, so to speak, including the consideration of complex non-economic factors (technology, culture, politics, etc.). The Rostow position was nevertheless somewhat lacking as a convincing study of the structural aspects of the change of the last stage. And paradoxically, his interpretation, which is very pertinent for the reading of economic systems still in a backward phase of their sequence, in which the paradigms of conventional economic theory are more appropriate, was lacking an in-depth 'economic' study of the implications of the change of this last stage. This study, by virtue of its historical-evolutionist approach, would have protected him from many persistent errors that the theories of economic growth (still founded on those paradigms) have been and are unable to avoid.

3.4 Sylos Labini's Answers

Most of the work of Sylos Labini on this matter still belongs to an economic approach.[53] In the part of his economic contribution that concerns the technological progress and its role in economic development and in what we call structural changes, Sylos Labini insists on the fact that in the long period, technical progress, even if represented as a necessary condition, does not constitute the main factor of economic development.[54] On the contrary, Sylos Labini, whilst stating that 'most modern economists consider these changes as a process which influences the economic life from the outside, that is as an "exogenous process"', argues that 'this point of view is not correct', since (even if 'in certain circumstances, the inventions can take place effectively in autonomous ways...usually they have been stimulated by war...etc.). Often, however, the invention is provoked by economic stimuli.' 'Anyway, the adaptation and the implementation, as well as the speed of diffusion of all inventions depend on the economic conditions; in the first place, they depend on the growth of the "market size"...which represent the general conditions of the technological change.' (Sylos Labini, 1984, p. 64 ff)

Having reaffirmed this old convinction, Sylos Labini rightly restates also that

the expansion of the market stimulates additional investment and, as a rule, the new capital goods are more perfected than those existing. At the same time, the expansion of the market promotes the introduction of new goods, which often satisfy the needs of a higher order – in the sense of the

German statistician, Engel – and for this reason they presuppose and increase in average individual income. From both viewpoints (capital goods and consumer goods), economic development appears as a self-sustaining process.   (ibid.)

If the expansion of the market represents, as Sylos Labini holds, the condition of the technological changes, the 'increase of wages compared to capital goods...and the variations in the relative prices of certain goods' (which include even the first increase if we consider the work as a good, too), represent the 'specific conditions'.[55]

Later[56] Sylos Labini again took up the theme of the relationship between economic impulses and technological progress, introducing a clearer distinction between autonomous innovations and induced innovations. Let us follow him in his own words:

> Most economists consider all innovations to be generated outside the economic system by autonomous scientific development. If this is so, then it is the task of economic analysis to study the effects of innovations rather than their origin. In the field of structural change, this point of view is shared by no less an authority than Joseph Schumpeter.
>
> A distinction, however, is necessary. The expectation of profit is a necessary condition for carrying out all sorts of innovations but cannot be considered as a specific cause or impulse coming from the economic sphere. Scientific progress is pushed forward by intellectual curiosity; in certain cases it gives rise to inventions that are profitable in given economic conditions and are transformed into innovations when certain entrepeneurs realize the practical applications that can be exploited for profit. Inventions of this type and the innovations which follow from them can be attributed to 'disinterested' or 'autonomous' scientific progress. Such innovations have made plausible the idea that technical progress should be considered as an essentially exogenous phenomenon. But there are innovations that are carried out only when certain economic stimuli come into play. We call the former type of innovations 'autonomous', the latter type 'induced'. ('Induced' innovations are likely to be based on inventions, which, in their turn, are 'induced' in the sense indicated.) Autonomous innovations are often major innovations and, as a rule, consist of entirely new products. They occur discontinuously and are thus the source of erratic shocks. Induced innovations are often of secondary importance from the scientific standpoint, as they have the nature of improvements and adaptations, but they are very important for the continuity and speed of economic growth. As a rule, they are process innovations or, if they are product innovations, they are only improvements of quality or design.

Induced innovations are stimulated by the expansion of demand or by cost increases. In a particular sense, innovations that are developed in the research laboratories of large firms belong to the category of induced innovations, since money spent for these purposes is comparable to other kinds of investments. Research and development (R & D) expenditure depends, in its turn, on the rate of expansion of demand in the market in which each firm operates; and this rate depends upon the behavior of aggregate demand in the economy as a whole and upon the efforts which the firm itself makes to raise the volume of sales: advertising campaigns and product diversification – efforts which will be more successful the more rapid the expansion of aggregate demand. Thus it remains true that aggregate demand is one of the two fundamental impulses behind induced innovations, the other being represented by cost increases.

... Innovations are to be considered as induced even if the economic stimuli are created or strengthened artificially by the government.

With the introduction of the dichotomy between autonomous and induced innovations, Sylos Labini tries to escape from Schumpeterian ambiguity, but it is not clear if he succeeds without provoking other questions. In fact he recognizes that the autonomous innovations are the most important from the scientific point of view, that they have an erratic character, etc., and that those induced are of secondary importance, and take the aspect of improvements and adaptation. They are important however from the point of view of the continuity and the pace of development. The induced innovations however, as they are determined by economic conditions, that is by the better opportunity of profits for the firms that adapt them or determine them (even if in differentiated terms between the short and long term), have been in any case the innovations that, from the traditional theory against which Schumpeter argues, are always included in the circular process of flow, that is in an adaptation of the investment (and its typology) to the circumstances of different economic impulses.

As we have seen, we cannot say that Schumpeter considered technical progress to be exogenous to economic facts: on the contrary, he contested the fact that the economic tradition would be such, in a static vision of development, without including this technical progress (making it therefore endogenous, as he himself argues against the traditional economy) within a dynamic economic explanation. He considered giving an economic explanation to the autonomous innovations of Sylos Labini, but not to those induced, as they have already more or less had their own economic explanation. And we have already seen that it is not by chance that from Schumpeter is born the economics of entrepeneurial invention, either of the single captain of industry as innovator (the unique, true entrepeneur) of original capitalism or the research laboratories of the big business of neocapitalism.

The present problem of technical progress is not so much to distinguish what is a typically economic impulse, and what is not economic (in other words what is endogenous or exogenous to the mechanism, usually the subject of the economic analysis). The present problem is to study the basic mechanism on which decisions are based which concern it. These mechanisms can be fed by factors that cannot be broken down by point of view (economic, technical, political, social, etc.); but by factors that are determined according to circumstances: the stage of development of the socio-economic environment in question, operators' motivations, governmental preferences and policies (influential among them unfortunately those of the military) etc., without trying to extract from all of that economic theories that are too generalized, which would perpetuate a endless discussion of false problems. Sylos Labini himself in an earlier writing of 1984 perceived (if I understood correctly) this need when he stated as the conclusion of a certain economic analysis that:

> technological changes consist in innovations in the productive process and in the product. In a direct way, the three conditions recalled above have an influence on technological change; but in an indirect way, those changes are conditioned by cultural, organizational and even institutional innovations; sometimes, legislation itself can represent, for good and for bad, an innovation of this type.[57]

And since technological change takes place in historical times, it is unavoidable, even for Sylos Labini, to draft a periodization of the economic development in four stages, which recall strongly those of Rostow.

The *first* is that of rural traditional society (which was analyzed by Adam Smith and which embraces the sixteenth and seventeenth centuries), in which the division of labour, from which technological changes depend, meets strong institutional obstacles, and in which free competition 'is not a reality but a goal to pursue'.

The *second* is that of '*competitive capitalism*' in which the trends of wages and prices have been 'very close to those predicted by Smith'. The development of investment goods becomes socially relevant; the sector of the investment goods becomes the main source of technological changes; it is the period when 'probably behind the most important innovations, we can find the triad described by Schumpeter, that is the inventor, the entrepreneur and the banker', etc. (this period could comprise, according to Sylos Labini, and in the same logic in cycles, *à la* Schumpeter, two long cycles).

The *third* is that of 'oligopolistic capitalism' (the same period as Schumpeter's 'trustified capitalism' and of the Marxists' 'monopolistic capitalism'), in which the Schumpeterian triad has lost importance; the individual inventor is substituted more and more frequently by a scientist or by a group of scientists who work in a laboratory for the larger corporations or in public laboratories; the role of the banking system changes, and even under the impulse of the public expenditure and by the expansion of the government bonds; and normally the innovations do not bring with them a legion of imitators, but more and more frequently are implemented by the already existing corporation. (Sylos Labini, 1984, pp. 77–8)

Thus, in this viewpoint, Sylos Labini outlined a *fourth*, further, stage that essentially interests our work; and he outlines it in a way that is tentatively more explanatory compared to that descriptive of Rostow: the stage whose hypothesis is justified by the technological and economic changes experienced in the last recent years, 'changes so rapid and deep', and to evaluate the importance of them Sylos Labini considered 'the recent evolution of the occupational structure'.[58]

Sylos Labini came to identify a radical change in the employment structure, in studying the persistent occupational crisis even in the presence of the remarkable advancement of the productive capacity and of the economic welfare of advanced countries. He came to consider that today's unemployment has nothing to do with unemployment in the era of increasing industrialization, when in spite of technological progress and increases in productivity, such phenomena were being translated into an expansion of labour opportunities. He came to imagine some 'new aspects of the cyclical development of the economy',[59] and overall a new way of conceiving the problem of unemployment.[60]

His consideration on this last, fourth, stage, that is, the consideration on the structure of employment and unemployment, on manual work and intellectual work, and lastly on the structure of industry (explosion of the small firms and enterprises) (see 1984, 1993) is so inherent and so introductory to the subject of this book that we will return more directly to it in the next chapters. For the moment, we will limit ourselves to observing that the constant reference to the changes in the structure of the final demand of consumers, makes Sylos Labini's answer the starting point from which our critical analysis of the contemporary structural change will develop (from Chapter 3 forward).

With Sylos Labini, moreover, the economic approach opens – or, so to speak, re-opens – to a wider vision, and then, perhaps more 'voluntarist' and less 'positivist', of the development and of history. And here we are meeting, inevitably, the historical, institutional approach, and its roots.

3.5 Beyond the Economics of Technological Change

Before examining the institutional approach, let us also continue to consider in a different respect the attempts to explain change 'economically'. They certainly derive from Schumpeter's critique and challenge against the traditional conception of development. At the same time, however, they arise also as a response to Schumpeter's ambiguous move of including the factors determining it (*innovations and innovator*) *within* the economic explanation. Yet this inclusion is realized by means of the surreptitious device of broadening the nominal boundaries of what is economic, without justifying what is 'economic' in the generation of inventions and innovations. In other words, he failed to explain them economically (a device that has been called a 'logical anacoluthon').

Thus Schumpeter resorted to 'cycle theory', considering the long-term Kondratief cycle (attributing the short-term ones to traditional static-equilibrium economics); but he never specified – despite a thousand pages devoted to the statistical enquiry of all long-term determining variables (prices, products, product change, etc.) – whether the cycle has to be considered as a determining cause of innovations, or, on the contrary, whether innovations have to be seen as a determining cause of the cycle. The predilection for the Kondratief, and for its more or less fixed periodicity, leads to the belief that he tended to consider the cycle as the cause of innovations (more or less clustered) rather than the contrary. But the latter view would reveal also a historical fatalism that is not easily reconcilable with Schumpeter's own personality, even if there is some reason to suspect this, considering his later analysis of the 'destiny' of Capitalism.

There have been attempts by his followers, especially by evolutionists and institutionalists, to develop not only the general topic of the relationship between technology and economic development, but also the problem of the economic explanation of innovations and even of invention (a problem that, as I noted above, was solved ambiguously by Schumpeter).

Thus, during the past decades, there has been an increasing number of studies on what I would call the *economics of innovation and invention*. I think that the foundations of these studies are in the extensive work made in the 1950s and 1960s in order to understand the economic and social factors of '*inventive activity*'.[61]

At one of the NBER's important conferences devoted to the topic 'How and When Inventions and Inventors Are Born', Jacob Schmookler presented the results of a big research project (financed by the Guggenheim Foundation) on 'Changes in Industry and in the State of Knowledge As Determinants of Industrial Inventions',[62] which concerned a very accurate (partly historical) enquiry on the 'most important inventions' in the most diverse sectors. But confronted with another contribution (by Fritz Machlup[63]) at the same conference, which proposed – likewise in the framework of the background question 'why do inventors invent?' – a theoretical scheme including some supply curves of inventions and inventors as a function of a set of aggregate phenomena, Schmookler necessarily stated (dissenting from Machlup's aggregate approach) that:

> so far as shifts in the supply of inventors are concerned, there are a whole host of familiar, unsolved problems: the effect of education on originality as well as on technical proficiency; the effect of ethnic and religious influences; the existence of secular changes in risk preferences and per-haps in the very recognition of risk; the effect of the shift from independ-ent to hired invention; i.e. the effect of the organization of risk-bearing; and the effect of the different degree of risk of failure for hired inventors as distinct from the risks of failure confronting, say, production engineer-ing or college professors. (Schmookler, 1962, p. 168)

Well, I do not think that in the past decades research has been able to 'solve' the aforementioned gaps concerning the knowledge of that set of *effects*; actually, I do not even think, frankly, they could have done so, except for what concerns totally particular and not generalizable circumstances and very limited viewpoints; and this would diminish the significance of any possibly achieved 'solution'.[64] *Vis-à-vis* such a confident positive research position, the value of Machlup's positive and neo-classical theoretical approach rises in my eyes (which at least has the elegance of an intellectual game)!

Is it not actually more 'scientific', then, to turn the problem and the approach upside down? Is it not more appropriate to think that 'empirical' research, instead of providing an answer the question of '*why*' and '*how*' inventors do invent, should answer to the question of 'what' the inventors can or should invent in order to solve some (social, economic, territorial, political) problems that a community faces? Would it not be better to define, considering every single case, project, programme and plan, *what* the inven-tors should invent, *given* the circumstance, rather than *how*, in general, they invent? What we need to know is in fact this: the circumstances, the objective *data* concerning each problem (project, programme, plan, etc.). But to know that, without previously knowing the goals, is useless, except to produce confusion and misunderstandings!

To mistake – in the field of social sciences – for 'scientific' (i.e. 'cognitive') what is not 'operative' (i.e. 'problem-solving') has been the big equivocation, error and ingenuousness of the social sciences from the past century onwards, which condemn them to an almost complete general uselessness, without betterment of the cognitive capacity itself.[65]

On the other hand – if we remain within the Schumpeter-type approach of knowing where the 'entrepreneur', 'innovation' and 'inventions' come from and what the relations among them are – if there is something sure (which seems to spring from the amount of research and attention devoted to these relations) it is that *no stable, 'standardizable', relations exist*, both because the (historical) circumstances in which these relations are produced do change and because the very nature of the actors we call 'entrepreneurs' or of the objects we call 'innovation' or 'invention' do change. In sum, the terms upon which one wants to build a *theory* of these relations – regardless if theoretically or empirically – change continuously.

The only possible theory is the 'operative' one (which the positivist approach rightly deems a 'non-theory'), a theory depending on problem-solving, given constraints and circumstances. A theory of programming, or planning.[66]

But a further sure thing that emerges from the many more or less empirical enquiries into the relations between inventions and innovations (the following diagnosis could emerge more clearly if we started from a different vision of the very goals of the research) is that inventions (assuming that it is possible to define them in a sufficiently omni-comprehensive way, and that this univocal definition is of any use[67]) are always born under two main stars: casualness and intentionality.[68] Since humanity – even if still believing strongly in providence, or in destiny or fate, or in good and bad luck – seems nevertheless more and more inclined (in the daily life of any individual as well as in the social management of groups and collectives) to try not to be dominated by events outside of its possibilities of control and programming, it is on the *cotè* of intentionality and programming on which the attention of scholars should focus. And on this *cotè*, it can be held that inventions, however born, have been always the result of *decisions*, *programmes*: from the individual ones of the single inventor or scientist, to the group ones, to those of social and collective research units, more or less linked to productive enterprises, which yesterday were directed by Schumpeter's entrepreneurs, today by Galbraith's or Drucker's managers or technocrats, up to the laboratories and public programmes of NASA or of military authorities.

The same is even more true if, in addition to invention, we consider innovation, which certainly is less subject than the former to the star of casualness and more to the star of intentionality, and thus more linked to the decisions and programmes of somebody (from the individual to the UN programme).

Therefore: if the 'programmatic' coefficient is the one that predominates in the history of inventions and innovations, why should we lose so much time in the search (more or less theoretical, more or less empirical) for regularities of behaviour that by definition never can be 'regularities'? Why should we try to scan the past or the present looking for ineluctable laws of development, when the events could be largely influenced by our own action, notwithstanding any alleged law? Why should we devote so much time to the discovery of parameters that can never be functioning but through arbitrary decisions? Why should we devote ourselves so confidently to the grasping of functional relationships among behaviours that, being necessarily 'empirical', i.e. ex post, do not have the 'necessary' requirement of repetition and predictability?

And – on the contrary – why should we not devote ourselves to the study of how 'problem solving' presents itself – at all levels and scales[69] – when there is the will to elaborate a strategy of innovation?

To be sure, the ambition to start from the definition of strategic objectives would generate the problem of how to make compatible in the first place the various goals of the research programmes related to the different scales at which they are elaborated. Yet the complexity we would face would not be more than that faced by the positive and 'empirical' researcher in order to give sense to his or her positive research; or to the complexity faced by a scientific community that aims to make sense of sets of researches conducted at different levels (in order to give them a plausible common result that has been absent so far, and in fact has produced only insurmountable controversies, and that for the planologist could not exist because of the wrong starting point). In effect, people have started by looking for something – the general validity of behaviours, i.e. a theory – that without the determination of objectives (i.e. of parameters for common evaluation) could not and cannot be evaluated.

In other words, and maybe with a simplification that should be considered only for its communicative functionality, the following argument could be developed. The point is to follow a path that is the opposite to the one followed by all research in the economics of invention.

Instead of asking *how* inventions are born and *how and how much* they influence or determine the innovations and under what circumstances does this happen, we should ask which innovations *would be necessary to solve* the (social, political, economic) problems of programming, and under what circumstances these innovations can *generate* (i.e. can be the determining factor of) inventions, which should be stimulated, spurred, and facilitated by 'targeted' research programmes?[70]

Schumpeter, who wanted at any cost to keep the explanation of development *within* an economic evaluation, had dealt a serious blow to the foundations of economics as a science, when he endogenized, i.e. included in the strictly 'economic' analysis (but considered by him different from that concerning circular flows or 'statics'), the factors determining change. He denied *traditional* economics the ability to explain *true* development and *significant* change, but confined its explanatory ability merely to temporary and local adjustments. He tried to give new foundations to it, moving it to another field, that of the real factors of development: of innovation and even of invention. But he did not realize, in my opinion, that there was an even stronger impediment that prevented economics from explaining development: that development cannot be explained by means of laws or objective regularities (his reliance on cycles has not produced any heuristic result), but by means of subjective and free (and thus unpredictable) actions;[71] and that economics – as any other social science – acquires value only as a tool for calculating the consistency and compatibility of complex decisions, among the most important of which there are those on scientific and technological progress. As the history of the past fifty years has clearly shown, actual economic changes such as the most important 'inventions' were born outside traditional economic factors, but mostly from non-economic decisions and choices.

Economics (as the other social sciences) would recover its functionality by limiting itself to be the 'guardian' of the rationality of decisions;[72] rationality intended as congruence between goals and means, and as maximization of their relation relative to the means, and not as discoverer of 'human behaviours' that remain unpredictable also when they are disguised as depersonalized phenomena: consumption, income gain, saving, investments, and in our 'Schumpeterian' case entrepreneurship, invention, innovation.

In brief, the economics of invention and innovation, like any other 'economics' (and like any other kind of positivist-type social science) – seen as the science of the relationship among ends and means, goals and instruments – can recover only if it transforms itself *into the science of political decision*, or into economic *policy*, or better, *planning* (even better, *planology*), without any illusion to achieve a scientific ground, intended as experimentally proven regularities, since these regularities simply do not exist.

The fact that any analysis of change should free itself from the aforementioned pseudoscientific assumptions and approaches, and become directly and decisively oriented toward the programming of change, belongs to the new emerging society, which will be the object of the analyses and considerations in this book.

4　THE HISTORICAL-INSTITUTIONAL APPROACH

However, let us return to the reappraisal of different approaches, and go to the approach I have defined as 'historical-institutional,' the one which equally tries to explain structural change, yet looks for its causes not in economic factors, but in 'institutional' factors, i.e. in the change of institutional social relations, mainly the property relations.[73]

In the 'historical-institutional' approach there is in the 'pole position', Marx's 'law of movement'[74] with all the variants generated by Marxist, post-Marxist, and quasi-Marxist literature. But, also, the theories of modern 'managerialism' (from Berle to Galbraith) have a good position.

4.1 The Marxian Approach

In line with this approach, it is the 'social relations' of production which determine the types and methods of production, from which it is possible to evince the main changes in the history of the economy. To use the famous synthetic words of Marx himself (which do not seem obsolete, at least as far as the 'historic-institutional' approach is concerned):[75]

> In the social production of their life, men enter into definite relations, that are necessary and independent of their will, relations of production which correspond to a definite stage of development of their material productive forces...At a certain stage of their development, the material productive forces of society enter into conflict with the existing relations of production, or – to formulate the same concept in legal terms – with the owner-ship relations within the framework in which they moved up till now....A period of social revolution therefore opens. With the change of the economic base, the entire huge superstructure is turned upside down more or less rapidly...[76] A social formation never dies before all the productive forces which it can contain are developed, and new and superior production relations are able to substitute it before the material conditions of existence are matured in the bosom of the old society. Therefore, mankind always assumes only those tasks which he is able to accomplish, as, with a closer look, it will always be clear that this task arises only where the material conditions for its realisation are already present – or at least about to become so.[77]

The primary factor of change, therefore, is the conflict of the material productive forces (*Produktivkräfte*) with the *existing* production relations (property relations, in legal terms), i.e., a factor exogenous to the mere relation of economic production: it is a matter of an emerging and contra-dictory 'social' relation.[78] But where does this emergence come from? In the preface to the *Critique* (transcribed above), Marx expresses himself some-what vaguely and, perhaps, in fatalistic terms:[79] these production relations in which men 'enter' are 'necessary and independent of their own will' and correspond to a 'certain stage of development' of their productive forces. It is this which has led some, with regard to the thesis of Marx, to speak of 'historical determinism': in that it is history which creates a social conflict on which the production regimes are developed and transformed. But the historical fatalism of Marx which denies the political will the capacity to determine events,[80] has caused others to speak of 'economic determinism' in that it is the economic relations of production which, unable to make up the operative frame of the material productive forces, go into crisis, taking with them the change in all the superstructures. In brief, for 'ideologists' (in the Marxian sense of the word) Marx is seen as *economist-minded*, explaining everything in economic terms (economic determinism); while for those who are themselves 'economists' Marx is seen as *non-economist-minded*, who, for explanations of the facts, draws from historical (imponderable) social factors exogenous with respect to the economic system and to the paradigm of the functioning of the economic system itself (historical determinism[81]).

4.2   The Marxian Ambiguities

Marx sensed the contradictions in his formulation and because he chose decidedly economic studies, he tried to use every method possible to go into greater depth in the endogenous factors of the evolution, the 'laws of movement' if not of known history, at least of the capitalist system.[82] And *Capital*, in its monumental research, represents the effort to understand, to penetrate, the vague and obscure side of its conception of history; to learn how 'necessary' the mechanism of conflict is between the capitalist (he who owns the capital) and the worker (he who owns the work), introducing surreptitiously a new endogenous element, of the economic type, an economic 'law',[83] within the economic reflection; and ending up by falling – himself – into the trap of 'positivist economics', which he had strongly criticized. He found himself, therefore, trying to formulate 'economic laws' (albeit only for the capitalist system) which were later revealed to be totally inadequate for the test of history, even if they were adequate to understand some aspects of the development of capitalism and of some of its important 'logic'.

Thus, while on the one hand, his 'economist-minded' line of thought (on which he stubbornly spent the whole of the second half of his life perfecting in a *complete*, ever more complete, theory of capital) became sterilized, at first in himself,[84] then later in his 'followers', in that the Marxist analysis of capital did not have real followers, but only objectors who highlighted – backed up by historical evidence – the inconsistencies and the factual denials.[85] On the other hand, the stream of thought which he abandoned (but on the basis of which he acquired fame and his reputation), that of the historification and institutionalization of economic development, had its most fruitful developments. To the point that it was possible to state that the whole of subsequent historical-economic thought – and a large part of sociology, not strictly psychological and positivist – can be defined as 'Marxist' (and not only in Germany) in as much as it was greatly influenced by his historical-institutional approach.

This is not the place for supporting and discussing the historical fragility and developmental ambiguity of the Marxist analysis of capital.[86] However we would like to immediately state the opinion that the fragility to which we refer is not that which the dozens of economists who have refuted the

Marxian theory of capital have knowingly highlighted. Rather it is that which is born from the conviction that also 'every' other theory of capital (like every other 'economic' theory) which is based on a *positive* generalization of behaviour and laws (as Marx himself ended up doing) has been shown to be inadequate by the test of history. And such inadequateness is true much more than in Marx's theory because the latter, at least conserved explicit roots in the history of capitalism, as production mode and social formation.

The two-faced Marxist Janus was thus unable to formulate a theory of the State and of the evolution of the capitalist society itself, other than one of a 'destructive' nature which looked towards the 'ideologies' of the past. His reticence in formulating recipes and of making predictions[87] shackled him in a sophisticated attempt at permanently updating his analysis of capital, to keep it in line with new visions and new realities which the development of capitalism offered – in the last third of the nineteenth century – while awaiting a total crisis of the old production method (capitalist), and a new production method yet to come to the surface (despite the many 'midwives' available).

This tenacity on the part of Marx and, above all, of his self-declared 'orthodox' followers, to not accept change, in order to keep 'ideologically' whole and valid the 'logic' of the analysis of the *internal* laws of the 'capitalist mode of production',[88] has in a way mortified and obscured the great role which the Marxian formulation itself had, as a matrix of the subsequent analysis of the evolution of capitalism.[89]

However, in 1873,[90] Marx accepts and diffuses a summary (more than an interpretation) of his approach to the historical change, that I assess as a document of special meaning for the survey of approaches to the change in which we are now involved:

For Marx – states the anonymous Russian reviewer, with whom Marx himself agrees, to such an extent that he reproduces a large part of the text without any objection – only one thing is important: to discover the law of the phenomena in which he is enquiring. And for him not only the law is important that rules over them, as far as they have a definite form and stay in a relationship that is observed in a given time period. For him, above all important is the law of its change (*Veränderung*), of its development (*Entwicklung*), i.e. of the transition (*Übergang*) from one form into another, from one order of that relationship into another. Once the law has been discovered, continues the Russian reviewer, Marx inquires into the details the consequences in which it manifests itself in social life ... For this purpose it is wholly sufficient to demonstrate the necessity of the present order of social connections (*Zusammenhang*) and at the same time the necessity of another order, into which the former must necessarily transit (*Übergehen*), indifferently from the fact that people believe it or not, that they are conscious of it or not. Marx considers the social movement as a process of natural history, driven by laws that not only are independent from the will, the conscience and the intentions of men, but on the contrary determine their will, their conscience and their intentions. But, some will say, the general laws of economic life are always the same; it makes no difference if they are applied to the present or to the past. Exactly this point is denied by Marx. According to him, such abstract laws do not exist...for him every historical period has, on the contrary, its own laws...Once life has survived a given stage of development, transits from a given stage into another, it begins to be ruled by other laws. In short, economic life offers to us a phenomenon which is analogous to the developmental history in other areas of biology. The old economists misunderstood the nature of economic laws, as they compared them to the laws of physics and chemistry. A deeper analysis of the phenomena proved that differences among social organisms are as deep as those among plant and animal organisms. Moreover, the same phenomena is ruled by different laws as a consequence of the different overall structure of those organisms, of the variations of their single organs, of the difference of the conditions within which they function, and so on. For example, Marx denies that the law of population is the same everywhere and at every time. He claims on the contrary that each stage of development has its own law of population. Together with the different development of the productive forces, the relations and the laws ruling them change. By posing to himself the aim to explore and to explain the capitalistic economic order, he is just formulating in a rigorously scientific way, the goal that any precise inquiry into economic life must have. The scientific value of such inquiry is in the identification of the specific laws which regulate the origins, existence, development and death of a given social organism and its replacement by another, higher one.

To this synthetic and insightful exposition of his own thinking,[91] Marx himself adds:

In expounding in such an exact and, for what concerns my personal application of it, benevolent way what he calls my real method, what else has the author expounded than the dialectical method?...[And concludes:] Dialectics...includes in the positive understanding of the present, simultaneously, the understanding of its negation, the understanding of its necessary decline, and thus perceives any emerging form in the flow of movement in its transient side. It is not to be intimidated, and is critical and revolutionary in its essence.

(*Nachwort* to 2nd edn of vol. I of *Capital*)

4.3 The 'Managerialist' Transformation

The 'institutional' change that drew the attention of these scholars was the passage of effective economic power from the hands of 'capitalists' to those of the 'managers' of industries and of the legal structures through which these operate, companies and corporations.

In a time of great social transformation, this phenomenon was considered as characterizing a good part of the structural (institutional) changes connected with those transformations. This gave rise to many different deductions, the most important relating to whether or not a change of such a kind represented a change to the capitalist system such as to radically modify traditional analyses of capitalism, in the first place Marxian and Marxist ones.

It is conventional to date attention to the phenomenon to a celebrated study in the early 1930s, which bears the names of Adolph Berle and Gardner Means.[92] The study showed, in clear and quantified terms, that in large enterprises the legal owners, that is the shareholders, were no longer either capable or really desirous to effectively control the enterprise. Financing requirements had exceeded the financial capacity of any individual owner or group of owners. Such enterprises had to be financed through investment by a very large number of individuals, none of whom owned enough to control the company or to be involved alone in its management.

That effective control, or power to decide on all the most important aspects of the life of the enterprise, and in particular on investment decisions, was in the hands of groups of owners with a very small packet of shares in the company was already well known. These managed to control the company notwithstanding the presence of a great mass of small shareholders uninterested in decision-making but only in the economic results of the enterprise, and specifically the dividend.

But Berle and Means showed that not even the controlling packet was any longer the basis for effective control of large enterprises. This had become the prerogative only of an impersonal bureaucracy of managers, self-legitimated in terms of ability and operating results. Their inquiry sanctioned the divorce between ownership and control of economic activities in the most important and most rapidly growing part of the economy. Berle and Means argued that the investor had replaced the owner and asked themselves to whom the management should be responsible.

Enterprises had thus ended in the hands of professional managers who were *employees*, not *shareholders*: businessmen and decision-makers without any legal title to ownership of the enterprise. Legal title was the formal foundation of all traditional commercial law, developed at the time when industrial society was appearing, in order to protect the rights of shareholders.

This phenomenon, which has been called the *'managerial revolution'*, was examined and commented on at length. It led to production of a significant literature[93] which often expanded beyond the boundaries of the large capitalist enterprise. In fact it coincided with the observation that even in regimes in which enterprises had lost their owners (communist countries) or were heavily dependent on governmental decisions on investment, becoming to some extent part of the state apparatus (fascist or 'corporative' regimes) they had come under the control of managers who were not owners. All that shed new light on the structure of industrial society.

Furthermore, since the area of activity of public sector non-profit organizations in performing economic functions had expanded, public sector managers and bureaucrats (under whatever regime) increasingly came to resemble the new managers of large industrial enterprises, forming a new dominant social class which brought about some changes in conventional patterns of social structure.[94] This was to some extent a revenge of sociology over economic approaches (based on the economic theory of the enterprise, born together with economic policy) and the legal-institutionalist one (based on the institutional role of ownership).

However, returning to the phenomenon of divorce between ownership and control of large enterprises, it ought to be said that in truth it had long been known.

As already pointed out, Karl Marx himself made it the subject of an analysis dense with prospective implications because it led to the logic of transition between capitalism as it traditionally formed and developed and its natural evolution into something new and different. Greater reference to Marx's accurate analysis of the managerial transformation (not widespread in the common debate for and against the Marxian theses) might lead to conclusions of some value.

First and foremost, as I see it, that transformation had already been included in the analysis of the 'overall process of capitalist production' which is the subject of the third volume of *Capital*.[95] In the 23rd chapter, Marx looks at the problem of the spread of managers in joint stock companies as a means by which the industrial capitalist manages to make money not only out of the workers (through the *plus value* of capital, the central theme of the Marxian analysis) but through 'pretended' wages of management.[96]

But in the 27th chapter, examining the function of credit in capitalist production, he tackles the topic of joint stock companies, already widely used in his time. Among their other consequences he sees that of 'transformation of the truly operating capitalist into a simple manager, administrator of other people's capital, and of the owners of capital into pure and simple owners, pure and simple monetary capitalists'.[97]

Thus Marx clearly saw that the 'function of capital is separate from the ownership of capital, and in consequence labour, too, is completely separate from ownership of the means of production and from the added value'. This separation leads him to conclude:

This result of the maximum development of capitalist production is a necessary moment of transition (*notwendiger Durchgangspunkt*) for re-transformation (*Rueckverwandlung*) of capital into the ownership of the producers, no longer, however, as the private property of individual producers but as their property as associates, as direct social property. And furthermore it is the moment of transition for transformation of all the functions which, in the process of reproduction (*sic*) are still linked with ownership of capital into simple functions of the associated producers, into social functions.   (Marx, *Capital*, Vol. III, Chapter 27)

It seems to me that there is no doubt. Not only did Marx foresee the development of capitalism into dissociation ('divorce') between ownership and control (which it seems we only became aware of in the 1920s and 1930s with the studies on the managerial revolution and on so-called neo-capitalism); but he also saw this dissociation as a 'necessary moment of transition' for 'retransformation of capital into the ownership of the producers' etc., that is, if I am not mistaken, into a form of socialist society.[98]

Furthermore, Marx comes to the point of stating clearly that 'this means suppression of the capitalist mode of production in the ambit of the capitalist mode of production itself', and clearly adds, 'therefore it is a contradiction that destroys itself by itself which, *prima facie*, presents itself as a simple moment of transition towards a new form of production' (ibid.). He also notes immediately that it (the new form of production)

> then presents itself as such also in its appearance. In certain spheres it establishes a monopoly and then requires the intervention of the state. It reconstitutes a new financial aristocracy, a new category of parasites in the form of conceivers of projects, of founders and directors that are such simply in name; a whole system of fraud and deceit that has as its object the founding of companies, the issue and sale of shares. It is private production without the control of private ownership.   (ibid.)

Are we really sure that this was written by Marx and that this is his prose, that it is not someone describing and criticizing the contemporary financial market?

No, this is someone who could see far into the transformation of the system, even if a certain political passion led him to confuse what 'ought to be', or what would be desirable, with the course of history. We are dealing with a transition and a transformation of capitalism which, if assessed on the political scale, took more than a century to mature fully (without, it seems to me, losing its essential characteristics, but rather confirming them rather remarkably). If assessed on the historical scale, like that of the industrial revolutions (first, second or third or whatever) there has been a rate of change much faster than has ever been known in the history of humanity.[99]

In spite of this explicitly 'managerialist' vision, Marx remained firmly attached to the primitive vision of the capitalistic process (in the opinion of both supporters and opponents and partly in his own). Looked at from this point of view, the divorce between ownership and control of the production process seemed to be a substantial *change of framework* compared to the Marxian approach that came to demolish the Marxian structure (and in part was true).[100]

However that may be, the 'managerialist' view continued, as we have said, to develop its analysis even post 1945, with much attention to many possible collateral effects. First and foremost, it stimulated a revision of the most established axioms of economic theory based on the behaviour of the capitalist-entrepreneur (using his own or borrowed capital) and who aimed, in substance, to maximize the return on capital (always called 'profit', as the basic category of economic logic) through combination of the other factors of production. In fact, if the motivations of the manager are different from those of the owner-capitalist, it is quite possible not to take account of that in theorems of economic behaviour.[101] But then a literature of every type aiming at defining the anatomy of the large enterprise from every point of view broke loose.[102]

Analyses multiplied on the evanescence of commercial ownership and on the emergence of a new class of managers. Was this a new class? With it, did the relationship between 'capital' as a factor of production and the various initiatives for investment change? How was the category (of managers) renewed; by co-option or in some other way? Were large enterprises of 'undefined ownership' controlled by managers a private fact or a public fact? Did the dynamics lead it towards expansion and decentralization or towards concentration and reduction? Was it more, or less, 'dependent' on government decisions than other productive sections of society?

Has the fact that the large enterprise has become the most conspicuous phenomenon of a society in evolution also made it the most talked about? A majority of the best-sellers on industrial or corporate sociology and economics have made management of the large enterprise the subject of analysis. How does it behave in relation to financial markets? What are its implications in research and in the search for innovation? How does it conduct the training of its personnel and how does that affect its relations with educational institutions (especially for higher education)? How does it appear in its industrial relations, with the workers, with trade unions, with labour legislation, etc.? How does it manage its relations with local and national political powers and thus with political parties and other movements and institutions?

One of the most extensive and informed assessments of the large enterprise phenomenon in all its implications, social and political, is to be found in

Giorgio Ruffolo's 1967 work[103] on the 'large enterprise in modern society'. In this work, the function of the managers of the large enterprise appears in an ambiguous light: on the one hand a constant pressure for growth not determined by profit nor even by a mere desire for power, but by an assumption of responsibility to society in its most important components; customers, employees, trade unions, marginalized groups and areas and miscellaneous policies (environmental, international, etc.); on the other hand, a rigid defence of its own autonomy and a certain aggressiveness towards both socially and politically representative powers. In brief, this work highlighted the contradictions between the dynamic and innovative nature of the large enterprise in the technological and economic areas and its conservative and authoritarian nature in the political area. The author thus developed guidelines both for a 'new constitution for the large enterprise' and also for it to function better within the framework of a planned democracy.[104]

In conclusion, the managerial transformation, nourished essentially by social analysis founded on legal aspects (ownership), has been a sort of prosecution and application of Marxian analysis. In spite of the apparent hostility that essentially pro-American 'managerialism' has adopted to a Marxist interpretation of the phenomenon, it had the same cultural roots. It is no accident that many of its structural claims, applied to the capitalist corporation operating in a so-called market economy, have given rise to a comparative analysis of the 'managerialist' type with the large soviet enterprises, emphasizing the similarities with the capitalist enterprise, in spite of the differences in historical origin. Highlighting the existence of an economic decision-making power that does not lie in ownership of the means of production (here in the shareholders, there in the state) 'managerialism' has contributed to showing the convergence of the two economic systems also from this point of view. In doing so, it has ensured a contemporary movement beyond both systems towards something new, which brings into question the traditional differentiating factors, reducing their importance, and it shows its function in moving towards a post-capitalist and post-communist society that find a certain bond in public and/or private sector 'managerialism'.

4.4   Persistent Unilaterality of the 'Marxist' Explanation

However, even if the 'manageralist' analysis seems to be the natural way out of the 'Marxian' analysis, and – inversely – it seems natural that the Marxian (and also Marxist) analysis should be converged in a more systematic analysis of the neo-capitalist productive system, in order to gain insight of its direct confluences toward 'post-capitalist' social structures, yet the mental catagories contraposing the capitalist system to the socialist one have remained very strong, and also very tenacious remains the wish to guarantee a Marxist identity of the analysis of the development of the modern industrial society. This constitutes the basis for a kind of 'fundamentalism' also of the Marxist culture, which has not helped for a rapid modernization either of the concept or of the political action of the movements that refer themselves to Marxism.

The 'Marxist' identity of the analysis of the development of modern industrial society is upheld by Mandel with the following observation:

> To say that the long waves of 'over' and 'under-accumulation' are equivalent to the radical changes in production techniques does not mean in any way that they are *caused* by such changes. The claim for this causality would lead to a mere tautology or to the type of circular reasoning to which Schumpeter fell victim. The scientific and technical innovations accumulate in a more or less continuous way... The *discontinuous* process of the innovations, unlike the *continuous* process of innovation-discoveries, cannot be explained referring to accidental causes or psychological reasons or to the fact that over-specialization and monopolies create the necessity for a periodic renewal of industries, stimulating the introduction of fundamental innovations whose application on a vast scale requires a relatively long time. The explanation may only come from the sum of all the laws of movement involved in capitalist production.   (Mandel's italics)[105]

This observation, from one point of view, puts the finger on the 'punctum dolens' of the Schumpeterian explanation (which we have above synthesized in the questions: From where comes the entrepreneur-innovator? How does demiurge of the economic progress come into being?), otherwise, put in relief by Sylos Labini himself. From another point of view the observation risks going back to a merely 'economic' and positivist explanation of the intrinsic law ('circular', as Schumpeter would say) of the capitalist development without discontinuity.

There are two simplifications which make the recourse to this type of 'Marxist' identity of the approach somewhat unjust and superficial. The first is that the consideration of 'technical innovation' as the mere primary cause of the change (as an 'exogenous' factor) does not seem to characterize even the thinking of the representatives of the 'pure' technological approach. I have never met any scholar of the history of the industrial revolution or of the history of technologies who has so naively believed that all change in the development is caused solely by inventions and technical innovation. Imagine, if you can, Schumpeter believing this! All historical-economic reflection (of the 'technological' approach like that of the economic and sociological approaches) has attempted to 'explain', perhaps too much, the complexity of development factors of industrialization, including even the demographic factor by trying to 'endogenize' – in some way – the innovations.[106]

The second unsatisfactory explanation is that '*the explanation may only come from the sum of all the laws of movement of the way of capitalist production*' – an explanation as naive or as vague as the 'technological explanation' itself.

It is significant enough that the Marxist 'law of movement' (the single explanation of the 'movement') has been substituted by the expression 'all the laws of movement' of capitalism.

In spite of this, it would be better stated what these *numerous* laws consist of,[107] without having recourse to a sort of logical schematism which conforms badly to the complexity of changes being examined. Furthermore, the risk is proposing – in antithesis to the 'technological explanation' (or to any other) – another, and only one, 'explanation', the 'law of movement' of the production capitalist mode, capable always of giving all answers[108] in any circumstances.

On the scale of the 'Marxist' theses (in particular those not always well illustrated) the impression remains that there is always the desire to impose a single explanation or causal interpretation of historical evolution, as if the 'scientific' approach to the awareness of historical events and the functioning of the economy may be characterized by the 'discovery' of positive 'laws' – like natural phenomena – of behaviour (in vain mitigated by the use of a dialectic logic), and as if the action of the social forces (workers, capitalists, interest groups and operators, ruling political class, and so on) were not able to have a specific effect within the complexity of factors underlying the development of industrial society.[109]

That approach of 'turning upside-down' which could be expected by Marxist tradition, when this tradition proposed itself as a 'theory of praxis',[110] and before taking the route of an exhausting analysis-contestation of the principles of the political economy, has been better implemented by sociology, which, instead, was started from a 'positivist' position, more inclined to discover some regularities of social behaviour of individuals, groups, and societies as such.

In fact, from the sociological approach, more than from elsewhere, springs a re-evaluation of the political and programmatic action even if of difficult identification, with a huge jumble of visions and positions.

5 THE SOCIOLOGICAL APPROACH

5.1 Does a Sociological Approach Exist?

Let us go to an evaluation of the sociological approach. In the 'sociological approach' there are (in an endless variety of cultivars) numerous *qualitative analyses* on the evolution of behaviour, ideas, life-styles, diffused in 'futuristic' analyses, more or less founded on technological bases, or economic or institutional ones, and also floating in the social scenarios, for which some strong suggestions cannot be denied. For example, in this variegated approach, one also finds the books by Bell, Toffler and Schumacher, limiting ourselves only to some best-sellers.

In reality, in the approach which we have, for brevity's sake, called 'sociological', one finds many different points of view, many philosophies of history and social evolution.

The sociological approach, therefore, with its multiple complex roots that range from historicist philosophy to psychology to political science, is difficult to define with any clear identity. One is rather dealing with a variety of very different approaches in which it is also sometimes difficult to find a reading key that explains factors of change. In fact in most cases one is dealing with a vast collection of comparative descriptions,[111] either (1) of cases coinciding with some historic transnational experience,[112] or (2) of cases coinciding with historic situations of idealized type models that do not adapt well to the multitude of circumstances to which one might want to apply them. These descriptive comparisons then allow us to draw conclusions that are so general that they do not even constitute a significant historical analysis.

It should not be surprising then that the sociological approach may appear as a residual approach to other approaches recalled, which are without order. This group includes: a) explanations that do not belong to one of the more defined approaches; b) complex explanations which do not deepen this or that explanation factor of the change (the drive for which has been the Holy Grail of many researches of the last fifty years on theories of development) but limit themselves to describe the changes in their multi-coloured, multi-faceted quantities; c) or in positive terms, the approach which summarizes all the others, escaping the rigid pretensions of causal interconnections but leaving the window open to history and to its indeterminable and tortuous path.

It should not even be surprising that in this indefinable approach we are compelled to discuss social change in very general terms; related to remote political and social roots, as did Daniel Bell, who more than others tried to confront the issue on the basis of sociological reasoning.[113]

For instance Bell recognizes that in this 'we are all epigones of the great master', and relates the opinion of another authoritative American sociologist,[114] that 'the fact that the conception of "post-industrial society" is an amalgam of what St. Simon, Comte, de Toqueville and Weber furnished to our imagination, is evidence that we are confined to an ambiguously defined circle which is more impermeable than it ought to be.[115]

And so, though I have searched, I have not found an author who is representative or sums up or is emblematic of this approach, but rather a great number of authors with an equal number of reading keys, some of little interest, others so obscure as to seem rather indigestible lucubrations. And I have not yet even found[116] an author in this eclectic *army* of describers who has produced a good explanation of the reasons why no approach to under-standing of historical change is possible, that everything depends on the whim of fate or the designs of providence; that is, in other words,[117] an author who has produced an ordered and comprehensible doctrine regarding this eclectic, disconnected map of the experiences and characteristics of evolution of contemporary society (without any attempt to explain them or even classify them according to some criterion).

Thus, once again, in order to find something that might resemble a socio-logical explanation of social change, I have to fall back on Max Weber's great work.

5.2   The Political Factor in Weberian Tradition

But referring to Weber does not mean only to Weber. It means opening up to the whole great experience of German sociology, rooted in German Histori-cism, in its turn rooted in German Enlightenment (*Aufklärung*) – in spite of some established, but no longer particularly up-to-date,[118] views that see Historicism and Enlightenment as antagonistic, especially in Germany.

Max Weber also tried to understand the element of transformation of modern society and to understand its direction. In his multiform, disordered and encyclopedic studies, there is a *leit motif*:[119] the purely political policy factor as a factor for change.

But alongside that, above all in his mature writings, there is the idea that political policy, becoming a profession, becomes ever more 'rational',[120] more technical. The 'technocratic revolution' thus finds Weber as one of its first modern prophets and theoreticians. It comes to represent the apex of a cultural process and hence of a structural change in modern society.

But he does not see only the political factor, as opposed to the 'economic' or 'institutional' factor in the process of 'rationalization'. His political factor comprises all the 'cultural', ideological or ethnic-religious factors that com-pose it (including the nationalism to which Weber was always very sensitive and which is to be considered an endemic disease of the last century that had tragic consequences in our own). Weber saved himself (though not entirely) from the eclecticism inherent in every sociological tradition precisely because he managed to propose, within the method of social research, that celebrated separation of his, between historical verdict and ethical verdict (or value) that constitutes one of the fundamental characteristics of his work.

Combining, as few thinkers of his time managed to do, an assessment of the ethical-political factor as not reducible to the materialistic (economic) factor with the meta-economic idea of power, the focus of his academic analysis became the relationship between 'technocracy' (that is, the rising 'power' of experts in contemporary society) and 'democracy' (that is, the rising 'power' of mass movements in the same contemporary society). And to this reading key he brought (or at least intended to bring) the analysis of structural change in course (in his time) and the sociological approach to analysis of that change (which is the theme of this rapid review of ours).[121]

5.3   The Technological Roots of Planning Rationality

But it would not be correct to root the 'sociological' approach only in the tradition of Weberian Historicism, and its annexes, without recording another great cultural offshoot of the Enlightenment (this time French), still more rooted in the origins of industrial society. I refer to the tradition of Saint-Simon and Fourier, which is far from extraneous to the birth of sociology as a modern science.[122]

In Fourier (also from the *polytechnicienne* root, in spite of modest family origin), the technocratic vision, awareness of the slow but certain march towards the 'rationalization' of mankind, is combined with a 'historic' vision of human progress. This vision, apart from its emphatic and schematic coating (which made it seem a utopia), concerns us closely, because it introduces a truly historical period classification, not very different from that of the analyses of change in many contemporary, academically more accredited authors. Fourier's *periodes* are incredibly effective anticipations of the 'stages' of economic development of modern historians (e.g. Rostow and Sylos Labini). And the most recent periods[123] prefigure many modern period classifications:

- The *fifth*, that of *'Civilisation'*, is clearly understood as that of the industrial revolution.
- The *sixth*, that of *'Garantisme'*, is clearly that of the Welfare State (which Fourier was far from experiencing) and which we can also relate to 'neo-capitalism' or to 'late capitalism'.
- The *seventh* is that of *'Sociantisme'* (or of 'simple association' or 'serio-sophie', where *serie* is the unit of volunteers who are assigned to the various social activities). (In Fourier there is an incredible anticipation of that transformation of the Welfare State into the Welfare Society with which we are concerned in our analysis, with the emergence, above all, of the associative economy, as a further stage in the evolution of contemporary society.)
- Finally, the *eighth* and last, that of *'Harmonisme'* (or of 'compact association'), in which the great principle of universal harmony is achieved.
- The Eldorado-like nature of the 'associative' vision did not reduce the predictive capability of this 'utopian', who, in his Saint-Simonian entourage, forged many historical champions of today's technological culture.

– It is not surprising that many interpreters of contemporary social evolution thus point out the contribution of the 'political' factor to contemporary social transformations and – as we shall see – focus on examination of the relations between 'technocratic' and 'political' power; nor yet that a theme increasingly developed is that of 'rationality' and in particular of 'technical rationality' (or also rationality of means) compared with 'policy rationality' (or rationality of ends).

5.4 Re-evaluation of the Political Factor

It is on these roots that both the training and further thoughts of many authors have developed, authors who, though sociologists or linked to the sociological study field, have enriched the panorama of analysis of change with some distinctive 'vision' of the role of political and planning management of the emerging 'new society'. Among these we shall choose the one with whom the vision of a 'post-industrial society' as a problem of identification but also of political management is most closely linked – that is, Daniel Bell.[124]

He, in fact, introduces something that involves political psycho-sociology into the conventional analysis of the passage from industrial society to service society. In his own words:

Industrial societies...are good producing societies. Life is a game against fabricated nature. The world has become technical and rationalized. The machine predominates, and the rhythms of life are mechanically paced: time is chronological, methodical, evenly spaced... [Industrial societies] are a world of organization – of hierarchy and bureaucracy – in which men are treated as 'things' because one can more easily coordinate things than men. Thus a necessary distinction is introduced between the role and the person....Organization deals with the requirements of roles, not persons...The watchwords are maximization and optimization, in a cosmology derived from utility and felicific calculus of Jeremy Bentham. The unit is the individual, and the free society is the sum total of individual decisions as aggregated by the demands registered, eventually, in a market.

(Bell, 1973, 2nd edn, p. 126)

Post-industrial society distinguishes itself from industrial society through more and more opposed characters. Bell identifies the new basis of the re-evaluationof politics and planning in such terms.

A post-industrial society is based on services. Hence, it is a game between persons. What counts is not raw muscle power, or energy, but information. The central person is the professional, for he is equipped, by his education and training, to provide the kinds of skill which are increasingly demanded in the post-industrial society. If an industrial society is defined by the quantity of goods as marking the standard of living, this post-industrial society is defined by the quality of life as measured by services and amenities – health, education, recreation, and the arts which are now deemed desirable and possible for everyone.

As a game between persons, social life become more difficult because political claims and social rights multiply, the rapidity of social change and shifting cultural fashion bewilders the old, and the orientation to the future erodes the traditional guides and moralities of the past. Information becomes a central resource, and within organization a source of power. Professionalism thus becomes a criterion of position, but it clashes, too, with the populism which is generated by the claims for more rights and greater participation in the society. If the struggles between capitalist and worker, in the locus of the factory, was the hallmark of industrial society, the clash between the professional and the populace, in the organization and in community, is the hallmark of conflict in the post-industrial society.   (ibid., pp. 127–8)

The conclusion is that post-industrial society is thus 'a communal society in which the social unit is the community rather than the individual, and one has to achieve a "social decision" as against, simply, the sum total of individual decisions, which, when aggregated, end up as nightmares, on the model of the individual automobile and collective traffic congestion' (ibid., p. 128). Post-industrial society increases the demand for policy decisions precisely because it is no longer an atomized society, that can rely on automatic self-regulating mechanisms, or on mere organization not targeted at objectives. And the objectives are extremely numerous, contrasting and conflicting, therefore requiring a more technical approach in addressing them; but that technical approach relates to social management, 'governance', the capacity to govern.

In summation, we have to introduce a dialectic consideration, as Marx would call it: the more society individualizes itself, the more it must socialize its choices in a non-standard manner:

In the national society, more and more projects (whether the clean-up of pollution or the reorganization of the cities) must be undertaken through group or communal instruments. In a tightly interwoven society, more decisions have to be made through politics and through planning. Yet both mechanisms, paradoxically, increase social conflict. Planning provides a specific locus of decision, as against the more impersonal and dispersed role of the market, and thus becomes a visible point at which pressures can be applied... [Every planning issue] cannot be settled on the basis of technical criteria; necessarily they involve value and political choices.

The relationship of technical and political decisions in the next decades will become...one of the most crucial problems of public policy. The politician, and the political public, will have to become increasingly versed in the technical character of policy, aware of the ramified impact of decisions as systems become extended....In the end, however, the techno-cratic mind-view necessarily falls before politics.   (ibid., pp. 364–5)

The sociological approach thus restores their importance in determining development to non-economic, non-technological and non-institutional fac-tors. The subjective, psychological and ideological factors are revalued. Leaving aside religious motivations,[125] the diverse domains of social psychol-ogy are explored, personal motivations and so-called 'values' are examined, without which it would be difficult to discover, to expose final causes (as Aristotle might have called them) with the ability to mobilize energies for the structural changes to be explained and/or predicted.[126] But can we honestly claim that these studies have given us good tools for analysis or good patterns for interpretation?

All we can say is that at least some of these studies have contributed to diminishing the weight of the exclusively 'positivistic' approach that was inherent in other approaches (economic, technological and institutional). Among sociologists – who themselves from Auguste Comte to Talcott Parsons have been firmly rooted in the desire to study the almost immutable laws of 'social physics' (an expression that says much about the positivism of sociology as such)[127] – critics of the positivist approach are now becoming much more numerous than in the other social sciences (especially economics, in which, apart from some strands,[128] the search for general conditions for the functioning of economic phenomena has become *sub specie aeternitatis*, without even the least discussion of the validity of the usual paradigms of economic rationality, which, as we all know, have their foundation in Bentham's utilitarianism).

The sociologists to whom we refer are those who have partially reversed trend analysis to emphasize how much margin there is for these trends to be powerfully influenced by a political or planning 'will'. And they have devoted themselves, in reference to the problems of application of this 'will':

- some interested in studying the technical problems of this application (and earning themselves the charge of being either 'technocrats' of social policy management or, worse, supporters of technical control of social policy);
- others interested in studying the political aspects of this application (earning themselves the appellation of 'politologists').

The sociological approach therefore which begins with a deterministic attitude (the factors that determine the change of structure in society are not this technical, nor is this merely economical, nor juridical-institutional, but essentially psychological, ideological and political),[129] in effect is open, so to say, more than the others to the transformation of methods.

In this way is also seen, in the most advanced kind of sociological approach to the change, even the issue of power, another theme dear to the sociological tradition. Who holds the power in post-industrial society? And how does one hold it?

Even on this point Bell is explicit. 'How power is held is a system concept; who holds the power is a group concept...Clearly when there is a change in the nature of the system new groups come to power. In the post-industrial society technical skill becomes the base and education the mode of access to power.'

The transformation occurs by public choice; but, so that public choice, necessarily public, can guarantee, as the market did before, a minimum of rationality, it is necessary that it is organized according to appropriate and predetermined procedures, capable of assuring the maximum discussion and evaluation of the alternative choice.

Bell says that 'the relationship of technical and political decisions in the next decades will become, in consequence, one of the most crucial problems of public policy. Politicians, and the political public, will have to become increasingly versed in the technical character of policy, aware of the ramified impact of decisions as systems become standard...In the end, however, the technocratic mind-view necessarily falls before politics. The hopes of rationality – or, one should say, of a particular kind of rationality – necessarily fade. There may still be, in the language of Max Weber, a *Zweckrationalität*, a rationality of means that are intertwined with ends and they become adjusted to each other. But this is possible only when the ends are strictly defined and the means, then, can be calculated in terms of the end' (pp. 364–5). But this is exactly the logic base of any respectable planning. The planner's rationality, his operational diffusion of the ends and means, makes obsolete the Weberian distinction between the end rationality (*Wertrationalität*) and that of the means (*Zweckrationalitaet*), which, if separated, represent non-rationality, and also two irrational, deficient modes of planning.[130]

It seems to me that the work of Daniel Bell can be considered a good synthesis of what has been done in this direction in the past three decades or so.

3 Structural Change: Towards a Convergence of Various Approaches

1 CONVERGENCE

1.1 Convergence as the Historical Synthesis of Change

Faced with the panoramic *excursus* in the preceding chapter regarding the extensive debate which has already gone on for many years, on the structural and social changes in the contemporary world, and considering the different structural change patterns and outlines which have emerged from that debate (either by approach, or by character and consequent denominations) we would ask ourselves: 'what can we say new that has not yet been said'? The question – which assumes an existential flavour especially if compared with similar questions that we can pose regarding many other fields of knowledge – can receive its own best answer only from the reader, at the end of this book.[1]

I will limit myself to two observations. The first is that the excursus with which I wanted to initiate our analysis of structural change in the aspects that I consider essential, has been motivated only by the wish to qualify our analysis with respect to that extensive debate, with a reading capable of marking the foundations yet also the differences. In other words, I have felt the need to recapitulate the whole of these approaches (obviously in a very succinct way and in the aspects considered most meaningful), in order to construct a building conscious of its foundations,[2] but also selective of the good foundations. The second observation (on which this chapter will be developed) is that, despite the differences in the approaches, we can ascertain something converging from the historical point of view; a convergence, moreover, confirmed by the great variety of interpretations that we have classified under the title of the most eclectic of the described approaches: the sociological one. I consider this convergence as a good base on which to construct at least the analytical part of our examination of the structural changes. Furthermore we will develop the problematic analysis of the political management of the changes, which is our greatest concern.

The most emblematic example of the converging of different approaches is the fact that even the strictest defenders of Marxist orthodoxy, who look only

69

at the evolution of the 'social formation' called 'capitalism', are prepared to admit that in capitalism something has radically changed recently; this despite recurring prophecies about its dissolution or collapse and extreme resistance to recognize also its internal deep transformations.[3] For example, Ernest Mandel, the tenacious Marxist 'ideologist', in his work on 'late capitalism' (*spätekapitalismus*),[4] agrees to speak of 'three ages of capitalism' understood as:

> the succession of long waves of under and over-accumulation (of relatively low and relatively high average growth rates). Each of the long waves of over-accumulation coincides with a revision and renewal of the industrial technology at the basis of capitalism, i.e. with a qualitative revolution of production techniques, different from the quantitative changes of technology which are a constant feature of capitalist production.
>
> (Mandel, 1971, p. 27)

In this sense, Mandel solemnly declares, 'it is clear that the long cycles of over-accumulation are in line with the 'industrial' revolutions, of which, in the course of the last 125 years, we recognize three, based respectively on the steam engine, on the electric motor, and on electronics.'[5]

We should thus ask ourselves, finally, where the difference between the approaches lies, if an analysis which claims to be 'Marxist' ends up with the same periodization of the great 'structural changes':

1. the 'technological' approach (for example, Schumpeter or Freeman), or
2. the 'economic' approach (the last three of Rostow's stages, in short, those of 'take-off', 'maturity' and 'mass consumption', correspond approximately – as well as chronologically, for the most advanced Western countries – to the *three epochs* of the 'industrial revolution' or the four 'industrial revolutions' of Sylos Labini), or,
3. the historical-institutional approach, of a 'managerialist' or Marxian type, which sees in the disappearance of the capitalist-owner a radical change of the 'social formation' considered: in its appearance (capitalism) the greatest historical revolution of civilization and of mankind, and in its disappearance (chapters 23 and 27 and others of the 3rd volume of *Das Kapital*; Mandel; 'Managerialism' in its last versions; Galbraith, Ruffolo, Hodgson and others) a last phase of capitalism (or 'neo-capitalism'), or *'re-transformation'* (to use the Marxian word) of capital towards the social capital moment, a particularly new moment, in the history of industrial organization. A 'last' stage of capitalism, with qualitatively different features from the preceding stages.
4. the approach by many authors classified here in the generic category of belonging to the 'sociological approach (like Aron, Gross, Touraine,

Bell, Giddens, and many others) who have anticipated pluralism not only in the classes or social structures of the post-industrial society (on the outlines of the Weberian and Parsonsian reflection), but also in the identification of the basic factor of programmatic approach to change itself.

1.2 A Comprehensive Vision of Social Transformation

All this only confirms, it seems to me, the inappropriateness of the divisions made in classifying the various interpretations of structural change (which I thought should be developed rapidly in this chapter as a basis for our future analysis). We had already seen many ambiguities in the most interesting authors selected from the technological and economic approach (Schumpeter) and the economic-historical institutional one (Marx). Furthermore, it is the whole category of sociologists that appears in an ambiguous position (but fortunate ambiguity!). And, if anything, a clearer and more justified taxonomic division emerges between those academics who take the position of an onlooker[6] in relation to futurology (what we can call the 'forecasting' or 'futurology approach') and those who take the position of the planner ('planology' approach').

From the convergence of those approaches the problem arise of not losing the essence of a synthetic vision of contemporary social change. De Masi (1985), the Italian academic I have already mentioned (Chapter 2, note 2) comes to our aid in this intention. On the traces of Bell (who proposed synthetic tables on the features of post-industrial changes), De Masi has extended the synoptic view to other studies on the structural change between the three epochs of pre-industrial, industrial and post-industrial society. I think it is useful to reproduce here a table, including some additions I took the liberty to include, concerning my own views (Table 3.1).[7]

2 THE CRISIS OF TRADITIONAL DISCIPLINARY APPROACHES

The ambiguities, on the one hand, and the convergencies, on the other, of the approaches examined, are both born therefore from the obsolescence of the validity and meaning of these approaches that we have chosen, in virtue of a conventionality that I myself believe to be of no utility, on the basis of the traditional disciplinary divisions of the social sciences. In other terms I think that it is much wiser to conclude that the ambiguity that we have highlighted along with all our reconsiderations of these approaches (technological, economic, institutional, sociological) must not be attributed, truly, to single authors, but rather to tenacious and fallacious habits to classify the approach according to the division of disciplines (economy, sociology,

Table 3.1 Comparison among the major characteristics of pre-industrial, industrial and post-industrial society

	Pre-industrial society	Industrial society	Post-industrial society
Periodization (D)*	Until 19th century.	From the middle of 18th century to the middle of 20th century.	From the Second World War.
World regions (B) and trends (A)	Europe, Asia, Africa, Latin America.	Western Europe, Soviet Union, Japan and others in successive possible stages of industrialization.	United States of America and potentially globalization.
Dominant economic sectors (B) (D)	Primary: extractive Mining and farming; agriculture; fishing; forestry; Self-consumption, primary sector.	Secondary: goods producing; manufacturing; processing.	Tertiary: transportation; utilities. Quaternary: trade; finance; insurance; real estate. Quinary: health; education; research; administration; leisure.
Key resources (B) (D)	Land Land, basic materials, prolificity.	Machinery Production means, basic product, patents, productivity.	Knowledge Intelligence, creativity, information, scientific and cultural laboratories.
Key institutions (D) (A)	Kingdoms (Empires), Church, Army, Patriarchal family, primary groups guilds.	State, corporation, firm, trade union, bank, parties, nuclear family, secondary groups.	Universities, research and culture institutes, mass-media organizations, banks, instable family, primary and secondary groups.
Axial institution (B) (A) Axial principle (B)	Feudality Traditionalism: land/resources limitation.	Private property Economic growth: State or private control of investment decisions.	Associative cohesiveness Centrality and codification of theoretical knowledge.

Table 3.1 (Contd.)

Dominant figures (B)	Land-owners, aristocrats, masters.	Businessman.	Scientists, researchers.
Central social actors (D)	Peasants, craftsmen, populace.	Entrepreneurs, workers, unions.	Technicians, women, scientists, information managers, intellectuals, 'prosumers'.
Occupational pattern (B)	Peasants, miners, fishermen, timber.	Workers, engineers, entrepreneurs, white-collar employees.	Professionals, technicians, scientists, entertainers, free-time operators.
Government order (D)	Legitimistic, dynastic, authoritarian, theocratic, regimes.	Representative democracies and welfare, rigid institutions, consociative democracy, real socialism, interventionist state.	Representative democracies, neo-liberalism and welfare, flexible institutions, participationism.
and Regimes (A)		Constitutional, parliamentary, national regimes (transitionally also totalitarian and ethnocentric) (national-centric order and inter-national order).	Federalistic, multi-national, multi-ethnic, multi-religious, multi-institutional, regimes (subsidiarity principle, with strong and planned federalism).
Technology (B)	Raw materials.	Energy.	Information.
Instrumentation (D)	Flexible instruments Hand-making.	Rigid instruments, assembly line tekne + logos machine-making	Electronics, information science biogenetic, intellectual and appropriate technology
Social locus (B)	Farm, plantation.	Business firm.	University, research institute.
Typical place (D)	Country, village, crafts-shop, manufactory (small is beautiful).	Factory, plant, office, city, urbanism, (big is beautiful).	Distributed information, electronic cottage, scientific laboratories, tele-work, urban life, diffused factoring (appropriate dimension).

Table 3.1 (Contd.)

	Pre-industrial society	Industrial society	Post-industrial society
Class structure (D)	Masters, serfs.	Bourgeoisie, Middle-class, proletariat.	Managers, dominant. Contestation movements, dominant.
Class base (B)	Property, Military force.	Property, Political organization, Technical skill.	Technical skill, Political organization.
Means of power (B)	Direct control of force.	Indirect influence on politics.	Balance of technical-political forces Franchises and rights.
Stakes and social conflicts (D)	Domination and survival, subordination and revolts, local wars.	Ownership of the means of production, plus-value appropriation, buying capacity, markets conquete. Class fights, industrial conflict, world wars.	Elaboration and implementation of planning models, knowledge management, know-how
Access (B)	Inheritance. Seizure by armies Social extraction; inheritance.	Social extraction; inheritance; merit; entrepreunerialship; connection's cooptation; career.	Education, mobilitation, cooptation.
Social mobility factor (D) (A)	Cast's succession; affiliative cooptation.		
Time perspective (B)	Orientation to the past.	Ad hoc adaptiveness. Projections.	Future orientation, forecasting. Planning.
(A)	Ad hoc responses.		

Table 3.1 (Contd.)

Time and space relations (D)	Orientation toward the past; tradition force; direct answer; time synchronized on the nature; time availability; sense of the beyond; local dimension; coincidence among living-place and work-place.	Short-time adaptation to the needs; medium-term designing; scientific assessment of times and their reduction; standardized or imposed time, based on machine; multinational dimension; living place separated with work place; time and place unity.	Orientation toward the future; Long-term scenarios and forecasting; time chosen and individualized, based on ourself; life based on the free-time; real time trans-national dimension; telematic and TV connections everywhere.
Design (B)	Game against nature.	Game against fabricated nature.	Game between persons.
Methodology (B) (D)	Common sense, experience. Direct experience; common place; trial and error; action and reaction; wisdom.	Empiricism, experimentation. Problem solving, finding; scientific organization of work; syncronization; concentration; centralization; 'One best way'.	Abstract theory: models, simulation, decision theory, systems analysis.
Cohesion factor (D)	Mechanic solidarity; 'Gemeinshaft'; limited size; common origins; faith.	Mechanic solidarity; ideology; class solidarity; 'Gesellschaft'; formal organization; aim; communication.	Programmed solidarity, communication networking; belonging feeling; aim; 'Global Village'.
Stakes and social conflicts (D)	Domination and survival; subordination and revolts, local wars.	Ownership of the means of production, plus-value appropriation, buying capacity, markets conquete. Class fights; industrial conflict; world wars.	Elaboration and implementation of planning models; knowledge management; know-how.

Table 3.1 (Contd.)

	Pre-industrial society	*Industrial society*	*Post-industrial society*
Challenges (D)	Children's mortality; hunger; diseases; 'materialist' needs; scarcity.	Energetic crisis, alienation, pollution, resources waste, anomy, social disequalities, wars, social and job security.	Quality of life, mental health, querying deficiency. Wars, post-materialist needs, environmental ecology.
Psychic structure (D)	Personality	Oedipal personality	Narcissist personality
Advantages (D)	Slow rhytms; equilibrium with Nature; self-management; poor bureaucracy; primary solidarity.	Mass-consumption; geographical and social mobility; dominance of Nature; egalitarianism.	Mass-Education, Accessibility to Informations, Free-Time; Invention of the Nature; Uncertainty's Reduction.
Disadvantages (D)	Poverty, serfdom; children's mortality; ignorance; physical toil.	Alienation; competitivity; waste; anomie; physical and psychological toil; exploitation.	Manipulation; hetero-direction; hetero-control; mass-deformation; marginalization; unemployment; physical toil.

* (B); by Daniel Bell
(D); by Domenico De Masi
(A); by Franco Archibugi
Source: See Note 7.

political science). In fact, these disciplines have lost, if they ever had them, any autonomous scientific content. Otherwise, it is not by chance that the authors who give the most meaningful contributions to the analysis of social and structural change are even those who have also been in terms of disciplinary belonging the most multi-faceted and in reference to whom it is more difficult to apply a precise 'disciplinary' label. If such is the case, they are those who, in a certain way, are outsiders in respect of their own academic and disciplinary communities.

In reality, the disciplines which are at the basis of the approach used are losing their identity even in their traditional field of 'positivist' analysis (the so-called 'economic analysis,' 'sociological analysis,' and 'political analysis'), in the fields in which these disciplines are born and grow, under the banner of the research of basic postulates concerning abstract and generalized behaviour, moreover referring to criteria and even laws of behaviour relative to the single individual (say, briefly, to the *Homo oeconomicus, Homo politicus, Homo sociale,* or *congregabilis*).[8]

Therefore, if such is the case, we should say that beyond the divisions by scientific discipline, the ambiguities are in the approach itself, which we have called 'positivist', common to all of them. This approach is much mitigated by the subject, the structural change, which is under analysis; it is a matter of a historical subject, and as such it is a great unifier of visions. In spite of it however, in spite of the potential unitary and evolutive vision that the same subject, the change, should impose, an operational vision still has not been decisively determined, a vision that frees the transformation from illusion to discovering the 'internal laws' of the development, and in order to, on the contrary, devote itself to the configuration of a manageable, organizable, feasible and working system of change.

And yet it is the last visions of the sociologists that could help us in this direction. In fact we could (and should) start from the clear historical perception of Max Weber, of the trend toward a rationalization of social policy, therefore implying a systematic confidence in 'reason'. It would be a matter of being confident in reason not only for the interpretation of nature but also of social reality; that is, confidence in the capacity of mankind to give itself any organization permitting it to control and regulate both nature and social reality (even if in different ways) and to lead it toward defined goals, along its multiple institutional realities, and in a coordinated and peaceful (not so much conflictual) vision of different interests and values. It is a matter of the vision, about the possibility of leading the social and economic development toward predetermined targets compatible with resources and means, in a comprehensive vision of a society which knows how to plan itself, even if starting from modes not very systematic or rational, but improving its performance with more systematic and rational modes.

For this reason, a more satisfying conclusive taxonomy for the analysis of structural change could be that of dividing these analyses in two categories:

1. Scholars who respect the futurology (inherent in our problem), taking the position of 'onlooker' (which we could define as the predictive or futurologist approach) and of interpreters of the future. In this interpretation these scholars can also be divided into many streams or schools.
2. On the other hand, the scholars who, abandoning the field of descriptions, explanations and interpretations, take the position of permanently improving the instruments by means of which, in any field of activity, from the most modest and private to the most loaded by responsibility and public, people could adopt the most rational and participative methods of decisions.

The political scientists from Weber onwards, who belong to the first category, are interested in the extension, or the factors that have contributed to the historical diffusion, of the 'spirit of rationality', and seek to know who the bearers of the spirit are (technicians, politicians, managers, etc.). In this way they surpass the old attitude directed to the identification of a rationality inherent in the formation of social classes (whose existence has been contested in advanced industrial or post-industrial society).

3   THE QUALITATIVE CHANGE

3.1   The Importance of Qualitative Change

Glancing at the synoptic Table 3.1, we observe on the one hand a substantial convergence in the periodizing passage from industrial society to something new and atypical with respect to what is usually known and accepted; but on the other hand, a vast description of characters which exactly from their quantity and their varieties risk losing and making imperceptible the possible connections among characters and their organization in a model.

Furthermore, Table 3.1 does not in any way express that essential change which we have just mentioned concerning the crisis of the traditional disciplinary approaches: that is, the passage from a descriptive approach to a programmatic approach.

In the first case the requirement to surpass the description in order to better grasp the interdependencies and to build an interpretative model, could lead us to a view that is too restrained by a single approach (technological, economic, and so on) that we assessed as insufficient and reducing.

The risk would be to see coming back through the window what we have thrown out the door.

In the second case the requirement to surpass the description in order to directly face the change to be implemented, without too much regard for that ongoing, could render rather useless any study of the factors explaining the change, or could only render it useful perhaps to increase the scope of the programmatic action.

Both of these dilemmas constitute two stones on which people often stumble in the social sciences and on which even we will stumble often in the course of this book. I sincerely believe that, even though we should never under-evaluate the importance and risk of these stones, we will not be able to avoid them altogether.

At the same time the awareness of the risk of falling alternatively into the excess of 'determinism' on one hand and in the excess of 'descriptivism' on the other induced us to focus our attention on the analysis of those contents of the changes that seemed to us to be more structural than the others.

In the first place, it should be remarked that an overly descriptive analysis of the evolution of contemporary industrial society risks missing some essential features which constitute the basis of 'qualitative change'.[9] Thus in our enquiry we have postulated that the most important changes, the structural ones, are exactly those qualitative, and vice versa.

In fact I am not so interested in discussing here the historiographical problem of contemporary industrial (or capitalist) society, which is by definition the *last stage* (or epoch, or phase) of the same.[10]

I preferred to limit and start my analysis from the main aspects in which the structural change manifests itself – in particular the change in the *structure of consumption* (Chapter 4), in *production activities* (Chapter 5), in the *labour market* (Chapter 6), and in the *role of the State* and public financing (Chapter 9) – in order to examine in the second part the political implications of this change.

In general, in our analysis we will put special emphasis on the changes relative to the *content* and *object* of the activity (consumption, production, work, public service) rather than to the *modalities* and *means* of the same. Otherwise we would not know how to place ourselves in the framework of approaches to the change discussed above: it would be difficult to select, *a priori*, the most suitable approach. Nevertheless it is possible to declare that the most relevant changes seem to concern the *contents* (rather than the modalities) *of production* – although logic would suggest establishing several interactions between the modalities and the contents of the production.

In short, the question '*Which* goods and services are or will be produced?' seems to us to have assumed much more importance than the aspect '*How* are they or will they be produced?', and not vice versa.

The significance of this methodological option will emerge several times in the course of this work. For the moment it will suffice to say that we prefer to start from the analysis of the factors which seem to us *substantial, real,* and *material,* of the socio-economic change; to then examine, if interesting, its *behavioural* aspects as well (even if the relations of causality do not always develop in this direction, and the semantic meanings are not always so clear).[11]

This starting from the material factors of development, new needs, new instruments to satisfy them and so on, seems to me to greatly resemble the concept of 'material productive forces' which (in the Marxist logic to which we have referred in the previous chapter) in their growth, or perhaps in their simple evolution, enter into conflict with 'existing' production relationships. But I am not sure of this, in part because the Marxist concept of productive forces is itself not very clear and is not well explained even by Marx himself.[12] Above all, the nature of these forces is not clear, except for the aspect that these productive forces are 'material'. Many have identified them with the evolution of production technologies, but the expression could also be used to mean various other phenomena connected with production; they might thus be understood also to mean material needs, goods and services, as expressed and requested by consumers as end users of production. Their evolution could be influenced by the evolution of tastes, and by all ways of life, the topic which we shall discuss at greater length in this book, and also by concrete, material modalities of production that this evolution might impose.

In this case the Marxian 'productive forces' would be the content and object of productive activity, from which we start our analysis. Therefore our analysis could come close to the Marxist approach, *mutatis mutandis,* and in ways still better defined and, obviously, updated.

We will start (in the next chapter) from a reformulation of the current concepts of *industrialization* and *tertiarization* and the transition between the two. It could be considered, on the hypothesis formulated above, as a change in the 'material productive forces'. In effect this change from industrial to tertiary economic structure will constitute the pillar of the considerations in the following chapters on the impact of that change on the model of society as a whole. Before the analysis of other impacts we will formulate arguments for a key concept to simplify and at the same time better understand the debate on economic policy (for any school: neo-classical, Keynesian, post-Keynesian or whatever); debate which in my mind has overly neglected, even in sophisticated reference literature, the structural change factors to which we are referring.

3.2   Value, Quality, Evaluation and Social Choice

However, if on the one hand an analysis too descriptive of the evolution of contemporary industrial society risks losing some essential outlines which constitute the basis of the qualitative change, on the other hand an analysis oriented too much to the qualitative changes necessarily involves a discourse on the quality and its criteria, on the so-called values which are presupposed by the analysis.

But can the quality be considered, even the social quality, as a matter to be dealt with in itself, according to what has been done in the centuries of history of philosophy and social and political doctrines? Or according to what a presently much more seasoned army of political scientists continue to do? Can our interpretative problem in matters of political science be conditioned to a discourse of values more or less absolute and still relate to certain ideologies?[13]

When we speak about quality, it is true, we also speak of values. And by now to speak about values means to speak about evaluation. And when we speak about evaluation we intend to speak about more or less rational choices of action.[14] What counts for individuals also counts for groups and communities (local, national, supranational).

The individual truly expresses his or her own values when faced with alternative concrete choices and with multiple values of which he or she could be the bearer, and faced with alternative possible causes of action or different available case-by-case means or resources or constraints, he or she chooses and acts on the basis of a decisional trade-off. An individual who applies only absolute values or criteria in his or her choices without taking into account as well the values in conflict, today is less 'rational' than the conscious individual who implements multi-valued choices and makes multi-criteria decisions. The former, in today's social organization, must be more feared, for better or worse. In fact he or she is the bearer, in respect to the latter, of a more simple modality of behaviour, even more limited. In Kantian terms we could say that this individual is subject to the ethics of the sentiment rather than the ethics of the intellect.[15] In current expression we can say that the former is more ready than the latter to assume behaviour dominated by 'passions', 'fate', 'belonging' (*religio*, in Latin), of every type: national, ethnic, confessional; with respect to values often reciprocally inconsistent. The individual of this kind is subject to emotional choices, normally more present in cultures that today we would say are 'developing cultures' in so far as they belong to a pre-modern stage (if by modern we intend the political and social culture springing from the democratic revolution, from the declaration of human rights, of the rights of citizens and from the basic values of liberty, equality and brotherhood).

Why should not the same scale of values be applied, *mutatis mutandis*, also to communities? Should not communities be distributed, as in our vision, in a progressive scale of rationality, according to the degree of multilaterality and of critical pluralism in their choices and decisions? Here I am referring to polyvalent communities, those that include an entire citizenship of reference (nations, states, and so on, and relative territorial governments), which can make decisions, in the sphere of goals and objectives and in that of management of the means and resources to achieve them, with more or less advanced levels of rationality, that is, by means of a more or less organized multi-criteria evaluation. The values defined by themselves in absolute terms, and expressed in general terms, and not in the function of specific processes of choice, are not only not operational, but even dangerous, because they can damage the well-being that, for the individual as for the communities, is always the fruit of a trade-off, of a sort of compromise between different objectives and therefore values. The individuals, like the communities, who operate in real time with actions which are oriented to an absolute objective, and not coordinated by other actions (oriented to other objectives), act in an irrational way, according to unilateral impulses which are generally harmful, because they constitute a waste of resources and a counterproductive effect, an operational stalemate, and so on. The well-being would not be achieved and the compromise performed would not be the best, but would only be dominated by casualness and chaos. In this case it remains to be totally and radically confident in the so-called design of Providence, but all this would be contradictory to the intention to build, consciously and rationally as far as possible, their own destiny, in spite of all uncertainties that are connected with this.

And all this despite this above-mentioned intention that constitutes the primary and normative character of mankind, either if represented by a single individual or by any other kind of community.

4   THE EMERGENCE OF A PROGRAMMATIC APPROACH TO CHANGE

Posed in the terms developed in the last sections, the analysis of change does not become an historical analysis, but only a programmatic one. This means that every analysis of structural change cannot avoid at the same time some policy purposes. Such purposes also invest the instruments of analysis of the ongoing transformations and of the prospective actions for the future.

Thus, the main policy purpose within which the analysis itself will be developed, is that which renders the political system capable of: (a) expressing its purposes more rationally; (b) obtaining a better consistency between purposes and actions targeted to implement and achieve them; (c) making the social conflict be more judicious and less unjustified; and (d) making the communitarian governmental actions more intelligent and effective.

In summation, it would be appropriate to allow values (absolute or relative) to play their role in every choice, in every particular circumstance and condition, according to the changing visions of individuals and groups over time, and so on. And even the transformation of industrial or capitalist society into something new could be the result of a planning process, if it is allowed to be developed, rather than being the result of a forecast, even if it is founded on a serious analysis of what took place before our eyes.

This approach, that I would like to call 'programmatic' or 'planological', presents itself in two phases:

(a) In one aspect this approach is the continuation of the mass of approaches which we have visited in our survey, because it assumes its convergence as an element of an enrichment and simplification for future decisions;

(b) In the other aspect this approach places itself on a totally different level, as an alternative to that mass of approaches; it places itself on an operational level, in which the disciplinary visions are put at the service of the objective, of the target proposed. In this way, we can avoid the stalements to which any partial vision tends to constrain us.

The structural change thus becomes no longer an object of analysis but an object of political operation.[16] The convergence of approaches that we meet in the interpretation is translated in a more effective convergence toward the political action to implement the change. In other words: the convergence is translated in the introduction and establishes a new more advanced system of political management; a system in which casualness is less at home and intentionality is the most practised; in which the invisible hand becomes more and more visible; in which change becomes less the object of *ex post* description and interpretation, and more and more the object of *ex ante* political decision.[17]

4 The Change in the Structure of Consumption and the 'Tertiarization' Process

1 GROWTH AND INDUSTRIALIZATION AS THE DEVELOPMENT OF MASS PRODUCTION

Now leaving the framework of the different approaches to the periodization of the evolution of *industrial society*[1] we will start from the assumption already formulated: that evolution is marked overall by an important transformation in the breadth and structure of consumption, production and employment.

Whilst the consumption of the *products of industry*, over the last century, has increased in enormous proportions with respect to the type of material goods that are accessories to the welfare of individuals and communities, and has replaced much consumption of products of 'self-production' or crafts, at the same time (whether because of cause or effect it is difficult to say) new consumption has emerged, previously unknown, or limited to very small portions of the socially privileged (castes or classes), and is today more and more in demand (and more available) to the world of the consumer.

Much consumption is *material*. It may be called 'new', but in reality it has substituted analogous older types (the automobile which has replaced the carriage or horse, the electrical appliance which has replaced the old domestic tools, broom, stove, etc.). Some material consumption (telephone, television, etc.) are genuinely 'new' and previously unknown.

But much of the new consumption of an *immaterial* type consists of 'services' (medical-health, education, information, culture, recreation, politics, etc.) which, although nominally existing in every type of human society, has assumed in industrial society a *mass* characteristic which is preponderant in daily life. It is on the analysis of this type of transformation of mass consumption that we believe we must in the first place concentrate our attention if we desire to discuss *structural change* in contemporary society.[2]

1.1 The Interaction Between Technologies and Final Consumption

In fact, although it is difficult to establish a precise relationship of causation between the various phenomena-variables of social evolution in the historical 'synthesis' of industrialization, we may say that the *interaction between technologies of production and final consumption* has almost always constituted the *heart of any structural change* in society.

And the 'crisis' which we are living through in industrialized countries – like many other important crises of the past, i.e. those of a 'structural' nature – seem likewise dominated by *a change in the relations between production technologies and the consumption structure*.

We assume, therefore, as a postulate of our future reasoning, that the evolution of technology has a sure, intelligible relationship with the evolution of consumption. We will describe some of the features of this relationship – albeit assumed as a postulate – without claiming or presuming that an exhaustive and explanatory meaning can be given to this description. It is already satisfactory that the description of the relationship (which implies inevitably some cause and effect relations, without it necessarily being absolute) may be convincing, allowing us to design a set of phenomena of the *structural change*, capable of sustaining some general theorization.

We will begin by exploring – albeit in a synthetic way – the *nature and characteristics of the structural change* on the basis of the relationship between the evolution of consumption and production technology. Subsequently, we will examine some aspects of the influences which the structural change, here defined and described, may have on some specific fields of economic life: (a) on development and transformation on the consumption side (Chapter 4); (b) on production activity and entrepreneurship (Chapter 5); (c) on the labour market (the behaviour of labour supply and demand) (Chapter 6); (d) on the crisis of public services and public finances (Chapter 9).

1.2 The First Phase of Industrialization: From Non-Mass Consumption to Mass Consumption

We will begin therefore by pointing out simply, that the commonly defined 'industrial revolution' has given us (or allowed) *mass production*.

But mass production has gone from being potential to being *actual*, on the basis of a more or less slow and 'critical' *process of adaptation* of production structures to the possibility of an expansion in consumption (or of the 'market', as is said), i.e. – in our sense – to the possibilities of *mass consumption*.

This process, which coincides with the process of 'industrialization', has been a very slow process.[3] It goes from Smith's 'pin factory' to present-day robotics, passing through Ford's 'assembly line'. As said, nobody can seriously think that the technical evolution which occurred during the entire process of industrialization is completely independent from the social and economic conditions which were determined during the period in question. On the other hand, neither does the frequent assumption of economic reasoning that technology is 'exogenous' mean that one should not necessarily recognize the historical 'endogenousness' of it: it means only to attempt to separate methodologically some reasoning, in order to make it more rigorous and heuristic.[4]

The interaction between *mass production and mass consumption*, therefore, should be theoretically, taken for granted. And it seems also to be found empirically (in historical data) everywhere in clear evidence.

We will begin from this postulate in order to proceed to a generalization (which could be considered a sort of corollary of the postulate mentioned). That is that *the more the conditions are created for mass consumption (effective demand), the more mass production becomes possible, and vice versa.* This affirmation-corollary of our postulate means, in substance, that the *potentialities* of one of the phenomena are not always in line with the *effect* of the other phenomena.

The potential of mass production (i.e. the presence in theory of the conditions for a strong development of the same) may find an obstacle in the absence of mass consumption potential (in the form of the buying power of the potential consumers, but sometimes because of the 'life style' of the same). Conversely, potential in mass consumption (buying power and willingness to change life styles) may find an obstacle in an adequate organization of mass production (although this case is, in the long term, less realistic).

However, it is well known that when an imbalance occurs between the two phenomena the classic 'crises' of *under-production* or *over-production* result, which are crises of *change* towards higher levels of income and economic well-being.[5]

Now, on close examination, it can be said that the 'process of industrialization' has almost always been resolved – albeit in different conditions and in historical periods – in a *process of adaptation of consumption to mass production*; by means of the reduction of unit costs (and an increase in productivity) which that process of adaptation made possible. If we call the consumption which preceded mass consumption, as a logical complement *'non-mass consumption'*, it can be said that this process of adaptation of consumption to production has consisted of a progressive transfer of increasingly important shares of *non-mass production* to *mass production*, and to a progressive substitution of *non-mass consumption* with *mass consumption*.

1.3 Industrialization, Productivity, Development, Redistribution

This rather reasonable and evident relation-function (which resembles more a type of relation which econometricians would call 'structural', even if not 'definitional', rather than 'behavioural') leads us to claim and realize that what we call 'economic development' has been identified up to now (and is still identified thus in a large part of the world) with the *industrialization rate*;

and this latter is generally identified in the rate of intensification of transfer from non-mass production to mass production mentioned in the previous paragraph.

This transfer has, moreover, guaranteed (and has been identified as) the *rate of increase in 'physical' production* (production per man-hour), realized both in the transfer itself of non-mass production to mass production, and in the constant (or cyclical, if preferred) technological innovation within mass production (from simple mechanization to cybernetics and robotics).

The rate of increase of the GDP, which is the usual indicator and the symbol of growth (in particular if considered 'pro capita'), is nothing other than the overall result of the physical gain of productivity obtained from the mass production sector. The overall result of productivity gains (which is the 'national dividend' as Pigou began to call it,[6] and which today more generally, and less meaningfully, is called 'national income'), which produces 'benefits' for the various subjects and social groups making up the community of reference (entrepreneurs, workers, families, pensioners, operators in the various sectors of the economy, etc.), produces them by means of mechanisms of 're-distribution' in all productive sectors, both in those in which the productivity gains are obtained, and those in which they are not obtained.

The redistribution by means of the said mechanisms of the transfer of benefits of productivity increases has also been the heart of economic reflection since it has existed, and is the heart of contemporary structural changes, to which we are devoting our attention (and to which we will devote the next chapters).

2   THE MOST RECENT CHANGES IN THE STRUCTURE OF FINAL CONSUMER DEMAND AND IN THE INDUSTRIALIZATION MODEL

Thus, the most striking change that – in relation to what has been said in the preceding paragraph – we would be induced to consider is that the *matrix* of all the other changes to be described is in the structure and quality of the goods and services produced and therefore consumed.

In particular, the changes in the structure of consumption patterns of the typical consumer *unit*, the household, are revolutionizing the productive systems of Western countries. They deserve some additional comments, even if in the past they have been the subject of many analyses (the shift of consumption towards services) becoming a common argument. However, the consequences, have not yet been sufficiently discussed.

We can start with the consideration that this change may in part be ascribed to the fact that in Western economies households consume an abundance of manufactured goods and have arguably reached a virtual saturation point. This situation of abundance and quasi-saturation undoubtedly derives from the extraordinary growth of labour productivity in agriculture, industry and mechanized and automated services (which should always be classified as part of the 'secondary' sector); progress achieved, notoriously, thanks to the application of science and technology.

Once, however, their basic needs for food, clothing, housing and access to mechanical (and now electronic) consumer durables have been met in a context of constantly rising living standards in terms of material ease and comfort, Western households are clearly demonstrating a preference for 'other' forms of consumption as their purchasing power rises.[7] But by its very nature and quality such consumption is unlikely to allow large productivity gains. For this reason they are no longer good enough *generators of profits for entrepreneurs* who must strive to achieve the best possible mix of production factors, notably 'capital' and 'labour', in order to make a profit.

We are obliged to make a reference to the authors who have carried out analyses of structural changes in economic activities related to technical progress and the development of markets. These analyses have taken on a classic status).[8], on the basis of which activities and production sectors are classified in 'primary', 'secondary' and 'tertiary' sectors (and some have also introduced the 'quaternary' sector).[8]

But here we would like, however, to recall in particular the different approach followed, for example, by Jean Fourastié, to whom our analysis is most closely related.[9]

According to this approach, the concepts of 'primary', 'secondary', and 'tertiary' are differentiated *in relation to the productivity rate inherent in them*. It may be stated that so long as primary and secondary sector production was still catering to widespread and persistent 'pockets' of 'under-consumption' (e.g. in the area of household durables and cars), there was every reason for the developed countries to continue along the path of industrialization with all the attendant changes that the 'capitalist' production system has undergone:

- a shift from artisanal to 'mass' production;
- continuous technological innovation necessitated by the constant effort to increase market shares or 'win' new or potential markets in the face of national and international competition;
- a constant propensity to save on the labour input per product or output unit (and a corresponding tendency to increase the remuneration of this labour input);
- and, at the same time, a steady upward trend in *total* employment, deriving from the total growth in the quantities and types of goods and services produced.

It should be pointed out that the model described above may be considered still valid for economies which have not yet attained the levels of industrialization of the most advanced market economies, i.e. those which *have not yet managed to satisfy the primary and secondary needs of the majority of their population*; here we are talking about the 'southern' economies of the developed world as well as semi-and under-developed countries. (Among these there are today the economies of Eastern Europe as well.) This model could also be of value to the more advanced economies if these were able to incorporate the still very strong needs of the 'third world' into their productive system and development dynamics, and to transfer adequate purchasing power and productive capacity to the latter. This highly complex aspect (to which I would refer the unclear concept of 'globalization') has however been consciously left out of our present analysis of structural change in advanced economies.

Continuing with the examination of factors of change in advanced economies it must be observed that once the Western industrial system had demonstrated its capacity to cater to households' primary and secondary needs by transforming the massive productivity gains into purchasing power, the conditions for a *new development model* were set (which many have called 'post-industrial'). This is based mainly on a *new consumption model*, or a new consumption structure, which could also be called 'tertiary' consumption (with Fourastié's meaning): in which old and new forms of essentially *intangible* consumption, namely the services, assume an increasingly dominant role. By intangible consumption we mean the kind of consumption, namely personal, whose provision over the centuries (in the case of *old* services) or for ever (in the case of *newer* ones), has and always will be incapable of improving the quantitative input/output ratio (i.e. productivity) and any improvement will be always in quality.

Concerning this new model of consumption, it has been pointed out that the hypothesis of continuous decline in manufactured (industrial) goods relative to consumption of services has not been confirmed by statistics for the evolution of family budgets.[10] Indeed, household monetary expenditure on 'services' does not grow as fast as that on 'industrial goods' in relation to the revenue increase. The most probable explanation, which seems confirmed by certain statistical information, is that as demand for 'new' services increases in proportion to the decrease in demand for 'goods', a *substitution* of old 'services' with new 'goods' takes place as well. The classic case of the replacement of old domestic services by new domestic appliances can be cited, as can those of the television for the cinema and theatre, recordings for concerts, computers for many personal services (book-keepers, typists, secretaries, translators, etc.); or, multimedia equipment, computerized learning systems, or health diagnosis can replace many other once personal services.

The industrial systems of developed countries have clearly demonstrated their capacity to 'invent' new products to industrialize (and consequently popularize) consumption of certain services which used to be quite personal (and thus also personalized and reserved to the top classes). The capacity to prolong the replacement of goods by services probably still remains, inasmuch as, after the post-war industrial progress and developments in automation technology, there are signs which invite belief that this capacity will reach a certain ceiling.

However, in all this there is nothing which denies the thesis of a fundamental evolution toward a *'service-society'*, in which either intangible services prevail over tangible goods to a new and greater extent, or in which human activities, i.e. essentially labour-intensive employment, is geared toward services rather than manufacturing goods.[11] The growth of tertiary employment and the decline in industrial employment – first relative, then absolute – is indeed a subject not contended either by people or statistical evidence.

And the fact that this increase of needs for intangible services takes the form of non-market activities by way of the informal economy or 'self-service', does nothing to detract from the thesis of the blooming of a 'service economy': it is merely a matter of one further important characteristic (as will be shown below, in Chapters 5 and 6).

3   THE HISTORICAL MODEL OF MASS PRODUCTION AND THE POLICIES IMPLIED (FORDISM AND KEYNESISM)

Before examining how 'tertiarization' modifies what we have called (in the previous paragraphs in this chapter) the 'process of adaptation' of production to consumption, we must know and interpret correctly how 'industrialization', and the historical model of mass production, have brought about, in their due time and way, their own process of adaptation of production to consumption.

3.1   Adaptation of Mass Production to Mass Consumption

What we have defined as the 'process of adaptation' of the production structures to the possibilities of an expansion of consumption has – on the other hand – characterized a good part of the economic events at least in this century (and in the advanced capitalist countries).

Mass production, in order to take root and develop, has attempted more and more to create its own effective 'effective demand', internally and externally to the countries interested and susceptible to adhere to its development. And the potentially infinite 'demand' is translated into an actual demand only when the consumers acquire the capacity of 'real' buying which derives from the distribution of the benefits from the increase in physical production.

The sectors (the industries) of mass production, in order to seize larger market shares from non-mass production (as long as this exists and survives) have had to increase therefore the general purchasing capacity for their own products, i.e. the purchasing capacity of the potential consumers or users of their own products (which on the other hand is the function of the real reduction of production costs, which derives, in turn, from mass production and its technological innovations).

It is a question, therefore, of a sort of circle, which is not vicious but 'virtuous' (as the person would say who forgets that in the etymon of the word 'vicious' there exists no pejorative meaning), between the increase of mass production and that of mass consumption (and which is represented by the process of adaptation mentioned).

3.2 The Discount of Future Productivity

In the past, Western industrial economies often found, in some periods, limitations in effective demand in relation to the potentiality of the production capacity: an attempt has been made to create, *pro tempore*, a buying capacity which went beyond simple possible adaptation, and took into account 'future' increases in physical productivity, stimulated by the same. It is not by chance that 'Fordism'[12] and 'Keynesism' are of the same time: both the *policy of high wages* and that of *high public deficit (and debt)*, are policies aimed at creating only 'fictitious' (or monetary) purchasing capacity *pro tempore*, but which are susceptible to provoking *increases in productivity* – in, and through, mass production – which are the *only real source* of purchasing capacity, and thus of expansion, thus wealth, thus dividend welfare.

The last great exploit of Fordism and Keynesism in the advanced countries was the post-war period, which coincided with the last 'great leap forward in mass production', which has been defined (to use one term) as 'automation', and which has ensured growth rates higher than any before known in industrial development: as high and vast, in the individual countries, as have been the 'margins' for the further expansion of mass production, or – in other words – how important has been the survival of non-mass productive technologies.[13]

3.3 The Negative Conditions for a Productivity Discount

But Fordism and Keynesism, as an expression, or rather emblem, of the discount and acceleration policies of future productivity, function only on the conditions that there are 'margins' and real possibilities for the increase of such productivity. Otherwise they are translated, rather than into a stimulus for the increase of productivity, into a possible discouragement of the same.

In this case, i.e. in the absence of real margins of productivity increase:

- the *'Fordist' enterprises* increase (labour) costs above income or marginal profit of production, without being translated into an increase in private consumption (of cars, for instance) and
- the *'Keynesian' state* (oriented to deficit spending) discovers that the public deficit accepted *pro tempore* becomes irrecoverable (by means of the overall increase in income, and in particular State income); whilst new pressure is created, on the other hand, for immaterial services, today prevalently public ones; and moreover a habit of having many public services 'free', a habit which nourishes waste and parasitism, with damaging effects for the efficiency of the entire economic system.

But in these cases the errors do not consist of 'taking longer steps than one is able' (anti-Keynesian neo-classical theories, and universal common places on financial balances) but rather doing this at a time (and at a point) when the foot is not on solid ground, but is hanging over the void (see the frequently tortuous post-Keynesian debate).[14]

3.4   The 'Margins' of Productivity Increase

But how are what we have called the *'margins' of productivity increase* brought about? This is – in my opinion – the heart of the question (in relation to the unpleasant aspects of the post-industrial crisis: scarce development and employment).

To the extent to which these margins exist, there are also possibilities of adaptation by traditional means (Fordism and Keynesism), even if they are not always easy to implement. For example, these margins exist, in general, in all relatively, but not completely, industrialized countries, in which mass production has not hegemonized the market, but there still exist extended forms of non-mass production and consumption of a *pre*-industrial type.

On the contrary, to the extent to which these margins no longer exist, because structural changes have been determined of a type which (we will see immediately) no longer offer these margins, the situation is completely new, and cannot be ignored. And the 'model of growth' will have completely different characteristics from those known (for which Fordism and Keynesism represented the most intelligent and brave adaptation). This is the case in all the advanced capitalist countries, just those in fact which have from the 1930s applied both Fordism and Keynesism successfully. This has allowed the potential and actual crises of over-production to be overcome in the countries where the highest points of 'industrialization' and technological innovation have been reached, to the extent that clear signs of 'de-industrialization' have arisen (in particular in employment levels).

Conversely, the same situation of an absence of 'margins' (for Fordism and Keynesism) can be produced in those countries where none of the effects of the industrial revolution have been experienced yet, and where mass production is not yet known (or is known only as the chance locating of 'Western' factories') without the creation of a 'local market' for mass consumption, whether small or large.

A highly indeterminate situation, in relation to the expansion margins of mass production, is that of ex-communist countries, in which there are better conditions of a further application of the Fordist and Keynesist models (because of the existence of strong margins of non-mass consumption), apart from one: the absence of entrepreneurship. If this hole is filled rapidly, and a class of industrial managers is formed which is able to apply a Fordist policy, as well as a Keynesian one, (by public policy-makers) on a national and international scale, it would have a good chance of success (as in the 1930s and 1950s in the Western countries).

In short, if someone asked my opinion about whether there are margins for Fordism and Keynesism in Sweden, the USA or even in Italy, I would say at this point, *none*; in Brazil and Korea I would say there are *many*; in a country in darkest Africa, *none yet*; in ex-communist countries, a *few* or *many*, depending on the availability of an entrepreneurial capacity which still seems to be lacking.

Naturally, the increasing internationalization and globalization of the economy, and the trans-national development of the mass production/mass consumption relationship, greatly alter the pattern of 'margins', as discussed above on national scales (and as will be said in Chapter 7). From this point of view, any generalization loses any heuristic nature, and becomes very arbitrary, and not able to avoid the obligation of following a 'case-by-case' pattern.

4 THE 'TERTIARIZATION' PROCESS

4.1 The Saturation of Material Goods and the Growing Demand for Immaterial Goods

Summarizing what we have said already, we can proceed to a further analysis of the characteristics of the change which lead to some firm conceptual points:

- production technologies and innovation offer possibilities of development of 'physical' productivity (production per man-hour), in particular in the production of *material goods*;
- electronics and information technology (IT) have furthermore offered opportunities for enormous increases in productivity in the service sector as well (for as much as it is a question of those services whose production

is measurable in *quantitative* terms: calculation times and operations, acquisition and diffusion of information, etc.).

- the possibilities of an increase in production are instead very limited in the vast range of production of *immaterial goods*. Here the physical productivity, which is measured in terms of quantity, is replaced by *quality*, which often has an inverse relationship with quantity.

4.2 The Need for the Differentiation of Consumption

In short, the 'affluent' society, which has arisen from the automation boom of the post-war period, has brought about a fundamental *structural change* in human and social needs in almost all Western industrial societies. The largely satisfied need for *material* goods has been increasingly integrated, at first, and then substituted by the need for *immaterial* goods, for which the production technologies have remained the same for centuries; or have changed from the method and quality point of view rather than that of productivity.[15]

Furthermore, the massification of consumption and the public systems of transfer and supply in all cases of need, whilst abolishing material discomfort, have at the same time increased also among ever larger strata of 'average' consumers, the psychological need for the differentiation of consumption, the need to leave mass consumption, not only as concerns some immaterial goods, but even for some completely traditional material goods as well.[16] The need has been generated – at first restricted only to limited sections of well-off consumers – for 'positional' goods – as they have been defined – whose enjoyment depends purely on the fact that it is not generalized.[17]

4.3 'New' Demand and 'Development'

The satisfaction of these 'different' needs is becoming prevalent in the overall set of needs to be satisfied, in more and more areas of consumption in advanced countries, and characterizes the *new* demand for goods and services. If, as is very probable, the population is not destined to grow much in Western industrialized countries, but rather to stabilize itself, it means that the additional demand for goods and services will be essentially oriented to – and thus induce – the growth of activities with a scarce increase in productivity; and thus a growth of activities with 'zero' development, if 'development' is measured with the indicators currently used. (We will return to this in Chapters 5 and 13.)

4.4 'Over-Industrialization'

If we leave aside, for the moment, the prospects of development in international and world commerce (to which we will return) for the advanced

Western countries (the OECD countries), the 'crisis' – which we have called structural, and which is seen to be chronic – seems marked by the *incongruence of a production system still founded on the search for a productivist 'development' which is no longer required, in fact, by emerging social needs.*[18]

In effect, there has been an impression, for some decades now, that the Western industrial system no longer knows what to 'invent' to stimulate the needs and demand for industrial products consumption, which has reached overall, as said, a certain *saturation*. The sophistication of products is enormous; the production of 'new', not always useful, products is also intense. But this has not prevented the relative decline of the most important industrial sectors, and in particular those which have achieved the most rapid increases in productivity. This allows us to speak about a general phenomenon of 'de-industrialization' of the post-industrial economy.[19]

(This does not exclude, however, that within these 'sectors', the companies which have accumulated the greatest advantages in terms of low production costs have not maintained important development rates of production at the expense of other less favoured enterprises in the sector.)

A 'tertiary revolution' is now being produced in place of the 'industrial revolution' which has dominated the growth of Western economies over a couple of centuries. Not surprisingly, therefore, characteristics and a model are forming of a *'post-industrial'* society, or *'service'* society, whose specific functioning we are obliged to isolate and interpret, despite its interwoven relationship with certain, characteristics of industrial society which have not been completely achieved.[20]

4.5   Towards a New Model of Society

Perhaps it would be better to speak of a *process of tertiarization* which is taking the place of the already known and acquired *process of industrialization*, but which presents characteristics and modalities different and sometimes opposite to the latter (this opposition of two processes deserves to be shown explicitly, even at the risk of some excessive simplification; this will be done in Chapters 7 and 8).

It is well known and received that a process of tertiarization is born on the basis of the achievement of an industrialization process, at an advanced level. A real process of tertiarization cannot be conceived without preceding industrial development which satisfies, with developed mass production, the fundamental needs of the society overall. This is somewhat obvious (but never heard as such in current discourses).[21]

A new society (which we could call a 'tertiary' or 'service' society) only appears when a process of industrialization has matured completely. (Excepting the cases of countries which, although they have not achieved fully a process of industrialization, develop a 'tertiary' role in the international division of labour: but in these cases a functional integration is had with other highly industrialized countries, for which reason we cannot speak of an autonomous service society.)[22]

But once it has appeared, the service society presents a model which is completely different from that of industrial society in the phase of its development and affirmation. The analysis of this model is fundamental for the interpretation of the crisis of change which the Western world is passing through. This analysis began, long since, at the political and in particular at the academic level. Although interesting theories have been developed on the subject, force of habit often (too often) leads to the utilization, in order to understand and face the critical problems which post-industrial (or, if preferred, 'tertiary') countries are going through, of interpretation schemes founded on the functioning of industrial society (which moreover is still functioning, albeit 'in crisis' and with a tendency to decline). This is, evidently, a mistake, loaded with wrong conclusions.

We will study the more evident features of this process of tertiarization in the next two chapters: in the fifth chapter we will develop the aspects of change of the *production structures*; in the sixth we will study the aspects connected to *labour demand and supply* and *employment* in general.

If the analysis of the structural changes allows us to understand the typical characteristics of this 'tertiary society' or 'service society', in comparison with those of the 'industrial society', we will be able to 'counterpose' the features of this service society with those of industrial society, as if they were two ideal-typical models, and not two realities in strict genetic connection (as they actually are, from another point of view).

The counterposition helps to understand clearly the actions and policies which are posed as the 'midwives' of a progressive evolution of the new society, and those which are part of a vision, and relative paradigms, linked to a society which although still dominant is in decline.

This will be the key to understanding the nature of the 'crises' and 'structural changes' which we will have identified, and provide the correct interpretative reading (which normally is far from the current and conventional one).

Thus a second type of analysis will proceed in two steps, the first a brief counterposed description of the two ideal-typical models: that of industrial society and that of tertiary society. The second step will be the classification of the effects and functioning of the two models in relation to the set of phenomena usually examined by the economic analysts: the labour market, production reorganization, investments, motivations, savings formation, financial flows, and so on.

5 The Change in the Structure of Production

The relative importance of the 'tertiary services'[1] (in terms of income consumed and employment generated) has already provoked the name *service society*, for a society which is coming out of the formidable increase in industrialization, and is now seeing a decrease, not only in relative but also in absolute terms (in the same way that agricultural employment declined with the emergence of the industrial societies). This development has resulted in a radical earthquake in *productive structures* (some have introduced the term 'tertiary revolution'),[2] whose salient features and consequences have been perceived and analyzed under multiple viewpoints which may be evoked as follows.[3]

1 VISIONS OF THE CRISIS IN INDUSTRIAL PRODUCTION

1.1 Various Ways of Recording the Crisis

The foremost and most useful way to read the various surveys, recordings and interpretations of the *structural* crisis of industrial production is to divide them in two categories: (a) those inclined to emphasize the *changes* which we can define as 'internal' to such production, more or less linked to the evolution of consumption as well as of productive methods and organization; and (b) those inclined to emphasize, rather than changes, *transformations*, which tend to modify radically the very nature of the whole industrial society.

It is difficult to ascertain clear boundaries between these two categories of analyses, also because it is difficult to identify a clear-cut difference between the two phenomena of change and transformation for which we have used words substantially similar also in semantics. Many short-term analyses, naturally belonging to the first category, end up grasping radical long-term effects. On the other hand, some more long-term-oriented analyses, which intend to sketch out social transformations of great importance (and legitimizing their location in the second category), as a matter of fact show themselves as more ephemeral than those we would put among the analyses of the 'internal' change of industrial society.

One is tempted to question whether, in this interlacing of readings, interpretations and meanings, the authors' personal characters are playing an important role, rather than the nature of the examined facts and phenomena.

It becomes not wholly illegitimate yet to take account of other, more subjective aspects of the debate on industrial crisis.

Among the analyses with structural tendencies one can then distinguish the pessimistic or 'catastophistic' ones which suggest a kind of collapse of the capitalist system due to its incapacity to restore equilibria, and more optimistic ones which, though not denying the disequilibria, underestimate their gravity, considering them part of a slow 'structural' transformation of the capitalist system.[4]

It is significant to observe that a certain economic alarmism (or sometimes even economic 'terrorism') concerning the crisis brings together those who are confident of the possibility of *short-term economic policy measures*, capable of restoring the old equilibria concerning employment, inflation, growth rates and the deficit, and those who do not share any of this confidence and dream of a *total overturning of the system*. The two tendencies are regrouping into a single conventional reading mode: that employment, growth rates, price stability and balanced budgets are good indicators of the economic well-being of a society, valid and utilizable. Their fear is not a crisis of the economic system, but only of its transformation into something different to which they are accustomed to see and to live.

On the contrary, the 'optimists', sceptical of the validity of traditional instruments of counter-crisis economic policy, argue that the indicators represent very little of economic reality and that they are rather signs of fundamental tendencies toward different equilibria, to be measured through other indicators. The 'growth rate' (of the GNP) and 'full employment' are the first indicators which must be considered outdated.[5]

In sum, the analyses of the crisis of industrial production can be seen from an infinite number of viewpoints, which can be more or less convergent according to the circumstances.

Yet perhaps, for our aims, what can be most interesting is to have a look to that part of those analyses which have emphasized the consequences of the crisis rather than its causes. And here we will offer a quick, selected survey.

1.2   The Crisis as 'Dependency Effect'

In this *excursus* on some selected readings of the crisis of industrial production we begin with the well-known one suggested by J.K. Galbraith (1958), who emphasized its so-called 'dependency effect', or, in other words, its self-referential character. Despite its old age, its being rooted in an era when the industrial crisis was far from evident, and its clear position among the analyses which do not belong to the visions of a social transformation but rather among the traditional ones on the need for 'more public and less private', Galbraith's analysis of the dependency of industrial society from the 'dependency effect' is nevertheless one of the most significant ones about the real factor of long-term structural crisis which deserve to be analysed.

The reduced need for material goods and the increased demand for immaterial goods (discussed in Chapter 4) has spurred the actors of the industrial sectors towards a multiplication of efforts in order to preserve a market for their products, trying to create ever new needs for material goods, resulting in a waste effect that is important, if compared with the overall appraisal of effective consumer preferences (even if a temporary, ie. short-lived, demand has actually been stimulated).

Now, a classic work on the effects of the misuses of 'consumerism', pushed by the apparatus of manufacturing production, is Galbraith's work *The Affluent Society* (1958).

Long before the perception of the crisis of the industrial system set in, actually in the middle of the period of post-war boom, this author was one of the first to describe the consequences of the production race far beyond the real needs of consumers.

Let me cite a few passages which I consider to be essential:

Consumer wants can have bizarre, frivolous, or even immoral origins, and an admirable case can still be made for a society that seeks to satisfy them. But the case cannot stand if it is the process of satisfying wants that creates the wants. For then the individual [one may ask if a printing error has not substituted this word for 'intellectual'] who urges the importance of production to satisfy these wants is precisely in the position of the on-looker who applauds the effort of the squirrel to keep abreast of the wheel that is propelled by its own effort.   (Galbraith, 1958, p. 120)

And further on:

As a society becomes increasingly affluent, wants are increasingly created by the process by which they are satisfied...Wants thus come to depend on output. In technical terms it can no longer be assumed that welfare is greater at an all-round higher level of production than at a lower one...It will be convenient to call it Dependence Effect...Among the many models of the good society no one has urged the squirrel wheel. Moreover, as we shall see presently, the wheel is not one that revolves with perfect smoothness. Aside from its dubious cultural charm, there are serious structural weaknesses which may one day embarrass us...[our concern for goods] does not arise in spontaneous consumer need. Rather the dependence effect means that it grows out of the process of production itself...This is not true of all goods, but that it is true of a substantial part is sufficient. It means that since demand would not exist, were it not contrived, its utility or urgency, ex-contrivance, is zero. If we regard this production as marginal, we may say that the marginal utility of present aggregate output, ex advertising and salesmanship, is zero. Clearly the attitudes and values which make production the central achievement of our society have some exceptionally twisted roots.

(ibid., pp. 124–5)

In Galbraith's subsequent works, aimed at drawing the future evolution of the 'industrial system',[6] a possible 'crisis' or 'withdrawal' of it is not regarded as a necessary consequence of the development of structural changes, but is, so to speak, 'optional', depending on the preferred policy choices. Says Galbraith:

If we continue to believe that the goals of the industrial system – the expansion of output, the companion increase in consumption, technological advance, the public image that sustains it – are coordinated with life, then all our lives will be in the service of these goals. What is consistent with these ends we shall have or be allowed; all else will be off limits... If on the other hand, the industrial system is only a part, and relatively a diminishing part, of life, there is much less occasion for concern. Aesthetic goals will have pride of place; those who serve them will not be subject to the goals of the industrial system; the industrial system itself will be subordinate to the claims of these dimensions of life. Intellectual preparation will be for its own sake and not for the better service to the industrial system.

(Galbraith, *The New Industrial State*, 1967, p. 398)

This conclusion anticipates what we will say about the effects of the crisis of industrial production in this and in the subsequent chapters. Yet it can already be said that, depending on the parameter of judgement that is used, the crisis is read in a different way, and with a different concern.

On the other hand, the very perception and evaluation of the crisis could be a function of the level of advancement of industrialization itself. Employing the words of an economics handbook, the 'marginal desirability' of industrial development can have varied indifference curves which are an inverse function of the level of advancement of the development itself. Not unlike the marginal utility of income, which increases the lower the income is, and decreases the higher the income is, so the virtues of the industrial system might be less appreciated the more such a system consolidates and imposes itself.

I consider these passages from Galbraith, despite their simplicity, particularly significant. Later, the critique of consumerism became more vague, more ideological, and lost the shine of the critical concept of the 'dependence effect'.[7]

1.3 The Industrial 'Diffusion'

The crisis of industrial production has moreover manifested itself with the crisis of mass production.

First to incur a historic crisis has been heavy or basic industry (steel, chemicals, cement, and so on), a crisis that subsequently pervaded everywhere – there more, there less – the whole production of material goods.

But what has attracted the most attention is the crisis of 'large-scale industry' as compared to 'small-scale industry', which has been parallel to the crisis of 'large firms' as compared to 'small firms'.

The identity of large industry and mass production is not evident always and in all sectors, although it is frequent enough.

On this topic a huge literature, both theoretical and empirical, has developed. We will try to summarize it within the limits of usefulness to the critical development of our analysis of change, with the help of one of the works we found more significant on the topic: the essay by Piore and Sabel (1984), 'The Second Industrial Divide'.[8]

First of all, according to these authors, mass production came to mean modern times, since it is the expression of a system of ideas that promises to explain how industrial society functions, where it comes from, and why it is how it is. It is the theory – dominant since the classical economists – according to which the increase of productivity (output per unit input) depends on an increasingly specialized use of resources (meaning a specific product).

But from a long time in the past – Piore and Sabel noticed – 'among the most discordant facts about the economy of mass production' there is the observation of the permanence of small firms and short-term production programmes in any phase of the Western countries' industrial history. Even during the 1970s (i.e. a decade when mass production had reached its most advanced levels) about 70 per cent of total production in metallurgical and mechanical industry in the USA consisted in small batches. This seems a result that does not conform to the perspective of all classical economists (from Smith to Marx and beyond) who were inclined to predict the progressive disappearance of small firms in favour of mass production. The regress (or non-progress) of mass production in comparison to small industry or 'craft' and the attempt to explain the permanence of small firms has produced also a kind of 'theory of industrial dualism'. It was developed on the basis of the following arguments.[9]

1.4 The 'Theory' of Industrial Dualism

Mass production (this is the common opinion) means the creation of general goods by means of specialized resources. The more general the goods are, the more extended the range of uses for which they can be employed, and the more extended is their market – yet the more specialized are also the machines, the more articulated and separated is the work employed for their production.

Thus an economic system organized according to this leading principle cannot be composed only of mass production firms, since the general goods they produce cannot be specialized enough to meet the needs of the firms engaged in mass production. In other words, the 'specialized' machinery requires that mass production cannot be itself produced by methods of mass production.

The machinery of mass production must, in fact, be built according to a logic that is the mirror image of the mass production: a production of specialized goods by means of general resources. Since the product is a specialty, with a limited market, production must be steadily reorganized; and the workers must have a range of abilities and a general understanding of the processes that were considered classical attributes of pre-industrial craft. So industrialization should, according to the theory of dualism, revive at least part of the craft sector – reorienting it towards its own aims.

A similar logic applies to whatever is the fluctuation or the constantly low level of demand that creates markets too insecure or too small to stimulate mass production. At the margins of almost all industries, therefore, small firms do survive providing a changing range of production items, or responding to emergent requirements. In exceptional cases, e.g. ladies' garments, most of an industrial sector is made up of this kind of firm.

In this way, dualism theory interprets modern craft production as a necessary complement of mass production. Its main claim is thus that (paradoxically) a second and opposite form of production is *inherent* to the logic of mass production.

Yet – according to Piore and Sabel – the theory of industrial dualism, so well-founded, acute, and sustained by however much evidence, is not able to explain wholly some characteristics which emerged from the historical observation of the industrial development up to the current 'crisis' of industrialization.[10]

First of all, in the theory of industrial dualism, technological progress in industrial society continues to be dominated – as in the classical theory which predicted the disappearance of craft – by mass production. Although craft can, in this perspective, 'participate' in the innovations generated by mass production (and sometimes grow with its own technology), it is not expected to generate a flow of technological progress proper to characterize autonomously industrial society and lead economic development. Mass production is seen as the technologically dynamic form and specialized production as its subordinate. Industrial dualism thus saves the classic rule providing an exception.

1.5 The Crisis of Mass Production and the 'Re-emergence of the Craft Paradigm'

The thesis that Piore and Sabel develop, instead, is that there is an *alternative re-emergence of the craft paradigm*, compared with the crisis of mass production, as a model to respond to the crisis of industrial production and technological advancement; and that this alternative produces – still in the industrial context – a second 'divide' of industrial history.

The thesis is imbued with a remarkable number of analyses of the development experiences of small firms following what they call the industrial 'dislocation' of the 1970s in many countries, such as Japan, Italy, West Germany, France, and the USA as well.[11]

But I am not sure to what extent the undeniably massive multiplication of small and medium-sized firms, which has raised so much clamour and attention in Europe (and in the USA) and hopes in the third world, is announcing a return to a 'craft paradigm'. As has been said above, many particular factors created favourable conditions for the growth of small and medium-sized firms:

(a)   The crisis of mass production under the form of a strong tendency towards high-quality branded products in most of the sectors of goods for final consumption, has surely reopened greater opportunities for the work of small firms.

(b)   Yet the large firms themselves found it convenient (and not only for competitive reasons) to 'decentralize' their own work, when technically possible, and to associate with small firms or even to create the latter.

(c)   It was not by chance that this integration of a new development of small firms and entrepreneurship happened in countries (and in regions within these countries) that had not yet reached full industrial maturity, but not in countries still far away from an industrialization stage, and is far less evident in countries where industrialization is very advanced or where the 'post-industrial' culture is advanced.

Since it is an answer that is in many cases so typical in some regions and countries, and in others so conditioned by some circumstances, can we believe that it represents a deep response to all challenges of social transformation that are forthcoming? In sum, can we believe that it can be seen as the most important phenomenon to characterize the transformation of contemporary industrial society? Is the large phenomenon of the expansion of small and medium-sized firms sufficient to let us declare a 'second divide' in industry's history?

1.6 Beyond Industrial Diffusion

Nevertheless, the phenomenon exists, and its analysis is very important in order to build a complete picture of the ongoing social transformations. The apparent quantitative regression of mass production and the undeniable quantitative progress of the small industrial firm compels one to pay due attention to the change which the two determine in the general framework of industrial activities.

In the first place, the relatively substantial increase in small and medium-sized enterprises producing tangible goods, seems to counterbalance the diminishing weight of the large enterprises, for which limited prospects of high profits provide less of an incentive.

Today these smaller enterprises can make do with lower profits in exchange for other advantages. Their cost prices are often lower mainly because of lower costs for labour (which in turn enjoys other benefits beyond those strictly linked to wages).

Technological progress, particularly in electronics, has made them less marginal than hitherto. Lastly their goods have a less 'mass-produced' quality and cater better to the more individualized tastes of the new consumer demand, including the demand for tangible goods and consumer durables.

In all countries abundant literature can be found – as already said – on the subject of the explosion of small enterprises during the 1970s and 1980s. With the years, small enterprise has become the anchor of the rescue-effort of 'job creation', for good and bad reasons according to the contexts, sectors and cases.

Categorizing the literature of works partisan to small enterprise there are two essential theses: the first insists on the *technological factor*, the second on *diseconomies of scale*. The first thesis concerns above all the advanced countries.[12] The second thesis, based on 'diseconomies' of scale under new conditions of production and markets, is better adapted to the less advanced economies, such as the European Mediterranean countries.[13]

In spite of this categorization, the technological factor and that of diseconomies of scale are often joined, which reinforces the evolutive capacity of small enterprise.

People have wondered whether the evident expansion of small enterprise is not the effect of a pure and simple crisis of industrial production, if, in other words, at least for a large part of this expansion, the case is one of 'pathological' rather than 'physiological' expansion, notably in the case of diseconomies of scale. One may also ask oneself whether this expansion renders an appropriate rationalization of industrial sectors in crisis more difficult, sectors which might themselves achieve strong increases in productivity to the general benefit of post-industrial society. Furthermore one may ask whether expansion of small enterprise in the industrial manufacturing sector has only created very precarious jobs instead of creating alternative opportunities for stable employment.

The answers to these questions only emerge through case-by-case analysis, carried out sector by sector and country by country; but without common and general conclusions. Here we will limit ourselves to pointing out that if it does not also respond to the quantitative and qualitative needs of final demand (that which will be even truer and more damaging than is foreign demand, as is often the case in the European Mediterranean countries), the model for development of 'widespread industrialization' may not result in anything but a response inappropriate to the structural crisis analyzed and to the requested model of society.[14]

1.7 The 'Decline' of Global Productivity

Another relevant phenomenon, connected to the structural change above indicated, is the steady narrowing of the total productivity of the 'mature' economic system, and the consequential narrowing of the area of activities obeying the rationale: *higher productivity equals higher profits*.[15]

Historically it was these activities that brought about the birth and development of the industrial and capitalist society, with all the major contributions to social well-being that followed, but which is showing signs of crisis: the contraction of these to a diminished sense of entrepreneurship (where profit is the spur), and a decline in the 'entrepreneur-investor' model with whose success the flow of funds system predominant today is associated.[16]

To this subject, a very important subject for our analysis, we will return in Chapter 11.

1.8 The Explosion of the Demand for Public Services

A macroscopic phenomenon is the growing demand for services (corresponding to the new needs, as said recursively) which by their quality and nature do not encourage the development of conventional profit-motivated entrepreneurship in the private sector, being directly reflected in a demand for 'public' services which may or may not be supplied free of charge.

As a result there has been substantial growth in the promotion and *public* production of services by the public sector which raises financing problems on a scale that contemporary industrial (or rather post-industrial) nations have never before known.

The expansion of the non-market sector occurred a long time ago in nearly all the OECD countries, where public spending expanded to more than half of national resources.[17] J.K. Galbraith's volume (1974) on the economy and public goals gives a lucid interpretation of the manifest tendencies of the growth of the demand for public services which would still deserve attention.

The connection between the expansion of the public service demand and the productivistic dichotomy of the activities, has not sufficiently attracted the attention – to my knowledge – of the scholars of public economics (except an essay by Baumol in 1967 on 'the Macroeconomics of Unbalanced Growth').

1.9 The Development of the Non-Mercantile Exchange

Lastly, another relevant phenomenon of the structural change under analysis is the growing importance of the activities developed outside the mercantile exchange and an expansion of the non-market economic sector.[18]

Changes in the structure of final consumption (with a relative saturation of demand for industrial products and rising demand for public services, particularly free services) also imply changes in lifestyles and living patterns.

The idea of working solely for gain is losing ground and this in fact would not seem to be widely affecting people's well-being at large. Even workers from the lower classes and the young are more interested in the conditions and nature of work; their preference is clearly to work for themselves even if they do not earn as much.[19]

Alongside and associated with this trend towards independent work for which demand is moving ever upwards in the personal services sector, an expansion is also taking place in collectively organized independent services, involving exchanges in kind rather than in cash and which may even extend to free ('voluntary') work.

The first place where independent work has developed is the household, i.e. the first economic institution of human life. For instance, studies on the role of the household in the real economy and in modification of the concept of development and well-being in the post-industrial economy have multiplied recently.[20]

But other areas and other occasions for independent work are gaining in importance for the future: small communities, clubs and associations, etc. are developing new activities and organizing themselves in new ways to meet needs in new areas of tertiary 'non-market' consumption which are not traditionally catered for by the public sector. The documentation on these new ways of organizing private consumption is already very significant.[21]

For the moment, in order to have an idea of the relationship that the non-market economy has today with the market economy (without delving into the subject of the techniques of 'new' systems of socio-economic accounting, a subject which will be taken up again, albeit succinctly, in section 3.2 of this chapter and in Chapter 13, section 5), we will recall that at the beginning of the 1970s Nordhaus and Tobin (1973) estimated that the value of leisure time and non-market work represented three-quarters of total MEW (Measurement of Welfare Economics, a total measure of economic welfare) in the US in 1965 (50 per cent and 25 per cent respectively). MEW, on its part, was nearly twice as large as GNP. Morgan *et al.* (1966) estimated that as early as in 1964, the US national product should have included unpaid work which would have increased GNP by 38 per cent. Sirageldin (1969), using the same model as Morgan, estimated that for the same year and country, households' disposable income was 43 per cent above the official calculations, due to domestic work. Subsequently, methods developed toward evaluation of the time spent in productive work in the household.[22]

To sum up, what we wish to point out is that for several decades, any examination of the inter-sectorial structural changes of productive activities (based on measurements both of employment and of the income of various sectors) cannot ignore, if it wants to maintain a minimum of significance, the changes that are intercurrent between the *market* economy and the *non-market* economy.[23]

However, this loss of meaningfulness of conventional economic accounting (SNA) as indicator of national socio-economic well-being or malaise, has not in any case altered its applications to the reasonings and prescriptions of quantitative macroeconomic policy; this fact puts the credibility and reliability of economics, as normative and applied science, into crisis.[24]

2   THE PRODUCTIVE DICHOTOMY OF THE ECONOMY

2.1   The Increasing Dichotomy between High-Productivity and Low-Productivity Sectors

This economic upheaval in productive structures (or tertiary revolution) which has been briefly outlined, has two *divergent* characteristics that denote the nature of the present employment crisis to which policy solutions are sought. These characteristics are:

1. on the one hand, an excess or surplus of products in the *high-productivity sectors* which have consistently been responsible for the high rates of growth recorded in past decades and which, despite the market crises, still display a strong innovatory drive, such as to generate further excess in the workforce;
2. on the other, such a crisis is provoked by increasing expansion in the *low-productivity sectors*. This cannot but bring about lower aggregate growth, and perhaps ultimately a steady state economy, as the relative weight and innovation capacity of the high-productivity sectors progressively diminish.[25]

The two divergent characteristics defined above – i.e. the excess or surplus of production in the high-productivity sectors, on the one hand, and the increasingly rapid expansion of the low-productivity sectors, on the other – produce a crisis that from several points of view can be considered 'progressive' in nature. We can say that it is a matter of a growth crisis, induced at once by growth in the productive capacity and efficiency of the industrial sectors and by the increasing material well-being of consumers who turn to 'new' forms of consumption, which unfortunately 'embody' rather lower rates of productivity.[26]

In spite of the range of interpretations in the analyses of the crisis, a general *consensus* exists in favour of recognizing that it is a matter of overproduction and the consecutive decline of profits.[27]

These special characteristics of the recurrent economic 'crisis' impart a unique quality to the crisis on the employment front, which should not be identified overhastily with the conventional concept of unemployment growth, as abundantly claimed.

2.2   The Employment and Incomes Features of Structural Change

In fact unemployment rates do seem to have reached historic levels in all the developed countries, the 'great crisis' apart. But in contrast with those crises, the high unemployment rates do not appear to be accompanied by any substantial *deterioration* in a household's *real living standards*, even in the traditional 'pockets' of poverty (existing in every country) which, despite the 'crisis', are tending to shrink rather than expand.

Returning to the line of reasoning about the present crisis of employment (that has been present for a long time) and the very limited role of its impact on change in real average household living standards, we can recognize that this could of course be mainly a result of the social security measures introduced and improved anywhere under the welfare state systems, to compensate for joblessness or short-time working, coupled with the rise (despite the crisis) in the incomes and purchasing power (despite inflation) of the 'not-unemployed', i.e. workers in employment.

One may thus paradoxically say that, in general, the crisis of our economies (in the last phase of 'tertiarization' or of mature capitalism) has been provoked by *excess* productivity (in the primary and secondary sectors, where productivity rates are high) and *simultaneously* by a productivity *deficit* in the system as a whole due to the relative increase of the tertiary sector, where productivity rates are low.

We must not forget, as we emphasize better in Chapter 8 (section 1.2), that the overwhelming increase of productivity in the 'productivistic sector' (caused by cultural and scientific progress) is largely dependent on the numerical increase (employees and outcome) of the 'non-productivistic sector', with their patrimony of 'intellectual' and 'scientific' factors not measurable in terms of *output-per-input*.

The tertiary output, with its low productivity rate, has been appreciated for its *quality* rather than its *quantitative* returns. The structural change with which we are dealing, therefore, has an immediate repercussion on the way of *evaluating* economic well-being.

3 CHANGES INDUCED IN THE CONCEPT OF DEVELOPMENT, WELFARE AND EMPLOYMENT

3.1 The Idea of a 'Steady State' Economy

The debate around how to evaluate economic welfare is not at all new.

For instance, since the last century, people started to evaluate in different ways the evolution towards a 'stationary' state of the economy, and to accept it less dramatically.

The historians of economy know well that a stationary state tends to be the rule in the history of humanity, which has concentrated development in exceptional periods, but not of exceptional duration. On the other hand, the idea that the growth rate of an economy could not be continuous and indefinite has often appeared in the thinking of classical economists, even if economics as a 'science' (so to speak) was born with the impulse of an extraordinary period of change and growth: the so-called 'industrial revolution'.

It is a fact (as seen in Chapter 2) that economic historians have counted many 'industrial revolutions' in the last two hundred years.[28] But the idea that we should pass through a 'stationary' economy has been appearing from time to time in the history of economic thought, as it was observed that economic growth could not continue indefinitely. It is time perhaps that we seriously reconsider that idea, at least in the terms used – more than a century ago – by John Stuart Mill when he stated:

> it must always have been seen, more or less distinctly, by political econo-
> mists, that the increase in wealth is not boundless: that the end of what
> they term the progressive state lies in the stationary state, that all progress
> in wealth is a postponement of this, and that each step in advance is an
> approach to it... I cannot... regard the stationary state of capital and
> wealth with the unaffected aversion so generally manifested towards it by
> the political economists of the old school. I am inclined to believe that it
> would be, on the whole, a very considerable improvement on our present
> condition. I confess that I am not charmed with the ideal of life held out by
> those who think that the normal state of human beings is that of struggling

to get on; that the trampling, crushing, elbowing, and treading on each other's heels which form the existing type of social life, are the most desirable lot of human kind, or anything but the disagreeable symptoms of industrial progress.   (Stuart Mill, *Principles etc.*, book 4, chapter 6)

And after having pleaded for better distribution of opportunity rather than growth of wealth, which effect would be to double 'the means of consuming things which give little or no pleasure except as a representative of wealth', he continued:

If the earth must lose that great portion of its pleasantness which it owes to things that the unlimited increase of wealth and population would expatriate from it, for the mere purpose of enabling it to support a larger but not happier or a better population, I sincerely hope, for the sake of posterity, that they will be content to be stationary, long before necessity compels them to it.   (ibid.)

And have we, posterity, taken account of this consideration? Stuart Mill carries on:

It is scarcely necessary to remark that a stationary condition of capital and population implies no stationary state of human improvement. There would be as much scope as ever for all kinds of mental culture, and moral and social progress; as much room for improving the Art of Living and much more likelihood of its being improved, when the minds cease to be engrossed by the art of getting on. Even the industrial arts might be as earnestly and as successfully cultivated, with the sole difference that instead of serving no purpose but the increase of wealth, industrial improvements would produce their legitimate effect, that of abridging labour.[29]   (ibid.)

John Stuart Mill's arguments are still valid, and rather prophetic considering when they were written (1848). His arguments are probably more valid today than they were at the time. This drives us to think that the limits to which he alludes are not particularly evident, as they have been superseded repeatedly in the economic history of the last century, with indisputable benefits to mankind. However, it should not be forgotten that: (a) J.S. Mill was more concerned with the kind of progress than with the quantity of growth as a whole; (b) he presumed the possibility of recurring cycles of progressing and stagnant economy in the long term, and considered the latter far from negative and abnormal, but rather to some extent normal and appropriate for *qualitative* transformation of the effects of the former; and finally (c) that he considered industrial improvements very important, provided that they produced legitimate abridgment of work rather than merely 'getting on'.

The application of a logic opposed to growth to today's industrial and economic situation seems an ideological denial which goes far beyond Stuart Mill's own position. For example, a modern author partial to the stationary state, E.H. Daly, nominates the minimization rather than maximization of physical fluxes of production and consumption as the appropriate objective.[30]

It seems that here one is walking into the trap of the logic of 'growthmanship',[31] merely inverting the values (from positive to negative) rather than going beyond the parameter (GNP) used as a measurement of society's well-being.

Would it not be more reasonable to abandon macro-economic indicators and the accompanying notions of maximization and minimization alltogether, and to carry out case-by-case and country-by-country research on *preferences which are worked out politically by the community* rather than by a blind and hazardous market? and define the appropriate indicators of such preferences, that are able to express them adequately? It might be wondered whether or not the growth of GNP is often indicative of well-being and that the achievement of other goals might be obtained with stationary GNP, yet a certain growth of GNP might represent the measurable effect of certain welcome 'industrial improvements' which could be subject to further research.

In general, it is nevertheless also reasonable to note that the expansion of activities and work with low productivity rates (Fourastié's 'tertiary') might bring about a strong reduction of the general growth rate of GNP, unless it is compensated for by adequate industrial improvements in the primary and secondary sectors, i.e. the sectors that are susceptible to high productivity rates. This would have a negative effect on employment, which indeed seems to be the case in the current economic crisis, without necessarily being interpreted as *regress* but rather, in the words of Stuart Mill, as *progress* in the 'art of living', or in more current terms, 'quality of life'. This is progress which must be accompanied by a policy of increased redistribution, above all of the 'given' opportunities to work (in terms of remuneration as well as burdens).

3.2   A Different Way of Measuring Welfare

But it is the current way of measuring progress and welfare that we must as soon as possible change in order to get out of the conceptual paradigms which lead us to talk about the 'steadiness' in the economy.

In effect, *steadiness in reference to what?*

It is true, productivity is in decline. But the productivity decline is considered as a quantitative relationship – 'Smithian', in the sense of the classical example of the pin factory, the famous example which inaugurates the 'treatise' that provided the foundations of the theory of business enterprise and of political economy in general – between production (output) and production factors (input).

But in the era in which it is argued that the main factor of production process is no longer *labour,* or *land,* or *capital,* or the *State* (which some decades ago some economists wanted to introduce in the 'factors' club), but *knowledge*[32] (seen as scientific progress or technical innovation), the productivity passes from being a quantitative relationship to being a qualitative relationship not measurable with conventional criteria and methods.

Or it is a question of 'measuring the unmeasurable' – like the title of a volume of essays collected by Peter Nijkamp *et al.*[33] The productivity measurer used traditionally is no longer suitable for expressing the value of output, production, knowledge, as welfare factors. To the extent that the 'knowledge' factor is applied to the production of material goods, traditional measurement may be attempted; but if we wish to apply it to non-material goods (or services) new criteria and forms of measurement are needed.[34]

As far as this production (tertiary services, both private and public) increases in relative importance in the sum of values which make up welfare, the indicator used becomes more and more obsolete and misleading: it continues to indicate a 'value' (output per man-hour) which is rather a 'misvalue' (i.e. a negative value) and to display as an *increase* what is rather a *decrease.* In such a way, bad indicators risk not only perverting values, but also inverting these, when they complain about a (monetary) decline that is, in fact, a real improvement and considering as (illusory) 'progress' that which in fact constitutes 'regress'.

From this point of view it is no longer a matter of pleading for zero growth or a stable or stationary economy, but of modifying the indicators through which growth and development are defined and by which one *inverses* the conception and value, positive or negative, of the real objectives to be grasped and measured. The structural changes may thus be evaluated in terms of the structures of activity and employment, but not in terms of GNP, which no longer expresses the value of well-being of post-industrial or tertiary society.[35]

This face of the current employment crisis is revealed not so much in terms of deteriorating living conditions as in an *increasingly inequitable distribution of working activity.* Boosting employment to achieve better living conditions without, at the same time, improving its distribution would be to go *against* the nature of things, and it would have an illusory effect that would be rich in negative consequences rather than positive ones.

In the real world of today, greater well-being cannot be achieved by *increasing aggregate employment* (in terms of total hours worked) but only through a better distribution of hours worked among the potential workforce, via a drastic cutback in average working time per person. Similarly, this higher level of material well-being can no longer be achieved by increasing the total volume of goods and services produced but only by redistributing their use and quality more fairly, and by channelling new jobs to activities that are socially useful and necessary inasmuch as they respond to needs so far unmet.

If we take into serious consideration these observations, we must acknowledge that a good part of the alarmist discussions made by economists in recent decades (which have always met with success in public opinion and with politicians always ready to expand the efficacy of certain clichés) concerning the level of employment or unemployment – as commonly understood – are obsolete. And they are the more obsolete the more recent they are: as if historical experience was worth nothing.

3.3   A Different Way of Conceiving and Measuring Employment

Actually, it is a real 'mystification'. When 'employment' (or 'unemployment') is mentioned, in reality one is not thinking of the labour that is delivered or the result of this labour, but of the 'income' that is (or is not) gained, of the purchasing power and the consumption that derives (or not) from it. Why should we not then speak directly about the latter, which is the real problem? And why should we not speak about income distribution? And – through income distribution – of welfare distribution?

If one were thinking – speaking about employment and far from any mystification – of the labour *to be delivered*, then the first question to be asked should be *what* labour, *which* goods and services, *which* jobs; in sum: *which activities* would be useful socially and individually, to such an extent that its 'provision' or 'creation' is desired. Useful to such an extent that it is preferred to employ human resources in such activities rather than leaving them in idleness, or amusement, or freedom of being and doing, however more desirable and beneficial than unwilling labour.

If this social and individual *demand* for labour does not show itself clearly in the market, and this demand does not stimulate and thus does not meet a real *offer* of work (i.e. truly socially useful work is not offered), then this can depend on two independent, but sometimes concomitant, factors:

(a)   on the one hand, on the reluctance by the labour offer for those demanded works (this is the case with the most burdensome, uncomfortable or 'heavy' work); and this would already be a good reason for not talking about unemployment in general, but about specific and qualified unemployment;[36]

(b)   on the other hand, on the lack of interest from that classical intermediary between the demand of goods and services and the offer of the labour necessary to produce them – the (profit-seeking) entrepreneur; and this is by itself a good reason for not considering that the for-profit enterprise is the only way to ensure a good functioning of the economy.

Reluctance, be it on the part of the labour-provider or the employer, means that in the market (in the idea that we have of it today and apply, and of which we try insistently to improve the potentialities) no necessity is evident to 'justify' a massive increase of labour provided, at least equal to the increase of the labour that, at least on paper, is declared as 'unemployed'. In sum, the author of this book must confess that every time he listens to an evocation of unemployment in these terms (and it is undeniable that the topic is currently dealt with in an almost obsessive way by everyone and everywhere) his logical mechanism breaks down. And this generates a vague sensation of being an outcast.[37]

Yet are there not other ways in which these social/individual necessities can be identified, and thus manifest themselves? Better: can it be held that, since they do not show themselves on the market, these necessities, these new needs, do not exist? Or: that new necessities, new needs, new potential consumption – which could spur a new employment of socially preferable labour, rather than the benefit of non-employment (not to be underestimated) – cannot be legitimately identified *in other ways*?

Even if free enterprise in the free market, in its historical development, is recognized as a basic tool to match, and to maximize the matching, between the demand for goods and services and the labour supply, it must be noticed that today,[38] because of some reason we are trying to understand, this tool is no longer sufficient, and must be accompanied by other tools.

Which can these tools be?

The first of these tools we have known very well for a long time: it is the state. It perceives and expresses a social (and political) demand for goods and services (actually, services more than goods) that is not satisfied by an adequate (entrepreneurial) supply in the market. Thus it substitutes for the latter and supplies employment for those services that display a lack of offer, because there is a lack of entrepreneurial offer, because there is a lack of increasing profitability.[39]

Yet the state has its limits. It cannot go beyond the limit which defines it as an integrator, not a hegemonic substitute for the functioning of the market. To begin with, if it were to substitute totally the market, it would lose its logical-functional identity.[40] And with this identity, some functional limits of the state become absolutely evident (the cases of its 'failure'). In the same way the meeting between needs and production totally founded on the market shows clearly the functional limits of the market (the cases of its 'failure').

Also in the mere quantitative relation of the transactions (exchange of real resources) that pass *via* the market, compared to those that pass, or could pass, *via* the state, the latter finds its limits. The fact that the state accounts – as said above – with its interventions (through transfers) for more than one-half of the total transactions of a community or society as a whole, compels the state to take care wholly of the real exchange between needs–products–labour, meaning there is a risk of not adequately satisfying individuals, not even where freedom and autonomy of choice for the market is a good revealer.

In sum, it is foolish to throw away the market for those matches it renders efficient, just because there are others for which it is not efficient; it is equally foolish to throw away the state for those meetings for which it is efficient and even indispensable, just because there are others for which it showed itself to be largely ineffectual.

And all this looking at the two institutions – state and market – at the best of their respective achievements: that is, not considering the phenomena, typical of each of them, of bad functioning, those 'pathologies' whose treatment has to be conceived and implemented *per se*, independently of their reciprocal relationships. We mean, for example, in the case of the state: bureaucratization, failures, embezzlement, which are inherent in certain operative mechanisms of it; and in the case of the market: the forms of market distortion, deterioration of competition, privileges, which inevitably manifest themselves in it.

But beyond the state, another tool of matching for the new demand for services and the labour supply is emerging. It is the sector that, in a rather provocative way, we shall call the '*do-it-yourself*' sector. To this new tool, this new 'third' sector (between state and market), we will here devote all our attention (to such an extent that it even provides the title of the present book: *The Associative Economy*). For we think – as we will elaborate later – that this sector compared with the others is destined to characterize more than anything else tomorrow's society, the 'post-industrial' society, and maybe the 'post-capitalist' one.

Actually, despite the provocative allusion to 'do-it- yourself', the point is not that any single consumer, composing the demand for new socially useful and desired services, will produce them individually, or inside the family consumption/production unit, as has been the case for centuries in all historical traditional societies, by means of interpersonal exchanges, which we will call 'gratuitous' since they do not take place in the market, by monetary means. It is very probable that during the next decades the 'intra-family' exchange (and consequently work), which dominated the basically rural pre-capitalist economy, and whose dimensions have strongly been reduced in comparison with extra-family exchange (and work) during the development of industrial economy (typically extra-family[41]), will again increase its dimensions in the post-industrial economy. In fact there are many signs of this.

Yet we are not referring to this intra-family 'do-it-yourself'. Rather, facing the crisis of service provision (due to various causes, as seen above) both on part of the state and on the part of the private entrepreneur, we refer to an inter-family and extra-family 'do-it-yourself'; a 'do-it-yourself' put into practice in several forms and in several degrees of association and organization, from the small 'community' of families, to the big territorial association – urban, regional, national, and even global – to which everybody, and every family, will entrust the task of satisfying his or her own 'private' needs, both material and immaterial (more immaterial than material); needs that are precisely those growing in contemporary society, with a clearly above-average elasticity relative to income. Needs that are no longer adequately met either by the market or by the state.

We are facing an emerging exchange of a new type, which does not take place through the market and through the traditional means of exchange, the 'official' money, guaranteed by the public authority. (But it is possible, as will be shown, that this new exchange will produce a special 'private' money, able to facilitate this new kind of exchange.)

We are faling an emergent exchange which does not happen either through the state, by means of that peculiar exchange tool (if it can be called so, considering that in it, coercive rule-making absolutely prevails over contracting) that is the taxation of private income/wealth, in exchange for the restitution of benefits (in proportion of the necessary provision of collective, non-divisible goods and services, or in relation with objectives of social redistribution of the income itself).

So this new type of exchange, of goods and services that are equally new, would still imply provision of *work*; yet it would be difficult, and only partially possible, to conceive of this work by means of the common concept of 'employment', and measured in statistics as employment (or, even worse, as unemployment), as already happens to intra-family or household work. The principal characteristic of this work is its being generally 'free', voluntary. It satisfies an emergent effective demand by all participants of the community.[42]

This new kind of 'voluntary' work should not be conceptionally confused with (or at least restricted to) the traditional charitable 'voluntary service', oriented at the limited demand for welfare of the most needy strata of society (a voluntary service that has always existed as an assistance against the excesses of hardship and social instability which the capitalist society, but also the previous ones, created in their progressive dynamism). We refer here to the voluntary form of free work, which derives from the exchange aiming at the satisfaction of the sometimes very refined, subjectively differentiated and 'personalized' needs that come from the whole society, when it has satisfied the needs we can call 'primary'. These are needs that, given the ever larger access to welfare by an ever growing majority of the people, and given the very nature of the services themselves, which are not suited for mass production, do not stimulate entrepreneurial supply, and the state is unable to provide them in the demanded quantity and quality.

Therefore, only 'voluntary' work, more and more generalized, can satisfy them. This kind of work is the one growing most qualitatively, that whose productivity, not measurable according to quantitative paradigms and frameworks, is the highest from a *qualitative* point of view.[43]

3.4 Policy Implications of the New Way to Conceive Employment

The importance of this new 'voluntary' work, however, for the evaluation of the total well-being of the society or community considered is becoming greater and greater. And it involves the very notion of social well-being, with all corollaries of measurement which are usually applied: first of all, the measure of the national product (GNP), which – as has been said above – continues to be used in any current, conventional talk about economic policy, though at the same time everybody agrees that it has a very limited significance, and its total integration becomes more and more urgent.

For example, if this new type of voluntary work (let us call it also 'voluntary' or 'free' employment) increases[44] compared to non-voluntary work, it is not at all evident that the total well-being decreases; on the contrary there are very good accounting reasons for claiming that it increases, even if the national product decreases (due to the way it is calculated). If on these new instances of conceiving work and employment no *permanent frameworks of statistical accounting* rise,[45] and we remain shackled with the old accounting systems, most of the current discourses on employment and unemployment risk being not only inadequate to reality, but also sources of totally wrong economic policy decisions. As already said, one will work for *regress* while thinking to act for *progress*. And solutions will be avoided in the name of a stability and improvement policy, while they could be the adequate solution for that policy.

Compared to the state sector and the (for-profit) business sector, this new work creates an operative 'third' sector. This third sector, in comparison to the firms motivated basically by profit expectations (by the entrepreneur), can be called the *private nonprofit sector*. And in comparison to the state, which is motivated by the 'public interest' and regulated by public law, it can be called the *'associative'* sector. This associative sector, so conceived, *modifies* – as said – *the conventional conception of employment*.

Above all, we must bear in mind the increasing existence of a non-paid employment which produces 'utility' or (non-monetary) 'income' – for the employed themselves and for other beneficiaries – which can *more than compensate* for the utility and monetary incomes lost.[46] This free, unpaid employment must more and more be evaluated in its interdependencies and 'substitution effects' with 'paid' employment, to which it can be, at the same time, complementary and/or integrative.

And also the more common concept of 'independent' employment, which is however gain- or profit-oriented, will change. This is in fact the important part of for-profit sector employment that will develop a strong *ambiguity* of meaning relative to non-profit sector employment; also because it is not at all excluded that the non-profit sector can develop (in its most extensive forms of organization) a strong employment of a traditional kind. But it would be also a mistake to limit the estimation of non-profit sector employment merely to paid employment (as is done in the first quantitative surveys on non-profit sector employment which are made on the international level as well).[47] In fact it is founded on a huge quantity of unpaid work. This unpaid work – provided also by those who can earn a partial remuneration – is of the utmost importance in estimating the sector's overall contribution to the social product and social well-being of the considered community.

6 The Change in the Labour Market

As a result of the developments described in the preceding chapter we can deduce the general consideration that the 'normal' relationship between demand and supply in the labour market *no longer operates as it did before*.

The demand and supply for labour no longer correspond: *not* because of the quantitative imbalance between the two items, *nor* because of the classic failing of communication (information, adjustment, accessibility, etc.) or other forms of 'segmentation' (as emphasized by the conventional analyses of the labour market), *but* because of the fact that they are no longer two comparable 'quantities', and so measurable in terms of reciprocity.

The paradigm of the old 'labour market' has become, even from the purely abstract or theoretical point of view, an obsolete instrument to even simply read and understand reality (which was the function to which already any theoretical economist had limited it).

The divergence between the two component terms of the labour market is, in other terms, a 'structural' divergence, and for this also conceptual, not simply quantitative. It has changed the nature, the source, itself of the demand and supply, to the extent that it would probably no longer be legitimate to speak of a true 'labour supply', and of a true demand for remunerated labour. We will try, however, in this chapter, to clarify the assumption, starting from two terms still conventional of the labour market, the 'demand' and the 'supply', and to underline here only two aspects that we consider essentials of the change and of the above-mentioned divergence:

– a new typology of the labour demand
– and a new typology of the labour supply.

I think, however, that a full understanding of this divergence can be attained only at the end of the analysis of all aspects of 'structural changes' and not only that of the labour market. In this chapter we will also try to draw some first conclusions on a new, specific, labour policy[1] which should be consequent in the light of a full understanding of the ongoing transformations.

1 THE BASIC DIVERGENCE BETWEEN THE TRADITIONAL LABOUR SUPPLY AND DEMAND

1.1 The Demand for 'Quality-Labour'

The demand for labour is traditionally expressed by a system of firms. But today firms need a labour 'quality' which is substantially different from that of the past.

Tangible labour, the 'labour-force' or 'quantity-labour' is less and less in demand. Today the way to substitute it with mechanical and informatic means can always be found.

We will not enter into the old question of whether the substitution of quantity-labour (work hours, human operations applied to machines, even the most intelligent involving control or selection) depends on the fact that this type of labour no longer exists, or whether, instead, this type of labour does not exists because it is not in demand.[2] It is a fact, however, that this demand for quantity-labour has been replaced by a demand for quality-labour.

And the demand for quality-labour implies a type of personal participation in the outcome of the production process which the traditional enterprises (and entrepreneurs) have never offered, and perhaps will never be able to offer, unless at the cost of the disappearance of the figure and role of the traditional enterprise (or entrepreneur).

1.2 The Personalization of Labour and the New Entrepreneurship

The demand for quality-labour implies, in other terms, a 'personalization' of the labour-asset as well (or of commodity-labour), which is no longer coherent with the enterprise of the past, which today still represents the paradigm of the enterprise.

Certainly, the process of industrial production still exists. But it is shrinking greatly from the employment point of view; i.e. from the point of view of labour, it is expelling labour-quantity. Paradoxically the entrepreneur (or enterprise) is disappearing, because they need from the market a type of 'labour-quality' of an 'entrepreneurial' nature; and the enterprise and entrepreneurship are, so to speak, expanding and spreading. In short the entrepreneur is disappearing because everyone is becoming, in their own way, an entrepreneur.[3]

Thus also the money-maker, the industrialist, who above all is a profit-seeker, is tending to disappear, as such, because everyone is becoming enterprising and profit-seeking (although not all – and this is valid both for the old industrialists and the new widespread entrepreneurs – are only monetary profit-seekers).

Naturally the large technologically advanced enterprise, almost completely automated, will not only exist in the future but will also widen its presence in any economic-industrial context. But in the enterprises aimed at profit, today it does not seem that automation and robotics are a privilege of the large enterprise; on the contrary it seems that they are becoming more and more a privilege of small industries.

Certainly, many of the enterprises operating *for* the market[4] will have a large role in service society, but nevertheless they will produce goods with a labour intensity tending to zero. However, the 'diffusion' of entrepreneurship will mean that not only industrial employment will decline more and more in absolute terms, but also that 'dependent' employment – that which by definition as well as by tradition distinguishes the so-called 'labour-market' – will tend to become more and more scarce, or at least to assume connotations which are completely different from those we are used to.

Then: about which labour market are we talking? About which kind of employment and unemployment? Which employer and which employee?

The nature of labour relations tends to particularize and diversify itself and tends to be more adherent to the singular, peculiar situations and circumstances. Therefore, it becomes more and more difficult to define labour relations and to define in a standard way the behaviour of its subjects. Perhaps it is the nature and speed of the ongoing changes that impedes us in providing a clear interpretation of the labour market. Perhaps we need to wait for the fulfilment of the entire cycle of ongoing changes to be able to look at a new 'model' of the labour market and labour relations. Anyhow, one thing seems sure: that the reading tools and modes which have we applied today to explain the current labour market are totally inadequate to the reality; and as such they are greatly misleading us.

What does this change depend upon? On culture, lifestyles?

It is difficult to answer in one way. It is certain, however, that all this modifies, in the production process, the traditional search, and demand, for quantity-labour.[5] The demand for labour-quality encounters (to use a traditional and still current language) a labour supply which is no longer prepared to work for the traditional system. At the worst, this supply tends to become an 'enterprise' itself, autonomously, and encounters, in doing this, far fewer difficulties than in the traditional capitalist production process.

The old type of production process, as said, today comes up against structural difficulties in increasing its outlets and is thus now only oriented towards 'rationalization' processes (which moreover encounter 'bottlenecks' typical of professional qualification and adaptation in the increased infrastructural mobility which they induce).

This is why a good part of current 'active' labour policies[6] seem destined to meet insuperable *chronic* difficulties; since they do not take into consideration that not only have the 'marketable' sectors of production changed (more tertiary than industrial sectors, more new technological products, more computerized working practices, etc.), but that the actual mode of production is changing the actual relationship process between the entrepreneur and would-be dependent worker. Both the traditional capitalist entrepreneur, at least as the 'employer', and the traditional worker, as employee, are disappearing.[7]

2   THE NEW BEHAVIOUR OF LABOUR SUPPLY

In any case, an expansion of this quantity-labour demand, which we considered obsolete at this point (even if largely still existent) should be able to count on – to meet and stimulate adequate supply – still essentially 'economic' motivations: i.e. the existence of primary and secondary needs. But these are needs which are not up to date with the current motivations of labour supply, in as far as they are needs which cannot find a direct possibility of satisfaction by means of recourse to paid work.

In short, today labour cannot be 'bought', i.e. obtained with money. It is necessary to look for it and obtain it in other ways. The worker who works only for money will be a bad worker. And moreover he is disappearing.[8]

In the production expansion programmes for an increase in employment, it is necessary to bear these motivational factors in mind; factors which are less incisive in all cases in which the employment crisis discussed implies a worsening of the average standard of living of the families referred to. But are we dealing with a case of this type, in mature Western societies? Has a real and absolute lowering of the standard of living been recorded as a consequence of the proclaimed emergency or occupational crisis?

From the point of view of labour supply there emerges a realization that the labour supply's propensity to work depends more on free and highly personal 'choices' than on 'needs' as such. And on a free choice of labour, greatly personalized.[9] The resulting tendency is a 'rejection' of industrial labour and, in general, of 'impersonal' work, and an aspiration by everyone for more 'rewarding' forms of work.[10] This phenomenon is particularly prevalent among the younger generation which is now entering the labour market with an incredibly higher standard of education than previously.

All this is at the basis of several 'paradoxes' that the current analyses claim to meet when – in the presence of exaggerated figures of unemployment (say, numbers enrolled on the employment agencies' lists), and particularly in critical regions marked by chronic unemployment – there is a contemporaneous weak response to explicit requests for more or less qualified industrial labour. On more thorough analysis, those paradoxes no longer appear as such; rather, other, diametrically opposed, phenomena deserve to be defined in such a way.[11] But critical analysis is not the preferred home of the platitude. The latter finds its true home in a system of ideas (paradigm) that reflects a previous situation and structure; when critical analysis has not yet found a new system of ideas (from which, probably, some new platitude will emerge in a distant future ...).

The type of labour supply thus available (including the 'official' supply expressed in the number of registered job-seekers) is increasingly oriented towards work with a 'qualitative' emphasis and a specific occupational identity and is generally ill-matched to firms' potential demand even in a situation of economic re-expansion.

It is by no accident that, notwithstanding the employment crisis, firms are often experiencing real difficulty in filling certain skilled jobs, even when governments are pursuing highly 'active' employment policies utilizing the most sophisticated labour market information techniques and media.[12]

On the subject of modifications in the behaviour of labour supply, abundant documentation can be found in all the research into labour economics which has highlighted the sociological and institutional aspects of the labour market. The situations of full employment that several countries experienced in the 1960s has evidently reinforced the analyses of the 'non-economic' behaviour of potential suppliers of labour. But the official increase of unemployment during the crisis of the 1970s and later, and recurrently up to the present, did not produce a return to 'economic' behaviour in the labour market especially by the labour supply – to the surprise of some, but not to others.[13]

This situation occurs in several industrialized countries where increasing unemployment (at least among younger workers) prompts ideas of 'non-economic' behaviour in the labour supply which goes beyond the segmentation of labour markets and which has more to do with the *way of life* of the suppliers of work than with their official status as job-seekers or as the unemployed.[14]

Here one is touching one of the most important subjects concerning forecast transformations of labour markets: the time of work (hours per day, week or year). It is opportune to note here that:

(a) The supply of labour demonstrates a preference for 'irregularities' in labour, above all due to preferences for reduced working time compared to the standard of 'formal' employees. On the other hand one must not forget that several studies have shown that part-time work as practised today in several countries is largely voluntary, on the side of labour supply.[15]

(b) The demand for labour, on the other hand, is generally resistant to the practice of part-time work, above all in manufacturing activities but also in services. If unions reflect a mentality tied to the full-time standard, negotiated by contract, and resist 'officializing' part-time work as well, this leads to an accentuation of the split between official and unofficial work, in place of a welcome integration of the two.

(c)   The sectors are increasing where the 'semi-employed' might be considered not to be 'under-occupied', but as employed in this full sense. These are the sectors of the informal economy where 'non-economic' considerations were prevalent; this means that the character of the 'informal' economy becomes more and more 'formal'.

(d)   An adaptation of the labour market to the new conditions thus implies complete flexibility in working time to the preferences of the interested subjects, with a digression from full to part time work being freely negotiated.[16]

Even if this seems to be the tendency – given that part- time employment in the OECD countries is the only employment which progresses, as full-time work sees grave stagnation, and even its decline[17] – it would be helpful if the institutional and contractual measures were worked out in order to accompany and favour this tendency, and *not* in order to obstruct it; since the several measures taken to favour employment creation have not provided for encouragement of part-time work or 'reduced' working hours at all; and since the fact that the latter – people being entrapped in a traditional concept of the labour market – is not considered a favourable factor for development, but rather an obstructing factor.[18]

3   THE CASE OF UNEMPLOYMENT: PERSISTENCE OF INADEQUATE MODELS OF INTERPRETATION

3.1   An Optimal Level of Disaggregation in Modelling

It seems to me that too little attention is paid to these phenomena today; for example, that current 'unemployment' is quite different from that which for decades has dominated arguments of economic theory and analyses of the labour market. At this point we should use two different words to designate these two types of unemployment, to ensure a correct distinction of the concepts in the unemployment debate.

One of the best attempts of in-depth analysis of the labour market in this direction is that of Sylos Labini, who has tried to subdivide the concepts of employment and unemployment in the most 'analytically effective' way;[19] he has developed more extended considerations, especially in terms of diachronic dynamics and structural change.

The subdivisions proposed by Sylos Labini are: (1) unemployed who were previously employed; (2) young people in search of a first job; and (3) people seeking jobs who do not belong to the labour force (housewives, students, pensioners), because, as justly stated, 'in many aspects these three categories of the unemployed require three different models of interpretation'. Sylos Labini suggests that to these principal subdivisions are added those of the economic sectors: agriculture, industry, private service and civil service. He insightfully warns us that an 'interpretive model' must take into account other types of subdivisions as well – for example, men and women, dependent work and self-employment, small and large firms. He also says that a final separation needs to be taken into account, between high-productivity and low-productivity economic sectors – a very important dichotomy which is often overlooked.[20] Sylos Labini is nevertheless opposed to further segmented and fragmented analyses 'which do not permit useful generalizations'.

It is very probable then that differences in behaviour and consequent 'interpretations' can be recorded in either the seeking or the offering of jobs for each of the variables (phenomena or categories) which Sylos Labini proposes to better understand the labour market. But what is it that we need to understand, and why?

In reality, to examine the question in depth, the only thing that needs to be understood is whether propositions on the matter based on an insufficient disaggregation do not risk leading toward erroneous conclusions. We well know what these kinds of conclusions are called: undue generalizations which lead to insufficient realism, not corresponding to reality.

The same thing can be of value for its logical complement: to discover that sufficient disaggregation which allows us to generalize in a realistic way. However, how do we consider this sufficient disaggregation (optimal disaggregation; not so extended to make a generalization impossible, not so reduced to make it fallacious)? Do we consider it dependent or independent from the actual circumstances of the world under examination? In other terms, do we believe that it is possible to propose a disaggregation which in any circumstances of the world of advanced countries (say the OECD countries, just to limit the field) can be valid? A disaggregation that cannot risk being misleading in one sense or another?

Let us again take the case of the disaggregation proposed by Sylos Labini: we have four categories of unemployed (or, reversely, of employed) which cross with four activity sectors which cross with four other circumstantial conditions.[21] And here we stop: because to go beyond could not allow any further generalization to which however we wish to arrive. To stick our nose into this phenomenological ensemble, without undue generalization, means building a hypermatrix of around one hundred relations or interactions (certainly some of which are null or without meaning). Would it be possible to manage such a casuistics in an understandable and meaningful way? Are we not affected by the doubt that, in these circumstances, any result would be only the result of our own taxonomy, that it is a result already included in the behavioral hypotheses which pushed us to the selected classification?

In sum, we should be careful not to project into historical analysis our actual point of view, which is not always the best critical method for understanding the (historical) events which we analyze.

Perhaps we should conclude that if we try to connect the possible behavioral diversities of each variable introduced, our interpretation is extended to such casuistics that, in spite of their apparent realism, lead us equally to that incomprehensible complexity which we wanted to avoid, and which is in practice unavoidable.

At this point, we can introduce the other legitimate and opportune question: why does it need to be understood?

In fact, for what purpose do we need to generalize, and generalize correctly? If our purpose is merely to understand what has happened in the past (in our case: in the labour market and in the evolution of unemployment) we only meet the problem of 'explaining' in an appropriate way, through the right connections, what have been the causes and the effects of determinate events (unemployment). We are faced by the classical problem of every historian.

The problem is posed in such a way: first we must not forget that, in dealing only with a historical problem, we face the derived problem of defining through which phenomenon the historical problem is manifest to us; and to do so we find ourselves, in the first instance, explaining which events we choose to represent that history to ourselves. In our case we well know which events we wish to explain: employment, unemployment, and connected facts. If we choose unemployment, and if the historical problem posed is 'why has it increased in recent decades?', then in this case we must first make sure that the basic indicator used in the past is the same as that used today. Now the key to the meaning of unemployment at the starting point and at the final point of the assumed diachronic period, is properly the key to the indicator: if it expresses the same phenomenon or not. If not, we are not speaking about the same event or phenomenon; but about two different phenomena, which are associated only by means of a word (nominalism). If yes, our problem is to analyze realistically under which circumstances and for which causes or reasons the time variability of the phenomenon (unemployment) is posed in relationship with other phenomena to which we can reasonably attribute a certain impact on the former.

But even for the phenomena/causes (in respect to phenomenon/effect, unemployment) the same difficulty is produced as before. Even for such phenomena (say: wage level, investment level, aggregate or disaggregate according to the taxonomy recommended by Sylos Labini) they should be passed through the 'examination of diachronic identity' about which we have spoken. In the long run, it is unlikely that they all should have kept their identities.[22] Anyway, if the answer is no, even in this case we are still in the said nominalistic error. If the answer is yes, we are able to build a reasonable explanation, and if we really want, an interpretation, of what is happening in the matter of unemployment in the historical period under examination. But nothing more.

3.2 Past and Future in Modelling Unemployment

If on the contrary our purpose is to extract from the historical analysis not only generic indications for the future, but even for prescriptions for the future,[23] this purpose finds itself in much harder and more insurmountable difficulties, logical and epistemological.

Here, in fact, on what basis do we establish the assumption that a correlation (or a correlational system which consists of a descriptive and interpretative model) we have believed established for the past, with all the doubt and limitations stated, could be valid also for the future? On what basis can we assume that these diachronic identities between phenomena, which have seriously been doubted in the past, could be sustainable also in the *ex ante* analysis, an analysis that intends not to be realistic but programmatic, not to 'explain' but to 'programme'?

Here it is not the case of insisting too much on the difficulties of any econometric analysis when it is directed to prescriptive purposes, based notwithstanding on a positive approach.[24] Here we would like simply to summarize the precariousness of economic analysis if applied without methodological clarity, in the matter of conventional economic policy. And concerning the analysis applied to the change in the concept itself of the labour market, the synthetic evaluation can assume the following approximate sequence:

– in the case of historical analysis, it is left to be proven that the phenomena (more or less theorized, more or less quantified) could always be the same behind common names and statistics;

– whenever it could be possible, the simplification of the reciprocal relations among those phenomena (choice of same, exclusion of other) and the assumption of an optimal level of aggregation (in the stated sense) make this model valid only for factual circumstances which have been at the base of its identification, but do not allow easy generalization in other situations and circumstances;

– finally, whenever the generalization proved possible, it would be valid only for *ex post* analysis of situations analogous among themselves, and not at all for *ex ante* prescriptions, based on positive and descriptive analysis.

All this of course has nothing to do with modelling conventionally, called decisional.[25] The decisional models in fact are not founded on behavioural relations, except in very rare cases of programmatic certainties or for reasoning which is only hypothetical or didactical. The major part of such models are founded on definitional, structural, and technical relations, that are exempt and indifferent to historical proofs and very extraneous to behavioural 'theories'.

3.3   Past and Future in Designing Employment Policies

In the case of interpretative analysis based on the confidence in a possible generalization, which has been the subject of the preceding comments, the problem is not so much to find an appropriate and optimal aggregation level, but rather precisely to understand what meaningful phenomenon in the long term can constitute a stable and sustainable change.

In this framework two approaches can be compared.

A first approach is that which is rendered sensitive to the occupational problem impending over the attention of the policy-maker and the public (especially over observers and operators such as political leaders, managers of economic activities, trade unions, etc.); such problems in any case can belong to a functional model of the labour market which has changed its structure and its traditional behaviour. The influence of such a model on the present depends on the fact that residuals of the past that must be managed until exhaustion, still survive. Certainly all this risks obscuring the perception of innovative strategies, and causing solutions to prevail which are ephemeral, imply the waste of many resources, and rapidly become obsolete.

A second approach presses to insist on the contrary toward solutions which have the advantage to be more in the line of the basic trends of change; and which assure that a greater consistency will presumably occur in the long run. But the same proposed solution risks being immature and overloaded with obstacles and resistances. The major resistance is in the fact that people still think with more conventional paradigms of easier and more simple ways of understanding. In such a way the risk is of an abortion of the propositive strategy, and in certain cases of a lengthening of the implementation time of the innovative events, just for the purpose of precipitation.

What we have described as change *in* the labour market (that corresponds more properly to change *of* the labour market), in close conjunction with the change in the other aspects of the contemporary societal system, can surely be impacted more by the second approach than by the first: but all this belongs to the nature of the analytical exercise implemented with this book; a book dedicated precisely to the long-term trends that can be forecasted, inside the present structure of contemporary industrial society and towards its transformation of character.[26]

Now, consistent with the indicated approach, I would be inclined to assess that most of the analysis and interpretations that are usually made on the behaviour of the labour demand and, consequently, on the causes of unemployment, are not so much in line with the present and future development of the labour market. And this independent from any opposed versions of them: from that of a Ricardian stamp (the labour demand depends on the competitive relation with the cost of the capital/machinery and the labour cost); or from that of a Keynesian stamp (the labour demand depends on the general level of the actual demand); or also from the Neoclassical stamp (the labour demand depends on the relation marginal utility/productivity and marginal cost for the firms; what in practice can be reduced more simply to the proposition: the labour demand depends on the marginal productivity of labour).[27]

Every one of these explanations or interpretations, even if applied to separate situations for each group of sectors or categories of unemployed, does not add anything to a dynamic concept of transformation; unless the approach comes to be radically reversed; unless we do not consider the explanations or interpretations limited to a particular stage of development and to determined institutional correlations (the actual 'historical conditions' required by Sylos Labini) to which those explanations are referred and to which we state that they belong.

For none of the explanations referred to above, today, in advanced industrial countries, projected into future decades, are there conditions which can make them subsist. Today, 30–50 per cent of the potential labour supply (according to the acknowledged paradigms of the labour market) possess a college degree, when no more than fifty years ago only from 2 to 5 per cent of that labour supply possessed one. Today agriculture covers just from 3 to 8 per cent and the manufacturing sector no more than 20 to 40 per cent of labour employment, when no more than fifty years ago the corresponding percentages were 30–40 per cent for each of the two sectors. These macroscopic structural differences indicate that the labour supply fifty years ago (for the first job or already employed, men or women, in agriculture or in industry, in small or large firms) were quite different from the present, in terms of aspirations, expectations, qualifications, personal or collective income available, and visions of the world.

As said, old behaviours, needs, and aspirations can subsist only in a few limited pockets of the labour market. And each of these limited pockets, more or less statistically noted, more or less deduced from theory, must be also analyzed in their 'historical conditions'.

Anyhow, one thing is certain: the unemployed of today are not the unemployed of fifty years ago. Imagine if they were the same as the unemployed of a century ago in Victorian Neoclassical England (Neoclassical in economic terms of course) or of two centuries ago in Georgian Ricardian England. The conditions of their external environment, basic needs, values and perceptions, and life expectations are completely changed. So the unemployment phenomenon, supported or not by statistical series, moreover of limited meaning and full of conceptual shortcomings, is totally different in these epochs about which, in ways different from the natural sciences, people have built their respective theories, soon becoming very arguable paradigms.[28]

All that, I repeat, does not mean that in the complex evolution of our advanced societies some situations do not still exist which belong to a past model. We must only ask ourselves if these situations and models help us to understand the lines of change, the dynamics of transition; and if they help us to give more appropriate answers to the policy problems.

4   TOWARDS A NEW, SPECIFIC LABOUR-MARKET POLICY

From the analysis of the labour market changes given above, it would thus appear that the only way to achieve feasible and effective employment growth is for labour demand – as far as it keeps the role of a determining factor in this growth – to assume *a new form* and to adapt to the conditions and constraints which would seem to characterize the labour supply.

In sum, I would be much more inclined to contrast the still dominant paradigm of an 'active' labour policy – based on the 'adaptation' of the supply of labour (and consequent educational efforts) to the new requirements of labour demand – with a different paradigm, still little adopted, founded on the adaptation of a new demand for labour to a new emergent 'supply' of labour.

To insist on the old paradigm means increasingly to risk failing to achieve the goal of adaptation. It also risks pushing toward a further divergence among the two component terms of the labour market. And where in such circumstance a kind of forced convergence of job creation has been implemented, through incentive measures and compulsion, in traditional sectors of production (I think of the case of the incentives and financial support to the automobile industry and its 'relaunches' as emblematic), the risk is that convergence may be ephemeral on the one hand, and on the other will produce extensive waste of resources and disappointment in terms of welfare, going against the real trends of societal change.

In fact, this artificially induced on almost 'dope-enhanced demand' for industrial commodities – just to guarantee and relaunch employment, as it is said – is not demand from new strata of consumers (until today kept away by their low purchasing power from the benefits of consumption, having marked effects on social welfare, and even on firms' and workers' productive capacity).[29] It is a demand from consumers that today have largely already benefited from a kind of over-consumption, and are only willing to extend the range of their goods and services in the direction of 'other' consumption, including an improvement in Mill's 'art of living'.

The changes described above in the structure of needs and in the final demand for goods and services appear to contribute positively to this type of paradigmatic adaptation and transformation. It is in the services and particularly in those not liable to substantial productivity gains and where technology is stationary, that the 'new' demand from the individual consumer and the community (which are overburdened by industrial goods) would seem to be concentrated. We are dealing with these activities where quality is more important than the labour productivity and which, with their highly 'personalized' nature, constitute the new behavioural constraints, the behavioural constraints deriving from the this 'new' labour supply.

Therefore the historical and structural conditions for matching labour supply and demand are present. What are missing are the appropriate instruments and policies with which to promote this match.[30] A policy of employment expansion, in the context of the structural changes discussed above, is doomed to failure if it does not recognize the need to focus efforts on devising these appropriate instruments and policies; in other words if employment policies do not involve the creation of a new activity model and new forms of labour input and performance.

To put it differently, an active employment policy should be 'active' not only in the sense that it seeks to steer the labour supply to production sectors with growth potential, and in the effort (always to be recommended but a little obsolete) to gear training policies to projected demand,[31] or finally to instal information systems linking structurally segmented labour markets. Such a policy should also, however, be 'active' in steering both supply and demand towards *new forms of production*, i.e.:

1. in the first place those which are capable of generating a supply of activities and hence a demand for labour for which conventional entrepreneurs by inclination or by motivation display little or no interest;
2. secondly, those forms of production that are capable of effectively responding to the expressed preferences of an unsatisfied labour supply, which, though sufficiently real to be recorded in the official statistics, is available for work only under special and more 'rigid' conditions than ever.[32]

Unfortunately, one must observe that despite several acknowledgments of structural change in the behaviour of the labour supply and thus in the labour market, the instruments and measures employed by official government policies aimed at increasing employment always refer to a functional *model* of the labour market which is rather theoretical and *largely outdated*. These policies consist of stimulating employment in existing and new companies, in lines of production which really match neither the consumption market nor the availability of labour.

Why do we not adopt policies (for an important portion of their impact, even financial impact) that can stimulate the autoconsumption, especially in the growing area in which the needs of production and those of consumption are joined in a more flexible or adaptable process?

Certainly, as Wassily Leontief pointed out in a masterly article in the *Scientific American* (1982), a welcome policy of 'labour sharing' can only proceed in company with an *incomes policy*,[33] which it would be very difficult to launch today without evaluation of the prospective impacts of technological change (as described and suggested by Leontief in this very article). It is well known that by incomes policy joined by *labour-sharing* one specifically intends *incomes-sharing*. On the other hand, Leontief regrets that since the last world war, in spite of waves of successful technological innovation, the working week has remained *practically unchanged for 35 years*.

Under such conditions it is not surprising that technological unemployment has seen parallel chronic growth. The working week to which Leontief refers is evidently the average one, which is approximately equal to the standard one; i.e. the 'formal' working week (Leontief's contributions concern the US, but the argument *more or less* applies to other OECD countries as well).[34]

Our point is that it will be easier (than in previous experiences) to achieve the welcome twin-track of work time- sharing and revenues-sharing if, on the one hand, one aims for sharing of working time realized along with *flexible distribution* of time rather than *diminishing its formal duration*, and on the other hand, one aims for a sharing of revenues, the concept here including certain *non-monetary revenues* (or so-called 'non-economic') pertaining to the informal economy.

But we will discuss this in Part II, devoted to the managerial questions of the change.[35]

First, I would like to further analyze the change with a more direct comparison of the features of the 'industrial society' in decline, with those of the emerging 'service society'.

7 The Service Society versus the Industrial Society

The emerging service society, which is the indisputed offspring of industrial society (much more so than the latter can be considered the offspring of agricultural 'rural' society, which it replaced), is assuming features which are antagonistic to those of industrial society. This antagonism deserves to be further examined.[1]

1 THE SUBSTITUTION OF LABOUR: A CONSTANT PATTERN OF THE INDUSTRIAL SOCIETY MODEL

(*a*) We have seen that the ideal-typical model of *industrial society* is founded on the development of physical productivity: it was born with the Smithian metaphor of the pin factory.

The social division of labour is the foundation of productivity, and to the extent to which human labour is substituted by mechanical energy and ability, the efficiency of human labour itself is multiplied, to the benefit of not only labour 'fatigue', but also of the incorporated cost in production and the availability of goods and products for consumption.

The constant substitution of human labour with mechanical labour is the basic objective of technology (from nineteenth-century machinery to current artificial intelligence), and the main factor of material well-being, for single individuals (Robinson Crusoe style), as for societies overall ('The Wealth of Nations').

The history of industrialization (and thus of industrial society) in all production processes – from agriculture to the extraction of minerals, from metal working to chemical processes, and from transport to commercial and banking operations, and in general administrative ones in the various 'service' sectors – is a story in which the intensity of labour in the production combinations labour/installations and/or labour/(fixed) capital tends to diminish (and its unitary cost to increase) and, on the other hand, the installations/capital intensity to increase (and its unitary cost to diminish).

The technological innovations and transformations in some sectors may also give rise to a revitalization of labour intensity; especially when they give rise to 'new products'. However, in time, the trend towards labour saving has always been the fundamental rule in industrial society.

2   HUMAN LABOUR AT ZERO PRODUCTIVITY IN THE SERVICE SOCIETY MODEL

(*b*) The ideal-typical model of a *service society*, conversely, is based on completely different principles. The basic difference is that the tertiary activities, by definition (*à la* Fourastié, as said previously) are not susceptible to realizing noteworthy increases in physical 'productivity': i.e. the quantity of service (output) obtained per hour-unit of personal performance (input).

Here we should nevertheless recall that the concept of 'tertiary' activity referred to, does not derive from a 'commodity' classification of sectors, but rather from an operational analysis of the production processes (what was stated in Chapter 4 should be recalled).

If in 'office' work, for example, the introduction of electronics and IT has reduced human operations and has allowed for improvements in the relationship operations carried out/working hours, then we would not be faced exactly with a process of tertiarization, but rather with one of industrialization and mechanization of some service activities.

In fact the concept of tertiary activity used here (which recalls that of those who first used it, for example, Fourastié) is applied to activities for which it is impossible to apply a measurement of the output in terms of quantity produced, or, if possible, such output does not suceed in being influenced, in its quantity, by the introduction of mechanical means.

An 'emblematic' tertiary activity is public administration. In fact, as is known, the traditional economic accounting systems – given the impossibility of adopting quantitative output measurements for this work – evaluate the product at the value of the paid labour, and the added value of these activities varies only with the variation either of the unit remuneration or of employment; and, by assumption, the added value by members of staff, i.e. productivity, of these activities does not vary, but is always equal to zero. If, paradoxically, we imagined that all employment was based on these activities we would not have, *a priori*, a zero growth rate. The income increases which would take place in the civil service would only be a 'redistribution' of the increases in output realized in the 'productive' sectors (which in our paradox would be the completely automated ones without employment).

The service society is brought about when in the great majority of activities which take place in it, increases in output per man-hour are not realized; and when in the sector of tangible goods in which they could theoretically be realized (by definition), a stop on the demand occurs because of a saturation of mass consumption and because of the shift of the demand growth towards services.

From an analysis of the behaviour of the two models numerous interpretative implications could be derived (to which here we will refer by way of example and by brief references).

3 ECONOMIC IMPLICATIONS OF THE CHANGE OF MODEL

3.1 Performance Indicators

(*a*) In *industrial society*, the GDP rate may be considered a good indicator of success in that it may represent a *proxy* of an increase in the purchasing capacity of desired goods by the consumer for which there is still an unsatisfied consumption.

(*b*) In *service society*, the GDP rate no longer indicates the performance of the production system, because it cannot be measured in terms of *output per man-hour*. And this is also independent of the fact that the resources destroyed are not accounted for (in particular the irreproducible ones) and some social costs, as is normally underlined and which is valid also for industrial society.

3.2 The Role of 'Investment'

(*a*) In *industrial society* the rate of investment (or of accumulation) represents the guarantee of being able to ensure the productive system's capacity to 'grow'; i.e. to progress in the productivity increase rate.

(*b*) In *service society* the investment rate is not a decisive factor: in some cases it may constitute a waste of resources if it is oriented towards unnecessary sophistication of industrial products. Since it is the quality rather than the quantity of services that indicates the productive process, it is probable that improvement effects may arise more from the current expenses (payment of workers and other current expenses) than from capital account expenses. (In education, in research, in health services, in recreation activities, and in cultural activities, which constitute the growing mass of activities in the service society, this is certainly the case.)

(*a*) In *industrial society* the predominant pattern of an increase in productivity is an organization which tends to concentrate itself and link up in a continuous production flow, profiting from the 'economy of scale'. On the strictly technological plane, as on that of economic-financial organization, the efficiency of industrial society is guaranteed by 'large size' and by the 'line': the assembly line, or distribution chain.

(*b*) In *service society*, the phenomena of differentiation and particularization effect the quality of the product and service more than the phenomena of unification and standardization. The foundations are created for a necessary industrial and operational 'decentralization', in the cases also where the logic of large size still resists. In the vast majority of services, furthermore – which are beginning to involve an ever larger market – the 'personal' characteristic is maintained which is by nature contradictory with regard to any form of 'impersonal' organization.

3.3 Basic Economic Motivations

(*a*) In *industrial society*, if progress is guaranteed by the increase in productivity, this is in turn sought for on the basis of an 'augmentative' interest in profit.

It is not by chance that capitalist accumulation and industrial society have been interactive phenomena and strongly integrated. And nor is it by chance that entrepreneurial profit has been considered the basic motivation of productive activity in industrial capitalist society; and that when, for various reasons, it declines, replacement motivations have been found with difficulty, whilst maintaining the productivity rate as the basic indicator of success. (The stakhanovism and the public aim of the non-profit enterprise constitute two types of 'exceptions' to the model, which are not always efficient and honourable.)

The Schumpeterian entrepreneur is the standard hero of industrial society, motivated by profit, who looks in product innovation or the production process for that rate of increase in productivity on which his rate of profit depends (and on the prospects of which the rate of investment also depends). The profit–investment identity, discussed in theory, in industrial society is nevertheless largely evident.[2]

(*b*) In *service society*, the absence of an increase in real productivity renders problematic the presence and efficiency of the profit motivation as a 'motor' of activity and investment.[3] The expectation of profit would have nothing more to base itself on. Other various motivations take over: social and professional recognition in the large range of activities, strongly personalized, which characterize the tertiary sectors.

The self-management of small business takes over from big business. Technological innovation is no longer exclusively aimed at a productivity increase, but rather at the improvement of the quality of the service and the subjective conditions of the service performance: it is more aimed at the benefit of the consumer and operator than at that of the entrepreneur.

In brief, the non-profit activities have increased their weight and influence on the entire economic mechanism, whether they are of a public or 'private' nature.

This fact is destined to make many economic theorems obsolete.[4]

3.4 The Motivation and Role of Saving

(*a*) In *industrial society*, productive investment is nourished by savings by means of the so-called 'capital market'. Private saving – by means of complex mechanisms of mediation – is channelled in those activities which, on the basis of fixed capital investments which it allows, ensure the highest 'yield' rates, in principle in proportion to productivity rates.

It is true that in industrial society as well, a separation has been operated between the motivation to save and the 'yield-productivity' of the same. This separation, which belongs to the last most advanced stage of industrial society,[5] has led to the decline of the private saver (and accumulator), i.e. of the entrepreneur motivated to save by his own entrepreneurial initiative. Saving has become almost exclusively limited to enterprises (for self-financing or for public contributions; this latter case is less infrequent than one wishes to admit) or to the state (active current balances), or an impersonal operation carried out by those seeking income or interest at largely current rates, without risk or uncertainty.

The self-financing of companies has become, however, an impersonal 'operation' as well, permitted – as is normally recognized – by the existence of oligopolistic market conditions; and accompanied by agreements and mergers, i.e. by a high rate of industrial concentration. This is in the design (often declared as well) to make today's consumer pay for the technological progress of tomorrow, from which there will be future advantages for tomorrow's consumer of productivity and profitability.

For the state, obviously, saving has never been motivated by profit, but rather by the public interest, which has already been a multiple of the private one (and has been financially fuelled pro-quota). This does not seem to characterize the model of industrial society more than happens for other models.[6]

(*b*) In *service society*, if the motivation for accumulation as an incentive for spending disappears, saving tends to decline as an institution and practice;[7] unless the motivation substantially changes. And in effect it is presumable that it tends to change (for reasons which will be shown in Chapter 11, and more widely discussed in Chapter 12).

In the public sector (in the service society) saving will always correspond to traditional criteria and motivations of public interest. In the service society it is not to be expected that the public sector will diminish its range of action, even if probably it will not increase it either.

In the private sector, since – as mentioned previously – the 'non-profit' sector and activities will expand, saving will essentially be aimed at providing the performance and consumption in this sector with more advanced instruments and technologies; and it will have more the nature of consumption projected in time, than of real productive investment.

If we had to give an explanatory analogy, the saving which will be produced probably on a vast scale in the non-profit private sector in the service society, resembles that which in families today as well (in industrial society) is identified in 'home-saving': by means of the purchase of a home for personal use, and not to put it on the house-buying market, like a normal capital loan (investment) seeking interest. It cannot be denied that this is saving, or that it constitutes an investment for the future: nevertheless the absence of the intention to make a profit from it, qualifies it as saving aimed at consumption, however long-lasting in time; i.e. it is saving which has a very different relationship with income production from that of productive investment in industry.

The rate of interest will have a reduced influence on the propensity of this 'type' of saving; and probably – despite the expansion of the tertiary sector – the activities which in the tertiary sector act as financial intermediation, will be destined to decline.

(*a*) In *industrial society*, moreover, the area of 'voluntary' saving has expanded together with the growth of per capita income, and displayed a strong propensity (or elasticity) relative to income. However, this propensity relates to a relatively small percentage of savers compared to the whole population (for the prevalence of dependent labour over independent labour), and the replacement of voluntary saving, quantitatively limited, by forced (state) saving. In industrial society the conditions ripened for the introduction of the totally different model of the society of services.

(*b*) In *service society*, the propensity (elasticity relative to income) towards saving decreases, the number of savers increases because of the relative growth of independent workers, and the forced saving will tend to disappear. The state is financed through public debt, but the part of this debt consisting of financial indebtedness (toward the voluntarily involved private sector) and not that part which is levelled down by inflation (which is forced saving). The financial market does not grow because the propensity to saving increases, but because the number of savers increases. In the model of the service society, when it is fully functioning, the importance of the financial market will probably fall, because the need for financial transfer between economic actors will decrease. The motivation for saving itself will change, to such an extent that we should ask whether it should still be called 'saving'. Rather than a form of income 'security' for the future, the motivation for saving will become a game for growing shares of savers; a kind of lottery towards which some of the motivations for gain will be directed, more and more frustrated in comparison with other more substantial personal motivation for professional improvement and for culture.

4 EMPLOYMENT TYPOLOGY

There is no doubt that the service society offers a completely different prospect to employment forms.

(*a*) In *industrial society*, the dominant employment has tended to model itself on forms and conditions of factory organization.[8] In agriculture and services as well, the reference model has become the factory. (We might think of administrative offices, which, in design as well – with the disapperance of walls – wish to give a impression of the scientific organization of work.) Industrial society has developed even more defined characteristics in labour relations: increasingly 'comprehensive' contracts, with ever wider articulations, but which are predetermined at the level of central coordination.

Industrial society is an employee society:[9] born from the disgregration and marginalization of independent labour (farm workers, craftsmen, professionals, 'landlords', etc.). In an initial phase, the old owners are turned out or eliminated (craftsmen, small farmers), and the industrial enterprise is more and more organized in its legal form of a corporation. Even family enterprises take on the form of corporations. But, subsequently, with the development of large sizes and concentrations, the small and medium-sized enterprises, with the relative individual entrepreneurs, become progressively replaced by 'managers' and 'executives', which are formally dependent as well on the corporation, but in reality are the bosses of the same. (This change has been called the 'Managerial Revolution'.)[10]

It is a phenomenon which has been largely documented and discussed (the famous 'neo-capitalism') and which finds its high point in the political affirmation of the great transnational or multinational companies or corporations.[11]

The economic and company concentration at which industrial society has arrived, has been further consolidated by the competition from public enterprise, whenever the state has decided to substitute large private enterprise, either because of the excessive power of the latter with regard to public interest (the case of nationalization), or because of the lack of the latter (this is the case of the 'late-comer', fascist or developing countries – in the process of industrialization, for which, without 'direct' state intervention no industrialization would be realized).

But whatever the motivations and historic circumstances of the industrial state, it is but a further confirmation of the general tendency of industrial society towards a generalization of the whole active population's state of 'dependence'.

(*b*) In *service society*, independent work begins to re-emerge, after its tendential dissolution, albeit in different forms. The 'labour market' does not become the tendentially dominant and hegemonic model, like in industrial society.

First of all the movement is accentuated and generalized towards a 'professionalization of labour', already announced in the last phase of industrialization, that of automation.[12] In the industrial sector as well, in fact, the first development of mechanization, which for a long time constituted a factor of degradation of qualifications (to the extent that man became the *bouche-trou vivant* of the mechanized process, to use a well-chosen expression invented by George Friedman[13]), has been succeeded by the latest development in automation, in which in the form of *new professions* inherent to the control of the entire process, labour qualification has been recovered.

But in the service society the movement towards a more extended professionalization is growing with the spread of the same extra-industrial activities and services (which are not susceptible to the quantification of *output*), all founded on individual performance of a professional type.

And in the same industrial activities, whilst in industrial society there is a tendency to absorb services within productive units (the large corporations equip themselves internally with impressive commercialization, personnel, legal, technical consultancy services, etc.) assuming professionals as dependents, in the service society the tendency is inverted, and takes up again the tradition of using 'external' consultancy services, in the general decentralization of the operations of many large operational services.

In the service society, by its very structure, the dominant model of reference is no longer the factory, but the office: and this ends up influencing the same industrial activities (even agricultural production, which is transformed into an *agro-business*). But strong tendencies are manifested also because the office is transformed into a 'study': and the study often is connected to the home. For this reason it is not totally senseless to anticipate the 'study-home', and (telematic) work from home – 'the wired home', or 'electronic cottage', as Toffler calls it (1980, chapter 16). See also on the subject a survey by R. Moran (1993).

In the service society the boom of 'services for production' is developing: marketing firms, advertising agencies, informatics, etc. But such activities, rather than going towards the large structure, are directed at the structure professionally self-managed.

In conclusion, the (employee) 'labour market' is being progressively substituted, as a relevant model of reference, by a 'professions market'.

5 'INDUSTRIAL RELATIONS' TYPOLOGY

The professionalization of labour, which, as stated, is becoming the dominant characteristic of the ideal-typical model of the service society, has some obvious implications in the conditions of labour supply, in particular with regard to remuneration.

(*a*) In *industrial society*, the problem of the economic and trade-union protection of the 'employee' has become more and more prevalent. The trade unions in fact have grown in number and importance. Collective bargaining has aimed at a greater participation of the dependent worker in the enjoyment of the benefits of productivity (sometimes, as said, even pushing wages 'beyond' such benefits, with a positive effect on productivity, because in this way 'labour saving' is stimulated, i.e. the introduction of machinary and technological innovation).[14]

And, since it is a society of employees, industrial society sees trade unions developing towards increasing size and stronger centralization; but they always have, as the main interlocutor, the employer, or the employer's union: even when the state has assumed a more important role of producer (of industrial goods and services) and thus of an employer. In the forms of tripartite organization, the state intervenes as a 'mediator': the essential comparison is between employers (including perhaps the state) and trade unions.

(*b*) In *service society*, the model of industrial relations would tend to change, even if the resistance of the institutional factors may delay its change (in these cases the trade unions assume an historical conservation role, rather than one of change).

With the need diminishing to protect employees, as such, there is an increasing need for the economic protection of professional relations. The main interlocutor of trade unions – which go back to being more and more 'professional' trade unions – is not the employer (who, as a profit-oriented entrepreneur, constitutes the driving force in economic development and productivity); but it is the collective or the community *as a whole* towards which the roles and remunerations overall of the various professional must be fixed. The trade unions should tend more and more to resemble professional associations which, together with economic standards (tariffs), fix also *ethical codes*.

In the service society, as a first movement, the trade unions would tend to decentralize as well, in articulations which adhere more to professional conditions. The proliferation of 'autonomous' trade unions may be the response to some rigidity in the traditional structures with regard to the tendency: however it is a response to a physiological need, and is not only a pathological phenomenon. Likewise non-trade-union forms of work performance (the so-called black labour market) are often a response to the new conditions of professional type performance, to which collective bargaining has not been able to give an adequate response; and thus it may be a progressive, rather than a regressive, phenomenon.

6 THE ROLE OF THE STATE

The change of model may have important implications for the role and functions of the state, and thus of the public economy.

(*a*) in *industrial society* the public economy has strongly developed. It is exactly the growing rate of productivity, and thus of development, peculiar to industrial society, which produces a need to 'compensate' the social imbalances which the acquisitive dynamic, *per se*, produces. The race for economic and productive progress (and for real gain which results for industrial society as a whole) must not be hampered by structural and social resistance (for example, by old 'corporative' structures, as in pre-capitalistic, not characterized by a strong productive dynamic). It is better instead to devote part of the growing income produced to 'repair' the damage of this wild race, and make it less wild, compensating those who suffer from it: and this by means of an assistance and protection-oriented regime, a sort of 'public collective insurance' against risks which inevitably intense development produces (but whose overall advantages certainly outweigh the disadvantages).

The productive dynamic of industrial society (technological innovation; entrepreneurial initiative; capital savings; i.e. constant marginalization of labour) requires the dismantling of any traditional social 'order', of any institutional 'enclosure' from which arises the constant incentive for better labour productivity, and thus wealth, of nations. The initial *faith* in the 'natural' readjustment of disequilibria, in the rebalancing 'invisible hand' of the free market, a confidence which has been demonstrated as perhaps excessive, has given way to a wiser policy of compensation and recovery of more extreme situations of imbalance and discomfort. The state, which started from a level of minimum intervention ('public order'), has progressively enlarged its sphere of influence, almost by means of an extension of the concept of public order, as a safeguard against the risks which social crises (poverty, unemployment, etc.) might bring to the social order itself.

Therefore, the intense social change, in the form of material economic development (which we have identified in the capitalist form) demanded (and still demands, in the situations in which it must still be fully realized, as in the third world and ex-communist countries) the free market, free enterprise, in short the maximum 'liberalism'.

But nothing has more demanded (and thus made possible) a wise compensating intervention of the state and a substantial enlargement of the role of the same, than the evolution of Western liberal-capitalist economies. In the main historic development evolution of modern economy, the industrial revolution (and industrial society which derives from it) calls for *free trade*; but in turn the maximum *free trade* calls for the state in defence of its dynamics.

The Welfare State was thus born from the industrial society. It protects with income transfers (of an insurance type, even if they do not take the form of actuarial equivalencies); and with free or semi-free supply or performance, thus creating those 'social' services which, on the other hand, become one of the forms of 'consumption' towards which the 'structural change' of demand is developing, both individually and collectively (as discussed in Chapter 4).

It is not by chance, therefore, that the more advanced forms of the Welfare State have occurred in the same countries, the same societies in which industrial society has arrived at its most advanced state, i.e. in which the growth rate of productivity has been more intense and achieved the highest levels.

But it is also true that the development of the Welfare State has further provoked 'tertiarization', i.e. (as said many times previously), the overall progressive decline of the opportunity for high physical productivity rates: those productivity rates which are, in turn the economic base of the possibility of Welfare State expansion (as well as its demanding factor).

There is a *threshold* in the development of industrial society beyond which the Welfare State enters into crisis as well: it corresponds approximately to the threshold beyond which it becomes no longer possible to increase the proportion of national income 'transferred' via the state to services provided freely or redistributed financially. This threshold is also that which marks, approximately, the *passage from industrial society to the service society*.

(*b*) The *service society* cannot satisfy the growing demand for social services via the state; i.e. by means of the public transfer of wealth from the profit-making sectors to the non profit-making ones, which some have called also productive and non-productive sectors. (This latter expression seems less correct to us: we would prefer '*productivist*' and '*non-productivist*' sectors, in as much as it is rightly linked to the opportunites for an increase in productivity, in the sense explained several times (and in particular in Chapter 5, section 2), whilst 'non-productivist' service sectors also have a 'production': of services perhaps, rather than tangible goods, but which is still a production; we will return to this in Chapter 8.)

And this cannot happen because, beyond a certain threshold, the weight of the *productivist* sectors becomes structurally inferior to that of the *non-productivist* sectors; the average productivity tends to decline (despite the fact that that of the *productivist* sectors may reach the highest rates ever known); and the whole economy becomes more 'steady'.

For this reason, the growing social demand for social services in the service society will have to find a way of being satisfied mainly by both market and non-market *direct exchange* (i.e. not via the state).

And the state, probably, will need to relatively restrict its field of action to the most acute social needs and to public consumption which is not *divisible*: more or less how it was during the beginning of industrialization and rapid development, with the increasing 'compensatory' effects required (discussed previously).

Nevertheless, among the 'indivisable public services' in the service society, the state will have to produce, in a new and extended way, those connected to a form of management of structural changes in the field of industrial relations: the passage from the 'labour market' (dependent) to that of 'professionalization'; which also means the passage from 'market' collective bargaining to 'income collective bargaining' or negotiation (among the various professional categories). But bringing income negotiation in society to this level implies the introduction of an overall planning process, albeit indicative, and carefully negotiated.

In the service society, in other words, the state will probably see the possibilities of *direct intervention* diminish, as producer of goods, manager of services, and redistributor of income. But it will probably have to increase its role as 'informer', preventive 'planner' of development scenarios, and organizer of bargained decisions on an overall national scale. This should be intended not in the (old) sense of issuer of commands and administrative rules, but rather as manager and controller of an (informatic) system for very articulated economic and social accounting (by social groups, professions, operational sectors, territory and institutions);[15] and as organizer of social bargaining or negotiation (which we call 'planning-type' negotiation), based around fundamental trade-offs which economic or social policy should impose.[16]

Obviously in the service society as well, the state continues to have an important role in a vast range of activities, in particular the indivisible and free ones. This would always leave the field to the validity of the theorems of *public* economics, in as much as it is distinct from an economics which is essentially *market-oriented*.

Nevertheless, the relative weight of the public role will diminish probably due to the advantage of the emergence of a (relatively) *new* sector of the economy, which is not the *public* one, nor that of the *private market economy*: it is the 'third sector' – which has been announced several times in connection to the analyses of the development of contemporary capitalist society[17] – which represents perhaps the most characteristic, emblematic and congenial sector, as well as the most interactive one, with regard to the ideal-typical model of the service society.

7   THE EMERGENCE OF A 'THIRD' SECTOR

The same relationship between economic institutions (firms, government, unions, etc.) tends to be configured in totally different ways in the two models of society.

(*a*) It has already been said that *industrial society* has essentially developed on the basis of sought-after mass production which, by constantly diminishing the unitary production costs, would permit higher and higher profits, compatible with wage demands and state taxation. In industrial society, stronger trade unions and a more extended state, although 'contractually' antagonists of the profit-oriented industrial enterprise, are its 'by-products', in as far as they prosper on the development of productive industrial techniques.

In industrial society, the industrial productive cycle reaches certain quantitative limits with respect to other human consumption and activities and this creates limits both to the search for profit as a basic motivation of the enterprise economy, and also for the development capacity of state activities.

(*b*) Between the private economy (or also public: but the experiences of *profit-oriented public corporations* have been up until now very debatable with regard to their ends), and the *non-profit oriented* economy, an economy has insinuated itself in the *service society* which is a hybrid: *non-profit* (like the public one), but also *private* (like the profit-oriented enterprise).

It is non-profit because the motivation to make profit is absent on the part of the operators. The majority to do not operate in the market, in the sense that they do not sell the services which they produce, because they are mainly the beneficiaries of them and because their action has humanitarian or at least 'social' goals. These cases of services which are developed *outside the market*, and which are therefore unknown to the current systems of economic accounting, tend in the service society to expand enormously. This growth is due also to the reduction of working time, and to the growth of an inactive population which nevertheless finds free time to develop personal activities (political, trade union, cultural, recreational, hobbies, and generically philanthropic and social) which are not considered 'economic' when to a large extent they should be, and enter into the well-being function both individual and social.

But in many cases the service society also develops many activities which, if also bought and sold on the market, do not have the aim, on the part of the producers, of profit, but only that of exercising an activity considered professionally useful to society (this in the field of educational, recreational, political, environmentalist activities, etc.). In this case, too, they are activities which do not respond to the logic of the business economy.

The operators of this sector are individuals who become *associated* for purposes that are not gain or profit (although sometimes they may obtain some reward for the work carried out); they become associated for purposes that are specific and inherent to the specific associative purpose. It is an 'associative' or 'cooperative' economy, whose functioning is still not well defined in historic experience but which most probably deserves a 'theoretical' analysis – an 'economics' – alongside those of the business economy and the public economy.[18]

From many points of view, this *associative economy* is founded on very similar behaviour to that of the *public economy*; and from many other points of view on behaviour quite similar to that of the *market economy*.

The current and potential extension of this sector of the associative economy varies from country to country, according to historic circumstances, and to the committment of the operators themselves; but there is no doubt that the factors which justify and postulate its development are inherent to the changes in the behaviour of the service society (as they have been briefly described here), in which the motivation of activities, the demand for consumption and the possibilities of financing free activities by the state change greatly in comparison with industrial society.

We mentioned above that, in the service society, unlike what happens in industrial society, the increasing social demand for social services can only be satisfied by means of *direct exchange* (both market and non-market). In fact, the sector in which this direct exchange takes place is the 'third sector', that of the associative economy. In fact it is doubtful that the social services now demanded from the state may arouse the interest of companies aimed at profit in the service sector, given the limited opportunities for income and profitability which these enterprises offer. It will however be for the interest and profit of the *users themselves* to respond to the *new demand*, generated by themselves, with forms of '*self-consumption*' and *self-management* of these services (paying perhaps a price as contribution to the realization of the service itself). This formula is destined to have a great development, in the most varied fields of service activities, and it is on the basis of this formula that the 'third' sector is essentially characterized.[19]

It is probable that in order to lighten the pressure for state intervention in the sector of social services, the state will be increasingly forced to promote and encourage the development of associative forms of 'self-consumption' and self-management of the services themselves, by ensuring its own initial contribution or the assumption of a part of the costs, in order to create in the sector the change towards a direct exchange between production and consumption.

It is pointless to say that many formulas of this type may *be promoted and realized by means* of a mix of public financial contribution and contributions 'in kind' (by means of *free and not monetarized* services) from the final beneficiaries of these services: as already happens in many recreational activities.

But we will return to this point more widely in Chapters 11 and 12.

8 The Process of Redistribution in the Two Models of Society

The antagonistic character of the service society, which is emerging, confronted with the declining industrial society, implies a somewhat radical revision of the concept, on which economic reflection is based, of the distributive mechanisms of labour and income. This aspect deserves wider and more specific consideration.

1 THE REDISTRIBUTION OF LABOUR AND INCOME

1.1 The Continuous Dislocation of Labour in Industrial Society

In *industrial society*, labour is distributed according to the demand which is born from productive activities, which in turn depend on the market demand.

But the market demand which is formed in industrial society is subject to criteria and constraints which technological progress and the search – by means of it – for an ever greater productivity and profitability impose. A permanent need for the adaptation of the supply to the demand for labour and for the conversion of obsolete qualifications into new ones is created. A regime of permanent dislocation of the workforce is thus produced which must flexibly, constantly, readapt itself to technological changes.

This process of continuous dislocation is determined in particular in the 'productivistic' sectors of industrial society (which, as said, do not include only industries but also many of the service sectors).

In industrial society, the expansion of consumption (which the reduction of real unit production costs permits) leads to an expansion of the demand for income and well-being, and facilitates the creation of new jobs in the low productivity (or 'non-productivistic') sectors, in the first place the public ones.

The *service society*, as said, arises when this process reaches a point beyond which a sort of feedback is produced, in as far as expansion finds its limits in the global productivity of the system. This is because the high productivity (or productivistic) sectors have reached a *minimum proportional threshold* in the entire productive system. The transfer of income from these sectors to the non-productivistic sectors is no longer successful either through the 'market' or through public finance. An *explicit process of public*

147

decision-making has to intervene (from the 'invisible hand' to the 'visible hand').

We would like here to examine more deeply some of the characteristics of the redistribution process and transfer in the evolution of industrial society, and the modification of this process in the model of the service society, by analyzing in particular its effects on inflation and unemployment (even though this falls a bit outside the main line of our discussion).[1]

1.2 A Misunderstanding about the Usefulness of 'Non-Productivistic' Sectors

First of all, however, it will be opportune to dissipate a semantic misunderstanding.

The fact that, in the development of industrial society, both income and labour are the object of redistribution and transfer from 'productivistic' sectors to 'non-productivistic' sectors, has led often to the belief that the non-productivistic are economically dependent (and in some ways parasitic) on the productivistic ones.

This produces a distorted vision of reality. In fact the expansion of the non-productivistic sectors is permitted by the increases in the productivity of the productivistic sectors (at least until the productive object of the latter responds to the preferential needs of the people); but also the increases in productivity in the productivistic sectors are 'allowed' – under certain conditions – by an expansion in non-productivistic sectors (if this corresponds likewise to the preferential needs of the people and if it is implemented in a favourable industrial environment). This happens in two ways, one direct and one indirect.

In the direct way the increase in productivity of the sectors which are susceptible to it, is to a large extent an effect of technological innovation or progress: which nearly always is the result of organizational, cultural and scientific progress. There is no point in mentioning how the latter is in turn a function of activities which do not only produce material goods, but also services: research, scholastic education, recreation and so on. Furthermore, it is useless to say how much the productive activity, in its technical innovation, benefits – as external economies – environmental protection, social and public security, administrative organization, design, marketing, etc., i.e. an (essentially 'urban') social 'infrastructuring', which therefore always presents itself as the cause and also the effect of not directly productive activities. Even the commercial and distribution services are normally considered a factor for the increase of productivity (and not only of profitability) of manufacturing industries.

In an indirect way, the increase in productivity in sectors susceptible to it (the sector which we have called 'productivistic') is allowed by the expansion of the actual market, of the purchasing capacity of the consumers, as said. And if it is not possible to obtain this expansion only with the expansion of income and the number of industrial workers and operators, it can be guaranteed by the expansion of income and the number of non-industrial workers (i.e. of the non-productivistic sectors).

The undoubted fact that it is the increase in productivity of the product-ivistic sectors which allows any 'redistribution' of income and employment, must not lead us to ignore or forget the close connection and interaction between productive sectors ('productivistic', or high-productivity rate sectors, or 'non-productivistic', or low-productivity rate sectors) in the promotion of the progress of productivity itself.[2]

1.3 The Weight of the Two Sectors and Differential Characteristics of the Distributive Process in the Two Models

What has been described above is valid likewise in industrial society and that of services.

The difference between the two models lies however in the implications which may arise from the relative weight which the two groups of sectors (productivistic and non-productivistic) have in one or the other model; and from the proportions of the process of redistribution which may derive from this different weight. It is on these points that I believe that it is opportune to dwell for a little while longer.

In fact my thesis is that, in the service society, the weight of non-productivistic sectors increases enormously (i.e. it exceeds a certain threshold which brings about the new model). And the consequence is that the transfer of income and labour becomes gigantic: it exceeds nevertheless a certain size threshold. (It would perhaps be opportune, and perhaps our duty, to say something more about this threshold, but reflection on this point is still premature.)

Some axioms could be established:

(a) *the more productivity increases in the productivistic sectors, the more the weight of the non-productivistic sectors increases (and vice versa);*

(b) *the more the productivity of the first increases and the weight of the second increases, the more the need to transfer income and labour from the first to the second is extended.*

It is therefore the *proportion of the transfer* which distinguishes the service society from the industrial one, and not the existence of the transfer itself. But, as said, before characterizing further this direct comparison between the two models of society, it is perhaps opportune to repropose an interpretation of the redistributive processes in industrial society useful for the comprehension of our thesis.

1.4   The Characteristics of the Redistributive Process in the Evolution of the Industrial Society Model

It is known that industrial society was born because, by means of an intense process of income and labour transfer, it managed to gain for all of society – in a more or less proportional way – advantages deriving from the substantial increases in productivity in industry.

The model of behaviour is known: we will reiterate it here in purposely simplified terms.

First the advantages of industrial productivity spread through the reduction of unitary prices (to the user or consumer) of industrial products.[3] It is the 'market' which 'redistributes' or transfers the additional real income (from improved productivity). (For indivisible public services it is the state – as always – which redistributes or transfers by means of tax collection.)

Subsequently, the reduction of unitary prices of products of the productivistic sectors (which is the 'natural' redistributive factor, as said) only occurs in 'real' terms, i.e. through inflation, and change in the monetary parameter. In fact the rigidity of the supply prices of the productivistic sectors due to a set of institutional factors (imperfect or oligopolistic competition, 'administrated' prices, 'price umbrellas' in favour of marginal firms, etc.) brings about an increase in the prices of the non-productivistic sectors, as much as it serves to keep enough balanced the relative price system, or – in other words – to rebalance the capacity for purchase of primary incomes (labour and capital) of the two sectors, to the new levels of real productivity.

This causes a general increase of prices (price inflation) which will be at as high a rate as is required to restore that real equilibrium, at the new levels of real productivity.

Therefore it can be said that the *redistribution* – essential in social equilibrium (at 'zero sum', a guarantee of not only economic, but in particular social and political stability), and very useful also for the possibilities of further growth (in productivity) – *in these circumstances* (institutional rigidity in prices, on which there is large evaluative consensus) *is guaranteed by inflation*. However, it is guaranteed by an inflation which is contained within certain rates which are 'equal' to those of the increase of the 'average' productivity of the economic system (as is commonly claimed); which is in reality the increase in physical productivity in the single productivistic sectors.

The task of the public 'economic policy' in these cases – as is upheld and theorized widely – is that of managing (by means of the use of instruments available to the government) to make sure that, in the absence of the possibility of containing nominal prices, at least their dynamics are contained in the limits of the process activated by the need to rebalance the real income in comparison to gains in productivity.

1.5 The Role of Inflation in the Redistributive Process in the Industrial Society Model

It is not true, in fact, that if nominal incomes increase on average within the limits of the average physical productivity of the system, inflation is not produced: because such an assumption does not bear in mind the redistributive 'factor' (which we have simplified) between productivistic and non-productivistic sectors. In order that inflation is not produced in those circumstances, it is necessary that the nominal prices of the productivistic sectors are reduced (in proportion to increase in the physical productivity of the same). If this does not happen, the need for redistribution implies an increase in prices (and relative primary incomes, or vice-versa) of the non-productivistic sectors, and therefore a modification towards the increase of the 'prices' parameter (or general index of prices), so that the system of 'relative prices' again finds its equilibrium.

Inflation becomes, in this case, the *guardian* of the equilibrium of the system of relative prices, the guardian of that *'zero sum' of opportunities and incomes* which is the physiological tendency of any society (therefore it is not surprising if *social equilibrium* is identified with the same).

If therefore the acquisition of additional monetary income is maintained within the limits of the increase in productivity (or, more 'Keynesianly', it is maintained within the limits of a reasonable expectation of an increase in productivity), inflation – if the nominal prices of the productivistic sectors do not go down (and if the real incomes of some other social sector do not go down, which accepts, by obligation or distraction, to be penalized in the dynamic process) – is inevitable: only that it is *physiological* for the guarantee of the system of 'relative prices' and the incomes systems.

In this case, therefore, inflation is not only a guarantee of social equilibrium, but also the instrument by means of which the benefits of development between productivistic and non-productivistic sectors are redistributed, as well as between the participants in the fruits of these.

And since such redistribution is in the majority of cases (but not all, and at this moment it is not relevant to discuss these) a guarantee of further development, it can be claimed that in the given circumstances – rigidity of the nominal prices (in decreasing) and the tendential 'zero sum' of incomes – *inflation is even a guarantee of development.*

Thus we should not underrate the 'positive' role that inflation may have (as an effect of the redistributive process of incomes) in the model of industrial society. And this by having recourse to the classical schemes of the functioning of the economic system: inflation guarantees redistribution, redistribution in turn guarantees an increase in purchasing capacity, and the latter guarantees the increase of productivity in productivistic sectors, which is the source of development.

All this is obviously because 'barriers' have been created in the distributive process; for which reason redistribution does not seem – apart from exceptions and particular attenuating circumstances – possible via the reduction of the (nominal) prices of industrial products, but only via the increase of the (nominal) prices of services and primary factors (and of taxes).

1.6   The Role of Inflation in the Redistributive Process in the Service Society Model

This positive role of inflation (or even simply the 'rebalancing' role mentioned before) *subsists only if there are expectations of an increase in productivity of productivistic sectors* (which are the only ones to obtain it): which is constrained, as repeatedly said, to two conditions:

(a)   that there are further technical possibilities of innovation and increase in productivity (and from this point of view it is necessary to say that scientific and technological progress may be infinite, even if they may temporarily go through, sector by sector, stationary phases; for example, an automated industry may go through periods of stagnant productivity);
(b)   (more important still) that there is an expansion of the production of the sectors in question, pushed by an actual growing demand in consumption of the products of the productivist sectors.

The conditions given above are those in fact which characterize *industrial society* in its expanding moments; and their lack characterizes, on the other hand, industrial society in its 'regressive' or 'post-industrial' moments, and thus – as we have conventionally called it here – the *service society*.[4]

In these conditions and phases (declining or *new*) of the service society, then inflation no longer has the positive role which it has been allowed to have, on the basis of the mechanisms peculiar to the industrial society described above. In these conditions inflation 'turns on itself' and no longer gets into gear with production development.

It remains indispensable as a redistributing and rebalancing effect of the *few and concentrated* increases in productivity (high singularly but low overall) which are produced in the service society, but its propagation goes far beyond its role.

Inflation, in the service society, is no longer 'physiological' (as said), but becomes 'pathological'; this happens not because the motivation for inflation of redistribution is lacking – in the way indicated – the benefits of the increases in productivity of the productivistic sectors; but because of the particular structural characteristics in which this need for redistribution manifests itself, respectively, in the two models of society (as we are to examine in section 2).

1.7 Models of Society and Theories of Capital

It is clear enough that the distribution I am referring to is the one among productive sectors, through exchange of commodities at given prices, and that I am not referring to the one between the primary factors of production within the sectors, i.e. between capital and labour. The latter is a 'classical' topic of economic theory ('classical', 'neo-classical' and, again, 'post-classical'); but, in my opinion, it is pertinent to the structural change we are dealing with, only if it is true (as it claims, yet with scarce reference to historical evidence) that this change is a function of the investment choices of capitalists, according to the relative advantageousness for profit-seeking entrepreneurs, and thus of the profit rate, and not, on the contrary, a function of other factors, such as the changes in consumer demand or in technology. As is well known, the first assumption produced an intense debate about the 'theory of capital' (opposing Marxist–Ricardian–Sraffian and marginalist-neoclassical theoretical economists). But, short of mistakes, I have not found examples of these debates which do not unfold – so to speak – *sub specie aeternitatis*, or that have gone deep into the relationship between 'theoretical capital' and the more realistic capital used – in diverse stages of capitalistic production – in diverse sectors of economic activity with a very diverse capital intensity (e.g. our productivistic and non-productivistic sectors). In our case, the inter-sectorial distribution includes both capital and labour, not excluding, though, different variable effects among the two sectors within it. Yet, compared to inter-sectorial distribution, the inter-factor one seems to us historically less significant and more subordinated (*ubi maior minor cessat*), except when one considers the latter – we repeat – the general cause of the former (for which, however, there are no relevant historical analyses).

The capitalists, possibly surviving in the non-productivistic sectors, become participants in the banquet of productivity increases of the productivistic sectors, like their workers and all other non-capital-income earners. The profit rate of this sector is stable, *routinière*, and we should ask whether it has the requisites to survive in such a stagnant condition. In fact, in the non-productivistic sectors of the service society the professional motivation emerges clearly as the motor of any personal commitment. But where the capitalist's professional motivation is the profit, the growth rate of this profit (and not simply the stable rate) represents the *raison d'être* of the pure profession of the entrepreneur-capitalist (who, on the other hand, is more and more hidden in the productivistic sectors behind the financial capital actors). Is it conceivable that, in a climate of *routinières* and stable profits and where the human and personal value of the achievements themselves become the *raison d'être* of the initiatives, a profit-seeking entrepreneurship can develop? In a climate in which the quality of work becomes emergent, and the owner of capital is to a large extent replaceable by those who contribute that quality?

Or is it not more reasonable to suppose a slow decline of this kind of entrepreneurship without prospects of increasing its productivity and profitability rates? In the experience of the *industrial divide* (which we fleetingly considered in Chapter 5) do we not find opposite cases of sectors of small and medium-sized firms that enter the sphere of the sectors marked by high productivity and with very strong rates of innovation and resulting profit rates, and sectors of small and medium-sized firms where professional quality does emerge, but whose profitability rates tend to disappear? And in the latter sectors of firms, is not the capitalist himself or herself a 'professional' motivated by interests which are very different from gain and profit?

In this sense, it can be said that also the conditions of profitability do influence the structural changes (together with the evolution of the demand for consumption and technologies), meaning that they can influence the permanence or the exit of entrepreneurs in the growing non-productivistic sectors. But it must be doubted that the theories of capital, of opposing 'schools', that have based their analyses on the assumption that the profit rate determines the change, were referring to this kind of circumstance.

In sum, we should ask whether the theory of capital, as has been discussed recently, is equally pertinent to the paradigm of industrial society and to that of the service society. And whether we should not, instead, go deeper into the structural conditions that can motivate the abstract behaviour which that theory seems to be seeking to determine by very generalized positive analyses, which fatally become only generic.

2   DIFFERENTIAL CHARACTERISTICS OF THE DISTRIBUTIVE PROCESSES IN THE TWO MODELS OF SOCIETY

Thus, as said in many ways, in the development phase of industrialization (i.e. of the passage of much production from the 'traditional' stage with very low productivity rates, to the industrial stage with much higher rates), the productivistic sectors tend to spread in comparison to the non-productivistic sectors. But in the development of industrial society, the productivistic sectors do not reach the point at which they tend, on the other hand, to regress proportionally, because of a certain saturation (as said) of the consumption of mass industrial products, in overall consumption.

In this way we have defined the *transition from industrial society to the service society*. In this latter model, perhaps the rates of productivity increase may also increase greatly; but they are much more 'concentrated' than before in some sectors which are exactly 'productivistic'; which reduces the rate of the average general increase of productivity.

Nevertheless, in the model of service society – despite the aforementioned average reduction of the productivity increase rate – the redistributive needs increase and – how can it be said? – the *intensity of redistribution* increases too, precisely because of the high level of concentration of the productivistic sectors, in comparison to the total amount of the productive system.

There is therefore overall *little to be redistributed in general, but where there is, there is a lot*. And *redistribution* in the case of service society becomes extremely important, and *strategic* for the survival of the system, since all the possibilities of obtaining improvements in income and welfare which were previously widespread in the capitalist production system, reside only in being able to spread, to the general benefit, the *limited but elevated* rates of productivity of the productivist sectors.

2.1 Further Analysis of the Transitional Relationship of Productivity – Prices from the Industrial Society to the Service Society Model

In the model of *industrial society*, in fact, the expansion of industrialization creates widespread possibilities of the increase of physical productivity (albeit with different gradations) in all parts of the economy where a mass production can be realized, a profitable accumulation of capital, and thus an advantageous search for profit. It is the need for redistribution which is 'concentrated' in the direction of and on the side of the non-productivistic sectors (which are both the traditional sector of the public services, and the traditional sector of 'non-mass' production activities which is undermined by industrialization and therefore becomes 'protected' in order to ensure its painless demise or its honourable survival, if the limited need for quality products survives).

But, apart from the need to redistribute to the advantage of the relatively concentrated non-productivistic sector, the model of industrial society is characterized by high productivity rates, which are not equal but *present in almost all sectors*, from agriculture to industry, from transport to the 'industrial' tertiary sector, etc. Redistribution occurs also *between* these sectors, but finds there everyone already participating, at least in part, 'on their own' at the banquet of productivity increases.

The redistributive mechanisms tend to realize only a 'flattening out' – and not always successfully – of the additional incomes (from productivity) for various categories of workers and operators (by means of the 'market' when the nominal prices of the non-productivistic sectors are increased; and by means of taxation on 'added value' or on 'income' to finance the non-productivistic public sectors).

In our analysis we are starting from a basic hypothesis, largely verified in real industrial society, that the nominal prices of productivistic sectors tend to stay still (if they do not increase) in the presence also of strong increases in physical productivity rates, which would instead justify their reduction. This is because of the strong tendency of any entrepreneur to 'profit' from (it should be said) any technical innovation – from the biggest to the smallest and most imperceptible – which he will introduce in *his* combination of productive factors, i.e. in *his enterprise* with the effect of reducing unitary costs.

On the other hand, we might also ask how the entrepreneur could be stimulated to look for and introduce new techniques and new production systems if there was not at least the expectation of obtaining *extraordinary occasional profits* at a much higher rate than the normal rate of interest, or even standard of average profit.

The case of a reduction of nominal prices of productivistic sectors, as a consequence of a marked increase in productivity, has taken place at times and in cases when some inconvenient competitor was to be 'expelled from the market' having not yet adopted similar productivistic innovations. Apart from the temporary nature of the operation this is a case which has been largely replaced by that of the oligopolistic 'trustees', and by that of price 'umbrella' policies which, with the presence of marginal firms, ensures high rent positions for the non-marginal firms and innovators. The case of a reduction of nominal prices following increases in productivity is practically by now only part of historic memory.[5]

With high rates of general price inflation, the productivistic sectors, if they benefit from productivity increases, have, if anything, increased nominal prices *less* so than the non-productivistic sectors; which means that they have reduced the 'relative prices'. But the non-occurrence of the reduction of nominal prices has meant that the necessary redistribution of the benefits of *their* physical productivity could take place only through inflation.

Thus the inflation is as high as is the gap between the nominal price and the 'relative' one. If the nominal price does not move (go down) the relative price will fall more than it would if the nominal price went down as well.

If the nominal price (of the productivistic sector) rather than diminishing, for one reason or another, were in fact to increase, then the *gap* between this nominal price and the relative one (which will express, in fact, the rebalancing of the relative prices) will be even greater.

In other words, the less prices in the productivistic sector reflect productivity gains with their reduction, the more the non-productivistic sectors will increase their nominal prices in order to rebalance the system of relative prices: and thus the higher will be the rate of general inflation. (To these factors, more than to others widely exposed in some theories, I consider there is to be attributed the rather widespread and recurrent fact that periods of marked inflation and turbulence are associated also with periods of strong structural change in the economy, and, vice versa, periods of monetary stability are associated with marked structural stagnation.)

In industrial society, at equal conditions,[6] therefore, the redistributive factor of the benefits of productivity is an inflationary factor, to the extent to which the productivistic sectors are not able to distribute these benefits through their nominal prices.

The gap between nominal and relative prices constitutes, simply, the inflation coefficient.

2.2 Factors and Circumstances which may Limit the Inflationary Effect of Productivity in the Industrial Society Model

Two factors mitigate the inflationary transmission described:

(a) the incomplete rigidity of nominal supply prices of the productivistic sectors;
(b) the incomplete rigidity of nominal supply prices of the non-productivistic sectors.[7]

The two phenomena, nominally identical, are located in very different contexts and are activated, motivated and regulated by very different factors. They must therefore be dealt with in a completely separate way.

With regard to factor (a), despite the hypothesized behavioural rule (and largely confirmed by past and present reality) there may be cases in which also the nominal prices (of the productivistic sectors) tend to decrease if in the presence of strong increases in productivity in the sectors in question.[8] Any distribution of the increases in productivity (where obtained), by this route, reduces the inflationary rate of the standard redistributive process described above.

With regard to factor (b), which is indeed more probable and realistic in many experiences, some non-productivistic sectors (in particular those destined to disappear in the period preceding their extinction but also some more stable and durable ones, or which are even capable of some dynamism towards growth) agree to not participate in the 'banquet' of productivity increase; that is, they agree to not adjust their nominal prices (and incomes) to the incomes of the productivistic sectors. All this is possible, but is articulated in a complex number of cases on which various factors operate.

First of all there is the (special) case of labour incomes which are created in the same productivistic sectors when in the presence of marked increases in productivity. The hypothesis that the workers of these sectors do not claim a wage increase proportional to these increases (and therefore to the rates of increase in profit and other possible capital incomes) is possible, but always problematic.

The matter would be less problematic if the workers and trade unions in the sectors with marked increases in productivity realized that such increases translate into a reduction of the nominal supply prices of the products involved; but if this does not happen, there will always be the demand on the part of the workers to participate in the banquet – more or less in proportion to their share or contribution – at least at the level of the productive units in which increases are realized.

On the other hand, it is more than probable, as has often happened, that the same entrepreneurs in the sectors in which marked increments in productivity are realized, prefer to have their own staff participate at the banquet (perhaps in differentiated forms because of the group's proximity to power and the relative advantage of managerial power, as happens in any 'autocratic' society worthy of the name) rather than appropriate – the entire value 'added' from the progress of productivity without transferring it on the prices. In this way the classic 'corporative' collusion is produced which may find a way of being accepted by the sectors less favoured by the progress of productivity, and by the non-productivistic sectors, at least for a certain period of time.

Obviously, we are referring here to the general case of productivity progress *in the presence of expansion* in the production of productivistic sectors, which is the standard case of industrial society; the general case of productivity progress in the presence of non-expansion, and even of reduction, of the activities of production (which are the known cases of restructuring and reconversion implying the general reduction of the workforce and dismissals) in reality has as an effect:

– either a paid surplus of workers: and therefore the measurement of the increase of productivity is confused and compromised (in the name of a solid redistribution of costs);
– or an effective reduction of the personnel: and therefore there are cases in which the remaining personnel benefit from unitary increases in wages as in fact their participation in the banquet.

If what we have called 'corporative collusion' (in comparison to the distribution of the benefits of productivity increases) is accepted by the others, then this is translated proportionally (as said) into a reduction of the inflationary transmission inherent in the redistributive process, since in this case there would be no such process.

But this case too is somewhat problematic. In fact a reduction of relative prices (and incomes) of the less favoured sectors or non-productivist sectors is very difficult if it involves homogeneous categories of workers. It is possible to not let some 'social' categories participate in the banquet (for example, the manual workers in comparison to professionals, civil servants in comparison to businessmen, etc.); but it is unlikely that proposed agreements on the 'gaps' in real wages (albeit camouflaged by a non-variation of nominal salaries) accompanied by an absolute worsening in living standards can be accepted by workers who are approximately homogeneous, professionally and socially (by education, social extraction, technical qualifications, etc.), but who operate in sectors with differentiated productivity increases.

In these cases, not even the known and debated 'segmentation' of the labour market exercises its effects much. Even if such segmentation is an indisputable reality from the structural point of view (thus separating women, migrant ethnic workers, what remains of pre-industrial social classes, etc.), and has distant historic roots, it does not serve to differentiate and exclude – if this is the case – the participation of such categories at the banquet of productivity (whilst maintaining the baseline differences).

And nor does the territorial separation of the labour market still exercise a role in the majority of industrial countries. Furthermore – if there were not all these reasons – trade union organization, which is a great transmitter of information and evaluations, would be enough to make impossible the passive acceptance of a reduction of the 'relative', i.e. real, incomes of some categories of workers in comparison with others (only because they belong to sectors with different 'productivity').

To the extent, however, in which a certain 'impermeability' of the labour markets permits the avoidance of the imitative and propagating effect of salary increases in the non-productivistic sectors, in comparison with those of the productivistic sectors, even this is translated into a reduction of the inflationary transmission.

2.3   Inflation and 'Unemployment-by-Productivity'

From the inflationary point of view, the factor which has on the other hand a definite effect of attenuation of inflation in industrial society, is 'unemployment-by-productivity'.

In effect, if the workforce 'freed' from the process of increase in productivity in the productivistic sectors does not find employment in 'new' productivistic sectors (which is the standard case nevertheless of industrial society) it cannot but weigh – albeit in a different way – on the (nominal) monetary incomes of the workers of the productivistic sectors. And therefore, whatever the stability or even increase in the monetary wages of the latter, the process leads finally to a reduction of the real wages and salaries of the workers in employment.

This is the case in which (nominal) monetary distribution results from the effects of productivity, without the push of the wages, salaries and incomes of the non-productivistic sectors. It is as if the obtained greater productivity (of the productivistic sectors) was distributed also to the non-productivistic sectors: but not by means of an increase in the wages, salaries and real incomes of these latter sectors, but rather by transferring the additional margins of real profitability (without allowances) to the new category of workers omitted from the productive process: the workers 'unemployed by productivity' ('Unemployment Boom' as somebody – Dahrendorf if I remember well – called it).

In this case the inflationary effect not only is attenuated, but is also eliminated: but on the condition in fact that the transfer of income realized is exactly proportional to the increases in productivity, and that the income and consumption of the unemployed does not exceed the real reduction of the income and consumption of the employed, whilst in the presence of their stability or increase in monetary wages, which become, so to speak, 'unitary family salaries' (per person, pro capita, by working hour).[9]

Any way of financing unemployment (allowances, integrations, etc.) which weighs on the incomes of productivistic sectors, without the benefits of productivity being transferred to the monetary prices, has however an inflationary effect.[10]

9 The Expansion and Decline of Public Services

In many respects employment in the public service sector corresponds most closely to the type of conditions described in the previous chapters, i.e. being able to meet both a new demand for services, and new aspirations on the part of the labour supply.

1 AN EVOLUTION IN THE ROLE AND CONCEPT OF PUBLIC SERVICES

But, first of all: what do we mean by 'public service'? The question, in spite of the apparent obviousness of the term,[1] does not fail to be controversial.

In fact, any kind of definition is unsatisfying because it must be 'neutral' about the substantive field and therefore limits of the 'public' role in comparison with the 'private'. And in order to be neutral, it must necessarily be either tautological or unmeaningful. The attempt of Samuelson, with his well-known suggestion to consider as 'public' any good indivisible and as 'private' any good divisible,[2] has received many objections; and quite rightly: because of its abstraction from the historical circumstances within which such a distinction can be manifest and applied.

For instance the first objection is related to the impossibility of finding the 'pure' public good in reality.[3] Other objections have regretted that Samuelson's formula would imply either an excessive restriction of the field of public intervention, or at least that any public intervention in the field of divisible goods (i.e. private) would be considered, by definition, an excessive extension or interference of the 'public' upon the 'private'.

And moreover, it being relatively commonly agreed that the field of 'public economics' includes not only the *allocation* of public goods and services, but also a *redistributive* function,[4] and a control of the social equilibrium through *economic policy* (employment, stability, balanced budgeting, etc.), it is relatively difficult not to extend the concept of public 'good' also to that of public 'interest'.[5] Why should an action to provide good legal security to the citizen and to the taxpayers be more a 'public good' than an action to assure their money or their real purchasing power? The conclusion we are tempted to draw from the long taxonomic debates (and/or political discourses masked as taxonomic ones) upon the role of the public sector,[6] perhaps is that the best way (more scientific and less scholastic) to face the problems of

161

the public function is to *plan* its operation according to each situation and circumstance, and then, in conformity with the objectives and strategies selected by that planning, to evaluate the optimal reciprocal boundaries and priority contents.

However, some trends and phenomena,[7] commonly recognized as matters of fact – beyond the taxonomies classifying what is public and what is private and the abstract discussion about what is the one and what is the other – seem to emerge from the historical evidence in the last half-century and in parallel with the changes which we have indicated in industrial society (structure of production, labour market, etc.):

1. the huge growth of public expenditure or outlays as a proportion of the national income produced;
2. the fact that the part of these growing outlays allocated to redistribution (transfer) has grown much more than the whole outlay.

As is well known, both phenomena have raised a great number of questions, among which:

– By what is this huge growth of the public function determined?
– Is it a reversible or irreversible growth?
– What meaning must we ascribe to the shift – within public expenditure – from the 'allocative' part to the 'distributive' part of the total outlay? What is the function of this shift? What are the causes of it?
– Is the 'distributive' part (whose weight has increased in the total) the 'cause' or the 'effect' of this huge growth of the total public function?

These and many other questions, surely of interest, have stimulated and nourished many reflections and many researches.

To the first question is related, obviously, the main question included in our own study path, that of the role the public sector plays in the general structural change, which we are analyzing, of industrial society into something new. Is it a determining role, or only subordinate?

It is impossible to deny that not even a sound transformation of the concept of public service has emerged from the whole literature developed on the subject.[8] However, it is also impossible to avoid noting that this transformation has remained only 'virtual'. The consciousness of the transformation has not had the effect of a radical rejection of the age-old theoretical question of the limits of public intervention and of the discussion about the theoretical equilibrium between the need for freedom (anti-state) and the need for justice (state).

This difficulty is well expressed by the persistence in political science theory of concepts and thinking that belong to periods that are really in the past; periods when the role of the state was truly different – in quantity and quality – from that of today.

This seems to produce – as in the case of conventional national accounting (SNA) discussed previously[9] – a kind of schizophrenia; on the one hand a person may recognize the fact that many schemes and paradigms of the past have no more sense; and on the other he or she continues to use them in the normal way, completely dividing his or her consciousness between theoretical and conventional.

It is symptomatic that – in concluding a 'tracking shot' on the history of the economics of public finance – a very influential author in this field, R. A. Musgrave, says:

> Over the two centuries here surveyed, the economics of public finance has grown enormously both in breadth and sophistication.... Yet, the basic problems have remained the same. The question of what public services should be provided, how they should be financed, and what role government should play in the macro conduct of economic affairs were visible to Adam Smith, and they still pose the basic problem. So does the fact that many issues in public finance remain inherently controversial.[10]

Apparently, those issues are seen and expressed with similar concepts and similar words. But it is difficult for me to believe that issues and visions on the role of the state have remained the same from the time in which the 'state' managed 5–10 per cent of GDP and today when it manages a good half of GDP. And I cannot believe that this macroscopic difference of role, which essentially is a macroscopic 'structural' difference in society, has no influence on the theoretical issues and problems related to the quantity, quality and sense of public services and is not faced at all (but nearly ignored) by the conventional negotiations of public economics.[11]

However, in our case, we will limit ourselves to commenting only on some possible implications (and perhaps causes) of the change examined on more general societal change.

2   THE MEANING AND EFFECTS OF THE EXPANSION OF PUBLIC SERVICES

Consistently with what has been said above, we will examine some of the most significant data concerning the expansion of the public sector in recent decades (OECD statistics data provide us with relatively comparable figures from 1970 till now (1995) – nearly the last quarter-century). I have selected some countries. Tables 9.1 to 9.4 show the last 25 years of the history of growth of the public sector, growth that has continued for the whole of the century, accelerating after the Second World War.

The data confirm what was already known, or easily forecast: a steady growth of the public sector; and all countries have arrived roughly at a public sector or 'general government'[12] that:

- 'outlays'[13] around 50 per cent of the Gross Domestic Product (with some exceptions) (see Table 9.1);
- manages 'receipts'[14] that are also around 50 per cent of the GDP (again with a few exceptions) (see Table 9.2);
- pays to its employees an amount which ranges from 8 to 15 per cent of the GDP (also with some exceptions) (see Table 9.3);
- employs a percentage of total employment which ranges from 17 to 22 per cent (also with some exceptions) (see Table 9.4).

The most important exceptions are for some countries (USA, Australia, Japan) that have always shown a public sector less significant than in European countries, in terms of all phenomena: outlays, receipts, employment (the level attained by outlays and receipts is around 35 per cent of GDP, and by public employment no more than 11 per cent of the total). For employment, this group of countries is joined by some countries of the other group (like Greece and the Netherlands).

Table 9.1   General government total outlays (as percentage of nominal GDP) (15 selected OECD countries)

	1970	*1995*	*Variation 1995/1970*
Australia	31.4[1]	36.2	4.8
Austria	37.6	52.5	14.9
Belgium	41.5	53.8	12.3
Canada	34.1	46.5	12.4
Denmark	54.5[2]	56.3	1.8
France	38.5	54.3	15.8
Germany	38.3	49.5	11.2
Greece	27.9[3]	47.4	19.5
Italy	33.0	52.7	19.7
Japan	19.0	35.6	16.6
Netherlands	41.3	51.4	10.1
Norway	34.9	47.6	12.7
Spain	21.6	44.8	23.2
United Kingdom	36.7	43.0	6.3
United States	30.0	32.9	2.9

[1] 1975   [2] 1990   [3] 1975

Source: OECD, analytical databank.

Table 9.2   General government current receipts (as percentage of nominal GDP) (15 selected OECD countries)

	1970	1995	Variation 1995/1970
Australia	28.5[1]	34.2	5.7
Austria	38.8	47.4	8.6
Belgium	39.3	49.9	10.6
Canada	34.6	42.2	7.6
Denmark	53.5[2]	54.1	0.6
France	39.4	48.9	9.5
Germany	38.5	46.1	7.6
Greece	23.7	37.1	13.4
Italy	29.0	45.0	16.0
Japan	20.6	32.0	11.4
Netherlands	39.9	47.7	7.8
Norway	40.0	50.9	10.9
Spain	21.9	38.3	16.4
United Kingdom	39.7	37.4	−2.3
United States	28.9	31.0	2.1

[1] 1975   [2] 1990

Source: OECD, analytical databank.

Table 9.3   Compensation of general government employees (as percentage of nominal GDP) (15 selected OECD countries)

	1970	1995	Variation 1995/1970
Australia	9.9	11.6	1.7
Austria	9.9	12.8	2.9
Belgium	10.1	12.2	2.1
Canada	12.6	12.3	−0.3
Denmark	12.9	17.1	4.2
France	10.8	14.4	3.6
Germany	8.8	10.4	1.6
Greece	7.7	11.5	3.8
Italy	10.0	11.4	1.4
Japan	5.9	7.4	1.5
Netherlands	11.5	9.8	−1.7
Norway	10.1	13.8	3.7
Spain	7.2	11.6	4.4
United Kingdom	10.4	8.6	−1.8
United States	11.4	10.1	−1.3

Source: OECD, analytical databank.

Critical Analysis of the Social Change

Table 9.4 General government employment (as percentage of total employment) (15 selected OECD Countries)

	1970	1995	Variation 1995/1970
Australia	12.1	15.2	3.1
Austria	13.3	20.7[1]	7.4
Belgium	13.8	18.8	5.0
Canada	19.2	20.7	1.5
Denmark	18.5	30.0	11.5
France	18.0	24.6	6.6
Germany	11.2	15.5	4.3
Greece	7.9	12.2	4.3
Italy	12.2	17.8	5.6
Japan	7.7	8.3	0.6
Netherlands	11.5	12	0.5
Norway	17.9	31.1	13.1
Spain	4.9	15.5	10.6
United Kingdom	18.1	14.2	−3.9
United States	16.0	15.5	−0.5

[1] 1990

Source: OECD, analytical databank.

Diversity, especially in Europe, has been reduced in the last quarter of a century by faster growth in the countries which were at a lower level at the beginning of the period, and a slower one in the countries which were at the higher level at the beginning of the period.

In this period, nearly all countries have seen outlays for *transfers* (payments in absence of an economic exchange, like social security, subsidies, and other transfers such as intangible asset and net capital transfers), that is, outlays having a redistribution aim, become relatively more important than the outlays for *final consumption expenditure* (essentially compensation of employees). (See Table 9.3.) As a whole, the percentage of the latter has declined significantly and in some countries very markedly in the period, while the percentage of transfer payments has shown significant and sometimes huge increases. This means that the expansion of the public sector in this period has been more in terms of welfare services than in terms of public activities or services.

Unfortunately, data of this kind do not give us any information about the 'real' output of goods and services to the citizen corresponding to this 'outlay', against the amount of 'receipts' entered as input. Only this comparison could give us the possibility of an evaluation of the real economic contribution of the public sector to the general output of a community (in our case, the national community): assuming but not conceding that GDP could be considered a good proxy for the general real output of a community.

But these data are sufficient to give us an idea of the role achieved – at an even faster pace – by the state in our Western industrial society, in *close connection* with the incredible pace of economic growth of the recent decades in the same Western industrial society. And this in the teeth of those, economists or not, who in the past (though they incredibly still persist today!) – when the state accounted for 10–20 per cent of economic activities – prophesied every kind of misfortune if the state increased, rather than decreased, its presence in economic life.

However, not everything seems to be satisfactory or problem-free in this huge expansion of activities and presence of the public sector. Even if the data do not give us any information about the real performance of public expenditure, everybody from any kind of profession, social group, and political faith, has the impression that something is wrong in the public sector. Everybody – inside and outside the public sector – observes that activities are not efficient, the organization is not working, that there is enormous waste of every kind of resources: labour, infrastructure, time, opportunities, money. The benchmarking of the private sector is without doubt the best. People leave the public sector either as users (if they can) and even as employees. The decline brings degradation. The degradation brings decline.

In recent decades, during the growth of the public sector, dissatisfaction has also been growing to the point where we can say that, more or less everywhere, there is a true *crisis* of the public sector, of public services, and of the Welfare State with which the public sector today identifies itself.

There are multiplying efforts in every country to repair the situation, to recover efficiency, to reform management and procedures in the public sector. The creation some years ago of the Public Management (PUMA) Committee (and corresponding department) in the OECD, has been an important 'clearing house' for these reforming experiences in OECD countries. The 'National Performance Review' and the implementation of the Government Performance and Result Act (1993) which introduced *strategic planning* into the US federal government, were epochal signs of renewal of the public administration, destined to leave an important trace in the history of Western countries.

3 THE CRISIS FACTORS OF THE PUBLIC SECTORS AND SERVICES

But before entering into the analysis of what we can do to face the expansion and, at the same time, the decline of the public sector, it is important to examine the 'structural' limits that the general change implies for the public sector activities and the structural factors which are determining the present crisis.

These factors are the same as the factors in the crisis of the Welfare State, but still deserve a short presentation and comments. As explained in Chapter 5 (section 1.8), I see the crisis factors as grouped in three categories:

1. financial limits;
2. lack of efficiency, effectiveness and performance measurement;
3. disaffection and dislike, on the part of users.

3.1   The Financial Limits of the State

The first group of difficulties and obstacles may be qualified under the blanket term *'government fiscal and financial limits'*.

Government tax pressure on the production of private resources for the purpose of income redistribution and the financing of indivisible (but also divisible) services has today reached intolerable levels, especially when it is borne in mind that the growth rate of the production of these resources (expressed in GDP) is slowing down.[15]

It is common knowledge that the elasticity of public expenditure with respect to GDP has long been (it not always) superior to one; and, moreover, that it tends to grow.[16] But (as correctly pointed out by the OECD study from 1978):

it could be argued that the achievement of high or full coverage marks a turning point. From that point, further decisions as to increased expenditure are of a different nature. They no longer need to be taken to fulfil the ideal of a minimum to everybody. In many OECD countries the access of all citizens to certain basic services and minimum income levels is achieved. Instead, new expenditure decisions have to stem from conscious policy decisions designed to increase resources per student, or to embark upon compensatory education promoting the chances of the less favoured members of society, or to raise the relative benefits of pensioners or for the unemployed, or to gear medical care programmes towards groups more in need of public assistance or whose health profile represents greater risks, and so on... There appears to be considerable scope for 'rationalization' of programmes to gear them better to their objectives, and this might itself be expected to release resources for further selective and targeted expansion to meet new needs and to make some further improvements, especially in benefit levels for the poorest recipients of assistance.   (ibid., pp. 30–1)

In Western economic systems public expenditure is obviously 'financed' by fiscal systems. Marginal variations aside, the elasticity of the state's fiscal revenue with respect to GDP, and thus the fiscal burden which falls on the private sector, is largely parallel to the elasticity of public expenditure with respect to GDP.

Even as far as the overall fiscal burden is concerned, we have reached a turning-point beyond which one must either conceive of other ways of financing ever-increasing public expenditure, or envisage other ways of the *non-public* financing of these services, for which demand is increasing.

The general political implications of such a situation, featuring a crisis of the conventional fiscal systems, has been analyzed in the much discussed work of O'Connor (1973, 1987). The fact that this work exaggerates the destructive effect of this crisis (repeating the thesis of the collapse of the state, already contested by Schumpeter at the end of the First World War, and which now can be even less accepted given the success of the Welfare State since the Second World War) does not mean that many of his considerations on the physical limits of tolerance of fiscal burdens are not entirely acceptable, above all in the face of a decline of the yields of private enterprise, as Schumpeter himself forecast in 1918 in a work on the financial crisis of the fiscal state.[17]

Even if the national and central government budgets are not in deficit, the tax burden on the economy as a whole has reached such proportions that, were it made any heavier, the government's main form of fund-raising, namely taxation, would lose all sense, and a radical overhaul of the whole system of government would be necessary. It is common knowledge, however, that equilibrium of both general and central government budgets is by no means 'real' and that it is easy to redress the balance in both cases by devaluing the currency in ever-increasing proportions.[18]

It should, moreover, be added that a policy of deficit spending – along well-known Keynesian lines – is valid in structural situations where the maintenance of a high overall demand has effects on the productivity of the supply 'apparatus' (in the sense that it stimulates investment combinations of factors of production that are more mass-production oriented, and therefore feature constantly increasing productivity rates[19]), so that a positive re-equilibrium concerning resources and allocations, *in time*, and dynamically, is eventually reached, and thus, in total (with certain inevitable changes in monetary parameters), a stimulating and positive effect on development is obtained.

But – as already pointed out (Chapter 4) – this policy of deficit spending is decisively less valid in a structural situation where maintenance of high overall demand (and the gap which develops between demand and real supply) does not have productive effects because demand is not mass-production oriented, but rather oriented towards quality production and services, with productivity growth rates which are close to or equal to zero, such as public services.

In this last situation the result – when a policy of deficit spending is applied – is merely one of chronic disequilibrium, not only in monetary terms (where these are calculated risks or acceptable costs) but also in real terms, without any *productivity-effect*.

However, from the moment when the chronic disequilibrium becomes a *contradiction in terms* and the real world cannot admit it, the real re-equilibrium is established, in a stationary economic condition, through real redistribution of existing opportunities. And deficit spending no longer has the role of ensuring redistribution of the benefits of productivity, although it is left with the (far from secondary) role of realizing *distributional goals* that are not necessarily formulated, expressed or negotiated.

3.2 Lack of Efficiency, Effectiveness and Performance Measure

Another group of obstacles to the development of public services can be identified in the *crisis of efficiency and effectiveness* of the same. In fact, everywhere – in some places more so, in some less so – together with the growth in demand for public services there has been a crisis in the ways of controlling its efficiency. This in spite of the fact that expansion has occurred under the pressure of a real social demand.

The social security or welfare schemes introduced in the post-war years in all the developed countries have shown that while such systems must often be on a large scale to standardize costs and ensure equality of rights (officially all citizens are equal), this tends to prevent the supply services from continually adjusting to real changes in demand preferences, even within a given social service.

This makes for *bureaucratization*: i.e. the development of obsolete or parasitic activities which reflect the interests of those attached to the institutions more than those of their users.

At this point it is useful to mention that important literature has developed since the 1980s on the topic of the crisis of efficiency and effectiveness in the Welfare State. Essentially our preferred selection are the works of an important OECD conference on social policies in the 1980s, published under the title *The Welfare State in Crisis* (OECD, 1981); among the reports of this conference, that by Rudolf Klein particularly highlights the risks and costs of institutionalization of the Welfare State, which would carry with it a kind of sclerosis and rigidity with respect to the new demands of society (Klein, 1981).[20]

Any criticism of the Welfare State mechanisms strongly provokes the sensitivity of its defenders. Certain critics have such a reactionary accent that this sensitivity is justified. But, as one of the co-authors (Le Grand) of the cited book on the 'future' of the Welfare State (Glennerster *et al.*, 1983) very correctly confirmed in the conclusion of his analyses of the disillusions of the system:

> nothing implies...that the welfare state should be dismantled and its key institutions handed back to private enterprise. There are excellent reasons for maintaining state ownership and control of health services, institutions of higher education, council houses and public transport...But the pre-servation of state *control* does not necessarily imply the preservation of existing systems of state *subsidy*. It is perfectly feasible to have one without the other. The state does not have to provide its services free or at subsidised prices. What is being argued here, essentially, is that redistribu-tion policy should concern itself less with subsidising services and more with 'subsidising' the *poor*.
>
> > (Le Grand, 1983; see also his interesting book on *The Strategy of Equality*: 1982).

The best way to control the efficiency and effectiveness of the public services is that of control and steering of its performances in every direction. But it is difficult to apply appropriate methods of measuring and evaluating such performances if they are not analyzed, defined and justified in a clear system of objectives related to a clear analysis of the best and desired way to achieve them, and to a linked system of means or resources necessary to achieve them. All that is called *strategic planning*.

To the meaning and usefulness of strategic planning we will return in Part II. On the methods of strategic planning, however, we will only mention here (because it is outside the aim of this book) that there is abundant technical comment and didactic literature which has been developed in the meantime.[21]

At this point it is opportune to conclude with three crucial aspects in the application of strategic planning in the public sector:

1. That any performance evaluation and measurements cannot but be based (in order not to be false) on the systematic application of strategic planning methods and procedures.
2. This systematic application includes its extension to the whole system of public sector agencies in the aim to set in consistency and coordination the efficiency and effectiveness of each of the multiple objectives within the governments involved.
3. Strategic planning (in order not to be fallacious) must take account, in a systemic and coordinated vision, of the objectives and of the available resources, on the scale of the entire societal organization of reference: including in this way the for-profit and non-profit private sector.

3.3 Disaffection and Dislike

The third set of obstacles is, apparently, an obvious variant of the second. The lack of efficiency and effectiveness produces dislike on the part of the user. But maybe there are some psychological factors which lead users to develop a kind of disaffection or rejection towards the free public services independently of the efficiency of the service provided.

Above a certain level of material satisfaction of basic needs it is possible that non-oriented consumers prefer more 'personalized' social services. This phenomenon, which occurs once a minimum level of tangible needs has been satisfied, is spreading throughout ever wider strata of the user population.

Even in the public tertiary sector these 'positional goods', for which a type of underlying economic theory has been outlined by Fred Hirsch, are gradually spreading through the system. This is giving an increasingly paradoxical (or perhaps not) result: the more the government seeks to expand and extend its action in order to fulfil social needs, the less these needs are subjectively satisfied.[22]

4 CONCLUDING REMARKS: TOWARDS A REFORM OF THE WELFARE STATE

An initial conclusion for this chapter is that the public sector in many aspects would be:

- the sector that presents the best requisites for satisfying the new social demand for non-material goods;
- the sector which, in the first phase already recorded, of the overall demand for non-material consumption, has actively carried out the role of almost the only subject (or entrepreneur) for the supply of such consumption;

Yet despite this, the public sector – for the reasons mentioned above – *is no longer able to extend this role further.*

If we then unify the conclusion of this chapter with the deductions made in Chapters 4, 5 and 6 (concerning the structural changes of the contemporary economy) we should be led to conclude that *neither of the two traditional sectors*:

- the *free enterprise sector* operating 'in the market' and 'for profit' (whose rules of behaviour are enshrined in classical political economy, and which is essentially a capitalist enterprise theory), on the one hand;

– and that of the *state* or *public institutions sector* operating 'outside the market' (whose rules of behaviour are codified in 'public economics' which has attempted to define an area of collective or public utility), on the other, has proved capable – for the reasons given – each sector for itself and in its own sphere of action, of producing the goods and services for which the stronger consumer demand is now emerging.

The general effect of this *incapacity* of the two traditional sectors of the economy – that of free enterprise and the public sector – to satisfy the real potential demand of the consumers, has been, first of all, to *slow up* the current expansion of these new emerging forms of 'consumption' and the relative production activities.

This has had, in turn, a deleterious impact on employment. In fact, until now manpower savings have been made on an ever-increasing scale in the sectors producing tangible goods (agriculture and manufacturing industry) as well as in the services lending themselves to quantitative automation (banking, communications, etc.). But today, these manpower savings – which used to be offset by job creation in the sectors producing new tangible goods or public services – are insufficiently offset by new job-creation in these two traditional sectors, whose employment potential has to all intents and purposes reached a ceiling.

As far as the level of possibilities of work in traditional sectors is concerned, the character of the evolution of the labour market was pointed out, long before the arrival of the crisis in the 1970s, by authors of the 'structuralist theories' of labour markets.[23] Evidently the structuralists' theses on the labour market (to which I am happy to have contributed in the 1950s[24]) found confirmation and thus credit among the conventional economists only after the crisis in the 1970s.[25]

Naturally, we consider that this is a general trend which does not apply to every case and which should be seen in relative rather than absolute terms. In individual instances and in absolute terms, job-creation is still taking place in the free enterprise and government sectors, but it must be stressed that this is no longer the *decisive* factor in offsetting the manpower savings which have resulted, and will continue to result, from technological progress in the goods-producing sectors.

As we have tried to explain in Chapter 6, the employment crisis which has afflicted the advanced economies for some time now, seems to be due *in essence* to this lack of a matching between labour supply and the new demand for consumption (and the consequent labour demand).

The crisis has become *chronic*, in as much as it has – despite some ups and downs – lasted for decades, and only slightly been compensated by the growth of the public sector, which has sometimes been excessive in comparison to the real size of demand and the connected needs for efficiency; but it has always been rendered acute again by the continuous development of work-saving advanced technology in capitalist enterprise.

It is a *structural* crisis because it has been forced by transformations in the *demand and employment structure*, despite the fact that such transformations are, for institutional reasons and reasons of habit, *slow to take place*, and slower than a rational and operational vision of social policy is prepared to accept.

The new social demand tends to put pressure on the social state in order to obtain the services it wants, without realizing – or only occasionally and case by case – the *impossibility* and *incapacity* of the same to satisfy it, at the size in which it manifests itself.

But even in the cases when this social demand would be prepared to turn to the 'market', it does not find a suitable supply of services, both because of the limited 'profitability' of the operations and the de-motivation of the traditional business man,[26] to which we have already referred, and to which we will return in section 5 of Chapter 10.

The logical conclusion to be drawn from this inability – on the part of 'capitalist' enterprises – to satisfy the new demand on the market operational level, and – on the part of public administration – on the level of the (social) state's operationality, is that – albeit with a delay – the new demand will be satisfied by a new form of production, which, for semantic simplicity, we can call, for the moment, neither 'capitalist' or 'etatist'.

What is the answer therefore? The new needs cannot be ignored.

We will find – as is happening already on a large scale – many 'deviations': for example, towards *extreme consumption*, stimulated by the tenacious supply of the capitalist enterprise, which attempts, with technological gadgets applied to final consumption, to maintain its market shares in the composition of overall household consumption.

But this cannot last indefinitely. Immaterial consumption, the symbol (according to a cliché, which is perhaps too clichéd) of an improvement in the *quality of life*, is being strongly re-proposed in contemporary society in response to growing and spreading 'technicalization'. Thus a new type of enterprise (or organization, or institution) cannot but arise which is neither *state, public* or even *'capitalist'* (or commercial).[27]

Part II
Critical Analysis of the Management Problems of the Change

10 Beyond the Welfare State

1 'WELFARE STATE' AND 'WELFARE SOCIETY'

The habit of distinguishing the expression *'Welfare State'* from that of *'Welfare Society'* is becoming widespread.[1] This distinction is called into play above all by those who wish to imply the idea or express the desire for an *overcoming* in some way of a certain 'crisis' in the 'Welfare State' – that based exclusively on the (redistributive) action of the state; in order to pass to a *'welfare society'*, i.e. to that welfare founded on a *more functional and fair society structure*: more 'integrated', as we argued in the Introduction, and therefore more politically and economically 'democratic'.[2]

One cannot help but notice how the relationship between the two expressions, like that between the 'phases' of development of contemporary society (which could in fact be designated with the two terms), is of a *dialectic* nature: having introduced the Welfare State (as a system of policies and state institutions able to guarantee the well-being of the poorer strata of society), the contrasting idea of a 'welfare society' is proposed, i.e. that which creates the same well-being but without the action and interaction of the state, in as far as the society itself will be more balanced. The second concept that is in antithesis to the first needs the first in order to define itself and develop, in a probably new synthetic model of society.

From this point of view, then, the expression 'welfare society' could be considered not only *integrative* and historically *complementary* to that of the 'Welfare State' but it would become even *antinomic* to the latter: for the 'welfare society' to exist it is necessary that first the Welfare State in one way or another is 'destroyed'; that state that until now has assumed the task of generalizing well-being only through an ever-increasing *redistributive* function and/or the supply of productive functions of (divisible and indivisible; individual and collective) well-being.

1.1 A 'Logical' Analysis of the Welfare State

There is in effect a logic that underpins the concept and practice of the Welfare State (and the *étatisme* that is naturally connected to it), which deserves a brief digression.

The Welfare State is born essentially from a logic and intention to *compensate* for the *negative* effects of development.

177

According to such a logic, in all fields (from unemployment to income and from knowledge to territory) development, by its existence, creates disequilibria; some go so far as to state that this development is nourished (that is, 'determined') by the imbalance and disequalities.[3] For 'political' (or 'social' or 'humanitarian', etc.) reasons the damage created by development (in terms of unemployment, social marginalization, regional or urban degradation, etc.) must be 'compensated' for with interventions on the part of the community (state), so as not disturb the 'free' occurrence of activities that in competition ensure development.

In the presence therefore of a sort of 'natural selection' or 'social Darwinism' that would govern the development of society, like that of nature, the (welfare) state assumes the role of 'guardian', only not just of the 'public order' (as was said of the old Liberal state) but also of a certain 'social order', with the protection of those excluded so that they do not create dangerous upsets for the existing order.

In this logic, the Welfare State would need inequality in order to justify *intervention*. In a society in which equality is strong we will need less state than would be needed in a society in which inequality is strong.[4]

In the welfare society, on the other hand, a *society of equals* (although hopefully *different*) would be sought. In this logic, society would arrive at such a point of 'affluence' that it would not have to 'redistribute', *by means of the state*, but simply 'distribute' within itself, perhaps even through temporary and localized conflicts and disequilibria, but finding in itself (and not in the leviathan state) the mechanisms of contraposition and compensation. This passage, this change, could be summed up thus: from (state) 'redistribution' to (societal) 'distribution'.

In this case the logic of the Welfare State would be substantially abandoned. In comparison to the *old* mechanisms of capitalism, that are in themselves 'accumulative', polarizing, and 'unbalancing', there would now be the installation and recognition of *new* mechanisms that have in themselves (overcoming the motivation of capitalistic profit) potential for *diffusion, decentralization, self-management*, and *equilibrium* (or '*neo-equilibrium*').

1.2 On Equilibrium, Disequilibrium, 'Market' and the Organizational Society

The word *equilibrium* is loaded with values; and attempts to render it 'aseptic', neutral with respect to values, have been in vain.[5]

The economic theory of the market mechanisms[6] assumes the balancing potentiality of individual transactions, without any state intervention;[7] and even against this state intervention (the so-called vendetta of violated nature), if it appears as an instrument of vested interests or simply of 'protection' of the most damaged (protection understood as the ultimate compensation for damages, and at any rate *not* to be avoided).

In the 'real' world however it has been realized that inter-individual relationships are conditioned by vested interests that are the rule rather than the exception. And that the 'market' mechanisms, far from resembling the theoretical ones, are governed by institutional interventions that ensure rather than a balancing potentiality, an unbalancing one, by their very nature; even those – as mentioned – of the (welfare) state, that whilst aiming at a 're-equilibrium' justify their existence only with the presence of an accepted permanent imbalance in social development.

The search for 'equilibrating' potentialities must therefore be aimed towards the identification and introduction of new institutional mechanisms, that are not the mere re-equilibrating intervention of the state, and do not, on the other hand, depend on the false (nonexistent) 'spontaneity' of the market and the 'invisible hand'. The new equilibrium, certainly, resembles the general equilibrium of the theory, with the difference that it no longer depends on the automatism of nonexistent (or at least not applied) principles of inter-individual behaviour, but rather on *organization*; it may be born as well, perhaps, from conflict, but it is concluded in an unintentional 'composition' (i.e. a contract); and it is therefore the result not of the 'invisible hand', but rather of a very visible hand.

This new equilibrium, in fact, and the ordered development that would correspond to it, would not be that which is realized *ex post*, by means of inevitable adjustments and compensations (as happens prevalently in the experiences of the Welfare State), but rather *ex ante*, by means of an efficient planning process and prior concertation (by plan negotiation).

2 MANAGING THE 'CRISIS' OF THE WELFARE STATE

Going on to revaluating rapidly, in the light of the above considerations, the factors of what has been defined as the 'crisis of the Welfare State' (in Chapter 9), we find the same elements which characterize its logic and nature (in the sense mentioned above).

The Welfare State crisis has been exposed as: (a) *a 'fiscal' crisis*; (b) *a crisis of efficiency*; and (c) *a crisis of affection*.

But, leaving aside the latter motives (which if well exploited could help the implantation of alternative policies oriented to give adequate answers to the first two mentioned motives of crisis) we would find that these two basic causes of 'crisis' are created by the Welfare State precisely because it is constructed on an old liberal logic of 'compensation' and transfers.[8]

For instance, it is on the basis of this logic that many public services continue to be *free of charge* (i.e. financed by fiscal transfer) without distinction, to everybody, when with a better policy of income transfer for the extremely needy (and, therefore, quite contained in size) they could be paid for by the other users, without great inequalities, but with considerable economy. A great deal of waste (which strongly characterizes sectors such as health and education) would be avoided, as well as a management which leads to parasitism and 'bureaucratization' (above all of public administration and in the para-governmental entities).

And it is on the 'basis of this same logic that the area of economically 'protected' subjects is becoming so widespread: the unemployed, the young, housewives, early retirees (whether with a 'golden handshake', or a miserable pension), the more or less permanently handicapped, those on unemployment pay, those employed in 'subsidized' firms (more or less public) kept alive by unjustified investment. There results a tendential decrease in the active population, and its concentration in increasingly reduced and rare portions of qualified workers who are 'highly-engaged' and 'highly-in-demand'. And it is from here that moon-lighting practices and social marginalization, or rather social 'segregation', are born.

This segregation (which we have spoken of in Chapter 1 and from which our analysis was started), in fact, is not only that of the non-workers, but also, and in particular, of those who work who are excluded from the benefit of 'free-time'. The non-workers, for better or worse, and rather better than worse, eat, dress, use public transport, enjoy themselves. These non-workers (who it would be difficult to call unemployed) constitute – in the families on which they rely – the most intense units of consumption, certainly more intense than those in the same families who work, and do not have any time to spend money or to enjoy themselves. Amongst these non-workers, there is an ever greater proportion of those who can afford, in one way or another, to *refuse* work, if it is not exactly up to their social aspirations; an ever greater proportion survive, in a relatively comfortable way (albeit some with a show of parsimony and austerity), at the expense of a family income or national income.

In fact, there is the widespread idea that with an appropriate 'reorganization' of the employment market and employment policy (programming, training, management of working hours, etc.) *work time could be equally redistributed*, as well as the benefits of the free-time which today's productivity and technology allow (but obviously not to all).

Undoubtedly, there is something that is not working in the known application of the Welfare State. We might attribute these dysfunctions to an excess of protective intervention or – as some prefer, and I would number myself amongst these – to the lack of a consequential development of some protective logic in order to go *'beyond' the welfare state*, towards a *'new'* way of producing and consuming, not strictly needing (or at least not so much) a redistributing state.

But there is undoubtedly something to be reviewed in the Welfare State: and the dispute as to whether it should be called a *crisis* or not seems frankly pointless to us.

In fact there is some sense in examining theWelfare State from the point of view of its complete implementation, and not exaggerating, as is often the case, the critical aspects.[9]

But it would be much more sensible to develop an analysis of its critical aspects from the viewpoint of a *profound change in its logic*: that connected with a concept of 'compensation' and 'redistribution', which is still a prevailing logic in Welfare State experience. It is to the difficulty in abandoning this logic that, in fact, the difficulties or 'crises' recorded today are connected. It is a logic which, despite its apparent reformist pragmatism, is showing today its true lack of substance, in as much as it is unable to guarantee the total establishment of the Welfare State, and a balanced compatibility between demand for services and available resources.[10]

This has been, all things considered, the limit of the experience of the 'socio-democratic' type (but 'liberal-democratic' as well[11]) in the so-called Western democracies, in particular European ones; but such a limit is today felt much more in the same European Social-Democratic circles, in which discussion and thought about a new model of society and on the feasibility of new institutions of a 'post-capitalist' type are flourishing.

In short, there is an ever stronger and ever more widespread need for further research into *what ways and means* could guarantee the survival of what good has been achieved by the Welfare State, and under *which conditions* it could be transformed into a *'Welfare Society'*, in which well-being is no longer the effect of state distribution, but is intrinsically 'organic' to the producing and distributing process of the fruits of social activity.[12] And without mincing words, by what means can it be transformed into a more 'socialist' society (in a society in which social and inter-individual inequalities are reduced to their historic minimum, if not completely abolished).

3 THE APPROPRIATE REORGANIZATION OF THE WELFARE STATE: SOCIETAL PLANNING

If the two crisis points of the Welfare State can be summarized as above, the answers seem somewhat obligatory. These crises can be overcome with the introduction of new forms of 'organization' and management, which allow:

(a) the reduction of the state's role of 'transferring' income (either in financial form or in the form of services) from the productive sectors (mainly primary and secondary) in which real productive capacity grows quantitatively and at a considerable rhythm thanks to constant technical progress, to the productive sectors (mainly tertiary) in which capacity grows only very slowly or not at all, despite the objective expansion of individual and social needs precisely in these sectors;

(b) the transfer of employment, not only from the sectors mentioned above with a high productivity rate to those whose growth rate is low, or nil, but also from those units *conventionally employed 'full-time'* to those *unemployed units* (units ever on the increase for structural reasons); and this by way of a generalized reduction of the 'individual' (conventional) length of the working-day; not only therefore according to the slogan 'working less in order that all work', but also, overall, 'all working in order to work less'.[13]

But the new forms of organization and management are those which allow the two following changes:

- 'non-state' transfer of income from the moment of production to the moment of consumption;
- 'labour sharing'.

In effect, it is not possible to realize such changes through the 'market', given the considerable institutional and social viscosity which have blocked the price system, and because of that process referred to by many economists as 'market failure'. In fact, those new forms of organization and management of the Welfare State have a name: *societal planning*.[14]

This planning is no more than a simulation, in a pencil and paper exercise, of the market, by means of a predetermined *collective preference function*; this can come from national democratic institutions, but also from various ways and degrees of social concert, *ex ante*, between social forces. It is probable that in the planning process, any hope of achieving balance depends ultimately on the willingness and capability of social forces to 'contain themselves' within the bounds of feasibility displayed by possible scenarios and by the results of the negotiations and contracts on which they will freely agree. But the same *new negotiation mechanism*, of bargaining *on* the plan, cannot be achieved unless – and the government's role in this is crucial – the same planning process is also carried out in its preparation and management phases.[15]

That planning – applied seriously – is an essential condition for moving beyond the Welfare State in the sense already described, is clearly understood by all those who first started talking of a Welfare State 'crisis' and of the need to go 'beyond' the Welfare State itself. For example, Gunnar Myrdal, in his book *Beyond the Welfare State, or Economic Planning in the Welfare State and its International Implications* (which was published in 1960, but includes also earlier works), clearly criticized both the 'nationalism' of the Welfare State, and its *lack of development* in terms of *comprehensive planning;* and it was these two directions that he thought it necessary, essential, to 'go beyond'.

On the second direction, the one which is here of greater interest, some of his simple, but profound, assertions deserve to be mentioned:

> Indeed, this planning *becomes pressing* as the edifice of the *Welfare State* rises. . . .
>
> It is, for instance, remarkable that the social security schemes, which are becoming increasingly expensive, were initially supported only by arguments of social justice and welfare for specific groups of people in need; . . .
>
> . . . As considerations of *these wider effects and interrelations* gradually come to the fore in public discussion, the explanation is mainly that these policy measures have by now become so numerous and important, and that they redirect the distribution of such a very large portion of the national product, that they *simply must be coordinated* with one another, and with the development of the entire national economy. Thus we arrive at planning in the modern sense. (Myrdal, 1960, p. 47; our italics)

And a moment before, Myrdal had also stated:

> as public and private intervention became more frequent and more far-reaching and closely related to the other constituents of this mighty process of social change, so there arose situations of growing complexity, contradiction and confusion. With ever greater impact, the need for a rationalising coordination of them all was pressed upon the state as the central organ for the public will.
>
> Coordination leads to planning or, rather, it *is* planning, as this term has come to be understood in the Western world.
>
> Coordination of measures of intervention implies a reconsideration of them all from the point of view of how they combine to serve the development goals of the entire national community, as these goals become determined by the political process that provides the basis for power. The need for this coordination arose because the individual acts of intervention, the total volume of which was growing, had not been considered in this way when they were initiated originally. (ibid., pp. 45–6)

We have quoted Myrdal because he is a writer who, by nationality and political leaning, can be considered to be an 'exponent' of the best experience of the Welfare State; and who has for more than thirty years directed and recommended 'going beyond' the Welfare State, in the right direction.

11 Beyond Capitalism?

1 SOCIAL DEMOCRACY, THE POLITICAL LEFT IN GENERAL, AND PLANNING

It is curious that during the most recent debates for or against the Welfare State,[1] about the nature of its 'crisis' and the recipes to revitalize or transform it, nobody remembered Myrdal's prophecy (recalled at the end of the preceding chapter) and nobody – remembering Myrdal or not – mentioned his recipe for avoiding that crisis: the progress of societal planning, as a modern tool of public and political management.

Such a planning, in fact, not only was not considered (as Myrdal did, and with him dozens of ingenious economists, including Ragnar Frisch, Jan Tinbergen, Wassily Leontief, Richard Stone, Leif Johansen, Karl Fox) as the only serious exit from the 'crisis' of the Welfare State; it is also completely absent, even as a possibility, from the minds of those broaching the theme,[2] almost as if it were an obsolete and outdated solution.[3]

And it is even more remarkable that now the lack of any acknowledgement of the need for planning is even more manifest among political, social and intellectual circles who seem the 'official' supporters of the Welfare State (social democracrts, trade unions, the 'left' in general), than among the traditional conservative Right supporting laissez-faire and free trade.[4]

All this indicates that the traditional Left prefers a potentially 'unlimited' Welfare State, but one potentially also on the edge of bankruptcy, rather than a Welfare State which 'can keep its accounts' with resources (via planning), and assumes responsibility for alternative choices in the social consumption it provides, which would lead it to a lasting, healthy and 'sustainable' management. Thus, they demonstrate faith in 'political laissez-faire', in which the adjustment of resources and the decisions on limits takes place on the basis of the principle of laissez-faire and power clashes, more than do conservative forces, traditionally supporters of laissez-faire.

On the other hand, the whole debate about the Welfare State in recent years has still the old, obsolete and boring flavour of '*déjà vu*', and seems to be stuck in the antiquated quarrel on 'yes or no' to state interventionism, and – within the Left – between reformers and radicals (or 'maximalists'), without being able to grasp the signs of a management reform of the state (which is called *strategic planning*), that goes well beyond the narrow terms of that age-old dispute. What is most disappointing is that the academic circles and literature (which unfortunately has lost in average quality in

184

parallel with its quantitative growth) tend to be the spokesmen – in a cultured version – of these quarrels, rather than refining methods and techniques of public management, able to really renew the quality of public choice.

Planning continues to be seen as a 'technocratic' tool of the central power against the freedom of choice of individuals and groups. Coming together with the recent crisis of the Soviet system, where economic planning seemed nominally to dominate (yet what kind of planning was it really?), it is not surprising that it became a politically 'dirty word', and that thus the politicians, but unfortunately also the academics more or less 'susceptible' to political fashions (or worse, those that introduced political fashions into the universities), carefully avoid uttering it, even with reference to its true and authentic concepts.

Yet it is impossible to escape the essence of things: and whether given any other name,[5] planning must be the line of advance of public management, from the level of single public agencies to the level of coordination among them, up to the level of coordination between the public agencies and the agencies of the private and/or public realm, on the national and the (today more and more pervasive) international level.

I will discuss later in this chapter the increasingly indispensable relations between the management of the Welfare State and planning policy, and in Chapter 13, summarizing, more generally about the role of planning policy in the historical renewal of the methods of political and economic management. I would like to emphasize here that most debates in political science, still linked to obsolete frameworks, seem to me a sign of the antiquity of the current debate, compared to a real 'frontier' approach to the topic. For example, the debate on the 'alternatives to capitalism'.

2 'ALTERNATIVES' TO CAPITALISM? A FALSE PROBLEM

The debate on the alternatives to capitalism recalls very wide and rich debates from the nineteenth century to ours. From utopian thinking to socialist, in all its variants, from all visions of a 'intermediate' society, liberal-democratic, liberal-socialist, corporative (fascist or catholic) itself in many versions, and so on, forever (I would say since its birth and its 'modelling', undertaken more by its adversaries that by its supporters) *alternatives* to capitalism have been sought.

Yet the very concept of an 'alternative' smells musty. It shows traces of an 'ideological' approach, long since rejected in words, yet hardly abandoned in deeds. It seems almost to have the force of a paradigm. And if the paradigm is not transformed, we will hardly avoid false problems today.

And yet today, and most intensely during the last decade, in the face of the crisis of communism and of the so-called 'real socialism' countries, the tendency to waste time on the question of whether there are serious 'alternatives' to capitalism is still very widespread.[6]

But by approaching the problem in this way, one is very far from the critical spirit which pervaded the present essay, which is inspired by what in earlier times (not very precisely) would have been called 'historicism'. Capitalism, and the 'market' as well, do not, and cannot, have any 'alternative', just as any other phenomenon in the history of humanity cannot. Nobody would try to discuss alternatives to Feudalism, to the Renaissance, to Enlightenment, to Nationalism, and so on. What is disputable is the property of the term, which for some has a wider and for others a narrower meaning; thus also 'capitalism' and the 'market' have an infinite number of meanings, and hardly generate alternatives, if not in the course of events.

When and where can capitalism be said to be really born?[7]And can it be said when it really died or will die? All is conventional. And we owe the most refined visions of this to the producers of interpretative frameworks, rather than to the historians, who tend to disintegrate, and to scatter any conceptual unification (and thus periodization) of this kind.

The ground is even more dangerous when these concepts are set against their alleged opposites, such as Capitalism vs. Socialism Central Planning vs. the Market, or further derivations such as Capitalism vs. Central Planning, and the Market vs. Socialism.

Yet history – the recent as well as the less recent – should have taught us how fallacious these oppositions are; and on the contrary, how a wide and diffused mix of character has for a long time predominated in the evolution of contemporary industrial societies, to the point that it stimulated many authors to present 'transversal' interpretations, as classification of 'economic systems'. For example, Rostow's interpretation (already considered in Chapter 2), leaving aside the 'social-economic systems', laid down the periodization and the reading of the different 'economies' by attributing to them a 'stage of development'. Kerr, Dunlop, Harbison and Myers (1960) proposed and applied *industrialization* as a key to the interpretation of the 'social-economic systems' (which was considered in Chapter 2 as well).

Instead of transversal interpretations such as those just recalled, synthesizing interpretations have been suggested: for example those of the 'mixed economies' (in the Western world) or of 'market socialism' (in the socialist world). These are interpretations and readings which showed themselves to be strongly anchored also to the persisting will to start from schematisms of functioning (possibly called 'economic systems', which on both sides have been made obsolete by the development of things).

In sum, the very approach 'alternatives to capitalism' sounds mistaken. The real problem is to grasp (beyond the oppositions) some common trends which emerge in the different societies, still more or less national, and more or less belonging to historical 'blocks' (themselves decaying), such as:

capitalist countries, with marked differences among the US, Europe and Japan; former Communist countries, with marked differences between more or less advanced levels of privatization; developing countries, with marked differences between the newly industrialized countries and the others.

The real problem – beyond the eternal comparative analyses that by nature tend always to emphasize more the historically insignificant (and thus useless) differences rather than the growing historically significant (and thus useful) similarities – is to be able to grasp among these similarities those that mark a force that I would call 'historically hegemonic', which can enable us to understand, and thus to govern, the future.

3 PLANNING AS AN ESSENTIAL CONDITION FOR THE PASSAGE TO A 'WELFARE SOCIETY'

Coming back to the relation between the Welfare State crisis and societal planning, we cannot ignore the widespread justification, amongst certain circles of the militant Left, for the non- conception of a Welfare State which would introduce methods of negotiated planning, which is that it would nevertheless be 'capitalist' planning and a capitalist 'Welfare State'.[8] There is undoubtedly some truth in this theory, which we developed here in Chapter 9, section 1.1, when we reflected on the origin and development of the Welfare State as an operation for 'compensation', and to a certain extent, safeguarding of the harm which the development of free market forces tends inevitably to produce.

But the transition from a 'planned society' to a 'planning society'[9] will not take place unless processes and procedures are introduced and practised which get the social and political subjects – whether rulers or non-rulers – used to governing their choices better and to achieve this by adopting the method of 'planning by learning', which is very bound up with 'learning by planning', and which is more than just a mere play on words.

3.1 On the So-Called 'Failures' of Planning

It is true that between the time that Myrdal thought that progress should be made 'beyond the Welfare State' by means of planning, and today, there has been a disappointing experience in almost all European countries.

But how can this experience be taken seriously? It is widely judged to have been a failure, and has been variously interpreted. Many quite rightly consider it fairly insignificant, precisely because it was so short-lived, inconsistent, and rapidly achieved that it hardly can be considered a true 'experience', historically effective, but only an attempt to introduce, more orally than by action, a method of government which did not find a serious method of implementation.

Politicians and political scientists have long squabbled over the causes of this, but the fact remains that it is not possible to seriously assert that something 'failed' if it never existed.[10]

Also, from the technical point of view, the methods of governments (and the related discussions) have drawn more from the national traditional baggage of 'economic policy', with its macro-economic models and its aggregated econometric models as tools, than from more recent planning technology, whose 'culture' is hard to introduce. A sign of this is the fact that many technological developments, achieved on a scientific basis, especially in some departments of planning offices in some European countries, but also in university research programmes, are still being ignored even in the official economic culture milieu of some countries.[11]

We will not go too far into the question of the modest significance of European economic planning experiences between 1960 and 1970.[12] But it is important to recognize that it is perhaps through these and their 'failure' that the debate on the solutions to be given to the problems of the *Welfare State* tend modestly to evade the only real way of providing an adequate solution to the need to distribute the benefits of technical progress and productivity in terms of income and reduced employment, without making recourse to an increase in the financial role of the state: namely through a *systematic planning process*.[13]

Such evasion becomes more significant when attention is turned to the numerous aspects of perverse malfunctioning of the Welfare State, and when it is suggested that its defeat can be achieved by a '*de-étatization*', for which it will be necessary to measure costs and benefits: a measurement, however, which is impossible without the *value parameters* provided by a national planning procedure.[14]

Furthermore, on the subject of moving on from a 'welfare state' to a 'welfare society', the fact that no mention is made of the fundamental need for planning, is due to the persistence of an archaic planning concept, understood as being an instrument of state 'authority', or rather of a central power, which stifles the initiative and the self-government of groups and the 'market'.

Nor is it to be excluded that the silence surrounding the need to plan, results from the discouraging evidence (this indeed historically effective and significant) given by the economies of Eastern European Communist countries, where planning was very much at home; though many writers have always – with admittedly excessive simplification – distinguished 'Western' planning (known as 'indicative', especially in France and Great Britain, whereas in Italy the term 'programming' was coined in order to ensure a good distinction) from the 'authoritarian' one of 'collectivist' or 'centrally planned' countries.[15]

In the ephemeral search for 'success', even words have a part to play; and woebetide all those who would use words which recall failures. But, despite the semantics of the political market, nothing changes: and the expected passage from Welfare State to Welfare Society is unattainable without an appropriate planning (on the basis of which are constructed the scenarios capable of making it possible and operational).

Certainly, the planning to which we refer is not the archaic mechanism of decision-making and centralized command, which the whole economic system must obey, albeit with a certain degree of freedom within its own structures. Planning, in the *modern* sense, is an instrument for the analysis of consistency and for coordination (see the phrase quoted from Myrdal) between multiple decisions, within one public agency or more, with the aim of *orienting* and *conditioning* (with the most varied direct or indirect means) towards situations and scenarios deliberated by the people concerned, scenarios which have been judged to be technically feasible and the most politically preferable by the appropriate decision-makers involved.[16]

The fact that there still persists, for various reasons (some of which are also pretexts), an archaic conception of planning does not say anything against the need to recognize its indispensability in overcoming the crisis of the Welfare State (even if something could be said about the credibility and information of those who still today cultivate such an archaic conception).

3.2 The Fundamental 'Operations' of Planning: Income and Labour Mobility Planning

If we recognize in a more advanced 'comprehensive management' of social and economic progress and in a more conscious social control in accordance with political preferences (in other words, in a more forceful societae planning), the condition for overcoming the crisis of the Welfare State, them the operational pattern for a passage from a Welfare State to a 'Welfare Society' must yet be outlined.

The discussion focuses – as has been said – on the determination of *how* (to what extent, and how it is to be formulated) to release a certain, qualified, redistribution of real benefits of increased productivity – to be hypothesized and/or programmed – in the economic system considered in its single components and sectors of production.

Such redistribution of real benefits will be carried out, as is known, by way of the purchasing power of the (monetary) incomes in different social sectors: and it is therefore to a *'real income' policy*, or better still, a *'planning' policy* for these sectors that we will refer here, when we mention (planned) 'social policy' of such redistribution.

It is essential therefore to arrive at such *income planning*[17] with the obvious 'agreement' of the social parties, in a process which I have elsewhere called 'planning collective bargaining' (by analogy with that which would substitute and integrate at the same time, i.e. 'market collective bargaining', practised more widely and more uselessly today).[18] Such income planning should contribute to the *guidelines* for all intervention, public and private, or only public, when aimed at correcting the effects of private intervention.[19]

From the 'jungle' of remunerations and incomes, a 'cultivated' system of these should be reached, even if only 'indicatively', so as to give flexibility to the system and by virtue of concerted assessment of the social and economic value of the different job positions (thus eliminating circumstantial and irrational privilege). Workers' unions – especially in their unitary and confederate forms – should contribute decisively and deliberately to the preparation of such an 'income planning'.

The other *pivot* on which the operational pattern of planning should turn in order to pass from Welfare State to *Welfare Society*, should be – as already mentioned – the redistribution of employment or work opportunities. Such redistribution could be carried out, as is known, through the redistribution of working hours amongst the various posts and between the different components of the active population, taking account of age, sex and geographical area for the different types of work.

Thus, the comprehensive sum of production needs – given technological and organizational conditions, hypothesizable and/or programmable – provides an amount of work and employment opportunities which can be distributed evenly, also so as to more equally distribute the complementary opportunity for leisure recreation or culture and for free time in general.

And it is to a policy, or better to a *'programme for redistributing employment'*, with all its connected implications in terms of sociological adjustment, of training, or professional retraining, etc., that we refer to when we talk of 'social policy' (planning) of such redistribution.

In fact, also in this case – as for income planning – *planning-collective bargaining* with the unions is fundamental in obtaining their cooperation, perhaps even their joint management, for the necessary employment mobility that such a programme inevitably involves, even if by guaranteeing that only this plan would lead to full employment.

The recurrent proposed 'Employment Agency'[20] would design the operative instrument for an employment redistribution programme; to be adopted only in the presence of, and through compatibility with, a comprehensive planning process, to thus avoid the risk of reducing the instrument itself to another organism for the distribution of 'protective' interventions, of the Welfare State type (and therefore susceptible to becoming bogged down in the crisis of efficiency affecting all the institutions of the Welfare State).

3.3 The Plan as a Decision Framework of Reference and as a Process

The plan (necessarily medium or long term: 5–10 years) which is thought to be essential in order to operate the passage from 'Welfare State' to 'Welfare Society' would assure the state's financial redistribution of a few incomes and services to the comprehensive management of a more balanced society, and thus be 'programmed' in advance to do this. Such a plan would therefore be a point of reference for all decision interventions made in the public sector, articulated however in a large number of 'agencies' and 'powers', central and local, general and sectoral, as happens in the complexity of political and institutional regulations which make up modern society.

The plan would obviously have *a preparation (decision-making) stage*, and an *implementation-management stage*.

The preparation (decision-making) stage, although involving all operational sectors in its choices and decisions, is concerned essentially with the role of those agencies representing community authority at the highest level, where *'particular'* interest should find necessary conjunction with the expected *'general interest'*.

Western parliamentary democratic systems, even if imperfect in their constitutional functionality, have not yet encountered, in practice or in political theory, any valid substitutes for them. But, if the *Welfare Society* is to be essentially a 'planning society'[21] (instead of a 'planned society'), and not the haphazard result of encounters/conflicts between interests of unequal weight, it would be necessary for its constitutional system, i.e. the political-parliamentary regime, to include and absorb, or rather express directly, the political planning process in its decisional-preparative stage (leaving the task of implementation and management to other level executives and other public authorities).

This would already be a first constitutional 'reformation' which would not give planning (science) a technical 'role' but would allow it to become *the very means of functioning and deciding of the political-public organism.*[22] While it is true that public planning constitutes an attempt to restore sovereignty to the citizen with respect to economic policies, which are today in the best possible case the result of uncontrollable 'market' mechanisms (which we know however to be controlled by more powerful economic forces), in the same way it would also restore economic sovereignty to those political organisms (Parliament) which today certainly give signs of deterioration, to such an extent as to cause doubts regarding their credibility, as well as their 'democracy'.[23]

Despite this, and despite the stressed importance of a constitutional reform which brings to the principal (elective) public organism the decisional-preparative stage of the plan, a reform which would give back vitality and credibility, and hence prestige, to the sovereignty of Parliament as the effective administrator of the community's interests including their economic ones; despite this, at the decisional-preparative stage of the plan, it should be possible also for agreement with other representative 'non-state' forms of an associative nature, of pre-eminent social importance, such as the unions and consumer organizations, to find a place.

This place for negotiating or extra-state bargaining should be found in even more diversified forms than has hitherto occurred. The state and civil society should find a way to express themselves in the plan, and in its process of conception.

At the same decisional-preparative stage, the planning bodies (which should be situated within and be dependent on the decisional political organs – Parliament) could also – together with the more or less formal negotiation which we have defined as 'extra-statal' – utilize other forms of analysis and evaluation of 'preferences' and of the popular demand, making ample use of modern methods of opinion polling and of 'market analysis'; this, with the scope of 'simulating' and predicting what has until now been considered the 'market': namely, the sanctuary of the consumers' sovereignty and the 'spontaneous' (*ex-post*) revealer and regulator of social preferences. Nothing prevents the consumers' behaviour, or that of the 'users' or that of the 'market', from being consulted beforehand, even in the presence of constraints which are more systematically perceived by the consumer himself: and all this would induce it (consumer, users or market) to make even more 'rational' choices than those made on the market on a case-by-case basis.

However, the Welfare State crisis and the planning that it requires lead to an upheaval of the operative mechanisms of the economy, in order to assure not only the maximum degree of choice to all participants, but even the effectiveness and functionality appropriate to the new motivations and new services and quality of life demands which are emerging (analyzed in Part I of this book).

4 SOCIAL BARGAINING, OR NEGOTIATION, AS A PREMISE FOR PLANNING EFFICIENCY

4.1 The Traditional Planning Operators

The plan, as we have said, has its own implementation-management stage. It is a question of *who* should supply and *how* to supply the goods and the services which the citizens and the community in general need, and which – in the scale of needs expressed (be it even with new methods of planning) – they have *preferred*.

Obviously, the implementation-management stage is, in the plan, intimately *interwoven* with the decisional-preparative stage. One cannot reasonably fix the objectives of *consumption* (and therefore of *production* of service goods) without knowing the operational conditions (constraints) of the production itself: and such operational conditions concern both *material availability* of resources *and* also the ('immaterial') *willingness* of subject-operators to act in the manner considered necessary.

However, as any forecasting and systemic methodology of planning recommends, it is always well to distinguish the two stages in such a way as to resolve, through a clear approach, the two fundamental problems of planning: those which Ragnar Frisch called the *selection problem*, and the *implementation problem*.[24] In the selection problem, the conditions to bear in mind are precisely the '*material*' availability of resources (land, employment, fixed capital, technologies, know-how, infrastructures, etc.). In the implementation problem, the conditions to be taken into account are the '*immaterial*' willingness of the subject-operators, or institutional actors of planning, which is equivalent to the 'how' of economic and social activity.[25]

Although interconnected (and in fact we have defined them as 'stages' of the self-same process) the two problems should not be confused, in a syncretic mess which on the way also wipes away the very 'process'; that process which should be a gradual change from one evaluation to the other (apart from the possibility of feed-back). To this end, the selection problem should be 'resolved', temporarily, independently of the *immaterial* willingness of the operators (even if nobody dares consider it irrelevant, but we agree that it is a determinant factor); and this in order to discover at a later stage (free from the constraints of preconceived ideas) which 'institutional framework' and which operational willingness is in conformity with the chosen objectives. It is at a later stage that it is possible to 'readjust' with efficacy the chosen objectives in the negotiations with the subject-operators, in which it will emerge on which conditions and with which objectives they would be willing to operate.

4.2 The Motivations of the Social Operators

The willingness of the subject-operators (which we have defined as 'immaterial') is the consequence of adequate *motivations*. The search for sufficient and appropriate motivations is an essential chapter of any serious planning.

The motivations of the economic operators have always been at the basis of every behavioural analysis and at the basis of the generalizations of 'economic theory'. The motivations have been so coded: *profit* as the motivation of the entrepreneur, *wage or salary* as the motivation of the worker, the *rate of interest or rent* for the capitalist or property-owner, the *vote* for the politician, etc. It has also been observed that in reality the motivations of each of the subject-operators are more complex than the 'theory' outlines, and this has given place to partial sophistications of the same theory. For each of the operators there have been noted some slight differences of motivation, which, even if not particularly relevant in invalidating the principles of the general theory in themselves, are relevant in highlighting the uselessness of applying those principles to concrete political and planning problems.

During the identification of adequate motivations in the case of planning choices one is so conditioned by the different factual circumstances (social structure and development of the countries or regions in question, institutional and behavioural characteristics of the operators in question, etc.) that it would not be very recommendable to apply theory to the behavioural schema, while it would indeed be advisable to conduct, for each single activity and operation, an *ad hoc survey* and an *ad hoc consultation* on the motivations of the operators.

For this reason, during the planning process, the operators should be identified, studied, polled and invited to participate on a case-by-case basis. The institutional framework can offer a vast range of situations, to which can correspond complex and diversified classes of operators. If we wished to simplify and outline, we should say that in our current Welfare State (and here we refer to those countries with a more advanced state of industrialization), probably exactly because of the affluence reached and because of the economic guarantees acquired, the incidence of the traditional 'economic' motivations (profits, wages levels and so on) is in general becoming weaker. There is, in fact, emerging – as a regulator of the activities of the operators – the incidence of other motivations which, not being yet able to define them all, we will call '*non-economic*' or '*meta-economic*' or simply '*political*', be they expressed in terms of individual preferences or in terms of collective preferences.

This is happening to the motivations of each of the traditional operators: enterprise, workers, and so on, for whom the profits, the wages, etc. are no longer the determining factor which induces them to activity (more or less dictated by the plans). But the new motivations also modify the institutional context or rather the conceptual categories on which traditional operators were previously identified, causing 'new' operational subjects, previously considered irrelevant, to emerge.

For example, the growing importance and diversification of 'public services' makes it clear that in this growing sector of activity, ever more strategic in development planning, and ever more full of new entrepreneurs and new operators, the categories founded on traditional economic motivations are no longer applicable, and, further, the very classification of the activities and of the connected operators must be articulated in a totally new and more functional fashion.

At the same time, the development of the consumers' use of tertiary, recreational and cultural services, has given place to the expansion of new activities performed outside the 'market', but nevertheless *not* 'public', with the formation of new operators whose motivations are still today largely unknown, but which certainly cannot be classed in the categories used up to now.

These changes therefore deserve a more organic reflection.[26]

In any case it is well to conclude that in the plan an articulation of these sectors, old and new, is essential, the more so in view of the complexity of the motivations which animate them, and which are, on the other hand, at the basis of success – at least of the possibilities of implementation and of management – of the plan itself.

Beyond the objectives of consuming (the consumers can also have complex motivations) which pertain to the decisional-preparative stage of the plan, a just (negotiated) equilibrium among the motivations of the operators, in their different and diverging roles, can also represent a fitting witness to that '*Welfare Society*', which today the Welfare State (still founded in one way or the other on the imbalance of those very motivations) seems to be unable to attain.

5 THE CRISIS OF 'ENTREPRENEURSHIP'

Thus, if one wished to examine more closely some of the characteristics of the crisis of the Welfare State, this crisis could be registered – under the profile of the motivations – in the demise of the *entrepreneurial spirit*.

5.1 The Crisis of Entrepreneurship as a Motivational Crisis of the Operators

The fall of entrepreneurship must be attributed to a series of factors, among the most relevant being that of the expansion, provoked by the Welfare State, of public services, which has shifted many socio-economic needs away from the area of *market-oriented activities* over to the area of *non-market-oriented activities*. And therefore profit-oriented enterprises have been replaced by public (or para-public) activities not oriented to profit, for which it has not been possible to substitute other valid motivations for their concrete and efficient operation, other than those of bureaucratic and autocratic social power.

On the other hand, there has been an important shift of activities, and above all of labour-employment, from sectors of production of material goods, to that of 'tertiary' products, i.e. production of services: this in the majority of cases has increased enormously the content of 'professionalism' as well as of 'personalization' present in the performance of work. And this has in general been to the detriment of the motivation of gain. Moreover this has also happened in the primary and secondary sectors, that is, in the production of industrial goods, with a generalized *professionalization of labour*.[27]

These transformations in the structures of consumer-trends, in the technologies of production, and in the quality of work, have given rise to the converging conclusion that vast classes of potential workers (above all in the younger age-groups of workers) are led to an explicit 'refusal of work' if they do not discover a sufficient content of professionalism in it.

And it is in this sense that the crisis of the Welfare State can be seen as a crisis of the traditional motivations.

And the way out of the crisis – if the 'crisis' may thus be labelled – no longer seems possible through the salvaging of old unrepeatable motivations: that of *profit*, for example, whose demise is certainly not for circumstantial reasons but due to the structural evolution of the activity as well as changes of *values*; or that of *gain* if it is no longer sufficient to adequately motivate the work.

It will instead be necessary to regain the motivations on a *new basis*, adequate to the structures and the values in evolution. And above all it will be necessary to assess the appropriate motivations in the various categories of activities and operators, some of which are only now emerging.

If the 'market' sector is in decline, this does not mean that in those areas in which it exists and persists the motivation of gain or of profit should be caused to be absent or mortified; on the contrary it should be recognized and satisfied, to avoid a paralysis of the (planning oriented) activity required.

It would also be an error to try to relaunch or to extend motivation in those sectors in which it is irremediably obsolete, such as that of public services, or in 'new' sectors which have been born in, and prosper under, the hallmarks of different criteria and values.

In the sector of public services and of public administration in general, efficiency – which seems more or less everywhere to have disappeared with the development of the Welfare State – is not given, as is well-known, by a condition of breaking even or of residual 'profit' in the comparison of costs against gains, evaluated at current 'market' prices. It is rather given by the extent of attainment of certain given objectives, compared with the certain means employed and the costs suffered. The regaining of efficiency in this sector, and therefore the regaining of certainty of its *social productivity*, will not be achieved by the introduction of 'privatization' as the criteria of administration, but rather by a programming of the expenditure (as has been said for some time now: a 'Planning Programming Budgeting System'); that is to say, by more appropriate measures of the cost–benefit ratio of alternative spending and by the ratio between expenditure and the result it produces. Only with the introduction on a vast scale of such measures of performances and planning, can the risk, already growing and observed, of 'bureaucratization' or of self-legitimizing administration of public expenditure (independently of its level of centralization or decentralization), be avoided.[28] Such a risk is inevitable from the moment that the public expenditure cannot be replaced by another expenditure made within the logic which belongs to private (profit-oriented) enterprises.

One can say that the more private entrepreneurship enters into a crisis, the more the area of 'public' or non-profit entrepreneurship widens. It is evidently a matter of an enterpreneurship which radically changes its characteristics.

5.2 A New Type of Entrepreneurship: The 'Private Collective'

The fall of entrepreneurship connected with the more recent evolution of the Welfare State has, in fact, roots which cannot be removed by trying to restore motivation of the conceptual categories (profit-making), criteria which derive from a social structure which is in rapid evolution (if not totally superseded).

In fact, it is not a foregone conclusion that the expansion of activity no longer motivated by profit or by gain and not operating in the 'market' (i.e. the activities belonging to the category or institutional sector of 'enterprise'), necessarily means the extension of the public sphere (that of activities which belong to the 'public administration' category or institutional sector) – a sphere whose extension is necessarily founded on state financial transfers, rendered operational by levies on the production of the private sector which imply an inevitable growth of 'étatism' (however 'decentralized' we might care to implement it).

And moreover, on the other hand, it is not even a foregone conclusion that the opportunity and the necessity to reduce the area of public intervention – in order to avoid the waste and the dysfunction of étatism – should necessarily mean a return to the motivation of 'profit' or of gain, in those cases where it is evidently inadequate for the type of activity in question.

For these reasons, the area of a 'third' sector of operation and activity is in fact rapidly spreading,[29] a sector lying between that traditionally defined as 'public' and that traditionally defined as 'private': a sector which relies on its own financial 'autonomy' and, as such, operates as does a private, independent, operator;[30] but whose objectives are *not profit*, but rather the management of collective interests and, as such, operates as a 'collective' operator – if not as a public one.[31]

This operational sector – to which one could give also the name of '*private-collective*'[32] – cannot yet have its own very precise boundaries, legal or functional, also because it is in a phase of great growth and change and has not yet its own consolidated physiognomy. It derives, on the one hand, from areas of '*privatization*' (in some form not yet clear) of the plethoric and inefficient sectors of the (Welfare) State. But it also derives from the growth of tertiary productive activities (often tied to direct consumption, and in particular concerning *new* categories of consumer goods) which do not aim at a profit of enterprise, neither individual nor company, and which therefore do not have 'lucrative ends', but which perform a voluntary *social action in different fields*: from the assistential to the recreational, from that of research to that of religious, political, and cultural solidarity.

In effect, all these areas of new activity – to which we will dedicate more attention in Chapter 12 – are growing enormously in terms of the material resources used and of the hours of work employed; and these are not taken into consideration in the accounting of the national product either in terms of cost or in terms of gain or income. They are in fact producers of individual and social costs and benefits and are not measurable in terms of market values, but rather in terms of artificial and inductive accounting. And obviously no governmental financial levy can be made to bear on this 'income'.

This 'private-collective' sector is naturally self-managed, even if its productive organization can imply hierarchical stratifications and more or less authoritarian managements (the case of religious communities is emblematic in this regard). In general, however, with respect to the processes of 'democratization' and of 'administrative decentralization' in great demand both in public administrations and in profit-making enterprises (especially if large), this 'third' sector does not encounter (because of its nature, that is, because of the nature of the productive processes to which it is bound) the difficulties which are encountered in other sectors from the point of view of efficiency and good organization.

Therefore this 'private-collective' sector is situated between 'étatism' and economy of private profit as an area of operational interventions which are characterized by a large degree of 'socialization' of the means and the ends of production.

The principle which guides it is not the *capital*, but the *association*.

However, it has nothing to do with the forms of association between public ends and private interest which have in the recent past been historically known and which have been 'theorized' by the political scientists as a *'mixed economy'*; and which are always founded on the merging of a public initiative of the general objective and a private 'operational activity' always motivated by profit. A classic example of this marriage is the particularly important Italian experience of partly state owned companies, which – despite public or semi-public capital (and despite the general objectives on which they have been taken over or created) – necessarily obey profit-making objectives on the pain of not being able to operate at all on a competitive market, and which are enterprises of common commercial law.

6 TOWARDS THE INSTITUTIONALIZATION OF THE 'INDEPENDENT' SECTOR

The independent, private-collective, or associative sector also has its historical examples: they are all examples of voluntary associations, as for example those of the foundations with welfare or cultural aims, those of religious associations which in some countries reach a substantial economic power, those of cultural, recreational and sports associations (when these are not business-oriented).

Political associations (parties and movements) and union associations (worker, employer and professional unions, etc.) are also an example of private-collective sectors which have already in the past assumed significant proportions, and which are destined to assume even more significant proportions in the future.

But the most significant historical precedent, and one which has already received some specific institutionalization in its own right in different forms and for a long time in all parts of the developed world, is that of the *cooperative movement*. Obviously the cooperative movement belongs to this sector in those cases where the movement and its enterprises have maintained, in a prevailing and coherent manner, their original 'social' objectives: i.e. where the objective of profit has not also become, even in a cooperative enterprise, the dominating feature, or rather where its operational dimensions have not excluded all forms of real participation by the partners in its management.

A complex array of new emerging factors, and first amongst these the so-called 'crisis' of the mechanisms of the Welfare State (as synthetically recapitulated in the preceding chapters), have created the premises, and in many cases the appearance of a proliferation of associative initiatives of this type, still not functionally defined and less still juridically so: their most indisputable characteristic is their ambiguity and hybridism and their non-applicability with respect to classifications hitherto well known and used.

In order to attempt to move towards a clearer definition of this sector and to avoid functional and institutional confusion, it is certainly worth proceeding towards some sort of 'institutionalization' of it: above all with the scope of distinguishing clearly its manifestations from analogous tendencies towards similar transformations (which in any case present themselves) both in the 'public' sector and in the 'private profit-making' sector.

For example, it has already been said that in the public sector and in its management there is a need for 'democratization' and for 'decentralization' which in certain cases could be – if taken to the extreme consequences of autonomy also in the financial sense (even if to some degree benefiting from subsidy in the same way as the *enterprise* sector and the *household* sector) – the prelude to its transformation in the private-collective sector. But, in the majority of areas, that need only goes as far as suggesting the introduction of forms of more decentralized or more *'participated-in'* management, perhaps even of self-management for certain defined tasks, on the part of both the operators and the users of the service in question.

This, just as the evolution of industrial relations in the private profit-making sector could lead to forms of *'industrial democracy'* of the *'co-management'* type, which would not however undermine the capitalistic nature of the enterprise (even if they would naturally modify its functioning).

In both these latter cases there would not be, properly speaking, a transformation into the 'third sector'.

6.1   The Relationship Between the Operational Sectors

We will begin by reflecting and by formulating proposals concerning the *particular requisites* which must be present before we can talk of an operational 'third sector' (distinguishing it however both from the experiences of democratization and of decentralization of public administration in general, and from the experiences of industrial democracy in the private sector). By thus doing, one should be aware that one will define an area of emerging *'socialization'* in contraposition to *'etatization'* on the one hand (with its more or less accentuated *'nationalizations'*), and, on the other hand, in contraposition to *'privatization'* of market power (which today assumes ever more the forms of corporate collusion or of oligopolistic concentrations, more or less trans-national, as may be the case).

The complexity of modern industrial societies, especially in their 'post-industrial' versions, that is marked by the great technological progress of automation, of information technology and telematics, and therefore by the large development of 'tertiary' consumption, excludes the possibility not only of accepting but also of forecasting the *absolute prevalence* of one sector rather than another. Social pluralism will also be manifested in the plurality of the forms of production, and perhaps, as never in the past, the different 'economic systems', which refer to one or other form (or social formation) of production, will *coexist in the same structure of a developed country.*[33]

Thus the unquestionable 'etatism' – inherent both in the experiences of 'real' communism and in those countries of the Welfare State, and which in different forms (and to different degrees) has coexisted and still coexists today with the market economy – will tend to review its 'hegemony', wherever this has been exercised.

And 'market capitalism' will do likewise, in those cases in which it has been – despite the Welfare State and rather in organic symbiosis with it – substantially 'hegemonic' through its own oligopolistic structures of power, to such a degree as to strongly precondition even the governmental structures themselves.[34]

6.2 The 'Third Sector' and the General Economic System

It can be agreed that the emergence of a 'third sector', in its great indeterminacy, which has been acknowledged (and the same definition of 'third' sector without qualification, bears witness to this), must be ratified in more precise conceptual and institutional terms because of the urgency of an 'ideological' reason: that of moving beyond not only the experiences of the real communist countries, but also those of countries which we could define as 'social capitalist' countries (with the support of the Welfare State).

This is the same reason why in the debates of the Left there is the search for a 'third way' to socialism. But the difference between the search for a third way to socialism and welcoming of the third sector is in the degree of hegemony which one wishes to give to the productive system which would characterize each of the sectors thus defined in themselves.

Each sector symbolizes – so to speak – a productive system.

The public, or state, sector symbolizes the administrative, integral collectivist system (which has been erroneously called 'central planning', bringing with this definition an archaic conception of planning). Wherever the public sector has hegemonized productive activities (in the communist countries) the 'communist way to socialism' has been the result.

In the same way, the private enterprise sector (or the public one working in the market and for the market) symbolizes the capitalist enterprise system (to whose 'laws' today even the small family firm and cooperative enterprises, which have lost their collective management, tend to submit). Here the capitalist enterprise system has hegemonized the productive activities, but an attempt has been made to progressively reduce the area of influence. Wherever the private enterprise system did not have the capacity to provide, in adequate quantity and quality, the required services and productions, the state has been progressively introduced. It has been introduced through its intervention in the social (Welfare State) and also productive field ('nationalizations', 'state enterprises', state shareholding and so on), in all cases in which it corresponded to the general public interest. The 'Social-Democratic or Labour way to socialism', or rather the Welfare State, has been the result. Some have also called this 'social capitalism'. This way, for the moment, has not modified the base of capitalist economy, and this has happened in all the Western countries of historical capitalism, in its long evolution, in particular those of Northern Europe, up to the current stage which some have defined as 'late capitalism'.[35]

Would the 'third way' imply the hegemony of a new sector – the private-collective one – over the traditional sectors (state and capitalist enterprise) such that it would mark the advent of a new 'system', which some have called that of 'Humanist Socialism', other of 'Liberal Socialism'[36] (to distinguish it from the homologous use of the words 'Socialism' and 'Communism') or simply that of 'Socialism' (taking for granted the clear difference from 'Communism')?

Since today the hegemony of the third sector is far from being a reality, it would represent a system devoid of an historic mode; it is the only 'unreal' system spoken about, although belonging to the future.

It is difficult, and certainly premature, to uphold today that the third sector (of which some features are now being noted and for which the aspiration is present to 'ratify' its institutional nature, and thus 'institutionalize' it in some way) may in the near future characterize the productive system and hegemonize to such an extent as to speak of a new economic system of production, different from the capitalist and communist ones (or collectivist or étatist ones).

But it would not be correct to exclude it either.

After all, despite the apparent political 'revolutions' (the French and Russian ones) with which the historians make the birth of the market economy or the collectivist economy concide, it is known that the *transition* from the 'corporative' system of production to the capitalist one, and from the capitalist system to the collectivist one, has been and still is very slow and never 'total': in that at any historic moment there has been and still is a survival of the old forms and anticipation of the new. And, in the end, a substantial cohabitation and coexistence is produced of all the forms which refer to this or that system. As now conventionally recognized by the scholars of comparative 'economic systems', the 'system may remain a conceptual expression, whilst the structure is by necessity real and concrete'.[37]

6.3 The 'Third Sector' and the Welfare Society

It is therefore very probable that for the foreseeable future the fundamental characteristic of pluralistic Western societies will, in their post-industrial phase, be hallmarked by a *combined active presence* of all three operational sectors mentioned,[38] even if one can at the same time presume that both the Public Sector (in a process of readjustment and decentralization) and the Private Profit-making Sector (in a process of objective reduction of its market areas) together will tend *to lose their influence in favour of the widening of a 'Private-Collective Sector'* (whose outlines and functions will become more clearly defined in Chapter 12).

Whether this tendency can be identified also in a search for a third way to socialism does not seem to us to merit concentrating too much attention. It seems a pointless question, similar to whether the Welfare State is in crisis or not.

One thing is certain: that this change in the Welfare State, in the sense that it is rendered necessary by its 'fiscal crisis' and crisis of efficiency, and by the search for a more egalitarian basis of production (which could identify itself in the emerging of the Third Sector), seems quite possible. But such a change – if it is to be without serious crises in the *modus operandi* of the two traditional sectors, public and private – is possible *only if the whole of the development and operational activity of the three sectors is kept under control by a planning procedure*, within which and on the basis of which are implemented those options necessary for guaranteeing an adequate functioning of the entire system. The functioning which must be guaranteed is above all that which is subject to the compatibility of resource usage and of the elimination of blockages and wastage.

A way out of the crisis of the Welfare State is therefore possible only if there is a substantial change in the model of society (or societal model). And such a change will only be possible if provoked by a new governmental control of the change and growth exercised by the planning process. It is only by calling upon the old operators (the state, in its multiple instances, the profit-making enterprises and the trade unions) and the new operators (the consumers and the 'third sector'), through an appropriate planning procedure for a more developed *negotiation* or *bargaining of planning activity*, that it will be possible to 'overcome' the limitations and the crisis of the Welfare State and to aspire to a social organization of the type which is implied under the name of 'Welfare Society'.

A 'Welfare Society' which, in the light of the logic and semantics discussed here could also be called – why not? – a 'socialist' society. For the moment we will satisfy ourselves by examining the nature of a post-industrial society which strongly recalls the features of a post-capitalist society.

12 A New Social Model: The Associative Economy

From what we have *considered* in the preceding chapter (section 4), we can begin to be aware that an emerging area of 'socialization' is being defined following the social transformations mentioned above. This area faces:

- on the one hand 'étatization' (with its more or less accentuated 'nationalizations');
- on the other hand, 'privatization' of market power (which today assumes ever more the forms of corporate collusions or of oligopolistic concentrations, more or less trans-national as may be the case).

As we have already said, the complexity of modern industrial societies does not give us the evidence that this area (of socialization) that we have seen to be *emerging*, could also becoming *prevailing*.

And it has been said also, that never as in the past will the different 'economic systems', which refer to one or other form (or social formation) of production, coexist in the same structure of a developed country.

1 THE EMERGING FORMS OF THE THIRD SECTOR

The third sector is emerging in several forms and there have been many attempts to 'classify' it in some way.

Before facing its 'taxonomy', we will recall – with a bird's eye view – some of the proposed classifications, in order to have first of all an idea of the breadth which we would give to its operationality.

1.1 The Third Sector in the USA

Let us start with the United States, which represents the most advanced country in the structural transformations of post-industrial society.[1]

Some years ago the different operational forms were classified, for instance, by an author[2] into four categories, which retain a significance not devoid of a certain conceptual interest:

1. the '*intentional communities*' or '*communal movements*', which represent the most radical forms, furthest from traditional consumption;[3]

204

2. the *barter or natural exchange forms* (limited in range but of great conceptual interest);[4]
3. a large number of cases of '*new wave co-ops*', as opposed to the more traditional '*old wave co-ops*', or the so-called '*employee owned firms*'. These new cooperatives were mainly occupied with *tertiary consumption* and they picked up old traditions of truly democratic management.[5] This last movement was supported strongly by a federal law, the Small Business Employee Ownership Act of 1980;
4. finally, there is the category of *communities and neighbourhoods in rural and urban environments*. This concerns local initiatives, which have vast fields of action and can be difficult to classify in accordance with general definitions. These include development of green zones and public gardens, creation of leisure clubs, restoring apartments, management of swimming pools, organization of voluntary work on buildings and above all the maintenance of houses, introduction to small scale solar power, management of schools in special fields (music, arts, theatre, languages, etc.), education of families in medical prevention, juridical information, social help, etc.

In the United States the term 'third sector' is considered synonymous with the term 'non-profit sector'. The existence of a non-profit sector as a category in itself is clearly recognized by the scientific world, by the operators in the sector and by public agencies. The recognition on the part of the legislator has in part relieved the American observers of the burden of developing its own criteria for the delimitation of the non-profit sector.[6]

1.2 The Third Sector in Europe

In Europe such initiatives exist, but are less developed. This is due to the general delay of affluent post-industrial society, which leads to new forms of organization and existence, and to the heritage of a different past, to a Welfare State which widely substitutes for private collective initiatives. Whichever way, the experiences along the lines of an alternative economy are also of great importance.

Most European countries have not developed their own concept which would cover the set of organizations which are distinguished both from public bodies and from the classic type of commercial enterprise, and thus when scholars or operators in the sector look for one they tend to adopt that of the 'non-profit sector' as understood in the United States. The situation is somewhat different in France, where from the previous century many of these organizations were bracketed under the term 'économie sociale'.[7] In France the expression 'third sector' ('tiers-secteur') is considered synonymous with 'social economy'.[8]

The characteristics of the social economy as commonly understood are summed up by the 'Charte de l'économie sociale', signed in 1980 by the most important operators and groups in the sector.[9] The basic principles of the French social economy are the following: (a) participation is voluntary and personal; (b) solidarity exists between members; (c) management has a democratic nature ('one man, one vote'); (d) the organizations are independent from the public power; (e) the administrators are not remunerated for their activities; (f) the goal of the organization is not profit, and if this is made it must be reinvested in the organization (but the cooperatives and mutuals can distribute it to members in the form of payment and price reductions); (g) the capital cannot be shared between the members, and if the company is dissolved it must be transferred to another non-profit organization.

The organizations of the social economy are generally divided, on the basis of their juridical form as well, into three large groups: cooperatives, mutuals and associations; the first two categories operate in the market, the third does not (from this derives the distinction identified by some authors between 'entrepreneurial forms' and 'associative forms').[10] Often added to the three main forms are trade unions, foundations, savings banks, enterprise committees, and others.[11]

The French social economy, therefore, includes economic subjects (cooperatives, mutuals) which in the United States are not generally considered as part of the non-profit sector (because they are not 'non-profit' enough), and excludes social bodies (religious communities, self-help groups) which instead are fully considered in the United States as part of the American non-profit sector.[12]

In France, the alternative movements are behind the relaunch of the *social economy*, which is essentially cooperative, a subject in which the government and public opinion are very engaged. The problem of a separate identity for the alternative movement with respect to traditional cooperation, heavily oriented to production of goods and the market, does not seem very pressing, perhaps apart from certain cultural initiatives.[13]

Also in France there is research into policies in support of enterprise creation.[14] Still in France, a debate has been opened on new forms of collective consumption and new models of work.[15]

In Germany, a line of research which deals with the third sector *per se*, i.e. as something different from research into its single components, is still underdeveloped.[16] Here there is a tendency to conceptualize the non-profit sector in juridical terms, identifying it vaguely with 'private entities of general utility' (*private Körperschaften mit Gemeinnützigkeitsstatus*).

A more precise attempt to develop a definition of the 'third sector' was that of Christoph Reichard (1988), which is interesting because it shows to what extent particular meanings are given to the same terms according to various national traditions – in this case German étatism. According to Reichard, third sector organizations are those which (i) enjoy sufficient autonomy from external influence (e.g. from the state); (ii) are not profit-oriented, but rather have goals of general interest; (iii) are structured in a relatively informal way and place the stress on voluntary work; (iv) act with solidarity in their relations with their members and customers; and (v) act on the basis of direct and reciprocal exchange, and not through an anonymous market. The organizations of the third sector act in an area outlined by the three traditional poles of the state, market and family.[17]

Staying with the German case (but the considerations are valid for other European countries), whilst among the experts on associative phenomena the sense is lacking of a 'non-profit sector' which beyond its multiplicity represents a unitary phenomenon, it is even more lacking in the organizations which make up this sector. An important cause of this absence is certainly the specific character which in this country non-profit organizations have acquired. In particular, in the field of social policy, into which a noteworthy part of the German third sector resources flow, a dichotomy has been produced between the old large social welfare organizations (*Wohlfahrtsverbände*), which enjoy numerous privileges from the state, and the recent spontaneous initiatives of local self-help, which have arisen in general from 'alternative' cultures and are keen on emphasizing their distance from the state.[18] Given the differences in size, finance sources, closeness to the state and in mentality which separate these two categories of subjects operating in the social field, it is difficult for the two movements to consider themselves as part of the same 'sector'. Nevertheless some recent signs, such as the tendency to the institutionalization of local self-help initiatives and their growing dependence on public transfer, indicate that this situation could soon change. Already in the 1980s in Germany nearly 12,000 alternative projects had been counted.[19]

In Great Britain, and in other European countries, the attention to the third sector, as such, is more recent, and it follows the vicissitudes of the cooperative movement. There are no special criteria of definition nor relevant experiences which deserve to be analyzed in particular ways.[20]

The institutions of the European Union have been aware for some time of the need to pay particular attention, in the context of its initiatives for economic development, employment and cohesion in the Union, to the potential of those economic actors which cannot be referred to the traditional profit-oriented enterprise, or to public bodies, and therefore form a 'third sector' of the economic system. The European Commission has to a large extent adopted the French usage and thinks in terms of 'social economy'. In its communication to the Council of the European Community of 18 December 1989, entitled 'Businesses in the "Economie Sociale" Sector: Europe's Frontier-Free Market',[21] the Commission observed that:

The hallmark of belonging to the [économie sociale] sector is the specific manner of organization of an enterprise's productive activity. The driving principles are the solidarity and participation (one member, one vote) of its members, whether producers, users or consumers, informed by a proud independence and civic purpose.

The enterprises are generally in the legal form of a cooperative, a mutual society or a non-profit association.

The sector thus includes organizations which form part of the economy because they engage in productive activities, applying resources to satisfy needs. They may produce market goods and services (i.e. sold at a price that at least covers their production cost), or non-market goods and services (supplied free, or at a price unrelated to their cost, the difference being made up by non-market financing, membership fees, grants, donations, etc.). They are enterprises operating in competition with traditional forms of enterprise.

On 28 July 1989 the Council of the European Community adopted a decision (89/490/CEE) for the improvement of the context of activities and promotion of the development of enterprises in the Community, in particular cooperative, mutual and associative ones.

With its resolution of 17 June 1992 relative to Community actions in favour of enterprises, in particular cooperative, mutual, and associative ones, the Council confirmed its commitment to support the consolidation of actions in favour of such enterprises and recommended that the Commission continue actions necessary to create a favourable context for their competitivity and to accompany their entry in the single market after 1992.

In 1994 the Commission asked the Council to approve a pluriennial work programme in favour of cooperatives, mutuals, associations and foundations in the Community.[22] In the programme it is observed that:

cooperatives, mutuals and associations occupy a significant place in economic activity in general and in the development of regions; whereas maintenance of the strengths and special features of the cooperatives, mutuals and associations sector will warrant a special effort in terms of analysis and optimization, more particularly as regards: its capacity for innovation and experimentation; encouraging the utilization by these enterprises of Community programmes specifically geared to enterprise development (the sector has a proven track-record in terms of networks and partnership arrangements and the mobilization of operators and consumers); its enhanced participation in the social dialogue and in the implementation of social cohesion policies, an area in which this sector has undeniable advantages.

[According to the document] What makes these organizations different is essentially the stressing of the following principles: primacy of the individual over capital; development of the individual (through training and culture); free association; democratic management; values of autonomy and citizenship.

It also points out that, more than any other type of body, associations are close to the specific needs of citizens and are thus able to respond effectively to greatly varied expectations and requirements. This is the justification for stepping up knowledge in the sector.

The opportuneness of promoting the positive potential of the sector emerges also from the recognition that it:

is particularly skilled in the field of social innovation, i.e. a field which it is very much in the Community's interest to recognize, promote and utilize. This can be done all the more easily and effectively given that a large number of firms in this sector constitute essential vehicles for Community policies. Whether the problems can be related to urbanization, economic decline, job loss, the increasing financial uncertainty among substantial sections of the population or the management of human resources, these entities come up with solutions which offer potential for renewal and which they disseminate – often with the support of the public authorities – by way of the kind of networks in which they occupy a very significant position.

An interesting documentation on new forms of self-management of collective services has been gathered through an inquiry in three French, three British and three German towns under the 'Programme for Research and Action on the Evolution of Labour Markets' promoted by the EEC Commission.[23]

From what has been said it emerges that the definition of the third sector is influenced notably by the surrounding environment. Nevertheless: since the comparison not only of the third sector in itself, but also of the evolution of contemporary industrial society in which it is emerging, is posed on a transnational scale,[24] which we will call 'general', the problem inevitably arises of a sort of general taxonomy of the third sector.

1.3 A Comparative Vision of the Third Sector

It is certainly not by chance that among the American experts the problem of defining the third sector arose urgently just when it was necessary to carry out a comparative investigation between different countries. The 'Johns Hopkins Comparative Nonprofit Sector Project', launched in 1990, represents the most advanced attempt up until now to compare the dimensions and characteristics of non-profit sectors in various countries (and reference will be made to its results in a following section).

The participants in the project, directed by Lester Salamon of the Johns Hopkins University of Baltimore, had to reckon with the problem that in a large number of the countries examined the legislation does not deal in a unified manner with non-profit organizations. To obtain comparable results a definition valid for all countries had to be established, which has been called 'structural-operational'.[25]

According to this definition, part of the third sector are organizations which:

(a) are formally constituted, i.e. which possess a constitutional act establishing the fundamental rules of its functioning and thus ensures them organizational consistency and stability in time;

(b) have a private juridical status;

(c) are self-governing, i.e. they are not controlled by profit-oriented enterprises or public agencies;

(d) do not distribute the profits deriving from their own activities, either to members or to employees, or to administrators: any profits must be reinvested in the activities of the organization;

(e) at least in part make use of voluntary work.

From the 'non-profit organizations' category, cooperatives, mutuals, and savings banks[26] have been excluded and trade union and professional associations included.

The 'Johns Hopkins' definition may be considered a formalization of the meaning attributed currently in the United States to the expressions 'non-profit sector' and 'third sector'.

2 THE EXPANSION OF THE THIRD SECTOR

The numerous attempts to define the third sector, as we have rapidly shown, have not managed to succeed in reaching a univocal and satisfying definition, not even with reference to the specific situations of each country and cultural environment. But even less satisfactory – as is evident – is the state of the information needed to estimate and evaluate the quantitative dimensions of the third sector in the general frame of the structures and the development of each country.

In this case as well, the state of the art – which is rather low everywhere, as we already said – is generally superior in those countries that are forerunners in the development of industrial (or rather post-industrial) society, and that are at the same time the countries in which the emergence and the awareness of the third sector took place earlier (USA, Germany, France, etc.).

2.1 Current Statistics: Employment, Expenditure, Activity Fields, Financing

Regarding the knowledge of the quantitative dimensions of the third sector, the data available everywhere is only rather occasional, unofficial, very different in source and meaning, and not comparable over diachronic values and over countries.[27]

We will only give some glances drawn from those statistical surveys we regard as more accurate, with more comparable data, and for the most significant phenomena. As we will say later in this study, the emergence of the third sector still needs – above all for those aspects of its activity which bear some relation with 'national accounting' – deep rethinking, based on the 'extension', and related 'integration', of national accounting to an assessment of 'non-market' activities and transactions and of 'no-price-markets', in which the third sector is the great protagonist.

Regarding international comparisons, the European Commission promoted the first EUROSTAT research on the social economy, which considered almost 269,000 cooperatives, mutuals and associations covered by the consulted national umbrella organizations, and which produced partial results.[28]

So far, however, the most important contribution to the knowledge of the dimension of the third sector has come from the above mentioned 'Johns Hopkins Comparative Nonprofit Sector Project', started in 1990, which examined seven countries thoroughly (France, Germany, Italy, United Kingdom, USA, Japan and Hungary) and another five less thoroughly.[29]

The authors of a concise report on the project gave a first impression of the scope of the activities carried out by non-profit organizations.[30]

From the same survey less impressive data are obtained with regard to *employment* and current *spending* in the third sector in comparison with overall employment and Gross National Product.[31]

A first comment which can be made about this information is that the overall size of the third sector in Western countries is relatively consistent: following the USA which reached 7 per cent, at the top of the overall workforce, are France, Germany and the United Kingdom, which all employ around 4 per cent, with Italy at a substantially lower level.

On the other hand, the research has shown important differences among the countries regarding the *fields of activity*[32] of non-profit organizations.[33]

If on the one hand, at least three-quarters of total expenses of the non-profit sector in all countries considered is concentrated in the four main fields taken together (education and research, health, social services, culture and recreation), the relative weight of these fields, as we have seen, varies from country to country.

Regarding the financing of the activities carried out by non-profit organizations, a common tendency is observable in all countries considered: the contribution provided by the 'classical' financial source, *private charitable giving*, is clearly lower than that provided by each of the other possible sources: *fees paid by the consumers* of the services provided by the organization, and *transfers by the public sector*. Even in the country where the proportion of financing coming from charitable giving is higher, the United States, it represents only 19 per cent of total third sector revenues, whereas private payments contribute 51 per cent and public transfers 30 per cent. In the Western European countries this situation is even more pronounced, and the differences are mainly in the relative weight of private fees and public transfers.[34]

The differences in the relative weight of financial sources between the different countries can be traced back to two factors. On the one hand, the fields in which non-profit organizations are active (education, health, etc.) have not the same weight in all examined countries. If each field, because of its peculiar characteristics, tends to couple with a particular form of financing, then at least some of the differences between the countries can be explained in this way. On the other hand, since the ratio between sources of non-profit finance in the same field is sometimes different in various countries, part of the difference must be explained also through 'styles' of non-profit finance that are specific to each country (i.e. economic, social and cultural context).

2.2 The Substitution Effect

Apart from the dimensions of the third sector, as pointed out by its importance in relation to some phenomena (employment, the product, etc.), it is necessary to try – in spite of the extremely limited data available – to grasp the emerging potentiality of the third sector in contemporary industrial society. We are helped on this point by some statistics that come from the USA and Western Germany, where information has appeared before that of other countries, and perhaps not by chance: they are the countries where the general conditions of the industrialization process tend to present 'newer' characteristics, and therefore more symbolic of the phenomena in general.

We have a distribution of employment for the USA[35] that begins from 1977 and therefore allows us to evaluate a possible 'evolution' of the total employment, from the point of view of the three principal sectors (commercial, public and non-profit) for the thirteen years from 1977 to 1990.

From 1977 to 1990 total employment in the USA increased by over 34 million; that is, over 34 million jobs were created, on a total in 1977 of about

103 million (with an increase, therefore, of approximately 33 per cent). Of these new jobs, over 23 million were created in the commercial sector (for-profit), a little over 5 million in the public sector and 6 million in the non-profit sector. In 1977 the non-profit sector represented 9.3 per cent of total employment and in 1990 it accounted for 11 per cent. But the most interesting effect with regard to the role of the third sector in creating new jobs in the USA can be understood better if, together with the employment change, distributed among three large chosen sectors, we look at the 'substitution effect' among them. In fact, the comprehensive increase of persons employed in the American market of 34 million in thirteen years, shows a development of the work demand, that can only repeat a rather standard pattern with regard to the previous structure; this can cause the 'marginal' variations to be little understood, though for the purposes of our reflection they can be the most interesting. If, to see beyond this simple effect of variation, we look at the relative substitution, the pattern is shown in a different way (see Table 12.1). If the commercial sector had grown at the same rate as the total employment, its employment should have been nearly 2 million more; in the same way, if employment in the public sector had grown at the same rate (during the thirteen years in question) as total employment, it would have been approximately 1.2 million more. On the contrary, only the third sector gained, by creating new jobs, more than it would have done in the general growth of employment. In other words, only the third sector has really 'subtracted' jobs from the other two sectors. If for 'new jobs', one intends only those jobs created in the internal infrastructural mobility of an employment system, under the same general employment conditions (no growth of employment), we must conclude that only the third sector shows any ability to expand.

The phenomenon is shown with even more interesting characteristics with the data on Western Germany.[36] In comparison with the USA, the German data have older bases (1960), allowing us to make an evaluation every 10 years up to 1990. Moreover, the structure of the commercial sector shows a distinct

Table 12.1   United States: substitution effect in the employment structure from 1977 to 1990 (in thousands)

	Variation effect 1977–90	Substitution effect 1977–90
Business, for-profit	+ 23028	− 1734
Government	+ 5211	− 1177
Non-profit sector	+ 6085	+ 2911
Total	+ 34323	0

Source: Based on data from Independent Sector (1992), table 1.5.

division into sub-sectors, that also allows us to watch what happens – and it is interesting – inside this sector. Lastly, it is a matter of a country (if only of different dimensions) that – like nearly all European countries – has not had such a high rate of population and employment growth as the USA, and, therefore – as has been said – the rate of substitution can be better evaluated between the three sectors that interest us.

In fact, employment in Western Germany has passed from about 25.7 million in 1960 to about 28.4 million in 1990, with the total net creation of 2.7 million jobs. This increase, with respect to total employment in 1960, represents an increase of about 10 per cent (in the ten years 1980–90, it was equal to about 1.4 million). This new employment, at the end of the thirty years in Germany, was generated only by the public sector and the non-profit sector, because the commercial sector as a whole lost 300,000 employees. The increase of the employed in the aforesaid sub-sectors of commerce and of the services for profit (equal in the 30 years to about 2.5 million) did not compensate for the reduction of jobs in agriculture and industry. The only expanding sectors were the public sector (+2.2 million approximately) and the non-profit sector (+900,000 approximately).

If we then look at the substitution effect, things seem even more significant. The commercial sector as a whole does not only lose a few hundreds of thousands of jobs, but loses nearly 3 million, to the advantage of the public and non-profit sectors (Table 12.2).

From the data examined, one could deduce that in the USA and Germany, the well-known process of 'tertiarization', common to all industrial countries – and known for a long time by now, from many analyses – is showing a somewhat new characteristic: *the ever more manifest replacement of the commercial tertiary sector with the non-commercial tertiary sector (public and non-profit)*. And on the basis of some signs that are still not completely obvious, but can be deduced from the universal crisis of public finances (budget deficit, public debt) of all kinds, it is presumed that a further tendency will be that of the relative substitution of the public tertiary with the non-profit tertiary.

The statistics concerning the third sector are still in their first stages in all industrial and post-industrial countries.[37] But there is remarkable enthusiasm for relevant researches that will soon give fruit and naturally permit more adequate analyses. But it seems to us that whatever data springs from the best statistics, above all in the sense of diachronic dynamics, and divisions into single activities, a leading line will emerge in all advanced countries: a growing third sector, on a difficult but relentless growth, which will have to be and can be faced with new instruments of economic and social policy, and also trade union policy.[38]

Table 12.2 West Germany: substitution effect in the employment structure from 1960 to 1990 (in thousands)

Employment Sector	Variation effect				Substitution effect			
	1960–1970	*1970–1980*	*1980–1990*	*1960–1990*	*1960–1970*	*1970–1980*	*1980–1990*	*1960–1990*
Agriculture	−1319	−859	−439	−2617	−1424	−904	−513	−2997
Industry	+490	−1266	−405	−1151	+120	−1528	−1030	−2515
Commerce	−4	+277	+283	+556	−145	+181	+15	+48
Private services	+569	+1037	+1299	+2905	+501	+975	+1082	+2653
Commercial sector total	−264	−811	+738	−337	−948	−1276	−443	−2811
Public sector	+880	+951	+374	+2205	−814	+891	+165	+1981
Non-profit sector	+146	+396	+331	+873	+134	+387	+282	+830
TOTAL	+762	+536	+1443	+2741	0	0	0	0

Source: Based on data in Anheier and Priller (1995).

3 SOME INTERPRETATIONS OF THE THIRD SECTOR

The emergence of the third sector, unclear and undefined but nevertheless overwhelming in recent times, has not failed to attract its interpreters. This book, with its analysis of the characteristics of the evolution of contemporary industrial society presented in the earlier chapters, constitutes one example.

Many interpretations are complementary to those offered in this book; others less so. We shall cite some in order to provide a full reconnaissance before dwelling at more length on policy recommendations.

The point of view from which the question of the existence of a third sector, beside the public and profit-oriented sectors, is generally examined theoretically is that of 'institutional choice'.[39] Attention is directed to the relative competitive advantages of the third sector in comparison to the state and market in particular situations of supply and demand. Attempts are being made to identify the services which neither the state nor the 'market' are able to supply, or do so in an inadequate way in comparison to the non-profit organizations. The existence of third sector organizations is explained in these approaches mainly by means of theories of state and market failure.

3.1 State Failure Theories

Burton Weisbrod (1977, 1988) has developed an influential theory on the formation of the non-profit sector based on the idea of state failure, and in particular on its incapacity to resolve satisfactorily the 'public goods' problem for all citizens.

Weisbrod observes that the state provides a quantity and quality of public goods determined by the political electoral process, and thus by the preferences of the median voter. In this way the demand for public goods expressed by large minorities is unsatisfied and the deviation from the average demand of specific groups is neglected. Lack of satisfaction may concern both the quantity of goods offered as well as their quality. The non-profit organizations fit into this space left empty, and deal with the demand for public goods left unsatisfied by the majoritarian mechanisms. When the demand is homogeneous overall, the state provision is preferred because the latter, thanks to taxation, is able to resolve the free-rider problems which arise in connection with public goods.

In a political unit, the greater the heterogeneity – in terms of income, wealth, religion, ethnic origin, education, and other characteristics which influence the demand for public goods – the greater will be the space occupied by non-profit organizations. The third sector is the product of the incapacity of the state to meet the needs and preferences of a society which is largely differentiated in life styles.[40]

Empirical studies have confirmed the relationship between social hetero-geneity and the development of non-profit organizations (in particular, between religious and linguistic pluralism and private non-profit education). The dynamic thesis is that as heterogeneous preferences and lifestyles increase, so will the presence of non-profit organizations.[41] One of the major difficulties in the theory proposed by Weisbrod is that it does not explain why not only public goods, but also many private goods are provided by non-profit organizations, and furthermore does not explain adequately why non-profit organizations should be in a better position than profit-oriented ones for resolving the problem of the free-rider. The theories centred on the failure of the market attempt to fill these gaps.

3.2 Market Failure Theories

American authors especially have developed hypotheses on the existence of non-profit organizations (in environments in which for-profit businesses operate or could operate as well) which are based on informational assyme-tries between the suppliers of particular goods and services and the potential acquirers or donors.[42]

In particular Henry B. Hansmann (1980, 1986, 1989) has proposed a well-known theory of the formation of the third sector based on the idea of 'contract failure'. Hansmann's argument starts from the theorem that when certain conditions are satisfied, the for-profit firms provide goods and ser-vices at the quantity and price which represent the maximum social effi-ciency. One of these conditions is that the consumers[43] must be able, without cost or excessive effort, (a) to compare thoroughly the offers of the various firms before choosing; (b) to stipulate with the firms chosen a contract which specifies precisely the goods and services which the firms must supply; and (c) to ensure subsequently that the firm has respected the contract, and if not, obtain some kind of remedy, of a legal nature or otherwise.

In the case of many products, such as industrial and agricultural goods, these conditions are generally satisfied; but in the case of other products, by dint of their intrinsic characteristics or the conditions of purchase and con-sumption, accurate evaluation by the consumer is not possible. The latter come across difficulties in identifying the most advantageous offer, or in making sure the contract is respected once it has been stipulated. In a situation of this type the market discipline is not enough to safeguard the consumer: the producer who knows the characteristics of the product is able – if he so wishes – to ask for a price which is excessive in comparison with the quality. It is in these conditions that it becomes advantageous for the con-sumer to turn to non-profit enterprises rather than to for-profit ones. Although a non-profit enterprise would also be able to obtain excessive prices for the product supplied, unlike for-profit enterprises it has no comparable incentive to do so. Having assumed the legal obligation to devote all income to service production, no one would take advantage of the gains which might derive from that type of behaviour. The non-distribution of profits constraint therefore represents for the consumer a further guarantee in addition to the market discipline, which in these cases has been seen to be insufficient.

For Hansmann the demand for a non-profit sector emerges therefore from the need for more 'reliable' operators in particular situations: the non-profit organizations seem more 'trustworthy'. The consumers need the safety offered by the non-profit constraint in cases such as the following: (a) donors buy services for unknown third parties, and thus cannot control the quantity and quality of the services (a good example would be donations to poor countries entrusted to non-profit organizations); (b) the person who pays knows the user, but the latter is not considered a reliable judge of the quality of the service (for example, homes for the elderly, nurseries and schools); (c) the consumers of a public good are prepared to contribute to the costs of its private production, but want to be sure that their contribution covers only the production costs, and does not also make a profit for the managers of the enterprise (e.g. associations for environmental protection and medical research); (d) the services are so complex that the final consumers cannot evaluate the quality, but on the other hand are so important that low quality would involve unacceptable risks (medical assistance).

For the fields (e.g. orchestras, theatres, universities, museums) in which the services are consumed by the acquirers who are able to judge their quality, Hansmann offers a special explanation, based on the voluntary discrimination of prices via donations.

Hansmann observes that non-profit organizations suffer from various disadvantages in comparison with for-profit ones, amongst which are the greater difficulty in access to capital, lower efficiency in functioning and slower speed in access and growth in expanding markets. The non-profit businesses represent a serious alternative to the for-profit businesses only in the fields in which the protection offered to the customer by the non-distribution constraint adequately compensates for those disadvantages. This is generally not the case for industrial goods, for which there are not serious problems of 'contract failure'.

The dynamic hypothesis gathered from Hansmann's theories is that the third sector will tend to expand in line with the growth in social needs which require 'trust' in order to be satisfied.

3.3 Non-Profit Economy and Ideology

Whilst the theories considered up until now concentrate on the 'demand side', other positions underline more the 'supply side'.

Estelle James and Susan Rose-Ackerman,[44] for example, have identified in the willingness of people motivated by a particular ideology (religious, political, educational, etc.) a necessary condition for the development of a solid non-profit sector. The founders of non-profit organizations are recruited mainly amongst those who aim to diffuse their beliefs in society, and this objective is in general incompatible with profit maximization. The element of 'entrepreneurship' thus takes on a central role. Furthermore, because of their ideological nature, non-profit organizations have more chance of attracting donations and voluntary work than do for-profit organizations.

According to these authors an approach of this type is preferable to the hypotheses of 'market failure' and 'state failure' of a microeconomic type, because unlike these it can explain the differences found between the non-profit sectors in different countries and socio-cultural contexts.

3.4 'Third Party Government' Hypothesis

The theoretical interpretations of the 'non-profit' phenomenon which we have looked at so far are greatly influenced by the characteristics of the American sector. In particular they stress its clearly 'alternative' nature in comparison with the public sector. It is a consolidated opinion that such a characterization does not lend itself easily to transposition to the European situation, where the links between the state and the non-profit organizations are generally tighter than in the United States.

But in the United States too some people have criticized the traditional view of the non-profit sector and in particular its alleged 'distance from the state'. Lester Salamon[45] is the author who has most insisted on the need to review this 'paradigm', as he has defined it. Salamon considers that the 'conflict paradigm', which supposes an inevitable conflict between the state and the private voluntary sector, and which considers that the expansion of the one necessarily involves the reduction of the other, strongly distorts the real American situation, and must be replaced by a 'partnership paradigm'. In fact throughout American history, and in particular in the period following the New Deal, public subjects at all levels, when faced with new responsibilities and also with constant general hostility to the bureaucratic state, turned largely to new or already existent non-profit organizations for assistance in the increased social tasks. Public financing has thus greatly overtaken donations as a non-profit sector resource. On the other hand, in the field where both sectors are present, the non-profit organizations are the main providers of services, and manage more public funds than the government agencies themselves.

The reason for these developments lies in the social advantage of being able to combine the strong points of the two institutional types. The partnership permits in fact the joining of the capacity of the state (scarce in the non-profit sector) to gather resources and ensure equity by means of a democratic political process, and the capacity of the non-profit sector (scarce in the state) to supply services in an informal, targeted and non-bureaucratic manner.

According to Salamon the fundamental characteristic of the American welfare state is the fact that it is based on the principle of 'third party government', on the basis of which the function of service financing, assumed by the state, turns out to be separated from that of service supplier, which the public organs prefer to delegate to private subjects – in particular non-profit ones.

3.5 'Functional Dilettantism' Hypothesis

In comparison with the approaches considered so far, which see in the third sector a real and efficient solution to the needs of society, Wolfgang Seibel[46] has developed an opposing theory, which has attracted much attention in Germany. According to Seibel the organizations of the third sector manage to survive whilst presenting, in comparison with state bureacracy and for-profit enterprises, serious efficiency and adaptability problems, and to a certain extent survive thanks to these shortcomings. The non-profit organizations in fact deal with social problems whose solution is particularly difficult (or impossible). The for-profit enterprises are not interested at all in entering these areas, and the public subjects are very willing to leave the field to organizations more or less independent from them. The continuous presence of unresolved social problems represents in fact a constant pressure on the legitimacy of the public institutions, who thus find it advantageous to 'unload' the responsibility for managing them on to non-state bodies, even if the latter are in no way able to resolve them.

In this way the third sector is made up of organizations which 'fail successfully', i.e. which act inefficiently and regularly fall short of their goals, but contribute at the same time to maintaining the stability of the political system with their function as a 'garbage can'. In exchange for this function the state generously finances non-profit organizations, thus ensuring their survival.

The essential characteristic of the third sector for Seibel is thus its 'functional dilettantism'.

4   A STRUCTURAL APPROACH: THE THIRD SECTOR IN THE POST-INDUSTRIAL ECONOMY

All these theoretical hypotheses have been criticized for one reason or another, and this is not the occasion to dwell on the debates which surrounded them.[47] It is enough to point out that they all seem to suffer from a certain staticness, i.e. they are not sufficiently linked to an overall vision of the changes in contemporary society. For this reason it is opportune to integrate these current theoretical hypotheses with an approach that is more attentive to the structural changes of advanced economies, whose elements can be summed up thus:[48]

1. If post-industrial society is characterized by the decline of industrial employment, this depends on technological development that permits ever higher levels of labour productivity and greater mass production with less and less personnel. But it depends also on the fact that consumption preferred by the consumers is tending more and more to be of the 'tertiary' type, thus creating little, if any, increase in productivity in the respective production processes. These are consumptions that induce productive processes with a high labour intensity. In these service sectors, which are prevalently personal, and in which the quality is prized more than the quantity of performance, productivity (in the traditional quantitative sense) is very low, and the possibilities of attracting entrepreneurship – which lives by the profitability which is connected to production innovation – are very limited. In short, post-industrial society is characterized by a declining entrepreneurship, at least of the 'traditional' sort, which seeks profit and is motivated by the same.[49]

2. Traditionally the state has taken on the burden of the demand that was unsatisfied by an entrepreneurial supply on the market. The various problems that have arisen because of the enormous expansion in public activities are widely acknowledged, and the economic and social unsustainability of further loading is taken for granted.[50]

3. In post-industrial society, unlike industrial society, the imperatives of a division of labour which, given the transregional and transnational nature of industrial production, is required for the achievement of high levels of productivity (and competitivity), no longer function. These imperatives still persist in the technologically more advanced sphere of industrial production; but not in that of the production of services, which today – whilst they cover an increasing role in the set of economic activities, and in the structure of consumption – are expressed on limited operational and territorial scales. With difficulty services are exchanged between regions and cities, and the productive units of services prefer a 'local' and 'human' scale. The need to 'personalize' that is proper to those who use the service rather than to the producers of the same, favours organizational forms of the non-profit type rather than the classic capitalist enterprise, which, we should point out, remains the institutional form most suitable for industrial production.[51]

5 FURTHER GUIDELINES FOR THE THIRD SECTOR

Thus the 'third sector' represents the line of development of modern post-industrial society, coherently with the process of great de-industrialization of activities and with the crisis of the Welfare State.

This is in spite of the fact that in recent times, notwithstanding the great attention that is being given to the third sector as a means for increasing job-creation opportunities, there seems to be little awareness of the role the third sector plays as a factor for the transformation of society and of contemporary economics. It is to this that we have dedicated this book.

A political objective, to which however the governments of all European countries do not seem yet sufficiently sensitive, is that of finding the way to *'facilitate' the growth of the third sector* through a policy which acts as a 'midwife' at the birth of this new model of pluralistic society (which we briefly outlined in the previous chapter).

We therefore will now look, in broad terms, at what could be the policies favourable to the development of the new model of activity and employment.

The natural and feasible development of this third sector – with respect to profit-oriented enterprises and the public sector – incorporating those characteristics of the two traditional sectors that are still valid, while discarding those which are no longer valid, is today hampered by a number of institutional factors which merit closer scrutiny. Very broadly, these factors may be classified as:

1. the lack, as yet, of a precise definition and conceptualization of the 'third sector', hence
2. confused and incomplete administrative and juridic regulation of activity and the economic institutions operating in this third sector, and, in any case, a current regulation which is decisively inadequate for the real operational needs, and consequently,
3. inadequate forms of financing.

These factors merit a few preliminary remarks.

5.1 The Need for a Better Operational Definition of the Third Sector

Therefore, as the rapid excursus in the preceding paragraphs demonstrates, it is undeniable that the third sector has been the subject of significant thought and a significant literature.

Nevertheless the bounds of the third sector are still very ill-defined. This constitutes in itself a major hindrance to the development of the sector.

Because of several differences in approach, the third sector may be taken to cover: both market and non-market activities; family activities and at the same time the reorganization of large production units along decentralized lines; crafts and cottage industry; cooperatives and charitable and voluntary activities; 'small scale' ventures and at the same time part-time activities, and sometimes even the 'hidden' activities as well as the illegal ones. The inevitable conceptual confusion that ensues totally deprives the concept of any precise significance and there is a resultant loss of functionality for the very activities that the concept should serve to identify in order to promote them.

Short of such an operational definition, the notion is reduced to a mere tool for interpretative analysis, rather academic in nature, useless as far as political intervention is concerned. While recognizing the complex nature of the phenomena of change (we outlined in the final part of Chapter 11) that are at the root of the emergence of this new and peculiar sector of activity it seems of primary importance that an attempt be made to de-code such a sector. In order to achieve this decodification we can use a kind of functional taxonomy of the third sector itself, and identify precisely (although in a broadly conventional manner) as different and alternative, (but not necessarily incompatible, rather largely *coexistent*) with the first and second sectors.

Also on this aspect of a more precise operational definition we will cast a rapid judgement, which will essentially arise from the further analysis of the specificity of such a sector with respect to the other two.

With respect *to business or capital economy* which operates *for* the market (not only *in* the market, in as much as this characteristic may be common – at least for factors of purchase – to the public and third sector as well), the third sector seems to be principally defined by the *absence of profit-making motivation*. This constitutes a very limited taxonomic criterion for this third sector, but we believe that it could bring great clarity and lead to a distinction of the roles resulting in implications of administrative regime to be used in its regard. In other words, in this type of activity profit would no longer be the main and decisive driving-force of the entrepreneurial combination of the factors of productions, but the basis of the enterprise would become *other* motivations, *other* aims, and *other* rewards.

For example, the cooperative movement has rightly been considered (together with mutual-aid activities and charitable voluntary action) as the forefather of the third sector. But the movement, on the basis of the proposed criterion, would today be considered part of such a third sector only on the condition that the cooperative enterprise – whatever its internal statute and whatever the relationship between the partners – does not have as its primary objective the gain and pecuniary profit of its partners, but rather the *attainment of social and associative goals*. We know that in its real evolution, the cooperative movement has substantially deformed (through imitation of the capitalistic system and often just to survive) its own original nature by absorbing a prevalently and often exclusively profit-making motivation. And we also know how this, in many settings, has reduced the cooperative form to nothing more than just one of the many forms of a conventional profit-oriented company.

Exceptions to this evolution are obviously all those cases in which the prevalence of associative objectives is different from that of profit: these are the cases (which are no longer, unfortunately, a majority) of *consumer cooperatives*, *building cooperatives* and more and more today *cultural, sport, etc. cooperatives*.

On the other hand, the third sector is also characterized with respect to the public sector by its *non-public* motivations, not aimed at the general interests, but rather by still largely 'private' motivations (even if very often they assume a collective form) which drive its activities. This implies that the meaning of the notion of the third sector cannot be reduced to organizational and operational and even managerial forms, which can be introduced in public services, if the action undertaken derives from public bodies and if the economic resources employed are exclusively public.

Nor is the *self-management by the users* of a public service sufficient for it to be included in the third sector: they must also undertake its *economic* and *entrepreneurial responsibility*.

It has already been said that the structural evolution of post-industrial society leads the third sector to absorb activities which today belong either to the first or second sector, but not to totally replace these latter. In the general expansion of the activity, the first and second sectors – that is to say also the activities of profit-oriented enterprises as well as the activities of public services – will also be subject to a certain degree of expansion. But in relative terms each of these will lose some of its own activities in favour of the third sector, the sector of the *communities*, of the *associations*, of the *cooperatives* which *are not aimed at gain*: the sector which we have preferred to denote as part of the *'social'* or *'associative' economy*.

The profit-oriented enterprises will undoubtedly see a reduction of their employees, both in relative terms and in absolute terms. This will occur thanks to the advances in productivity of labour which such enterprises, by virtue of their own dynamics, will tend to achieve through the acquisition of technological innovation, and also due to the decrease in the growth of demand for industrial products, the satisfaction of which (demand) is the prevalent orientation of such enterprises.

The state, for which there will remain good motives for growth, will probably see its own employees increase only in absolute terms, but their relative weight will diminish with respect to the employment-capacity offered by the third sector, as a result of a process of *de-étatization*, which we have said is inevitable for many services which have hitherto only been thought of as public.

5.2 For a New Institutional Regulation of the Associative Economy

From the administrative point of view as well as from the fiscal one, the juridical position of *activities without lucrative aims, or 'non-profits'*, is in all countries still in a rather elementary state. A more precise regulation and one which is more advantageous fiscally (taking naturally into account the possible speculative deformations of it) would allow an expansion of such activities with guaranteed effects on employment, even if such effects are already present today in 'hidden' or 'underground' forms or simply through 'informal' and economically 'invisible' activities, to use current terminology.

Certainly in every juridical system there already exists the notion of 'association' or that of 'community'; and in some regimes, the foundations have been endowed with greater juridical and fiscal functions with respect to others.

But in all regimes the need is felt today to intervene with a more *up-to-date regulation*, which should take into account the particular developments which in fact the associative economy has had with respect to business economy. In other words a new *law of associative economy* should be placed side-by-side with traditional *commercial law*.

A while ago, Delors and Gaudin[52] have in this regard proposed – with reference to French law (valid in a certain measure also for other European systems, as for example the Italian one) – the introduction, for those goods and services destined for sale, of a new statute of enterprise: the enterprise of 'associative labour' (*entreprise des travailleurs associés*); and, for those services which cannot be destined for sale, another type of enterprise still more fitting: the 'association for reciprocal services' (*association à services réciproques*). These latter forms – which regard more strictly the economy of the third sector, at least in the sense in which we have here defined it – would contribute to give a minimum of juridical and social rules to activities which are in any case in great expansion: all those activities in which each member of the association finds himself being at the same time both entrepreneur and supplier of labour and sometimes even user of the services supplied; and also, in different measures and forms, the financial investor of the same.

A new statute, of the type evoked, should define the conditions for the application of the above-mentioned associative forms, the modalities for exercising an eventual arbitrage within the very association, the rights and duties of the employees and eventual dependent professionals. Moreover such a statute would be the place in which to define the relationships of these specific associative forms with the external economy, in order to avoid all forms of unfair competition with respect to the conventional business sector (especially if in a regime where such types of activity have been granted fiscal benefits).

And it would indeed be most desirable that this new statute should stem from a new legislative initiative of the European Community. It would then start off with, on the one hand, a character already harmonized at the Community scale, and could constitute the most salient aspect of the policy for a new 'European social space'.

Certainly, the idea of establishing, through European Community Legislation about to be born, this new and important institution of the third sector – a sector which has not yet found just recognition, legitimization nor citizenship in national legislation – represents a new and precise 'European' prospective. Furthermore, it would be one of the most interesting forms of the creative rienforcement of economic and social cohesion of the Community.[53]

It is therefore important to point out that the enterprises of the social economy – which for some years have been united by a European Confederation, the European Federation of Workers' Cooperatives, Social Cooperatives and Participative Enterprises (CECOP)[54] – have promoted the signing of a 'European Charter of the Social and Solidarity Economy',[55] taking their cue from the French initiative we referred to in section 1.2. Probably all the efforts of the trade union organizations ought to converge on this in order to address the dissatisfactions associated with the need for better definition of the roles and borders of the third sector.[56]

On their part, European trade unions, through the European Trade Union Confederation, have started to take the problem of a commitment to the third sector seriously, promoting a conference in London at the TUC headquarters and inviting CECOP and its associated organisations, among others, to discuss a 'new partnership'.[57]

6 THE FINANCING OF THE ASSOCIATIVE SECTOR

The associative sector, in order for it to develop, has, above all, need of financial support. And, if for this support one thinks of public financial support, this is not surprising; nor should it seem in contradiction with what has already been said in Chapter 8: namely that the difficulties in expansion of the public sector (difficulties which are, among other things, one of the factors of expansion of the third sector itself) are totally unable to break through a certain upper threshold of public transfer as set by the national product.

Public forms of financial support for the associative sector – of whatever type one might think of – nevertheless represent a transfer effected by the state through the means of fiscal instruments. But such a transfer by the state can have different weights.

In all countries – some more, some less (according to the industrial 'seniority' of each of them, which is in its turn a function of the degree of extension of the public sector present in the economy) – public finances destine a part of their resources for the financing of the private productive sector: above all for capital interventions, but also on current accounts, in order to favour this or that industrial policy considered of *national interest*.

One should not forget that we live in an epoch in which we ask ourselves whether a serious economic growth can still be possible (simultaneously) in all countries; and whether the consumption of industrial products is of priority today among the range of factors of social well-being; and whether they will be anyhow the most *demanded* by the 'market' or whether they will not rather be widely substituted by a growing demand for social services.

In this framework the associative sector constitutes in all respects a productive sector which furthermore has the requisites for matching the real needs of a changing society.

And also from the point of view of containing public expenditure, the opportunity emerges to reserve a certain place in the system of future transfers for the associative sector – just with the aim of reducing, in the future, the burden of that public expenditure, which would become inevitably overloaded in the absence of the associative sector.

6.1 Possible Forms of Public Financing of the Associative Sector

Public financing of the associative sector can be of widely different forms.[58]

As is known, the associations, not having lucrative goals, do not obtain capital easily (except for the case of foundations). For this reason, they do not even have risk capital to offer as a guarantee of eventual financial loans.

State intervention should thus foresee supplying initial capital, even as 'sunk' capital.

In order to avoid the degeneration underlying supplying capital to associations of an uncertain duration and even more uncertain success (above all in the present phase which is still an experimental one), the most adequate form could be that of capital granted in leasing (with or without redemption of the capital good itself, after a determined period of lease). The price of the lease could also include the cost of insurance against the eventual loss of the capital. Naturally such a model of intervention has to be studied on a case-by-case basis with reference to those different operational sectors in which the associative activities might develop.

Numerous associative activities could ensure contributions in the framework of the collective goods placed at the free disposal of the population. In these cases public financing would assume the form of contracts for services, with direct subsidies from the state, in all its agencies (establishment of social-security, local communities, etc.). Also in this case, which already represents numerous experiences, the contractual forms to be adopted should be adapted to the typology of the services offered. The general objective would be that of avoiding the wastage of resources, but also that of arbitrage in their use, and so attain a greater participation in their management by the users. In fact, a 'sub-contracting' management by the state of many subsidies which today are directly distributed by the state itself, would have the great advantage of better articulating public participation and of 'drawing it nearer' to the real interests of the users (without considering the positive effect of a better civic education of the users themselves).

Such a sub-contracting management would include both the form of the concession and that of the co-management and control of associations, or consortiums of users according to predefined standards and parameters. In every foreseeable case of public financing, careful attention, above all at the level of political authorities, should be given to the definition of the objectives to be followed and of the criteria with which the services allocated by contract should be managed. Every decision relating to objectives, criteria and priorities should be public and publicized, with the intention of avoiding speculation, arbitration and illicit collusions.

Three types of contract have been identified in this context: that of *first-time establishment*, that of *innovation* and that of *delegation*. The first would serve the associative unit in installing its infrastructures: the aid could be that of a certain financing of either premises or machinery, or even of specialized personnel. The second, which would be continued for several years, would have the function of allowing the experimentation of new fields of action, and would be susceptible to verification of validity at a predetermined time. The third – applied to the case of sectors with a more consolidated existence – would imply that the public administration entrusts the associative unit with the primary purpose of performing a predefined task and offering a service well-defined beforehand.

6.2   New Forms of 'Private' and at the Same Time 'Collective' Financing of the Associative Sector and its Statistical Recording

But public financing is not the only form of possible finance for associative activities. Obviously, because the associative sector is a private sector, even if non-commercial and *non-profit*, nothing is more logical than for this sector to be financed by private forms. The most noteworthy are: the no-charge performance of labour; the legacies and patrimonial contributions on the part of large fortunes and large enterprises; the participation fees of the association members (clubs, unions, etc.); and lastly the forms of private collective savings, as is the case of the mutual-aid societies, of the building cooperatives, and of collective investment funds.

The experiments have until now been financed with these forms. In many of these cases, the no-charge labour of the association members, inseparable from the activity itself (which does not always employ people from outside), greatly reduces the employment-effect of such activities.

But one must not underestimate the interrelationships in the associative sector between employment-effects and income-effects. In fact the participation in the associative economy, through no-charge labour, allows the acquisition of non-monetary (therefore invisible or intangible) income which however has the effect of diminishing the need for monetary income, and therefore the supply of wage-making jobs.

This effect of reduction of the demand for monetary income produces in fact a slowing-down of the real supply of work in the monetary (official) market of work itself: and above all a slowing-down of full-time work, corresponding in practice to the average of the formal working-hours, annual, weekly or daily. Such a slowing-down is still stronger if we consider certain segments of the official labour market: for example, young people, women and the elderly. This phenomenon however is not reflected in the official statistics of the market of work and employment, and above all it does not get transferred to those of unemployment, since this preference for voluntary work or unremunerated is taken into consideration neither by surveys on employment, nor by the lists of employment agencies.

Because the virtual reduction of supply of labour is expressed primarily in a reduced availability for full-time work, or a greater supply of part-time work, this phenomenon does not appear in the official statistics which continue to register an indifferentiated and unsatisfied supply of work, when in reality this supply is very differentiated and very much conditioned: as is manifestly evident when concrete opportunities of job positions, made available to those signed-up on predetermined lists, are subsequently abandoned by these on the short-list in the face of the real conditions of the work itself.[59]

In order to correctly evaluate the phenomenon we are talking about it would be necessary to heavily correct the meaning of employment and unemployment statistics.[60] Associative economy implies a non-remunerated occupation (monetarily speaking) which diminishes the worth of a demand for remunerated employment. A non-active person could be – with the development of associative economy – a person who is in reality only partially inactive, because employed in an informal manner, but not as a result of this any less productive or less remunerative (from an informal point of view).

In this regard it appears pertinent, even if not exhaustive, to use the definition 'informal economy' to designate associative economy. In this age of post-industrial society in which an informal economy (informal because not formally perceptible in official systems of accounting of production and employment) develops rapidly, the formal value of employment (and of non-employment or of unemployment) is not the same as it was in the age in which society was becoming industrialized, in which the informal (non-monetary) economy tended to disappear and in which the exchange of goods and services, and therefore also of employment, tended to be monetarized. Until associative employment (including that which is not remunerated monetarily) is also taken into account in employment and unemployment statistics, the worth of employment (and of unemployment) of today will be very different from that of the age of industrialization: according to our personal estimation its worth should be roughly halved.[61]

And as long as associative employment is not also accounted, the employment-effect of the increment in the associative sector will be – as other things belonging to the change in post-industrial society – buried, or hidden or simply distorted.

However – to return to the theme of the different forms of financing – private financing of associative activities, above all of the new ones and of those connected with the new emerging social needs, might also find other forms even less conventional than those cited above. Reflection in this regard is not yet at a very advanced stage and the various opinions are not all unanimous, not even among the partisans of the third sector and of the associative economy; but we equally feel we should insist here on a new form of private-collective financing which for a long time has been considered efficient and the driving-force of great social developments: the *trade-union funds for investment* (to which we will dedicate the following section).

6.3 Trade-Union Funds for Investment

Substantial financing of the associative sector could be assured by mobilizing the savings of the wage-earners themselves through the contractual capability of the trade unions and the associative power that they represent. Amongst other things the trade unions are one of the most significant and representative expressions of the associative sector, employing, directly or indirectly, a considerable amount of manpower, with salaried employees and other collateral activities. Thus in its contractual activity for guaranteeing ever higher wages, the trade union performs a role which influences considerably distributive processes.

In the first place, the trade union tries to allow those working in sectors with a high degree of productivity to participate in the profits of those same sectors.

In the second place, by pushing for the wages of workers in sectors with a low degree of productivity to equal those of workers in sectors with a high degree of productivity, the trade unions modify the relative prices of each of the sectors, in such a way that the entire social context comes to benefit from the advantages of the increment in productivity attained in those sectors with a high rate of productivity (since the prevailing market structures prevent a generalized redistribution of such advantages through the lowering of the price of products belonging to those sectors with a high degree of productivity).

In the third place, the trade union influences the distributive processes, by negotiating with the governments the level and the progressive curve of levies, be they fiscal or of the social-security type, upon the income (of workers and non-workers) and by negotiating the direction of allocation of public resources which are so levied.

Now, it is well known that in the usual framework of economic policies it is always asked of the trade unions to contain their wage demands within the limits which must not exceed the average overall rate of increment of productivity at the level of the entire economic system. The principal argument given is that wage increases are translated, almost entirely, into additional final consumption, while savings and investments have their source substantially in income deriving from capital.

If one does not assure an adequate margin of profit for the enterprises, investments are discouraged and unemployment is produced: so it is said. The trade unions often object that it is not to be taken for granted that profits must necessarily be the exclusive source of investments; nor is it to be taken for granted that wages are necessarily converted into final consumption. Basically it is from this objection that the idea was born of instituting *trade-union funds* – managed by the trade unions themselves – which gather together the *contractual savings* of the workers, that is to say the savings established during collective bargaining, both at national level, and at sectorial, regional, or even company level.

Some have seen in trade-union or wage funds for investment the means for transforming the capitalist nature of today's economic system: i.e. to create a capital 'without an owner';[62] however, proposals and discussions in this regard are much more numerous than corresponding implementations. And even in the heart of the trade-union movement there exists much hesitation regarding this: above all among those who prefer the trade-unions in their traditional role, as administrators of the employment market through collective bargaining, or, as negotiators with government on the measures of general economic policy.[63]

The exercising of responsibility in the matter of financial activities, on the part of the unions, used to raise much diffidence and it is claimed that they would have neither experience nor adequate structures for it. And in effect, the formation of union funds for investment would be of limited value and meaning if such funds should then only be channelled into the ordinary financial market, nourishing the demand for capital at market rates, and if such uses should be remunerated with the normal profits of a financial enterprise.

The trade-union funds could, however, constitute exactly an alternative channel of financial accumulation, by its nature different from the profit-making sector of the capital market, and could be suitable for financing precisely the activity undertaken by the third sector, itself also without profit-making ends. Obviously the modalities of distribution and assignment of the funds to the initiatives of the third sector should be further studied with much care; they should become the object of mechanisms still entirely to be invented in a logic of financial engineering.

7 THE ROLE OF THE TRADE UNIONS IN THE MANAGEMENT OF THE LABOUR MARKET AND OF THE NEW FORMS OF PRODUCTION AND EMPLOYMENT

The creation of an instrument, such as that of trade-union funds (with the implications for employment which would derive from it), for the promotion of the 'third sector' is based on a general review of the role of the trade-union, which seems, however, to still meet with much resistance and misunderstanding, tied up with the conservative spirit which still permeates the structure of the trade-union leadership. It is worth briefly stopping on this argument as it would imply one of the most relevant changes of post-industrial society.

In such a society, in fact, the worker finds himself covering different roles, to a much greater degree than before, when the social roles were much more rigid. The trade union cannot fail to reflect on this situation; it must follow the workers it represents in these new and multiple roles, unless it wishes to run the risk (a risk already experienced by the more conservative unions in the industrial world) of losing the convinced adhesion of the workers themselves.

The trade union is in this way obliged to represent in some way not only the worker as such, but also the worker as consumer, the worker as saver, the worker as user of public services, and lastly (with the expansion of the associative phenomenon which we discuss) also the worker as a member of auto-consuming communities, or rather – which is the same thing – of auto-producing communities, essentially of services. The intervention of the trade union in these fields does not imply an incompatible duplication of the social functions of the state, but rather on the contrary a duplication not only compatible but also desirable because coherent with a pluralistic conception of modern political society which has a need to counterbalance the growing powers of the state.

Here it is worth underlining that the spread of the institutional and functional tasks of the trade union slots into the necessity of managing in some way the containment of a growing (and moreover impossible) 'etatization' by means of the promotion of substitute activities, at the same time both private and collective, outside the market or, better, without profit-making goals. In other words, it slots into the growth, already amply described, of the third sector or 'Associative Sector'.

The trade union would become in this way the promotor of the development of activities (and therefore of a supply) in the tertiary services, and quaternary generators of new occupations (at low capital intensity levels), activities which in the traditional capitalistic market would not find adequate conditions for development, due to their general inability to stimulate entrepreneurship; while the state could not develop them due to the financial limitations already mentioned.

In this way the trade union (which already represents in its own right an important institution of associative economy) would become the promotor of the development of other institutions of the associative economy itself. And it would furthermore rediscover a very strong tie with its own origins, which are connected and contemporary with the mutual-aid movements and co-operatives, which become justly considered the forefathers of the third sector.

It would only be a question of relaunching this organic binding together of the three movements (trade unions, cooperatives and mutual-aid 'societies') with new forms suited to the new circumstances and to the needs of collective consumption of post-industrial society. A trade-union fund for investment (national or articulated on a sectorial or spatial basis), thus conceived and so oriented, would constitute the basis of a specific financial circuit, much more suited for operating in the non-profit sector, in as much as it is itself not regulated by the principles and the logic of profit-making as is the ordinary capital market.[64]

8 PROMOTION OF THE ASSOCIATIVE SECTOR IN THE FRAME-WORK OF A COMPREHENSIVE PLAN OF DEVELOPMENT

Naturally, the growth of a so-conceived third sector – as a sector of the associative economy – and the development of the most appropriate forms for its financing, cannot but call for a favourable and promotional policy from governments and, in the European case, from the Community.

As we have said, there are numerous legislative and administrative governmental measures – implying expenditure or not – which could create the institutional conditions favourable for the development of an associative economy. In effect the state, which, thanks to the development of an associative sector, could register a relative decrease of its own services distributed directly by itself, would not however see diminished, but rather increased, its function of overall planning (of which we spoke in Chapter 11).

And in the framework of this function, the comparative development of public services and of services supplied by the associative sector and the comparative use of the financial and economic resources in the two sectors, should be justified by cost–benefit evaluations at a level of 'societal' economy in its entirety. And all this in order to be sure that the destinations of the resources (which some can consider 'distortions'), outside the verification of the market and not dominated by profit-making logic, correspond to 'societal' welfare functions (as 'collective preferences functions') which are also well-defined.

The analysis and evaluation of the investments in the third sector could be partly based on the developments attained in the theory of public economy, and on the criteria and techniques of determination of value and prices outside of the market[65] (prices already widely applied in the case of public investments); and in part they could give rise to new criteria and techniques for the associative economy itself.

All this can occur by introducing strategic planning and result evaluation systems and procedures in the non-profit organizations.[66]

13 New Policies and Instruments

We will now attempt to conclude our analysis, in particular that devoted to the 'management problems of the change', by proceeding to a sort of condensation of a large part of the arguments dealt with, and by providing a small *'summa'* of the management policies to be adopted.

1 NEW TASKS FOR THE PUBLIC SECTOR

The changes that are taking place in the structure of contemporary industrial society, as found in the principal Western countries (examined in the previous chapters), imply and are at the same time linked to profound *transformations in the character and modes of public intervention*.

The history of Western capitalistic societies is characterized by a *constant increase in the magnitude and scope of public intervention* (constituted by all the diverse institutions foreseen by public law: the state, local authorities, public agencies, etc.).

This simple fact in itself constitutes the 'historic proof' of the fallacy of the theory of laissez-faire, with regard to that of the opportuneness of the public regulation of social development. If the thesis were true that the intervention of the state damages economic progress, and thus also social progress, the history of capitalist societies – which have recorded numerous successes in the last two centuries – should be that of a constant economic and social stagnation or non-progress, if not regression, given the dizzy growth which public intervention has had in particular in this century. We might wonder on the other hand whether this substantial increase in the role of the public economy has not constituted an essential factor in the socio-economic progress of capitalist societies. I believe that none of today's theoreticians of laissez-faire would be prepared to claim that contemporary economies could have large growth rates without the intervention of the state. And this bears witness – as historical proof – of the mistake of the old critics of public intervention, who claimed it was harmful, even when this intervention hardly covered 5–10 per cent of the Gross National Product!

The increase in *scope* is characterized by the fact that the incidence of services promoted and supplied by the 'public hand' (which is by definition a 'visible' hand[1]) has been increasing above all in connection with the great possibilities of allocating to immaterial – usually, but incorrectly, called 'tertiary' – services the increasing quantities of resources and manpower made available by technical progress and the impressive increments in physical productivity achieved in the material goods production sectors (agriculture and industry).

Summing up what we have said in the previous chapters, once primary needs were satisfied, even with considerable population growth, effort was then addressed, with greater resources, to the satisfaction of the immaterial welfare needs (education, health, environment, recreation, etc.) that were previously satisfied at possibly more sophisticated quality levels only from a certainly far more limited portion of the population. This obviously gave rise to a constant increase in the utilization of real resources, labour *in primis*, in the public service sector. There was thus a steady rise in the numbers of medical staff, teachers, sportsmen, writers, and civil servants of every class and rank, 'intellectuals', and generally all those who, in one way or another, directly or indirectly, are paid or subsidized by the state through taxation of the product and income of the entire economy.

The increase *in magnitude* is in turn characterized by the fact that there has been an extension, in both quality and quantity, of the protective system provided by the state against all social hazards and afflictions (unemployment, disablement, illness, and finally old age). This has naturally resulted in the introduction of increasingly novel, large-scale and extensive social assistance schemes, to such a degree as to be accused of disincentivating personal initiative and enterprise. These comprise all the various forms of 'income maintenance' introduced by the Welfare State, and essentially consist in the withdrawal of resources produced by those who take part directly in the production process, for redistribution to those who do not.

But we have also seen that the Welfare State has entered an 'overload' crisis. And this deserves a *completely new attitude* by the supporters of public intervention and the Welfare State, which has nothing to do with the old *querelles* about *laissez-faire* and public intervention.

2 THE FINANCIAL LIMITS OF THE STATE

As we have already described (Chapter 8), the point has been reached at which the process of 'free' (i.e. solely fiscal) provision of the new social services, and the process of 'transfer' of income (again by fiscal means) for the various, increasingly widespread forms of '*income maintenance*', have brought about a 'financial' incidence of the state on the overall real product of each country that could not easily be further increased.

At the same time, *it is by no means certain* that the 'real incidence' of social services utilized and consumed by the population should not or could not further increase in the overall consumption structure, as the expression of either an authentic preference on the part of the final consumers themselves, or of a *collective and political preference* expressed by the legitimate inter-preters of popular sovereignty.

In other words, what cannot be increased is not the relative amount of real resources supplied in the real social services, but only the role of financial intermediation played by the state, because it is a source of distortion between the real wants and the real preferences of different social categories; and is in addition a source of squandering and unnecessary bureaucracy, which often produces social costs that are disproportionate to the benefits ensured.

2.1 General Alternatives to Public Intervention

To ensure instead the desirable expansion of social services and resource utilization in the overall resource utilization structure, it would be necessary to avoid placing the corresponding burden on the taxation system, in order to avoid the inflationary repercussions (or feedback) that tend, indeed, to nullify any reform in the resource utilization structure.

Paradoxically, it is not excluded that such rape of the state budget pushes it towards an increase in (monetary) public consumption, a cutting back in social consumption, and induces, through public expenditure and transfer, a resistance to desiderable decline of real consumption of material and indus-trial goods (from food to electronics), which, on the contrary, is increasingly 'oversatured', 'saturated' or 'saturable'. And this provokes a 're-launching' of inflationary mechanism.

With more sophisticated *comprehensive programmes of resource utilization* – established in a central planning framework, as illustrated in Chapter 11 – instead of directly taking on the management of these services, the state could develop formulas to enable the general objectives identified to be achieved by the mobilization of *other direct financial channels*, based essentially on the initiative and direct management of the users themselves. Such channels, possibly promoted or regulated or incentivated through public finance, would involve the utilization of 'private' incomes (this is the 'third sector' which we have dealt with in Chapters 11 and 12).

Thus, instead of pursuing a course of generalization, public intervention could more usefully:

(a)   on the one hand, restrict itself to the most needy cases and sectors (in both social and regional terms, i.e. those in which cultural and institutional factors rule out the autonomous assumption of civil and economic responsibilities in the fields of social consumption);

(b) on the other hand, commit itself to 'promotional' action, incentivization and guidance, that is to say to a *planning* and *programming* rather than to a *direct operational* role.

Generalization should be pursued in an increasing proportion of social consumption and services in respect of industrial goods production; and should be pursued not in a direct manner, but instead through the freely chosen action of present or potential users, in the forms preferred by them, possibly with collective management.

Instead of further extending free social services – or services with generalized 'political' prices, i.e. costs borne by the state budget – these should instead be concentrated on only truly *indivisible* services (as they are classified by all conventional handbooks of 'public economics': see Chapter 9). On the other hand – with appropriate initial incentivation – the role of moving towards self-management and financing of such services, above all the 'divisible' ones, should be left to collective (but 'private') forms of association.

In 'real' terms, this would still involve the management of the same quota of resources (the fiscal measures would still weigh equally on private income): if it is desired that this quota should increase to the benefit of *certain* social services, it may be wondered whether it would not be more efficient to act directly on the spending behaviour of the users and beneficiaries, rather than through the imperfect and imponderable instrument of taxation.

It would be necessary to find out how to 'block' the expansion of some expenditure sectors, and foster the birth or expansion of others: and this can obviously be all the more easily achieved not only as the total amount of funds available increases, but also in proportion to the clarity and precision of the overall picture with regard to total funds available and all necessary and desirable items of expenditure; or in other words, to the degree of articulation and sophistication of the planning method employed.

Indirect 'instruments' of public intervention, if goals were clear and quantified, would certainly not be lacking.

2.2 New Criteria for Managing Public Intervention

In many of the traditional sectors in which services are provided 'gratis' by the state, characterized by *indivisibility* of consumption, new management criteria should be adopted. As a first step, it would be necessary to introduce advanced techniques for measuring the performance, output and effectiveness of the service provided. And in those cases where this output can only be evaluated on the basis of the users' subjective feeling of well-being, it would be advisable to introduce forms of user self-management of the service, though still in a public finance framework, linked to objective quant-itative criteria.

In those cases in which, on the contrary, the service can only be evaluated in an 'objective' and political fashion (justice, defence, institutional system, public order, civil defence, etc.), modern forms of output and productivity evaluation should be introduced, with advanced cost–benefit analysis meth-ods, with the aim of using rational methods to minimize the amount of resources used to achieve politically detemined public ends.

Where their use is possible, forms of self-management of public services are instead the best instrument to ensure the maximum efficiency of the service itself from the users' point of view.

The transformations that are taking place in the structure of contemporary industrial society imply, therefore, a decrease in the importance of the accumulation and investment process in agriculture and industry, with respect to that which is to be obtained in the service sector. But this also tends to modify the operational model according to which the accumulation and investment process has hitherto taken place.

Indeed, with due exceptions, the accumulation process has until now been guaranteed by the profit-making expectations of the 'firms' – public and especially private – operating in the 'market', with profit as the indicator of success and essential motivation.

In widening the scope of economic activities towards 'self-managed' services (whether self-financed or otherwise) the weight of *non-profit-motiv-ated* investments tends to increase enormously. This does not mean, how-ever, that there is also a reduction in the importance of the investments themselves and of the related accumulation of resources: the process of setting aside and saving income earned and produced must therefore be attained outside the usual financial channels, motivated by profit and interest rates.

This, therefore, envisages a new important role to be played by financial sectors, linked, with regard to both the collection and the utilization of resources, to 'new' activities, outside the normal financial capital markets. Totally new institutions will consequently be required, such as Trade Union Investment Funds (dealt with in Chapter 12).

Public economy grew up (in the Welfare State) to assure fair redistribution of the benefits of development and compensation for the inequalities pro-duced by development itself. Public economy has aimed to ensure equal opportunities and access to services for *everybody*.

But the nearer one came to this goal, the more a widespread need emerged for differentiation and autonomy of choice. This is basically the reason for a certain disaffection towards the services provided by the state, which have at the same time become more costly in proportion as efforts are made to render them more attractive to their users.

In this situation of sought-after differentiation and growing standardization, in the dichotomy between what is wanted and what is obtained, the reality of waste has crept in.

In order to assure their availability to all, many services have been brought to levels not totally demanded; while the shortcomings of others have at the same time induced the more prosperous classes to replace them with private services more in keeping with their specific expectations. In other words, waste has become inherent to the 'public' nature of such activities, to the intention of providing a service available to *all*. And this is so without even considering the *processes of 'bureaucratization'* (that is to say, unnecessary work produced by the mere existence of bureaucratic relationships), or rather assuming them to be neither more nor less likely to occur than in the private sector (which is clearly a 'heroic' assumption).

This difficult situation with regard to the public economy is combined with the increasing importance (in the structuring of 'needs' and the demand for services and also for goods) of what can be described as 'positional' goods and services, in the sense in which Fred Hirsch uses the term: goods and services which are perceived as being useful only because they are *not* accessible to everybody.[2] This creates a decidedly paradoxical situation: the more the state attempts to satisfy everyone, the less satisfied everyone is.

A reality such as this can no longer be overlooked by social reformers. And it means that new approaches are required for social reform itself, the aim of which is to offer equal opportunities to everybody. Any reformist attitude that fails to take these new facts into account, and instead sticks to the old vision of the state's role as provider of undifferentiated services that must be the same for everyone, would be the most effective ally for the dismantling of the Welfare State, going in exactly the opposite direction to people's real needs. Such an attitude would be uselessly conservative.

In those cases where the public economy produces wastefulness and dissatisfaction, it should be replaced by a free initiative and free enterprise economy: but – and this is the innovative and 'social-oriented' aspect of such an approach – these should be initiatives and enterprises not motivated by gain/profits, and would operate outside and beyond the market.

All this has therefore contributed, in all likelihood, to cause historically obsolete operative situations to survive and even to flourish unnaturally. Out of the hatred for the public economy and the state dominance which it engenders, a policy of anachronistic and inefficient 'privatization' is adopted. And vice versa, out of hatred for the market economy and the capitalist power it produces, excessive and inefficient encroachment on the part of the state is accepted and defended.

3 THE FUTURE OF STRATEGIC PLANNING

Therefore the 'associative' economy could constitute the *new* developing sector in post-industrial society, and could determine the characteristics, by its own values and modes of operation, of a *new type of society* (neither capitalistic nor 'étatist', but what we could term 'social'? or 'socialist'? or, at best, 'liberal-socialist'?).

This does not imply that the public sector, the state (in all its articulations and local ramifications), on the one hand, and the market on the other, shall not in future still have a very important role to play in the overall economic system.

3.1 The New 'Regulatory' Role of the Public Sector

The state, in particular, must increasingly perfect its *role as the regulator* of development in the public interest; a role that in the capitalist nations it has hitherto performed somewhat dubiously, falling largely under the thrall of the logic and philosophy of the market economy (which must however be admitted to have been the most notable source of progress and social change from the time of the industrial revolution onward).

This role is today facilitated both by more extensive political means of intervention available (acquired by the state in the more recent evolution of political systems), and by greater understanding and theoretical knowledge of the processes and mechanisms of the relations and transactions operating in economic and social systems (such as the fundamental improvement in statistical information and the construction of economic, social and demographic accounting systems, etc.)

This regulatory role should be performed above all by determining *ex ante* – through appropriate forms of 'simulation' – the scenarios resulting from possible or desirable changes in consumption patterns, the quality of life, and the social structure of behaviour and relationships, and inducing operators to *negotiate* preferential choices in relation to these scenarios, upon which their respective lines of action can be based.[3]

In Western industrial nations, which are also the most technologically advanced, the state would still appear to be very far from capable of assuming this regulatory role, and still appears to be restricted to that of *ex post* 'recorder' or 'notary' of the market economy; and this market economy is today rather dominated by the large-scale producers of the 'meso-economic' sector, which is fundamentally monopolistic or oligopolistic, generally on a multinational scale, causing this economy to be something quite far from the theoretical concept or ideal type of a 'market economy'.[4]

In the above nations, the state plays, at most, a remedial role, 'patching up' the various faults that develop in the mechanisms of this 'market' economy, i.e. 'capitalist' type; although by now the faults to be repaired have become so numerous and have required such large-scale remedial action of a social nature (pollution, job debasement, health problems, unemployment, delinquency, urban congestion, environmental degradation, etc.) as to create a 'parallel' demand – the public economy – which is overwhelming that of the market.

Indeed, in the capitalist economy, both the state, and also the trade-union movement, in spite of the various powers they have accumulated in the slow and lengthy evolution of the system itself, appear to be two institutional 'carry-overs', two 'by-products', of the system, existing indeed only as *repairers* of the system itself and, in a sense, opposed to it by reason of its faults.

No matter how 'independent' the State and the unions have sought to become – above all in the Welfare State – their development has been up to now a function of the 'crisis' of the system in which they operate.

3.2   Central Planning and Direct Intervention

The non-capitalist (and really 'democratic') state must instead seek to play an *autonomous leadership role*. And, in order to do this, it should not just *wait* until the spontaneous mechanisms of the market produce 'situations' to be dealt with, either for better or for worse, but should instead begin to control such mechanisms with the purpose of orienting them to work in the interest of popular and political sovereignty.

There has long been a word for this type of preventive management of social development, and this word is *'planning'* (and when carried out at the level of an entire national community it is called *national* or *central planning*).[5]

But in spite of the enormous increase in all Welfare State countries of the state's powers and means of intervention, the only thing that it has not been possible to establish in those nations is *a modern central planning system*.[6]

And this is perhaps because it would have been the only means of overcoming the substantial *'subordination'* of the state in relation to the capitalist system itself, and its *ex post* vicissitudes.

It may be added that the reasons for this behaviour are neither mysterious nor beyond explanation. The more the state is burdened with 'reparatory' activities, made necessary by the emergence of various critical situations, and the more it must engage in 'constrained' direct management, the more its margins of choice and operation are restricted and the more existing constraints – starting with its own financial resources – are predominant and determinant.[7]

On the other hand, the more the state is freed from direct management functions, the more it can develop those planning and programming functions, that should be more properly its own, in order to recover and decisively acquire *prior decisional autonomy*.

In any case the state, in its 'reparatory' role, is proving increasingly incapable of effectively controlling the most important 'crisis' factors: unemployment, public deficit and so on. And this is because the state is not yet capable of understanding in detail, let alone governing, the interrelational factors between the various economic phenomena, and is not able in an adequate manner to simulate their operation for control and decision-making purposes.

A highly detailed knowledge of these interrelations, and the adoption of adequate choices in relation to overall development and its specific components which are the constituent factors of a strategic planning process, would reverse the traditional approach, which for simplicity's sake we will term 'economic policy', which aims to govern only the 'aggregate' quantities of the system, with central government 'instruments' only.

The consistency between the overall (and therefore aggregate, according to the chosen taxonomy) quantities is not in question, at this point. It is indeed obvious that every evaluation and planning approach at *disaggregate* level must prove consistent and compatible with regard to the reference aggregate quantities.

But although the *structural* relationship between aggregate and disaggregate variables (according to a given taxonomy) must necessarily be in the form of equations and identities, this is not the case with 'behavioural' relations: the functional behaviour of an aggregate variable is not necessarily identical to that of its component variables, and may therefore be 'different' in its substance and form. That is to say, it may differ according to the typology of the variables that constitute the aggregation.

Any *ex ante* evaluation or decision carried out at the aggregate variables level will therefore be evasive of problems and choices that should be made at the disaggregate level, and that could be far more significant than those illusorily made at aggregation level.[8]

Knowledge and control of the interrelations between the 'disaggregate' variables of the system (and the degree of taxonomical disaggregation will, in fact, be determined by the complex set of problems that dominate all planning processes) will shed light on the 'invisible' functioning of the market that economic theory has always sought to deduce and codify; in other words, it will make the hand described as 'invisible' become 'visible'.

Planning thus provides the means to control the 'invisible' functioning of the market, rendering it 'visible' and susceptible to prior determination, by reason of choices negotiated under the sponsorship of the state between the institutional operators, through *prior control* (*ex ante* and not *ex post*) of the various transactions constituting the economic process, and their consequences.

3.3 Articulated or 'Systemic' Planning

This is why modern planning is not public intervention planning, as always believed, by both its supporters and its opponents. When conceived in this manner, indeed, planning could not help but be associated with the authoritarian extension of the direct production role of the state. And as such, its fortunes were linked to those of 'étatism', in its successes and its failures.

But modern planning is not, on the other hand, merely 'indicative', as it has long been preferable to describe it in contrast to the 'authoritarian' or 'imperative' type, and also with the intention of emphasizing its capacity to coexist and even integrate with the market economy (the planning approach 'à la française' is the best known example of this indicative planning).

Modern planning is essentially *systemic*, in the sense that it seeks to include in its *analysis and prospective evaluation framework* all variables considered relevant, and is articulated into a *series of partial pictures and models*, which must however be reciprocally consistent. This is because it is not possible to express all the variables considered to be important in a single picture or model.[9]

Planning has as its principal instruments, as is obvious, the plans themselves. And planning is *systemic* insofar as the national plan (and perhaps a supranational one), the synthesis, is the point of encounter and verification (as regards compatibility) of a numerous series of plans, of a sectorial and spatial (by fields of activity and regional areas) and even institutional (by more or less aggregated operators) character.

The formulation of the plans is based on the independent evaluations of the operators concerned; indeed systemic planning is, in fact, a service provided by the state so as to render *consistent* and *efficient* in relation to *each other* (the condition for their success and even their implementation) the various plans of the various operators, whether public or private, sectorial or territorial.

None the less, the state as sovereign political authority can and should formulate general guidelines, to be complied with when the various plans are brought into mutual consistency.

The problem of *how* to ensure that the sub-state plans are in 'conformity' with these state guidelines, or with each other, vertically and horizontally, in cases of clear incompatibility or conflict, is a problem that will be solved 'politically' and subsequently: through appropriate forms of negotiation, arbitration and political decision. Two factors are essential and will determine the effectiveness of such a planning system (as a 'system'):

– the arbitration and relative trade-offs must be based on sufficiently clear and well-defined frameworks and scenarios;

– and even the individual plans, independently formulated and subsequently brought into conformity through arbitration to a 'systemic' logic, must make *explicit* the extrasystemic reference data on which they are constructed (data which are either taken into account in the 'higher level' plans, or developed hypothetically by the plans themselves).

The modalities used may vary from one case to another. In some cases it may be sufficient, for example, to employ *persuasion* to ensure that the plans are made to conform, or the plan's self-adaptation. In others, some public operators may prefer *incentivation* or *command*, by means of legal or administrative intervention, which would involve 'authoritarian' action.

In conclusion, as outlined here, modern (and systemic) planning is not, in itself, either authoritarian or indicative, because this involves the tools available of relations between decision-makers and not the actual formation of decisional content; in other words, it could adopt 'authoritarian' norms or else merely provide recommendations (just to select two extreme solutions) according to circumstances, and according to the implementation prospects resulting from the evaluations made by the institutions concerned, even during the negotiation process.[10]

In this context Shonfield's phrase (Shonfield and Shaw, 1972) about a desirable planning which should be 'more than indicative and less than imperative' seems a little too 'naive' and reductive; but this expression captures the meaning of the type of planning which we have attempted to describe and develop further in this chapter with greater articulation.[11]

4 PLANNING-ORIENTED COLLECTIVE BARGAINING

Of all the implementation procedures, the most important is clearly negotiation or *bargaining*, which we shall call '*planning-oriented*' bargaining in order to distinguish it from the type that has long been in existence among operators and political bodies, but which is performed without any plan being present, and constitutes '*market-oriented*' bargaining (although often with regard to a 'political market').

If it did not seem at first sight (and only at first sight) to involve a contradiction of terms, we would prefer to speak of a 'planning market', because this would clearly express the concept of a plan (or plans) negotiated between the operators involved, within the framework of, and in conformity with, plans at higher 'system levels', and it would also express the concept of its implementation by *means of agreements*.

Which level allocates	Authority: whose preferences prevail	Central preferences	Mixed preferences	Peripheral preferences
M a n a g e m e n t s y s t e m	Decision, making by the Centre	1. Central, direct (a) Perfect and direct central allocation with consumption rationing (b) Central and direct allocation with free consumer choice	4. Central and market oriented, direct Direct allocation of investment based on central preferences and direct allocation of resources for current production based on market principles	7. Market oriented, direct Market oriented, direct allocation based on profit criterion in market prices
	Decision-making mixed	2. Central, direct and indirect Central direct allocation (as in 1) with built-in mechanism for indirect allocation (as in 3)	5. Central and market oriented, direct and indirect Central-direct allocation of investment and market built-in for current production	8. Market oriented, direct and indirect Market oriented direct allocation of investment and mechanism of market allocation of current production
	Decision-making by the Enterprise	3. Central, indirect Central, indirect allocation through mechanism based on shadow pricing (possible versions corresponding to 1 (a) and (b))	6. Central and market oriented, indirect Corporation market regulated by government	9. Market oriented, indirect Perfect competitive market

Figure 13.1   Resource allocation models

In addition, the term would clearly express the intention of somehow substituting in place of the traditional concept of the 'market', in an abstract sense, as a place (of a highly mysterious and uncontrollable character) in which transactions and their terms are spontaneously and 'naturally' determined,[12] the concept of a 'market' as a place for negotiation, agreement and stipulation, 'administration' and management agreed upon between relevant powers and actors, both public and private, as well as unions and companies.

The latter concept seems to us to be far more appropriate to the desired future condition of greater *collective and prior control of economic social development*.

Today's 'administered' market, dominated by 'mesoeconomic' forces, needs *planning-oriented bargaining* to restore an active role to excluded and subordinate forces, which, as we have mentioned, include the state and the unions, which still operate in an 'auxiliary' position. It therefore needs a proliferation of 'plans', as a result of this plan negotiation, to restore congruency to the objectives of economic and social development.

Planning-oriented bargaining has already been prototyped in many Western European countries. *'Contrattazione programmatica'* in Italy at the end of the 1960s, the *'planning agreements'* foreseen in British industrial legislation, and the French *'contrats de plan'*, especially in the version recommended in more recent official documents issued by the French government, are all examples indicating a widespread need to achieve a negotiated system of intervention in which decisions are made by agreement between the central government, industry and the unions. But if these experiments are to overcome the historical limitations they proved to have, it is necessary for them to be introduced into an ordered 'process' of central and multi-level plan construction, of the articulated and systemic type described above.

In other words, it is necessary for planning to become the *predominant system of organization and control of decisions so that planning-oriented bargaining* can operate in conditions that are no longer characterized by haphazardness, inadequate instruments, and ultimately by absolute precariousness and ineffectiveness.

To achieve this improvement in the planning-oriented bargaining (which is substantially lacking as yet in all countries), it would be necessary to establish clear public planning 'procedures', specified by the legislation (and perhaps also by the Constitutions) of the modern nations, which foresee an orderly and well-articulated process of plan formation and negotiation, at all levels, with reasonable but definite time limits; and this would be done for the purpose of 'launching' a complex 'planning system', from which the new form of economic and social development evaluation and decision-making would be brought forth.

5 PLANNING-ORIENTED SOCIAL ACCOUNTING

Such *socio-economic frames* of reference are essentially *accounting frames*. This is why a new and modern systemic planning, of the type forecast here, is based on a new system of *social accounting*. This would be based essentially on two innovative developments:

1. Firstly, it will be 'extended' to include 'non-market' transactions, given the importance which these transactions have acquired in the formation of social product and social well-being, which can no longer be overlooked and must be taken into consideration in accounting terms as well.
2. Secondly, it will include projection into the future, since it will express not only the *ex-post* recording of a social reality, but also the foreseeable and desirable quantifications, based on *ex-ante* plans, of the same social

reality, these quantifications being, in turn, the scenario within the framework of which the various operators will situate their actions.

As regards the technical aspects of this *extended* social accounting, it has to date undergone some discussion, and initial application, encountering the first difficulties. As well as being perfected from a conceptual point of view,[13] it also requires a lot of work to be carried out to create adequate *information tools*, which are at present insufficient in all nations with regard to those costs and benefits that cannot be measured in terms of market prices (social costs, environmental costs, etc.).

However, the development of the relative accounting technology will be interactive, i.e. a condition, but also a result of the development of the political demand for planning.

In the budget forecast and scenario-construction field also, considerable work is required to perfect the techniques concerning simulated projection or conditioned forecasting. But here it seems that technical progress is today considered far more important than political progress, and that this work has become excessively academic, and risks the futility of unnecessary and unproductive sophistication because it is not applied to concrete situations and circumstances by appropriate decision-making centres, which would instead render its methodologies more concrete and effective.

The stable political introduction of a central planning system would most certainly improve the situation enormously. It could also represent an opportunity for important scientific progress in this matter.

6 PLANNING AND THE NEW UNIONISM

The introduction of a central planning system of the type described above would indispensably require modifications in the practices of both the company system and the union system. Planning-oriented collective bargaining would become the fundamental occasion of such adjustment.

Planning would give firms a kind of vast 'market analysis', on the basis of which they would orient their investment decisions, in a manner that would, however, be agreed with other firms and institutions.

This will involve studying, one by one, the cases in which product competition between firms is less harmful than beneficial (and, in this case, would be appropriately encouraged); and the cases where, on the contrary, its negative effects would lead it to be replaced by suitable forms of agreements. These agreements should be developed along the same lines as the industrial 'trusts' that have in many cases given rise to large-scale concentration of investments, and high efficiency and productivity in the most highly developed phase of capitalism; with the difference that here this would take place with the blessing of the government, the unions and the consumers, and above all in accordance with the planning system's objectives.

Planning would provide the unions, with regard to their collective bargaining practices, with a new way of negotiating wages and other working conditions, with greater attention and effectiveness with regard to the acquisition of real income and real wages.

The trade-union officials' job would certainly become more difficult, but also more effective. The unions could at last achieve a real 'presence' in the seats of economic policy decision-making, instead of one that is, as has been the case up to now, episodic, symbolic and substantially ineffective, also because the government itself is not able with its present instruments and procedures to negotiate with the unions on a basis of concrete prospects and well-defined operational analyses.

The overall 'responsibleness' of the unions would certainly increase.

The constraints regarding the compatibility of resource and income distribution choices would be more clearly apparent, and would have to be taken into account in negotiating wages. But in this case the issue of constraints would not be illusory, 'to be taken on trust', as in current economic policy declarations applied to a market economy without planning, but would instead involve quite operational, and therefore hard to evade, commitments; also because the accounting systems – if the proper accounting technology, as outlined above, is applied along with 'systemic' planning procedures – would fully reveal the costs and benefits of alternative solutions, and the contradictory and negative effects of any broken undertakings.

In other words, the approach, one of conflict but also of negotiation, would consist in a *trade-off* between alternatively quantifiable solutions, and not on matters of principle or general evaluations without corresponding operational reality.

Social conflict, which today the unions tend to 'discharge', with success, outside their own structures, would to a large extent – an appropriate and concrete extent – be 'internalized' within the union movement's structures, if and insofar as it would be concerned with the distribution of available income among different categories of employed persons. This could certainly make it harder to handle the interests of the various categories of workers on a *'federative'* basis. The first important stage of planning mediation and negotiation (once the constraints specific to each plan have been fixed) would take place *within* the unions, which would become a powerful instrument of political self-management. From this point of view as well, the unions would have a harder life and would find more demanding management requirements; but with more responsibility their power to affect reality would be greater.

For these ends, it would also be advisable to increase the *independence*, both political and formal-institutional, of the union movement – as a force in the 'associative' economy – in relation to the other public institutions, in order to preserve a fundamental dualism (or pluralism) of powers, even where the fields of interest converge.[14]

To obtain these concrete results in this mediatory function within the union front between different categories of workers, with regard to planning and income distribution, the unions would have to master the entire range of distribution and choice problems specific to planning, without being able to delegate elsewhere the responsibility of providing generally compatible solutions (although this responsibility must finally remain with the competent public and politically sovereign institutions).

In order to master these problems, the unions must *master* all planning issues and evaluation techniques, and particularly social accounting and forecasting techniques. In other words, they too must for their own purposes have the capacity to simulate development plans.

This would seem to be one of the most significant outcomes of the new course that a serious planning *reform* could take. It would involve completely new modes of union action, while offering a substantial opportunity for renewal, in the operational *impasse* in which the unions find themselves in the present phase of evolution of the capitalist system.

This would in fact solve many of the problems faced by a union movement that does not have any scope for action credible for its own worker base, due to the above-mentioned *impasse* between, on the one hand, a claim-pressing movement that has now reached an absolute ceiling, and on the other a collaborationism that, failing changes in socio-political structures, risks bringing complete discredit upon the unions, and, in any case, makes them into accomplices in the economic, if not political, debacle of the present democratic system.

Planning reform, in other words, in the terms indicated here, could give a new image to the presence and function of the unions in post-industrial society, in which the role of the 'associative' economy tends to increase; in which the 'market', and consequently the employment market also, tends to acquire completely new characteristics, given the new nature of its jobs (increasingly 'tertiary'); and in which even the role of the 'working class', as traditionally conceived, is undergoing complete transformations.[15]

Thus one could almost speak – with even more justification than in other phases of the history of the trade-union movement – of a 'new unionism'.

7 PLANNING AND THE ORGANIZED CONSUMER MOVEMENT

The introduction of a central planning system, of the type outlined above, finally implies definitive consolidation of the consumer movement (or consumerism).

The extreme development of mass production has already removed the power to control product quality from the individual consumer; and the emergence of tertiary (service) items of consumption of a 'public' nature have led everywhere – especially in the most industrially, and consequently 'tertiarily', advanced nations – to a strong *consumer movement*, which greatly resembles the birth, a century ago, of the analogous workers' movement, which arose as an answer to the challenge of loss of control over the quality and conditions of employment and the development of industrial work.

In a manner very similar to the development of the union movement, the consumer movement grows in proportion to the 'market's loss of significance. With industrialization, in the past, such loss of significance affected an atomistic labour market, which guaranteed a certain balance between the bargaining parties' powers, and thus the unions arose, obviously increasing the rigidity of the labour market and making it a place characterized by *administered relations*. Monopolistic development of production and 'tertiarization', especially of a public type, have introduced a 'market' of *administered prices*, in which the consumer has been deprived of any contractual (market) power: and this has brought about the birth of the *consumer movement*, which will grow all the more as the last vestiges of the traditional 'market' are dismantled.[16]

The new emerging role of planning will tend to introduce new forms of economic transaction, as we have said; in which the operators' decisions should be negotiated *ex ante*, and thus administered prices should reach their highest and most generalized level. The presence of a strong organized movement representing the interests of the consumer-operator, in the planning negotiation and agreement process, becomes essential, because the state may only take on this representative function (as it should have previously done) in an indirect and complex manner.

The consumer-operator (which is essentially constituted by the household-operator, but also by new complex consumption units, especially of a 'tertiary' and 'quaternary' type, emerging from the *associative* economy or the 'third sector' of the economy) must play a fundamental role in planning-oriented collective bargaining, in terms of income distribution and consequent 'relative' prices policy.

Above all, in the phase of planning that involves the definition of its social and structural goals, consumers must play a decisive role with regard to decisions about the final utilization of resources, that is to say the structure of the final demand for goods and services, which comes to be the essential motor of the entire productive process simulated by the plan (obviously taking into account the constraints and conditions of the supply of production factors).

Planning, so as not to risk becoming only a form of corporative mediation between 'producers' (enterprises and workers) – with the presence of a state that is not always strong enough to withstand them, requires the presence of a strongly organized consumer movement: which is, in any case, rapidly growing, due to the historical factors mentioned above, in almost all advanced nations, through the initiative of cooperatives and unions.

The rise of the associative economy (already outlined in Chapters 11 and 12) will necessarily further strengthen the organized consumer movement. Indeed the operative units of the 'third sector', and above all the predominant types that operate in the tertiary and quaternary sectors, are units that tend to unify the moment of production of a service with its moment of consumption: in other words, they are very much 'self-production' and 'self-consumption' units.

None the less, they will constitute a strong final consumer presence on the traditional 'market' for the items for which they cannot be both producers and consumers. And these units will be far more inclined towards associative organization for the purpose of exercising contractual power than is the case with families.

And it will probably be these new consumption units that will decisively strengthen the consumer movement and assure its effective presence in the planning process, which must however be properly worked out in the context of *planning reform*, which we hope develops in all advanced countries.

8   THE 'DEMOCRATIC' MEANING OF STRATEGIC PLANNING

Socio-economic planning, understood in a modern way, far from representing a threat – as would-be interpreters of it would have us believe – to the liberty of the consumer, would, on the contrary, be the way *to give back to the consumers their real sovereignty over choice*, thus preserving it from the constraints of occasional and limited opportunities and the pressing conditions of supply.

The citizens/consumers, as well as the citizens/producers, would have the possibility, with their direct or indirect participation in the elaboration of plans, at any level, as well as with the harmonization and selection of decisions regarding at plans at various levels, of participating in choices made for themselves and for the societies to which they belong, which would be much more influential than the manoeuvring of their limited and, on the whole, narrow purchasing capacity in the strongly limited and conditioned markets in which they operate.

The markets in which they operate, if and when they operate, are without doubt good indicators of the consumers' preferences. But they could also have other ways of revealing preferences and participating in much more vast choices, in all the cases in which the markets do not manage to be a good ground for choice.

The citizens could be directly called to express themselves, with organic surveys that are technically coherent with the procedures of selection and evaluation peculiar to planning processes, and much more widely and in a much more organized, frequent and coordinated manner than is the case today.

With the IT achieved today, a good information system on the opinions, preferences and aspirations of the citizens (whether they be consumers, producers or contributors) would cover a range of 'replies' that would be deeper, more coordinated and much more *revealing* than the occasional and episodic operationality of the markets.

And indirect participation as well, by means of subjects called to representative roles, whether 'public' (elected by the legal political bodies) or 'private' (various category and 'stakeholders' associations and social groupings), could be greatly improved – in particular in making explicit and transparent the motivations and implications of the votes of the representatives (consulted permanently in all decisional fields) and the technical constraints of compatibility between the various decisions.

The coordination, selection, executive control which strategic planning implements are, in fact, essentially ways in which an attempt is made to 'rationalize' individual choice as well, either directly or through representatives, relating them to the possible structural constraints and contradictions. This 'rationalization' would simply make the operationality of the social bodies more aware, less instinctive, and more 'intelligent', without having to lessen their participation by means of only a 'technical' management of planning. And it would have the role of educating the capacity for choice and democratic responsibility of the citizens.

But an information system on the preferences of citizens and their representatives may only function when a system of planning founded on suitable decision and procedure models is in existence.

From this point of view, the development of a modern system of strategic planning constitutes an improvement of the level of citizen participation in the management of society overall, and thus of the degree and quality of democracy of a political system.[17]

Notes and References

Preface

1. Myrdal (1960), first published by Yale University Press. Our quotations are from the British reprinting by Duckworth, 1961.
2. And it has been ignored even by recent works which have used – and perhaps abused as well (I would like to believe unknowingly) – as a title the same expression used by Myrdal (see, for example, Pierson, 1991), without grasping the profound innovative significance and change in the conventional conception of the Welfare State, incorporated in the expression 'beyond' in Myrdal's work. See also Nicholas's (1992) large survey of the contemporary literature on the same subject.
3. Or – as others prefer – public policy or management, regulation, socio-economic programming, and so on. I advocate not renouncing the use of the more correct word 'planning' just because of the too easy references to the historical case of Soviet planning, the wrong identification with the authoritarian style, and other subconscious motivations and roots not well identifiable which have made the word 'planning' a 'dirty' word.
4. Archibugi (1991).
5. In the Chapter Sources the writings are listed in which I developed, in the past, parts of the analysis and reflections which have found a to be hoped organic and unitary exposition in this book.
6. Among them I would like to quote, for the interested reader, and linked to some final chapters of this book (Chapters 11 and 13), the following:

   - *Accounting Framework for National Economic Planning*, published (in Italian) in the 1970s (Archibugi, 1973), as a consequence of a practical experience of a new national economic accounting for planning (witnessed in this epoch in Italy with much disappointment); an updated English edition of it is in preparation.
   - *Introduction to Planology: Towards a Multidisciplinary Convergence of the Planning Sciences*, which analyzes critically many strands of thinking in the economic, sociological, town-planning, system engineering fields, leading to a new concept of the planning discipline (Archibugi, 1992a); also forthcoming in an English edition.
   - *Strategic Planning and Economic Programming*, recently prepared in co-operation with other scholars, as a renewal of the teaching programmes of the (Italian) Postgraduate School of Public Administration (Archibugi et al., 1998); also forthcoming in an English edition.
   - *Treatise of General Planning*, under preparation, which represents in didactic form the synthesis of various studies and research paths aimed at the birth and the 'neo-disciplinary' development and training of a new professional figure of planner. (According to the syllabus of a special Seminar held with the cooperation of the (Italian) National Research Council in 1993.)

1 From Social Protection to Social Integration

1. The literature on the evolution of social welfare and the Welfare State is boundless. Among many works, I refer the reader to some recent works consulted: the collection of essays edited by Dixon and Scheurell (1989); Flora (1986); Tomasson (1983); Baldassari, Paganetto and Phelps (1995); and the books by P. Thane (1982); Flora and Heidenheimer (1981a and b); Ashford (1986); De Swaan (1988); Ritter (1991); and Rimlinger (1974). For Great Britain, in particular J. Hay (1978); for Great Britain and Germany, the papers collected by Mommsen (1981). A more recent work by Christopher Pierson (on a claimed 'new Welfare economic policy') collects recommended documentation on historical studies into the Welfare State (Pierson, 1991). The work by Pierson also constitutes an accurate catalogue of the various recent and current positions on the Welfare State crisis (seen from all angles) but loses its way – in my opinion – in many political issues that are at the margin of the main critical challenges of the Welfare State's future. Still from the point of view of the historical evolution of the Welfare State, I would mention, for Great Britain, the numerous works by Richard M. Titmuss which constitute, at least for the early post-war period, something half-way between historical analysis and political protagonism, on the part of an author who has had a great influence on the Welfare State in his country (see for all his works, the 'essays' of the 1950s, collected in 1958, and a further collection of essays in 1968 and 1979), and for this reason a remarkable impact on the experiences of many other European countries, which have always taken Great Britain as a reference point on this subject.
2. Many scholars prefer the term 'social-democratic', in order to distinguish more precisely this latter from the social policies of 'real socialism', i.e., that of Eastern European countries up to a few years ago (for more extensive comments on this point, see Pierson, 1991, chs. 1–3).
3. On the paternalist character of the Welfare State, as conventionally intended, see, for example, Andreas George Papandreu with an essay on 'paternalist capitalism' (1972), and C. Pateman on the patriarchal character of the Welfare State (1988) and Nielsen (1994). In general terms, a development of this argument can be found usefully in a report of a British Commission (see Dahrendorf *et al.*, 1995).
4. On this point I would like to mention the large collection of arguments edited by B. Jossa (1989), for a volume of the eighth series of the *Biblioteca dell'Economista* (*Library of the Economist*) of the publishing house UTET, a volume dedicated precisely to the 'theory of economic systems'. The paper which engages this topic the most is without doubt by F. Volpi (1989), which summarizes the argument on *The Economic System and Modes of Production*. (On the 'economic systems' see note 33 of Chapter 10 of this book.)
5. Or, if we prefer, less social segregation, marginalization or disintegration.
6. Sometimes the semblance emerges as well, in some countries of the 'third world', of a refusal of modern industrial society, and its inevitable corollaries (consumerism, commercialization, life styles, individualism, etc.). It is probable, however, that this 'refusal' is only to be attributed to some ruling classes (above all religious hierarchies) who feel that their age-old material and spiritual supremacy and authority is compromised by the influence of Western culture. It is not the first time in the history of humanity that the local *ancien régime* has allied privileges and fanaticism against the natural aspiration of the masses to

assimilate less hierarchical innovative roles. We might also ask if the irrational refusal of the 'Western' model does not derive also from a neurotic sensation of the material distance of realization which the situation presents in relation to acquisition (and the possible occurrence of the 'love–hate', 'attraction–repulsion' phenomenon, well known in psychology and found in Aesop's more 'familiar' version: the fox and the grapes).

7. For an approximate and general reference to the significance of this expression (now largely used and abused) it is obligatory to mention the works by Bertram Gross (1966 and 1967), Kahn and Wiener (1967), Alain Touraine (1969), and Daniel Bell (1973). See also how even I used the term in 1957 (Archibugi, 1956). After several decades of discussion on the possible connotations of a post-industrial society the moment has perhaps arrived to characterize its physiognomy with more 'autonomous' semantics. See below (in Ch. 2, Section 1) the reference to some substitutes for the term; in Chapters 7 and 8, having to contrast the new model with the ideal-typical model of industrial society, I have used – without much imagination, but without avoiding an autonomous definition – the expression of 'service society'. In the whole of this book, we will develop an overview on the literature concerning this 'new' type of society, especially in its *economic* structure reflections; and – as the title of the book suggests – we will conclude by defining this new type of emerging economy – preferentially – as an 'Associative Economy', a phrase that better defines its character as against that of the Capitalist Economy, for which it is becoming an historical replacement. Anyhow, even the question of denomination will be developed step by step as we proceed in the description of the ongoing changes that are the subject of analysis and management guidelines in this book.

8. More considerations in a book of papers concerning the evaluation of the Welfare State in a historic perspective (Schottland, 1977). For a comparative assessment of Welfare States, see a recent book edited by Bent Greve (1996).

9. There has been interesting debate on the comparability of the American Welfare State with the European one: see Skocpol and Ikenberry (1983); Skocpol (1987); Weir, Orloff and Skocpol (1988); Baldwin (1996); and, finally, Pierson (1990). See also, for a different point of view, Uusitalo (1984). On the comparability of models see, in general, Boje (1996).

10. Reports on the subject are not lacking, either on the international scale or at the level of individual countries. Among essential reading, see recurrent and always up-to-date and interesting studies of the OECD (in general: 1981 and 1988b; for the elderly: 1988a, 1992, 1995d, 1996a; for women: 1985c; and for the handicapped: 1994a). See also an insightful essay by A.B. Atkinson (1991b), who systematically occupied himself with the subject (see also Atkinson ed., 1989 and the survey of literature in Atkinson, 1991a).

11. For some considerable time the phenomenon has been the subject of numerous analyses. See an old study by the United Nations (UN, 1956). A 'classic' writer on the subject is Sauvy (1956), and in Italy, Somogyi (1979). But the subject has continued, naturally, to be of permanent interest. To remain in the range of more official international inquiries we recommend: a report for a World Assembly of the United Nations held in Vienna in 1982 (UN, 1982); and other UN reports and studies (UN, 1991; 1992 a and b). See also other important works of OECD on the social and economic implications of ageing on the social securities systems (OECD, 1981; 1988b; 1988c); and on the labour market (OECD, 1994c; 1996a, b, c). Among the wide literature, see: an assessment by Hagemann (1989); another, more prudent, in Thane (1987); and

financial evaluations of the problem in Pampel and Williamson (1989), and in Atkinson, ed., (1989).

12. A review of the policies of social redistribution of income in long-term planning can be found in the documents of the Economic Commission for Europe (UN-ECE, 1974 and 1979). See also the comprehensive collection of papers edited by Davidson and Kregel (1989).

13. The need for and the characteristics of a 'planning society' in comparison to a 'planned society' will be more widely discussed later (in Chapters 11 and 13 in particular). Also see the definition of 'planning society' in Faludi (1973, last chapter); and also in the Report, below recalled, of the US Advisory Committee on National Growth Policy Processes (1977)).

14. Further observations on the deception between 'active' and 'non-active' are to be found later in this work (section 3.1 of this chapter and section 3 in Chapter 5).

15. Ernest Mandel defined them thus in his work *Der Spätkapitalismus* (translated into English with additions as *Late Capitalism* (1975) and translated into French as *Le Troisième Age du Capitalisme* (1976)).

16. There is much literature on the socio-economic effects of automation technology, from which it is difficult to make a selection. I gave an analysis in the 1950s of the situation which was published by the Italian National Research Council called 'Le relazioni industriali nell'epoca dell'automatismo' [Industrial Relations in the Age of Automation] (Archibugi, 1956), and now republished in its complete form (forthcoming). On the relationship between modern technological evolution and automation, see the more recent outstanding contribution by Wassily Leontief on 'the future impact of automation on workers' (Leontief and Duchin, 1986).

17. The paradox lies in the (inflationist) disequilibrium, which in the short term seems to penalize the most fixed and therefore smallest incomes, and is – in the medium and long term – the instrument for the participation of these incomes in the 'banquet' of increased productivity (we will return to this point more widely in Chapter 8). See, for wider considerations, an ancient work by Phelps (1972).

18. On this point a strong stand can be found in a report (named 'Maldague' from the name of its chairman) by a study group instituted by the EC Commission (of which the author was part, among others, such as Jacques Delors and Stuart Holland) on the structural causes of inflation (see European Commission, 1976), and the specific contribution to this Commission on the 'cognitive control of inflation' (Archibugi, 1975) with the comments by Caffé (1978, p.202). On the nature and role of inflationist processes in post-industrial society we will return in particular in Chapter 8.

19. For more information on the relation between poverty and social security systems, see the important works, some already quoted, by Anthony Atkinson (1983, 1989, 1991b). For the measurement problems of poverty, see the works of Amartya K. Sen (1976, 1979 and 1983).

20. See Zandavalki (1994) and Tsakloglou (1996a and 1996b). Also OECD (1988a, 1988c, and 1996a) and the collection of essays edited by Atkinson (1989).

21. More work exists on these points since the 1970s: for instance, Niaudet (1973); but the most updated information is in the quoted Atkinson (1989 and 1991b).

22. Although we can be attentive to the different objective proportions of poverty, we still cannot forget that poverty, like 'happiness', is a relative situation, which must be considered in its historic relativity.

23. At the request of a smart commentator, I would define as 'women's frustration rate' the relation between expectations of 'emancipation', always increasing

thanks to the formal achievements of parity in the civic and moral consciousness, and the effective economic and social opportunities to satisfy them.

24.   Further considerations are in Rein (1985). A literature which is aimed at
      underlining the Welfare State as a system that underprivileges particularly the
      women (Wilson, 1977; Barret, 1980; Pascall, 1986; Pateman, 1988; Langam and
      Ostner, 1991; Orloff, 1993) has been developed in the past decades. While the
      connections between women's conditions and the Welfare State are not so
      evident, it is arguable that an excess of protection could jeopardize the insertion
      of women in the activities (as I myself had the occasion to argue in a paper
      published in the ILO journal, at least as concerning Italy (Archibugi, 1960)).

25.   Someone might ask himself whether a society where all are marginalized is
      conceivable. The answer is yes, because what is relevant here is the 'sense' of
      marginalization, and not the philological correspondence of the word to a
      'reality' measurable in terms of quintile or decile of statistical distribution. If
      this was so, a traditional society, where the distribution curve (of any kind of
      pertinent variable: income, consumption, or other tangible goods) is very flat
      for a large amount of total target population, could be more suitable than the
      pluralistic society where the distribution curve shows a more elastic distribution
      of the target population. The distribution curve is not bad or good *per se* but in
      relation to the structural absolute conditions of any real society to which is
      referred.

26.   On the problems of social policy for the elderly a wide literature exists. One of
      the latest works of the OECD is a survey on the critical policy challenge of
      ageing in the OECD countries (OECD, 1996a): about the 'flexibility' of the
      retirement age, see an older OECD work (OECD, 1971). Furthermore, on
      some new views that have emerged about elderly protection, see OECD (1995d
      and 1996a). See also the well-known, important book by J.S. Berliner (1972).

27.   On the entity of the migration phenomenon, see always the OECD studies
      (1993 and 1995e).

28.   For these aspects, we suggest that the reader skip directly to the final chapter of
      this work.

29.   Stimulating considerations are in some recent studies by the OECD (for
      instance: 1991; 1994b; 1995c; 1996b, c and d).

30.   See OECD (1991). Some (only some) insights of Illich (1971) meet my con-
      cerns.

31.   In effect this 'myth' of industrialization has more and more been limited to the
      regional areas of a country considered under-developed. I would say that an
      inverse relationship may be established between industrial development and
      the presence of the myth.

32.   It is doubtless that everywhere in the OECD countries, in present times, a re-
      evaluation of household work is occurring: see a recent OECD study (1995b).
      See also the collective book edited by Anderson, Bechofer and Gershuny
      (1994).

33.   On the flexibility of the labour market, see another study by OECD (1989b).
      See also an interesting early study by A.A. Evans for the OECD (Evans, 1973).

34.   On the introduction of flexible methods of reduction of working time, see an
      OECD study (1995a).

35.   The discussion on the need for a guaranteed income started to develop in the
      1960s and has not made particular progress since then. See the collective
      volume edited by R. Theobald (1965). See also Stoleru (1973). The discussion
      has been taken up more recently in Europe through a wide intellectual move-
      ment named BIEN (Basic Income European Network), coordinated by some

scholars of the University of Louvain (Belgium): Christian Arnsperger and Philippe Van Parijs. Periodic conferences are organized (the first in Louvain-la-Neuve, in 1986, the last in Amsterdam in 1998) and a very interesting documentation by countries is collected (the Website is: http://www.espo.-ucl.ac.be.html). See also a book of essays edited in Germany by T. Schmid (1984), among them one by Dahrendorf. This last author has declared his strong support for the minimum garanteed income, with arguments which have not changed the perspectives opened earlier in the 1960s on the subject. See also Chapter 10 of the book of essays by Dahrendorf on 'neoliberalism' (1987). A vast source of information on the subject is the study by A.B. Atkinson (1991a).

36.   This is the reason why I am perplexed about the proposals for a 'negative income tax' in order to confront the problems of poverty, since these policies would still be numbered in the framework of *'protectionist'* interventions, without demanding their strict coordination to active policies of employment, aiming at the redistribution also of the workload in productive processes. On negative income tax, see the classic work by Green (1967).

37.   It is strange that, notwithstanding the common acknowledgment that modern labour policies need a strategic overview (see for this an interesting essay by OECD, 1996b), people are generally yet reluctant to recognize that this strategy implicates appropriated studies of economic programming.

38.   On this point the reader is referred to specific works of mine (Archibugi, 1973, 1974, 1996). This will be dealt with more thoroughly in Chapters 11 and 13.

39.   The accounting schemes for this new policy of planning have been studied; and particular mention should be made of the application of Richard Stone's 'social matrices'; see his report, prepared for the United Nations, *A System of Demographic and Social Statistics* (UNSO, 1975).

40.   I deal, of course, with cognitive and informative type planning, which could be also the guideline for possible means of persuasion (incentives, financial help, and so on).

41.   See OECD (1996a).

42.   On the flexibility of the retirement age, see an early OECD study already quoted (1971).

43.   See a paper of mine (Archibugi, 1978d) on the subject.

44.   But the backwardness of the 'serious' experiences of planning elsewhere, the non-existence of organs and instruments dedicated to this type of work, the amateurishness of those who talk about planning, are such that we have to despair of realizing, in the short and medium term, a sufficient factual knowledge in order to sustain a process of operational decisions in the framework of an integrated planning. We will return to this in Chapters 11 and 13.

45.   For this consideration see further a contribution of Rudolf Klein (1980b).

46.   However, essentially founded in 1987 by a republican group of Congress members as a tool for 'guiding change and strategic planning for Members of Congress, their staff and the public'.

47.   Within the 'National Commission on Supplies and Shortage'. The Report is entitled: *Forging America's Future: Strategies for National Growth & Development* (US Advisory Committee on National Growth Policy Processes, 1977). This Committee was composed of eminent economists, scholars and well-known managers. Among the economists was the Nobel prize winner Wassily Leontief.

48.   See a sort of three-sector triangular logo used by the Congressional Institute (<http://server.conginst.org/conginst/plan105/pla_main.html>).

2 Structural Change: A Reappraisal of the Various Approaches

1. For an assessment of the present status of the *theory of structural change* (and a large cataloguing of the relevant literature), I can suggest the essay by Moshe Syrquin on the 'pattern of structural change' (Syrquin, 1988). Less useful to our aims is on the contrary another approach to the structural change represented by a traditional Ricardian–Marxian–Sraffian problematics synthesized in the work of P. Leon (1967) and L. Pasinetti (1981).

2. Even the literature to which we are referring is now endless. In the course of this chapter we will make a severe critical selection. Two recapitulatory contributions by Italian scholars who deserve greater recognition in the international scene: those by A. Colombo entitled 'Le società del futuro: saggio utopico sulle società post-industriali' [The societies of the future: an utopian essay on the post-industrial societies](1978), and by D. De Masi, with the title 'L'avvento della società post-industriale' [The coming of post-industrial society]; the last contains an interesting introductory essay by the editor to a collection of papers on various authors (like Jungk, Galbraith, Bell, Touraine, Toffler, Inose and Pierce, Gottmann, Dahrendorf, Gorz, Gershuny, Offe, Kahn and Wiener, Thurow, Naisbitt, Illich, and many others) of the literature mentioned above (De Masi, 1985).

3. To enter into such a subject, means to find oneself in the open sea of historiographic debate, of historic causality, of historic synthesis. Certainly this is not the place to do that; but at the same time, one should not forget that many of the approaches to the change to which we will do rapid and propaedeutic reference in this chapter, are largely interrelated with the critical-historiographic debate mentioned above; and that many epistemological shortcomings that people meet, drive properly from a scarce familiarity with that debate. Personally, without troubling the great representatives of critical *Historismus* (from Dilthey to Weber, from Troelsch to Simmel and Croce), I have found it useful to read two compendia. respectively, of the German tradition and of the French. The first, by Arthur Spiethof (a well-known economic historian of the Schmoeller School and also pupil of Max Weber), is a collection of the author's methodological writings translated into English (1948); the second is an essay by François Simiand (1903) (an equally well-known French historian of the beginning of this century, belonging to the group of scholars around the Journal *Revue de Synthèse Historique*). [Both these works have been republished: the first under the inclusive title of 'Pure Theory and Economic Gestalt Theory: Ideal Type and Real Type'; and the second under the title 'Causal Interpretation and Historical Research' in an English version, with various writings of economic history, edited by Lane and Riemersma (1953), a section of which is devoted to methodological writings]. To these essays we refer the reader for a framework of all the critical-historiographic questions.

4. A few years ago, an author amused himself by classifying in the literature at least 64 different 'theories' concerning the stages of economic and social development (Marien, 1976). The same author, active in future studies, has then classified the analysis of the vast material collected and indicated, in two main streams: the first, technologist, oriented to emphasize the organizational, technical, and centralistic aspects of new trends; the other, 'ecologistic', which emphasizes on the contrary the individualistic, naturalistic, and decentralistic aspects of those trends (1977) More recently Marien (1996) developed, again for the World Future Society, another useful bibliographic work on the very abundant

literature concerning environmental problems and sustainable development. The dichotomy of the two trends, however, must not be exaggerated, as will be more apparent in the following discussion in this book. In fact, the most critical manifestations of futuristic thinking express a dialectic fusion of the two opposed concepts, towards better and more advanced syntheses, and the antinomies technology/environment, centralization/decentralization, and others such as 'from the top'/'from the bottom'; from which others arise, such as state/market, plan/no plan, and others even more complex, such as necessity/freedom, theory/practice, analysis/synthesis, and so on. These are antinomies that the advanced scholar, though assuming them in his or her technical baggage, leaves to common language.

5. This convergence (especially the analytical one) is not odd, all considered, if we bear in mind the above quoted interpretation schemes by Spiethoff and Simiand, or, more generally, the basic critical-historiographical debate, to which I have made reference, but also necessarily excluded from our analysis (and which does not allow any disciplinary division of the approaches, such it has been here developed for practical reasons).

6. All the histories of technology are a largely unconscious expression of this approach; see, for instance, Singer (1952) and the monumental history of technology (in 8 vols) by Singer *et al.* (eds) (1954–84), and compendiums of larger scientific findings (for instance, Forbes, 1960).

7. It is commonly believed (Bezanson, 1921–22; Coleman, 1956) that the first to use the expression, with an historical periodization meaning, was Arnold Toynbee (uncle of the more famous historian) in a work interrupted by his untimely death, and published in 1884 under the title *Lectures on the Industrial Revolution in England* and reprinted in 1956 under the title *The Industrial Revolution* (see Bibliography). However, the expression has been used also by Friedrich Engels – the intellectual partner of Marx – in his work on 'The condition of the working class in England' (Engels, 1845, pp. 11 and 355). And also by Stuart Mill in his *Principles* (orig. edition, 1848, p. 581), and even by Marx, twice in the first volume of *Capital* (edition 1967).

8. Symbolized by the application of Hargreaves's spinning-jenny, of Arkwright's continuous spinning-frame, Crompton's mule, the mechanical loom invented by Cartwright, and finally – but most importantly – Watt's steam engine, as any good history book on the 'industrial revolution' tells us: see the classic works by Mantoux (1928) and Ashton (1948); (see also previous Ashton's works of documentation (1929 and 1937). See also the recent contributions by Deane (1967) or Landes (1969). Also very important is an essay by Maurice Dobb on the 'industrial revolution and the nineteenth century' (1945), although the approach of this latter includes it more in the 'institutional' approach.

9. For a synthesis of the debate among the historians and between historians and economists, see D. C. Coleman (1956), pupil of Postan and Ashton. The question has been examined by me more extensively in an early essay from 1956 (Archibugi, 1956).

10. A classic of the 'second' industrial revolution is the (posthumous) book by H. Pasdermadjian (1959). The author already asked himself whether the 'second' industrial revolution was not about to give way to a 'third' revolution, that of nuclear energy, electronics, and cybernetics. See also on the third industrial revolution the cited work by Landes (1969).

11. We can make reference to the more 'classic' scholars of the historiography of the English Industrial Revolution – for instance the already quoted Mantoux and Ashton and, moreover, Hobsbawm (1968) and Musson and Robinson (1969).

12.   The endless and recurrent history of the 'capitalistic' forms of production is a classic of the modern historiography, perhaps motivated by the need to contrast the easy assumption of Capitalism as an emergence and a characteristic of the same 'Industrial Revolution'. For all, see the beautiful three volumes by Fernand Braudel (1982–84), *Civilization and Capitalism*.

13.   Drucker, (1993, pp. 17–18). An undoubtedly technological approach to the structural changes is that which Drucker has developed in many of his numerous books. One can especially see that in *The Practice of Management* (1954), in *Managing for Result* (1964), in *The Effective Executive* (1967) and in *Technology Management and Society* (1973). I consider Peter Drucker an acute anticipator of the evolution of the capitalist system and of the structural change of contemporary society, and many economists and sociologists would profit well by taking him in greater consideration before developing their theoretical evaluations.

14.   In fact, Schumpeter, since his first work, the *Theory of Economic Development* (1911, trans. in English, 1934), has identified radically this wrong position with all the economic theory traditions (from Smith and Ricardo onwards). Moreover, from the physiocrats onwards:

> they focused directly on the great fact of the circular flow. To describe it, to outline its small wheels or gear, has been their main aim, their sole, purely scientific, goal. However, to describe the circular flow, means – *ipso facto* – to describe the static economy.... If we investigate the arguments of Adam Smith, we find there, substantially, only economic verities of static nature ...That the core of the theories is a statics of the economy becomes even more clear in the following authors, first of all in Ricardo...In the congeries of researches which make up his work, he undoubtedly does merely outline the basic lines of a statics, the elements of a circular flow logic. [And further:] 'the great reform introduced by the subjectivistic doctrine of the value left intact the static character of the theoretical construction...No description is more static than Leon Walras' one, in whose hands the principles of the theory crystallized in the most rigourous form never assumed before by our science. The authors of the Austrian school too...do not describe anything else than the circular flow of the economy. (Schumpeter, 1911, Italian translation, 1971, p. 63).

In short, for the Schumpeter of 1911 only the following authors are saved:

(a) Stuart Mill, because of his explicit distinction of a static analysis (oriented to provide the 'economic law of a steady and unchangable society'), from a 'theory of movement', which should be distinguished from our theory of equilibrium, i.e. a 'Dynamics of the political economy from a Statics'; from which Schumpeter disagrees only because he thought himself 'to be able to demonstrate that the static condition does not include all fundamental phenomena of the economy, but that the life of a stationary economic system is different in its essence and in its basic principles from the life of a non stationary economic system'.

(b) Karl Marx, for these aspects of his theoretic construction where

> he tried to deal with the development of economic life also by means of economic theory. His theories of accumulation, of impoverishment, of collapse, result in fact from purely economic arguments, and his vision aims always to penetrate theoretically the development of economic life as such,

and not simply its flow in a determined moment. The bases for his theory have however an absolutely static nature, they are therefore the bases of the classics.

(c) the American J.B. Clark *(Essentials of Economic Theory,* 1907) whose merit is – according to Schumpeter – having consciously separated 'statics' and 'dynamics', and postulating a special theory of dynamics. Thus Schumpeter added, later, in chapter 2: J.B. Clark saw

> in the dynamic elements, a disturbance of the static equilibrium. This is our view too, and also from our standpoint an essential task is to investigate the effect of this disturbance and the new equilibrium which then emerges. But while he confines himself to this and just like Mill sees therein the meaning of dynamics, we shall first of all give a theory of these causes of disturbances in so far as they are more than mere disturbances for us and in so far as it seems to us that essential economic phenomena depend upon their appearances. In particular: two of the causes of disturbance enumerated by him (increase of capital and population) are for us, as for him, merely causes of disturbance, however important as 'factors of change' they may be for another kind of problem just indicated in the text. The same is true of a third (changes in the direction of consumers' tastes) which will later be justified in the text. But the other two (changes in technique and in productive organization) require special analysis and evoke something different again from disturbances in the theoretical sense. The non-recognition of this is the most important single reason for what appears unsatisfactory to us in economic theory. (Schumpeter, 1911, Italian translation 1971, p. 63)

From these 'insignificant-looking source flows' Schumpeter tries to develop a new conception of the economic process, which overcomes a series of fundamental difficulties and thus justifies the new statement of the problem in his text. He declares that the statement of the problem is more nearly parallel to that of Marx. For according to him there is an internal economic development and no mere adaption of economic life to changing data. But his own structure covers only a small part of the Marxian ground. [Schumpeter, 1911, Engl. translation 1971, p. 60]

15. I presume we can state that systematic research activity on the matter has been developed only from the 1960s onward – as the authoritative opinion of Simon Kuznets testified at the conclusion of the 1960 NBER Conference on the 'socio-economic factors of inventive activity' (see NBER, 1962 and Kuznets, 1962). From these debates in this time a vast amount of research was developed, and also some general systematization. See, in chronological order: J. Schmookler (1962), who played a central role in the conference of NBER cited; and then N. Rosenberg (1976 and 1982), and Nelson and Winter (1982); Nelson, editor of the proceedings of the NBER Conference, was also the author of an important critical survey on the 'state of the art' as far back as 1959 (Nelson, 1959); and furthermore, also Stonemann (1983); and lastly Freeman and other scholars of SPRU (Science Policy Research Unit) of the University of Sussex (Freeman, 1982; Freeman and Soete, eds, 1990); and also the volumes of essays edited by Dosi, Freeman, Nelson, Silverberg and Soete (1988) on the relations between 'technological change and economic theory'; and by Di Matteo, *et al.* eds, (1989).

16. I think that all of the research in the preceding note (of which I mentioned only the most summarizing literature known and consulted by me) is representative

of this examination. The whole constitutes the reference point for the key debates on the economic theory of technological change, the meaning of which I will come back to in section 3.3 below.

On the relation between science and technology, see furthermore the excellent works by Archibugi (Daniele) (1985) and Dosi (1985).

17.   On the wider historical phenomena, see the works of Freeman (among them his papers cited, 1982), and the essay in cooperation with others (1982). See also the preceding works by Pavitt (1971 and 1979). Furthermore see the very interesting collected essays by Archibugi (Daniele) and Santarelli (1990) on singular historical cases of the relationship between (technical) invention and innovation (economic effects), and some cases which represent some economic 'micro-histories' (of such importance as the steam engine, the railways, electrical transmission, chemical applications, the transistor, and the computer industry!), from which one extracts, among other things, that the classical dilemma 'demand-pull' or 'discover-push' of the economics of technological development (as many other theoretical dilemmas of development economics are) is a useless dilemma, which depends on many historical factors that cannot be put in the framework of a specific theory, not even the evolution theory (about which see the above cited Nelson and Winter, 1982). See for this purpose also the conclusive essay in the collection by both editors, Santarelli and Archibugi (Daniele) (1990).

In section 3.5 we will discuss the capacity of such approaches to bring more than a deeper knowledge of what has occurred in the different cases of history of technological innovations, in their different 'casuistics'.

18.   Thus Kondratief expresses himself clearly in 1922, at the end of his long statistical analysis of the 'existence' of long waves:

> With the data available it can be supposed that the existence of major economic cycles is very probable;...and it can be stated that if they do exist they are a very important and real fact of economic dynamics, a fact whose reflexes are seen in all the principle branches of economic-social life. But if major cycles exist and if they cannot be explained by fortuitous causes, how can they otherwise be explained? In other terms, the problem arises of a theory of the major cycles. (See Kondratief, 1935.)

Kondratief published his views in three versions between 1922 and 1928. His concept of capitalistic economies oscillating around a long-run dynamic equilibrium position came to be regarded, in Stalin's time, as anti-Marxist heresy. In 1930 he was sent to a Siberian prison camp where, according to Solzhenitsyn's *Gulag Archipelago*, he died: Kondratief is reported to have been rehabilitated in the Soviet Union in 1987 (according to a note in the magazine *Science*, 9 October 1987, p. 149).

19.   A work by Paolo Sylos Labini (1950) does him justice and, furthermore, provides an enlightening vision of the further development of the 'economic' approach to the development of capitalism, especially in the work of Schumpeter.

20.   The variables on which Pareto constructed his series are amusing to recall: the movement of French, British, Belgian and Italian foreign trade; Italian emigration; the takings in Parisian theatres; the sums collected at the Clearing House in London; gold production (Pareto, 1913).

21.   This phrase by Pareto which we consider very important with regard to later developments (Kondratieff and Schumpeter) of the theorization of long waves,

was written in a context of analysis of the undulatory movement of social phenomena (in the *Treatise of General Sociology*, 1916), a type of analysis which always attracted Pareto. However, we should in fact not forget to consider the theory of economic crises carried out from his *Cours* (1896–97, chap. 4 of Book II) which precedes by about 20 years the *Treatise of General Sociology* (1916).

22. For a complete evaluation of the more recent debate on the long waves, see the works presented in some Conferences on the subject: Copenhagen, June 1989, with the theme: 'Recent Developments in Business Cycle Theory: Methods and Empirical Applications'; Brussels, 1989: 'International Colloquium on the Long Waves of the Economic Conjuncture'. A useful overview on the more recent views of the question, to which I owe very much, is that by Di Matteo and Vercelli (1992).

23. For this kind of conclusions – and also for sources of other information here recalled – I am indebted to Di Matteo and Vercelli (1992, pp. 10–15).

24. And published, as already said, in 1911. The text here referred to is in the English edition, first published in 1934, and again by Oxford University Press, 1961, except the parts omitted in the English edition but which can be found in the Italian translation of the German edition (1971), to which I also refer.

25. To which he devoted the first long chapter of his 'theory'.

26. To which he devoted the second, pivotal, chapter of his theory.

27. The carrying out of new combinations [of means of production] we call 'enterprise'; the individuals whose function it is to carry them out we call 'entrepreneurs'. These concepts are at once broader and narrower than the usual. Broader, because in the first place we call entrepreneurs not only those 'independent' businessmen in an exchange economy who are usually so designated, but all who actually fulfil the function by which we define the concept, even if they are, as is becoming the rule [1911! present author's note], 'dependent' employees of a company, like managers, members of boards of directors, and so forth, or even if their actual power to perform the entrepreneurial function has any other foundations, such as the control of a majority of shares ... On the other hand, our concept is narrower than the traditional one in that it does not include all heads of firms or managers or industrialist who merely may operate an established business, but only who actually perform that function.

(Schumpeter, 1911, Engl. edn, 1961 pp.74–5)

Here Schumpeter expounded at length the reasons for his 'restrictive' concept of 'entrepreneur' and 'enterprise'; and concluded:

The carrying out of new combinations, ... the entrepreneur's essential function, must always appear mixed up with other kinds of activity, which as a rule must be much more conspicuous than the essential one. Hence the Marshallian definition of the entrepreneurs, which simply treats the entrepreneurial function as 'management' in the widest meaning, will naturally appeal to most of us. We do not accept it, simply because it does not bring out what we consider to be the salient point and the only one which specifically distinguishes entrepreneurial from other activities. (Ibid., p.77)

This restrictive use of the words 'enterprise' and 'entrepreneur' has not been kept enough in mind, in my opinion, even by the Schumpeterian literature. We will see later the consequences (Chapter 11) when we will describe the changes in the 'entrepreneurial' motivation. In any case, in order to improve the definition of the Schumpeterian concept of 'entrepreneur', Schumpeter himself sends the reader to the entry 'Entrepreneur' written by himself, in a 'Dictionary of the Political Sciencies' (of his time): *Handwoerterbuch der Staatswissenschaften.*

28. And Schumpeter explains further: 'In contrast to the condition of the "circular flow" this does not mean in itself that year after year "the same" things happen; for it only means that we conceive the several processes in the economic systems as partial phenomena of the tendency towards an equilibrium position, but not necessarily towards the same one.' (ibid., p. 62)

29. It seems that many of the specifications referred to here were introduced in the revision of the second chapter of his early work (1911), on the occasion of the English edition (1934). And it seems that with such a revision Schumpeter intended to succeed in making the essentials of his position understood, and to preserve it from misunderstandings. He thought he could make it understood by abandoning the adjective 'dynamic' (which he had used in opposition to 'static'), to designate the change different from that of mere adaptation (towards equilibrium) to the change of the data of economic evolution (among which Schumpeter included, as seen: natural changes, the growth of population and wealth, etc., and, as we will see in the next section, even every autonomous variation in the needs of customers). Since it is presumable that even the states of scientific knowledge and inventions (always distinguished by Schumpeter from innovations in his taxonomic scheme of technological progress) have to be considered as 'data', it seems that Schumpeter has by himself prepared the base of his own interpretations. As a determinist (and exogenous) factor of development, only enterpreneurial innovation remains for him.

30. Here a classic anacoluthon, familiar to epistemologists, is produced: what is stated under a condition, is denied under another. Within the classic or neo-classic paradigm of equilibrium, the factor 'innovation' is exogenous (it is extraneous, determined outside); but within the Schumpeterian paradigm the innovation becomes again 'endogenous' to economic theory. This is one of the cases in which the interactive relational concepts (in our case those of endo-genous/exogenous; but this applies also to other abused examples, such as: equilibrium/desequilibrium; economic/diseconomic; etc.) do not have much sense if the paradigms or simply the assessment criteria or parameters are not made explicit when they are used.

31. The specific meaning of the statement is in the adjective 'new' (which implies therefore the innovation). Sure, Schumpeter says, 'To produce means to combine materials and forces within our reach . . . . In so far as the "new combination" may in time grow out of the old by continuous adjustment in small steps, there is certainly change, possibly growth, but neither a new phenomenon nor development in our sense. In so far as this is not the case, and the new combinations appear discontinuously, then the phenomenon characterising development emerges' (ibid., 1961, pp. 65–6). It is only to this case that Schumpeter reserves the expression of 'new combinations of production means'.

32. On the contrary, regarding risk, Schumpeter tended to say that the one who really takes risk is never the entrepreneur, but rather the capital lender, who risks capital, or the means of production: 'Risk obviously always falls on the owner of the means of production or of the money-capital which was paid for them, hence never on the entrepreneur as such' (ibid., p. 75n); while the entrepreneur (unless he is the capitalist himself) risks only his prestige and image.

33.   the class position which may be attained is not as such an entrepreneurial position, but characterised as landowning or capitalist, according to how the proceeds of the enterprise are used. Inheritance of the pecuniary result and of personal qualities may then both keep up this position for more than one generation and make further enterprise easier for descendants, but the function of the entrepreneur itself cannot be inherited, as is shown well enough by the history of manufacturing families. (ibid., pp. 78–9)

34.   Rightly, Xavier Greffe (1992, p.49) says – about this Schumpeterian position – that we should use the words *'entrepreunerial situations'* or *'événements'* rather than *'entrepreneurship'*. Under this point of view the reasoning is similar to that of the theory of catastrophes, where changes are seen as qualitative variations or jumps, rather than marginal movements.

35.   Since the beginning of his reasoning about the basic phenomenon of economic development, Schumpeter stated that: for development, one must intend only 'those changes which are nor forced upon it from without' (see the text quoted above).

36.   See the enormous amount of research in the economics of innovation. An exhaustive treatment of the topic can be found in the works of Freeman, and his followers in the research unit on Science Policy (SPRU) at the University of Sussex (Freeman, 1974; Freeman, Clark and Soete, 1982; Freeman, 1984).

37.   Paradoxically, the Schumpeterian theory is affected by the same error which he – *mutatis mutandis* – accused the traditional theory of having: saying how the economic process (the circular flow) was working (and what it was), but not being able to say where the true change was coming from, what its determinant factor would be.

38.   In fact from this point of view we should point out that the 'theories' of economic development seem to have given up being 'theories', as we can see roughly from what is claimed by almost all the authors chosen as the 'pioneers' of economic development, in an (almost celebratory) collection of their essays of retrospective evaluation on the theories of economic development, which the World Bank published in 1984, edited by Gerald M. Meier and Dudley Seers (1984). The book collected the post-war essays of ten authors who are leaders in these theories: P. T. Bauer, Colin Clark, Albert O. Hirschman, Arthur Lewis, Gunnar Myrdal, Ràul Prebisch, Paul Rosenstein-Rodan, W. W. Rostow, Hans Singer and Jan Tinbergen. On the other hand, these disappointed and sincere analyses are accompanied by other, pitiless and comprehensive analyses on the birth and death of the economic theories of the development, including those by H.C.Arndt (1978), on the *Rise and Fall of Economic Growth*; Dudley Seers's essay on 'The Birth, Life, and Death of Development Economics' (1979); A.O. Hirschman (1981), 'The Rise and Decline of Development Economics', the first of his *Essays in Trespassing* (1981); Deepak Lal's *'The Poverty of Development Economics* (1985); the review of literature on economic development commissioned from I.M.D. Little by The Twentieth Century Fund (1982) and defined by Rostow as 'a kind of critical memorial service'. And Walter Rostow himself in the last two chapters of his monumental work on the 'theorists of economic growth' (from David Hume to the present) (1990) (20th chapter: 'What Don't We Know about Economic Growth?'; 21st chapter: 'Where Are We?') provides a frank, desolating panorama of the present status of development economic theory.

39.   We are talking, evidently, of Rostow's most important work *The Stages of Economic Growth* (1960), in which emerges the systematic description of the

five stages that have made it famous, even if it had been prepared and, so to speak, anticipated by the preceding work, *The Process of Economic Growth* (of 1952). Furthermore, definitely to be recommended is his more recent monumental work, *Theorists of Economic Growth from David Hume to the Present, with a Perspective on the Next Century* (Rostow, 1990), which represents a sort of great notebook on the development of economic doctrines, seen from the angle of growth theories. In this work there is an overall reconsideration of his own theory (chap. 18).

40. For this self-definition, see the already quoted chapter 18 of his latest work on the evolution of theories of economic growth (Rostow, 1990).

41. This opinion would place Rostow among the followers of the technological approach, but its reasoning works out entirely within the ambit of economic reasoning.

42. We recall that the 'long-cycles' of Schumpeter (*Business Cycles*, 1939), which he called 'Kondriateff', were placed as every 50–60 years (the 'short' ones, or 'Kitchin', were 2–3 years, and the 'medium', or 'Juglar', about 9 years).

43. Kuznets was in the 1950s a 'classic' of the quantitative analysis of development (1956–67), with his conclusive theorizations (1966) updated in Kuznets (1973b).

44. On Rosenstein-Rodan, the comments are well known on theories concerning the 'big pusch' (1961).

45. See, by Chenery, in addition to his classical work, *Structural Change and Development Policy* (1979), also his excellent essay on 'Growth and Structure', in Chenery and Srinivasan (1988). In the same year in which the book by Rostow was published, an authoritive group of labour economists, Kerr, Dunlop, Harbison, and Myers, merged their research, formerly separated, in a common book: *Industrialism and Industrial Man; The Problems of Labor and Management in Economic Growth* (Kerr *et al.*, 1960). They proposed an interpretation of the change from many points of view, but overall from the point of view of the typology of industrial relations, in connection to the industrialization process. The key of historical interpretation of this group was very similar, therefore, to that of the growth stages or development stages, from Rostow, as far as development and industrialization mark their identity. Both the visions, or paradigms, opened a window to a very undefined future. Kerr, Dunlop, Harbison, and Myers did risk, however, outlining a post-industrial future: they limited themselves (see the last chapter of the cited book) to designing a vanishing 'pluralistic industrialism' where differences fall into a generic confluence without trend indicators (for the rest, it was not so different from Rostow). The character of the post-industrial society, evidently, did not reach a stage of significant perception.

46. Rostow deals with this in the final chapters of his major work, *The Stages* etc. (chs. 8, 9 and 10), and in his subsequent work *Politics and the Stages of Growth* (1971).

47. Rostow (1990, p. 429). He declares recurrently his limited enthusiasm for the economic growth models, and recalls how since his first book on the *Process of Economic Growth* (1952), he had claimed that

> conventional economic theory suffered from four weaknesses that rendered it grossly inadequate as a framework for studying and teaching the history of the world economy as it had evolved since the mid-eighteenth century. First, conventional economic theory provided no mechanism for introducing non-economic factors into the analysis of economic growth systematically when it was quite clear that economic growth – notably in its early phases but, in fact,

throughout – could not be understood except in terms of the dynamics of whole societies. Second it could not accommodate within its structure the process by which major new production functions were generated and diffused. It provided no linkage between science, invention, and the production process. Third, mainstream theory provided no credible explanation for trend periods, longer than conventional business cycles, in the prices of basic commodities relative to manufactures. Fourth, it provided no credible linkage of conventional business cycles to the process of growth. For a historian, it is palpable that cycles are simply the form growth historically assumed. The separation of cycle and trend – of the Marshallian short from the long period – is an act of intellectual violence that cuts the heart out of the problem of both cycles and growth.

But at the same time he recalls how '1950 was a time when mainstream business-cycle theorists were ringing the changes on the interaction of the multiplier and the accelerator, thereby effectively separating growth from cycles, relegating innovation to exogenous investment'. And he recalls how his first book, *The Process of Economic Growth* (1952)

responded to these four problems by an extended consideration of the interweaving of economic and non-economic forces centered on propensities that summarize the effective response of a society to the economic challenges and possibilities it confronts (Chapters 2 and 3); by an analysis of the complex linkages among science, invention and innovation that generate the flow of new production functions, including the sequence of majestic, innovational leading sectors that distinguish modern economic growth from all past human experience (Chapter 4); and by relating business cycles (Chapter 5) and secular trends (Chapter 6) to the process of growth thus conceived. (all quotations are drawn by Rostow himself in his last work: Rostow, 1990, pp. 428–31)

48. Without this opening Rostow would have to be classified among the authors of a strongly historicized 'technological' approach. And that is the normal approach of the historians who are mistrustful of any specific interpretive philosophy of historical development or a 'determining factor' as reading key of the process itself, as is the habit of the economist. With this opening, he places himself in that hybrid but wise position in which he seeks a main explicative factor, refuses any too forced generalization, and bases himself on the formulation only of interpretive schemes that are rather more classificatory than explicative. It could be said that he tends to pass from the position of the economic historian to that of the 'historic' economist (or historicist, or institutionalist, or evolutionist).

49. Rostow himself here quotes his image (suggested elsewhere) that 'economies made their way through history, overshooting and undershooting their optimum sectoral paths, like a drunk going home from local pub on Saturday night'. And relating this conception with that of some other scholars close to the same, he states that his 'respect expressed for J. M. Clark's extended analysis of the meaning of "balance" and Arthur Burns's measurement of cyclical distortion as well as my regret that Hirschman did not go beyond his praise of unbalanced growth to develop the notion of dynamic balanced growth that he acknowledged as an implicit norm in the course of his analysis' (Rostow, 1990, p. 431).

50. But if this were the case, this 'intrusion' would be welcome!
51. In his 1971 work in which Rostow wrote widely on an application of his key to reading the political events of the moment, he discussed again the future after the last stage of growth (the age of the car, which symbolizes .that of mass consumption), but he does not go much further in the analysis: 'A decade after [the considerations that are reported above] we know a bit more about the problems and possibilities of this further stage of growth which we could call: the search for quality' (p. 230). Some presuppositions are clear: 'the employment shifting is made up of two elements: the low increase rate in productivity in the service sector taken as a whole; and the high elasticity with respect to income in the demand for certain services. It is to the latter that we must look in order to discover the economics of the search for quality' (ibid.).

    He too therefore shows himself at the time already attentive not only to the development of the sub-sectors of the services linked to consumerism (for example, those linked to the car: such as car repairs, car rental, car supplies, petrol stations, etc., which however already at the time – Rostow noted – 'decelerate development with the passing of time'); but above all attentive to the development of sub-sectors such as medical services, equipment for recreation, foreign tourism, education, religious spending and social assistance. And many of these expenses are also effected by means of a more extensive legislation which increases its weight in public budgets (federal and others). And it is the increase of these spending sub-sectors which he claims help us to define an aspect of the search for quality. Afterwards remarks on some structural changes do not stimulate him to further synthetic visions on future society, as at the time others did successfully (for example, Bell, to whom we will return) leaving a fertile soil for debate. Rostow did not fail to note the effects of these changes in various directions, in which he slipped into discussing a bit of everything in a very interesting way: problems of justice and public order, the race problem in the United States, the youth rebellion of those years, the political relations of the United States with the rest of the world, etc. but without constructing any organic vision of the transformation under way.
52. The extensive literature on 'growth models' and on the theory of growth, whether old or new, which developed from the 1930s to the 1960s.
53. Even if, his approach, which is not different from Schumpeter's and Rostow's, can appear in the eyes of the aforementioned same authors or their readers as very heterodox, in regard to a traditional or conventional economic approach.
54. Sylos Labini (1984, p. 69 of Italian edn).
55. Sylos Labini, (ibid., pp. 70–1).
56. Sylos Labini (1993, p. 202 ff). More arguments for a theory of 'induced inventions' can be found in Samuelson (1965). One of the most extended and, in my opinion, unsurpassed treatment of the entire subject of technological change by successive authors is in a classical work by Nordhaus (1969).
57. Sylos Labini (1984, p. 72).
58. Sylos Labini (1989). The arguments take up again in a summarizing way from chapter 9 ('Technical Progress, Unemployment and Economic Dynamics') in Sylos Labini (1993).
59. Sylos Labini (1993, chapter 5).
60. Ibid., chapter 8.
61. A big clearing house of the ideas on this topic was the important conference in spring 1960 at the University of Minnesota sponsored by New York's NBER, the stronghold of the empirical studies and the American institutionalist school heir of Wesley C. Mitchell's economic thought. The title of the Conference and

of the resulting book (NBER, 1962) was: *The Rate and Direction of Inventive Activity: Economic and Social Factors.*

62. Schmookler, 1962, p. 168.
63. Machlup, 1962, pp. 143–67.
64. In fact, an impressive quantity of scientific production occurred in the decades in question (more or less in the line indicated by Schmookler and, anyway, by all people that in front of the traditional 'theoretical' analysis have always been partisans for a more patient 'empirical' analysis). We will recall such production with the most prestigious and authoritative names among the scholars of the matter, and with the indication of their most relevant and summarizing works. For instance, Nelson: 1967 (with Peck and Kalachek), 1982 (with Winter) and 1987; Freeman: 1974, 1982 (with Clark and Soete), 1990 (ed. with Soete), 1997 (with Soete), 1993 (ed. with Forey); Heertje: 1977, 1988 (ed.), 1990 (ed. with Perlman); Mansfield, 1968; Stoneman 1983, 1987, 1987 (ed. with Dasgupta), 1995 (ed.); Dosi, 1984, 1988 (ed. with Freeman, Nelson, Silverberg and Soete); Scherer, 1986; Cantwell, 1989 and 1993; Silverberg, 1994 (ed. with Soete); Archibugi D., 1997 (ed. with Michie) and 1998 (ed. with Michie); and many others that would be too long to record (and for which we refer the reader to a survey by Christopher Freeman (1998)). These works in fact have been accompanied by an endless variety of analysis and evaluations spread in the journals of economics (some of which have been created *ad hoc*, just to represent the specialization of the subject). We cannot say that such empirical studies, which from many points of view are very 'historical' studies, have not increased knowledge about how facts occurred; and that they do not give us some interesting visions. But certainly, they do not help us in formulating a 'theory' (or theories) of the invention or innovation; rather, on the contrary, they help us to abandon the idea that such empirical studies could be useful to formulate it. In the empirical enquiries by now, we find reasons and material to support everything, and also the contrary of everything.

Reading Freeman, we learn (on the basis of enormous quantities of studies) that 'the strong emphaisis . . . on firm-specific technological knowledge accumulation should not be taken to mean that exogenously generated scientific discoveries and advances play no part in technical innovation at firm level' (Freeman, 1998, p. 23). But at the same time we learn also that 'much empirical research has also shown that another major determinant of innovative success lies in the nature and intensity of the interaction with contemporary and future users of an innovation' (p. 25) (which are logically the antithesis of the scientific research). Then, at the same time, we learn (from another huge series of studies) that 'had already shown that good internal coupling between design, development, production and marketing functions was one of the decisive conditions for successful innovation' (p. 27). And on the basis of the realization that there is a gap of productivity level between firms of the same sector, of the same size, and with the same markets, there is clear evidence of 'the central importance . . . of firm-specific knowledge accumulation' (among which are the internal educational programmes). Other numerous researches have 'shown' the prevailing importance of the so-called 'incremental' innovation; whilst a good group of other researches, on the contrary, have shown the importance of the 'radical' innovation. Then in order to recompose the logical bickering, it has been applied to a 'master key' taxonomy: the innovation has been ranked 'on a five point scale from: systemic to major, minor, incremental, and unrecorded' (p. 30). In such a context, all this wide empirical research, by its benevolence, cannot but lay bare 'the sheer variety and complexity of innovations'. Variety which people also want to classify 'by industry...by degree of novelty and cost...by technology...and by type (product, process, organizational, system)' (p. 30). Exactly: in order to deny the possibility of any generalization, of any 'theory'.

It is the case that the empirical research is often invoked to respond to theoretical questions to which it is not possible to give an empirical answer, but only a theoretical answer. Instead of using this empirical research to face concrete action problems (in our case political action), people think it can serve to formulate some behaviorial objective regularities (on which, eventually to build improperly even prescriptions and policies); regularities which, on the contrary, cannot exist because of the 'variety and complexity' of the casuistics put in evidence even from the empirical research itself. We must therefore ask ourselves: How can all this analysis be useful to us? Freeman, as a conclusion to his survey, which he himself defined as 'biased,' on the literature on the economics of the technological change, very acutely states:

> A century ago, the 'Methodenstreit' divided the German economics profession and raised many similar questions. Whilst the neo-Schumpeterian would probably not wish to be identified with Schmoller, or the neo-classicals necessarily with Karl Menger, the basic questions of how much does history matter, the role of country-specific institutions, and the limits of universal generalizations about economic behavior are still with us. Schumpeter attempted (and according to most accounts failed) to bridge the warring camps in the Methodenstreit. It could be a fruitful experiment, although difficult to set up, to see if interdisciplinary assessment could make any contribution to the dilemmas of the economics profession today.
>
> (Freeman, 1998)

In summary, he suggested employing the giant energies in people and resources that are allocated in so-called empirical researches (but always related to a positivist paradigm) in an inter-disciplinary cooperation based always on an attempt to draw from the reality of social behaviour – and technological innovation *is* a social behaviour – some regularities or laws, historically undiscoverable. Instead, my opinion is that the same energies employed in empirical research would be much more fruitful if limited (in the mean and interpretation) to the strategic objective and to the empirical analysis of the factor, and limit conditions which 'historically', that is with time, place and social organization determinations, constrained the operation in question – in other words, with operational purposes in a problem-solving approach.

This does not mean conferring on such researches a general value from their starting point, but only a pragmatic value. I would prefer to call this approach a 'planological approach'.

65. For a broader treatment about the way I consider the relation between a 'planonogic approach' confronting the historical contribution of all so-called 'social sciences' (sociology, economics, political science) I refer the curious reader to one work of mine (actually permanently in progress) of which a draft edition has been published by the Planning Study Centre in 1992 (Archibugi, 1992a).

66. For this kind of theory, in its general aspects, but not applied to the economics of invention, I refer the reader to my work cited in the last note.

67. On this, the pages devoted by Simon Kuznets to the definition of the inventive activity, introducing the 1962 NBER Conference cited above (Kuznets, 1962), seem to me simply 'masterly'.

68. And it would be otiose today to state what role in per cent and probability the one or the other star had or can have. Also because a minimum of familiarity with philosophy (or even a minimum of commonsense and life experience) suffices to know that this is an eternal dilemma to try to solve it by means of 'empirical' enquiries on inventive processes in the manufacturing industry.

69. These scales and levels being the same that differentiate the analyses (and their results) about the relations among inventions, innovations and circumstances, about the 'effects' that Schmookler (see above) proposed as research agenda to the economists of innovation and of invention as well.

70. And all this beyond that 'K factor', *casualness*, which we know pervades any human decision, and that anyway would make arbitrary any discovery of causality, or functional correlation, that could result from our (empirical or theoretical) enquiries.

71. As has been said above, this is true regardless of the nature of both the innovations and the innovators: as it is well known, the innovators (or entrepreneurs) are today research bodies and decision units that do not correspond to the old character of the entrepreneur, even though limited by Schumpeter only to the character of the innovator.

72. By means of apt accounting tools, based on relations that in econometrics are called 'definitional', or 'structural' or 'technical', rather than 'behavioural'.

73. 'Relations of production' in economic terms and 'relations of ownership', in legal terms, in the Marxian language.

74. Indeed, more precisely: 'the economic law of movement of the modern society' (*das oekonomische Bewegungsgesetz der modernen Gesellschaft*) as Marx called it in the Preface to the first edition of *Capital* (1867).

75. The following passage is taken from the famous 'Preface' to his *Contribution to the Critique of Political Economy*, published in Berlin in 1859, which Marx himself considers the conclusive work of the long studies of the economy which, undertaken prior to the events of 1848–9, were 'taken up again from the beginning' (following numerous personal political pilgrimages between Germany, Paris and Brussels) in London in 1850, on the 'vast selection of material on the history of the political economy gathered in the British Museum'. It is well known that the period from 1850 to 1867 (the date of publication of the first volume of *Capital*) is the period of Marx's 'long silence', broken only by the *Critique of Political Economy* which closes a vision of the historical-economic evolution of society and introduces a paradigm of thought (which I would define historical-institutional, while other well-known definitions are: 'historical materialism' or 'dialectic materialism', and of which further mention will be made later) on which he bases the 'critics' on conventional political economy. It is indeed notorious that the first volume of *Capital* (and what is more, the mass of notes which went on to form the second and third posthumous volumes) represent the development of a formulation already incorporated into the *Critique*. A good display of the intellectual maturation of Marx prior to *Capital* is in E. Mandel (1967). I avoid referring the passages from Marx to a special edition of his different works. I have preferred to quote them through their internal paragraphation (given the limited amount of the quotations).

76. In the same passage, shortly before, Marx had stated that altogether the aforementioned 'production relations make up the economic structure of society, the real basis on which a legal and political superstructure is built and to which determined social forms of awareness correspond'.

77. It should not be forgotten that at the time of writing this famous introduction, Marx had almost completely matured his system of ideas on the capital: already two years earlier he wrote to Engels: 'I'm working like mad, through the night, to summarize my studies of the economy, so as to have clarified at least the basic outlines prior to the flood' (which was a European revolution predicted by Marx as the consequence of the serious financial and economic crisis of those years). The notebooks, published posthumously in 1939 under the title *Grundrisse* by the Marx-Engels-Lenin Institute in Moscow, were already completely written, and it was on them that Marx based the *Critique* published in 1959 and later a large part of the material which was to appear in the three books of *Das Kapital* (1967), the second and third volumes of which were edited from his notes by Engels and published posthumously.

78. Indeed, things are not so easy. There is even a dispute between 'Marxologists' on how to interpret the famous passage of the preface to the *Critique* quoted above. Some emphasize the primacy of 'material productive forces' which, in the course of their evolution, enter into contradiction with existing social relationships of production. This is the basic thesis, for example, of G. A. Cohen in a very thorough examination and revision of *Karl Marx's Theory of History* (1978). This would classify Marx more under a 'technological' than under a 'historical-institutional' approach. Others object that in many passages of Marx's monumental work it is said that the evolution of productive forces, too, may depend on the social relationships of production, and that all the relative 'novelty' and specificity of the Marxist approach lies in having emphasized how greatly the change in production relationships can release new productive forces. There is no lack of ambiguities in Marx on this aspect, too. Then there is always the problem of thoroughly studying and defining the meaning of the concept of 'productive forces'. What are they? Inventions? Innovations? And what is their origin? Their interaction with the economic structure, in turn dominated by the production relationships, make them a rather historical-social factor.

    An exegesis of Marx is not our greatest desire at this moment. We can limit ourselves to emphasizing on the one hand a persistent ambiguity in his thought, but also the irrelevance of this ambiguity in relation to the approach to change we have already glanced at. And perhaps what seems an ambiguity to us, when looked at from the point of view of coherent but rigid analysis of the primary factor of change, may constitute a good basis for interpretation of the multiplicity of factors that may preside over it in the various historical and institutional situations in which it occurs and of the impossibility or fallacy of wanting to bring it down to a theory of history, whether the Marxist one or any other.

79. Nor in the text of the *Critics* can we find more clarification the subject, even because the preface is actually a postface, in which the author tries to express in an essential way the most important comprehensive results of the book.

80. 'Even when a society managed to see indistincly the natural law of its own movement... [Marx will tell later in 1867 presenting the *Capital*, to which he assigns 'the ultimate goal' to reveal that law of movement of modern society], it can neither jump (*ueberspringen*) nor eliminate by decree (*wegdekretieren*) the natural phases of development (*naturgemaesse Entwicklungsphasen*). But it can render more rapid and soft the throes.' The philosophical basis or the theory of history in Marx have been the object of extensive literature (at times too demanding even for a mind like that of Marx which was very complex and very polymath). See, for instance, the quoted works – differently oriented by G.A. Cohen (1978) and by Jon Elster (1985, especially chapter 5).

81. This 'figure of Janus' is by no means new in the evolution of every form of thought and it falls to all scholars who contest the paradigms, or the conventional line of thought, of their respective disciplines, or who move in a substantially transdisciplinary field (who are also those scholars who produce real progress in scientific thought in each field). Anyway, we must pay attention here to the risk of the same anacoluthon found in Schumpeter's reasoning (see above, section 3.2).

82. Otherwise, in *Capital*, we can get an attack of indigestion of 'economic' laws; at a rapid excursion we could recall (indicating volume and chapter in which they are mainly treated): 'the law of value-labour' [I,1]: 'in the relations of exchange...of products,...the worktime socially needed for their production, impose itself as natural regulating law (*als regelndes Naturgesetz*), as, for example, the gravity law, when the house crashes on our heads'; the three laws of 'surplus value' [I,9]; 'the laws of capitalistic appropriation' [I,22]; the 'general law of capitalistic accumulation' [I,23], to which are related also 'the capitalistic laws of population' [I,23], that of 'increasing growth (*steigenden wachstum*) of the constant part of capital in proportion to the variable one' [I,23]; and, lastly, those of 'wages and the wider labour market' [I,23]; the 'laws of capital centralization' [I,24], which Marx presents as the 'immanent laws of the capitalist production itself'.

Then, in the second and third volumes of *Capital*, the output of 'laws' continues: the laws about the general circulation of commodities [II,4]; and, over all, among the most discussed: 'the basic law of capitalistic competition' [III,1]; the laws of 'the general rate of profit' [III,13]; that of the 'tendential falling rate of profit' [III,13]; that of 'the increasing labour productivity' [III,15]; that of 'sharing of surplus value among capitalists' [III,48]; and, finally, again that 'of the development of the capitalist mode of production...by separating more and more the means of production and concentrating progressively in wide groups the means dispersed of production, transforming the work in wage work, and the means of production in capital' [III,52].

The expression 'law' (*Gesetz*, only rarely substituted by others, such as *Regel*, *Grundregel*, *Tendenz*, etc.) is somewhat abused in Marx, enough to rouse suspicion of a colloquial habit more than a really scientific language (as many superficial critics of Marx or, on the other side, some over-sophisticated exegetes – see Dumenil (1978) – have intended).

83. In the preface to the first edition of *Capital* Marx declares that 'the final aim of this work is to reveal the economic law of the movement of modern society' (and we know that he considers bourgeois-capitalist society to be 'modern'). He accepted the closing-off of the analysis of any other external historical factor in the formation and circulation of capital and dedicated himself entirely to the analysis of the internal law (or laws?) of movement of capital.

84. It is a well-known fact that, after the first volume of *Capital* was published, Marx abandoned any further development of his theories; the posthumous writings seem to have all been created and developed before 1867; the third volume of *Capital* (Engels tells us in its preface when he published it in 1894) had been prepared in draft form between 1863 and 1867.

85. Indeed, we should say that the Marxian theory of capital has been put in crisis by history, not because it was wrong (at least at Marx's time), but because the institutional conditions on which it was based have changed. And here, it seems to me, is the gist of the Marxist logical mistake (but even of many institutionalist-evolutionist modern economists): it is not consistent to treat in 'positive' terms an institutionalist-evolutionist vision or approach. See Hodgson (1988).

86. What is more, in the notes for the third volume of *Capital* there are, in the last chapters, passages which show how Marx himself was aware of his own fragility. However, this matter will not be treated here, but rather in an essay covering just this subject which I hope to complete shortly. A good starting point is the paragraph 'The Two Schemata of Marx' (pp. 54–63) in Bell (1973), where he said: 'If we seek to chart the stages of development of capitalist industrial society, we have to begin with the predictions of Marx. But in so doing we are confronted with a conundrum, for in this view of the future, there is not, as I shall try to show, one but two schemata, and it is to these two divergent schemata that most of the theories of social development are responsive.' Further considerations around this topic may be found in Giddens (1981).

87. But he did not even stop, at least up until the 1860s, lightly forecasting 'crises' and 'breakdowns' of the capitalist system, and advising the social democratic movement in its political programmes or fighting them.

88. Which in many ways is the most 'anti-Marxist' way of thinking.

89. Even if defined by dogmatics as 'not orthodox', in my opinion, much more orthodox than the 'orthodox'.

90. In the Post-scriptum (*Nachwort*) of the second edition (1873) of the first volume of *Capital* (at the beginning of the last ten years of his life, in which he had been prevented from working intensively by his illness, even from arranging for printing his numerous writings concerning the other two volumes of his great work). Marx in polemics with many reviewers of his book (first edition) quoted a focused and essential assessment of his own historical method from an anonymous Russian reviewer (translating it from Russian, perhaps by himself, since we know for certain that in this epoch he begun to study several matters – chemistry, physics, and even Russian). I would be inclined to consider Marx's recall of this review, through the expressions of his reviewer, with which he agreed, as a kind of return to the historical-philosophical foundations of his vision, a way out from the meanderings of his theory of capital, from the 'economic' positivistic-oriented debate, within which he felt he had become become ensnared and disoriented. In short, I would be inclined to consider it as a last message, nearly autocritical, summarized by the exhumation of the 'dialectic' evolution concept (very familiar in his youth) to be applied to his own economic theory.

91. Which Marx translated and reproduced because 'it could be interesting for many readers to which the Russian original is inaccessible'. And he did the right thing, since it is really very interesting! Even if neglected – as far as I know – by the most esteemed Marxiology.

92. Berle and Means (1932). Peter Drucker has called this 'one of the most influential American books of this century' (Drucker, 1993, p. 71), and, given the publicity ructions, perhaps it has been.

93. A selection in chronological order would include: Chester Barnard (1938); R.A. Gordon (1945); George Hurff (1950); J.K. Galbraith (1952, 1967); Edith Penrose (1959); and Sargeant Florence (1961). But one should not forget Thorstein Veblen's book on 'absentee ownership', published in 1923, well before Berle and Means's study.

94. One cannot but recall a piece, celebrated at the time, written by J. Burnham, *The Managerial Revolution* (1941) which greatly widened its horizon from the large enterprise to a sociological concept of power, much influenced by Weber's approach. More recent treatments on the subject have been developed by Chandler (1977, 1990).

95. Published posthumously in 1994, not entirely complete and 'finished' by Engels at least thirty years after it was written (again in the form of notes and material for reflection).

96. 'On the basis of capitalist production, in joint stock companies a new fraud develops in relation to the managerial salary, since alongside and above the effective manager there is a quantity of directors and controllers for whom in reality administration and control become a simple pretext to defraud share-holders and enrich themselves' (*Capital*, III, chap. 23).

97. And adds 'And when the dividends that they receive include interest and entrepreneurial gain, that is the total profit, this total profit is pocketed solely under title of interest, or a simple indemnity of ownership of capital, an own-ership that now, in the real process of reproduction (*sic*) is as separated from the function of capital as, in the person of the manager, this function is separated from ownership of the capital' (ibid., chap. 27).

98. Here Marx even says, 'before continuing, this important observation from an economic point of view must be made: since profit presents itself here almost exclusively in the form of interest, such enterprises are possible even when they damage the pure and simple interest and this is one of the reasons [does this seem trivial to you?], of the causes, that resist the fall in the general rate of profit, since these enterprises in which the constant capital is in such a huge proportion compared to the variable capital do not necessarily have an influ-ence on levelling the general rate of profit' (ibid.).

   In other words, Marx already saw how his law on the tendency of the general rate of profit to fall (on which he expanded in the third section of Volume 3 of *Capital* with rigorous deductive logic in the paradigm of the capitalist process of production) is gilded by the re-transformation of capital and the reduction of total profit to mere interest. There would be much to say on this point and many objections to make, but I shall restrain myself because it would lead us away from our theme. However it remains clear that in this chapter Marx amply anticipated not only the divorce between ownership and control, but also the halt to the fall in profits, because the profits are no longer themselves, but something else, something closer to interest than to profit.

99. Friedrich Engels, editing Marx's writings quoted above, thirty years or more after they were written (in his 'supplementary considerations' (*Ergänung und Nachtrag*) to the volume, better known *simply* as *Nachtrag*, he states that volume 3 was written in 1865), added a note in parenthesis (always in the same chapter 27) in which he affirms, among other things, the following: 'Since Marx wrote the above, new forms of industrial organisation have been de-veloped that constitute the joint stock company to the second and third power', and, emphasizing that this development was in line with the trend to monopoly concentration in Marx's process of capitalist production, he con-cludes that in many activities competition had been replaced by monopoly, 'and thus, to our great satisfaction, the future expropriation by the entire society, by the nation, is prepared' (Engels, *Nachtrag zum III Band des 'Kapital'*).

   That the concentration of capital (by trusts, holdings and finally through the stock market – for which Engels in *Nachtrag* provides a historical update to 1895 in relation to this chapter of the volume), and the divorce between own-ership and control of the production process were two processes intimately connected in Marxian logic, I believe there should be no doubt. It was one of the end points reached by the maturing analysis of the functioning of capitalist production as a whole. An aspect which, perhaps, is still to be studied, is whether he did not suspect that this conclusion of his analysis in its entirety did not lead the whole theoretical structure he had built on the process of capitalist production (in the first and, as a corollary, in the second volume of *Capital*) to creak on the level of historical change. That could justify his difficulties in completing the chapters of volume 3, especially those concerning the social implications of these trends (seventh section of the volume, dedicated to the distribution of income); naturally without underestimating the conventional justification of the most respected biographers (in the first place Engels himself) based on the disease that affected him at the end of the 1860s.

However, we know (from a letter to Engels dated 22 April 1868) that Marx considered the book practically finished at that date and was making plans to deliver it to the publisher Meissner. What prevented its publication until his death 14 years later? I wonder if, together with his numerous and increasing health problems and political commitments (which according to Engels prevented Marx from completing a final draft of the last two volumes of *Capital*), there might not have been a certain dissatisfaction on the author's part and that the latest conclusions (and perhaps the latest events) relating to the development of large joint stock companies needed to be brought into greater coherence with the general plan of *Capital* and required some 'revisionism'.

100. This does not eliminate the fact that a little book *If Marx Were to Return*, written by Berle (1965) for the American government information office (USIS) in 1965 with clear propaganda aims, shows that the author was not very familiar with the third volume of *Capital*.

101. In this case, too, the best known and more representative books on a new economics of monopoly and oligopoly (therefore including the new behaviour of managers) are works on the theory of monopolistic competition (H. C. Chamberlin, 1933) or imperfect competition (Robinson, 1933). Marris (1964) deals directly with the economic analysis of 'managerialism'. But I consider the work of Paolo Sylos Labini on the relationship among oligopoly and the technical progress, one of the best summaries of the economic behaviour of the new managerial enterprise (Sylos Labini, 1956).

102. The literature on this topic has become immense. Samples from its origins can be selected from among the works of those who later perfected it (see Berle 1954 and 1959; and Berle and Harbrecht, 1960; Means, 1962) but after the Second World War the managerial transformation was adopted as the emblem of the 'new capitalism' (especially American and in its transnational dimensions), both by its exponents and its detractors. I will recall, among the most significant, only Galbraith (1952, 1967); Drucker (1946); Lilienthal (1952).

103. Unfortunately only in Italian (Ruffolo, 1967).

104. See in particular the final chapter of the book on the 'large enterprise and the plan' as conclusion of the part dedicated to 'social control' of the large enterprise.

105. Mandel (1971, p. 47). Ernest Mandel has recently passed away. To him I have been personally tied with solid, esteemed roots, due to long brotherhood of study and political action. Ernest Mandel has to be considered one of the most authoritative scholars of Marx, with his *Treatise of Marxist Economy* (Mandel, 1962, English translation 1968). His critical independence of thinking is testified by a life dedicated to contest the stupidity, and also political criminality, of Stalinism, to keep pure the memory of the socialist expectations throughout the Trotsky movement of the 4th International, and to safeguard the nobility and the intelligence of Marxian thinking from the deformation of the intellectual and political dishonesty of the Stalinist 'church', incapable – for mere

opportunism or for political sectarianism – of any authentic, intelligent and courageous self-criticism.

106. Schematizing – sometimes in an incorrect way – the opinion of others, seems to bring about the validity of one's own opinions, but does not favour, in the end, even the quality of the argument upheld. More general considerations in Blaug (1990).

107. Laws which, as seen in section 4.1, are considerable. Until, it is suggested, that they are a linguistic expression of any logical reasoning, rather than an unavoidable mechanism of the capitalist development. See also another essay by Blaug (1980).

108. The ambiguity produced by the desire to conserve the Marxist identity of the analysis of capitalism and by the necessity to update such an analysis and make it converge in the recognition of the great change under way, also plays some bad tricks. Thus Mandel in the work cited on late capitalism, at the beginning (p. 8) denies that it is a 'new phase' (*keine neue Epoche der kapitallistichen Entwinklung*), but at the end of the work (p. 488) he speaks of this 'new stage in the development of the capitalist way of production' (this linguistic incoherence was noted by Bo Gustafsson as well (1979) in the introduction to a volume of essays on post-industrial society).

109. It is a real shame to see the great contribution of critical analysis contained in Marx's works used without adapting it to more detailed analyses, and in particular without updating it! Marx's critical spirit would have wanted to do this, even after a few decades of impetuous transformation of the Western economy (between 1850 and 1870), considering he left unpublished the most important writings on the 'law of movement' of capitalism: i.e. the chapters which are not always very coherent with the earlier parts of *Capital*, but which are loaded nevertheless with a great capacity of analysis projection and clear-sighted assessment of 'real' capitalism, which was being transformed in front of his very eyes. It would be incredible to think that he would not subject his theories to severe critical analysis and updating, after the last hundred years of the history of capitalism.

We can imagine with considerable difficulty that Marx himself, already thoughtful and critical, in his last years, on the validity of the assumptions of some of his writings, could be happy to be lifted up again from oblivion, after more than a century, as gospel of new poorly informed generations of hurried and sectarian readers, his study's notebooks of the *fifties*, named *Grundrisse*!

110. Of which the most well-known expression is that of Marx's 11th *Thesis on Feuerbach* (1845): 'Philosophers right now have only interpreted differently the world; now it is a matter of transforming it' (Marx-Engels, *German Ideology*, 1846, Appendix to Part 1.)

111. Even if they are often brought to the scale of major national cases. For a general panorama of the state of the Sociology I would suggest, among several works, the books by Giddens (1995 and 1996).

112. For example, the continental European style as opposed to the Anglo-Saxon, the European as opposed to the American, the Scandinavian as opposed to all others, or the Dutch (inevitable when one descends to the scale of national or local experiences and when Switzerland is so isolated as no longer to arouse any comparative interest).

113. The main work of Daniel Bell, that on the coming of industrial society, is not only that which contributed in a substantial way to conceive the character of contemporary change and to the fortune of the term 'post-industrial society', but also that which tried to take into account the origin of sociological

reflection and of all cultural factors which may intervene in the identification of a new society. See overall chapter 1 of that work, dedicated to the theories of social development.

114. Edward Shils in a writing from 1968.

115. Daniel Bell (1973, pp. 54–5). But at the same time Bell observed: 'The one figure Professor Shils left out, strangely, is Marx, perhaps because we have all become post-Marxists.' See on the subject the last work by Ernest Mandel (1993).

116. But perhaps due to my lack of information; for which reason I invite readers and colleagues to help me by pointing out works that meet the requirements indicated.

117. In the name of that trash-bin of all the disappointed hopes for rational progress of ideas, the so-called post-modernism. Anthony Giddens has repeatedly developed this thematism in a prudent and clever way (Giddens, 1976, 1990, 1991). Some interesting annotations are to be found in a paper by Abrahamson (1989).

118. The tradition is for Historicism, and German Historicism in particular, to be critically set against Enlightenment in all fields from philosophy to historiography, from art criticism to politics etc., and that it should be presented, from the start, as a sort of 'struggle against reason' (Antoni, 1941, following in the footsteps of the idealist vision of Benedetto Croce and many other students of the culture of Romanticism and Idealism). In reality, more attentive analyses of the *Aufklärung*, or German Enlightenment, (especially in recent decades) has revealed, on the one hand, a more 'critical' Enlightenment (starting from Kant himself) aimed more at discovering the sense of history; and on the other hand, a less irrationalistic German culture than appeared from some cultural stereotypes founded only on some currents of nineteenth-century German thought. This question, which was the subject of some studies in my own youth, especially those of a historical philosophy nature, is clearly outside the scope of this chapter, if not of the book, except for one not insignificant aspect: that German Historicism, in its rediscovery of its Enlightenment roots, is at the base of a historical-dialectic vision of social and economic evolution which, through Marx but not only Marx, has permanently produced that reflection on history and historiography which is one of the foundations – in economics, in sociology and in the social sciences in general – of the lines entirely different from the 'classical' or 'neoclassical' ones of a positivist stamp: Weberism in sociology, the historico-institutionalist school in economics. For further development on the argument about the incredibly important role of the German Enlightenment, allow me to refer to some component writings of my unpublished PhD dissertation on 'Reason and History at the Origins of the Modern Critical Conscience' (in Italian, 1949–50); and a more vast, recent and informed contribution by another Italian scholar, Eduardo Tortarolo (1989) on: 'Reason on the Sprea: Historical Conscience and Political Culture in the Berliner Enlightenment' (in Italian).

119. Carlo Antoni, in his fine essay on Max Weber – unfortunately poorly known internationally even among authors who write on Max Weber – remarked that 'Weber's specific topic was a of technique of power, of "political policy as a profession"' (Antoni, 1939, p. 128).

120. More than once Weber identifies Western culture as a culture of rationalization, a culture made up of 'rational accounting, rational technology, rational law, and with these a rationalist economic ethic, the rational spirit and the

rationalization of the conduct of life'; and aims to discover the 'origin' of all that. He looks for it in a comparison of the religious ethics of Christianity with that of the other great religions of the world.

121. More elements on the Weberian 'rational society' in Ferrarotti (1985 and 1989).

122. Auguste Comte – recognized father of sociology – started out as an Assistant Professor to Lecomte de Saint-Simon (and co-writer of his Lectures to the Ecole Polytechnique, 1814–16). See also Saint-Simon, *Oeuvres Completes* (new edn, 1975); Comte, *Oeuvres-Completes*, 1844–1895. (New Ed. 1976).

123. The earliest ones are *Sauvagerie* (a sort of pre-history of humanity), *Patriarcat* (an epoch characterized by agriculture and livestock husbandry), *Age barbarique* (in which clans and tribes are replaced by the nation and in which empires and cities develop). Fourier's works have been recently republished in a very complete edition (Fourier, 1971).

124. Bell (1973, pp. 127–8).

125. The studies, strongly influenced by religious premises, even if conducted by the authors with delicacy and discretion, reveal a bias so strong as to be immediately discredited by everyone. 'Extended' Western culture is so far advanced that a creeping fundamentalism now makes everyone intolerant. How welcome it would be to have 'pure' religious values, not materialized by positive and historically determined religions! And how this form of cultural-religious syncretism could make us reassess the search for new, truly universal values in a meta- historical cultural brotherhood!

126. See for instance the well-known 'Silent Revolution' by R. Inglehart (1971 and 1977).

127. *La physiologie sociale* is a title of a work by H. Saint-Simon (1965) and 'Phisique sociale' was also the title of a relevant part of the Course in 'philosophie positive' by Auguste Comte (1976).

Even if it would be unfair not to recall that Comtian, Spencerian positivism and their epigonies did not concern the social sciences so much as science in general, and therefore develop in a methodological and epistemological position in relation to the philosophical theory of knowledge as a whole.

128. For example, those of institutionalist or evolutionist economics which, in turn, is not exempt from the fall-out from the same epistemological error or its classical or neoclassical interlocutors of wanting to explain the phenomena by analysis of more or less historical institutions. But this is a topic that is outside the present subject.

129. But the attitude that it is not different from other approaches in the (positivist) methods modifies it only for the determinant factor. On this point see the general further observations by Giddens (1974). The influence of post-industrial society on economic thinking has been studied already by some works of F. L. Block (1985 and 1990) and Block and Hirshorn (1979).

130. The absorption of two Weberian rationalities in a single process, is one of the clearer results of the modern science of planning (or planology). Its initial expressions are represented by the conceptual division and distinction, in a single planning process, between the selection problem and the implementation problem, on which Ragnar Frisch (1974) has engaged himself insistently; and with him many of his followers (Johansen, 1977–78; Archibugi, 1979). About the principle of a correct notion of the methodology of planning we will say something more in Chapters 11 and 13 of this book, but a systematic treatise of the subject is in other writings, which will be given in the notes of the chapters indicated.

3 Structural Change: Towards a Convergence of Various Approaches

1. An advanced evaluation by the author would not be so useful, and for certain aspects could be also misleading.
2. To avoid the risk also of inventing things already well-known in the literature or to induce the idea that I could: a risk that is always present when we do not take enough account of the 'state of the art'.
3. For instance, a contribution belonging to the said Marxist orthodoxy and, which for other aspects I consider informed and relevant, is that of M. De Vroey (Undated).
4. Mandel (1975).
5. Mandel employed a good part of his last years to reflect upon the evolution of capitalism, to contest the theory of 'long cycles', but also to acknowledge the contribution which this theory could give to the explanation of a persistent survival of capitalism itself. See, for this, his essay on the 'long waves of capitalistic development' (Mandel, 1980 and 1981), and his contribution to a collective work about the 'new results of research on long cycles', with Alfred Kleinknecht and Immanuel Wallerstein (Kleinknecht *et al.*, 1992).
6. The expression is from Ragnar Frisch, in a masterly work on methods of prospect analysis that remains unsurpassed for its clarity of ideas and advancement of techniques (Frisch, 1962).
7. The basic tables, of which Table 3.1 intends to give a revised and integrated version, are at p. 117 and p. 359 of *The Coming of the Post-Industrial Society* by Bell (1973) and also at pp. 47–50 of *L'auvento post-industriale* by De Masi (ed.) (1985). My own integration is the result of considerations which will be developed in the course of the present work; therefore they will be fully understood only at the conclusion of reading this book.
8. *Natura nos sociabiles fecit* (Seneca); *Homo sociale animal est* (also Seneca); *Homines natura sunt congregabiles* (Cicero).
9. This is the value of a work by Giorgio Ruffolo (the same historian of the large corporation evolution and challenge) on 'Social Quality', in which the trend toward a post-capitalist society is constantly referred to as a 'social option', and a large role is reserved to reforming political commitment (Ruffolo, 1984).
10. Last, obviously, in a chronological sense. Whether it is 'last' also in the 'typological' sense, i.e. if we are not going to have a so-called industrial society anymore, or if (late or mature) capitalism after this last exploit is going to give way to a *new* society, which we will not be able to call 'capitalist', is a much debated question which deserves some more lengthy considerations, but which goes beyond the scope of this work.

    We will deal with this topic in Chapter 11 when I will outline the contents of a society defined as 'post-capitalist'. If by this denomination we mean that we have moved or are moving away from capitalism, or that we are still within it, but with characteristics completely different from those in which the term 'capitalism' was coined, then, frankly, it is a question that does not excite me very much.
11. In other words, the assumption that some phenomena constitute the 'structure' of others, called 'superstructural', would deserve to be discussed at a level which goes completely beyond the subject of this work. (In any case, a good treatment of the subject can be found in Giddens, 1984.)

    In an old essay of the 1960s I tried to 'redress' the widespread and conventional question of social behaviour solely in terms of class conflict among the ruling class and subordinate classes, introducing also a consideration of the other material conditions, i.e. life style and consumption (Archibugi, 1966). I tried to explain – during the youth's contestation of that time – that some signals of behaviour, apparently 'over-structural', and related either to new forms of associative life or to new consumption, were having an impact much more 'structural' than people could or would think. However in a political environment obsessed with the idea of 'power', I was unheeded, even in a restricted ambit of my own cultural relations. I think now that it was during those years that the basis of social transformation was created (in the more advanced countries) and that today it has become 'common place' (the post-capitalist economy), and that is the substantive focus of a renewed attention with this book.

12. It seems to me that one of the authors who has devoted the most attention to the clarification of this concept is Cohen (1978), already cited, in his book on the 'theory of history in Marx', and especially in chapter 6; but his theses have also been disputed.

13. In this sense, I am referring to *The End of Ideology*, another book by Daniel Bell which, some time ago, has entertained us (Bell, 1960), as characteristic of the society into which we are entering.

14. Certainly I do not wish to enter into the debate on 'rationality', what it is, if it exists, what are its limits, how it expresses itself, etc.

15. I am referring especially to the *Lessons of Ethics* by Immanuel Kant (1782), which in its treatment of the subject, as a work of maturity, can be considered one of his most precise and conclusive works.

16. This political operation will be the object, as mentioned, of the second part (especially Chapters 11 and 13). The more technical and organizational aspect of this political operation, which we could also call simply 'governance', and which concerns planning as a method of governance, will be dealt with in another series of works (of mine, as of other authors) that will be indicated in the cited chapters.

17. An important work in this direction is that by Arrow and Raynaud (1986). See also usefully an ancient approach by Daniel Bell (1966), and a more recent and stimulating work by Heilbroner on the 'visions of the future' (1995).

4 The Change in the Structure of Consumption and the 'Tertiarization' Process

1. We will shortly discuss this expression. Nevertheless we are referring to those countries where the manufacturing industry has manifested its most advanced and marked forms, in substitution of agricultural activities as main sources and opportunity for employment, output and income.

2. There is immense literature on the analysis of the transformation from rural to industrial society. In particular, I would cite the works by Karl Polanyi (1944) and Raymond Aron (1961, 1962, 1965).

3. Naturally the concept of 'slowness' depends on the historical parameter adopted. Here we are referring to the process of that 'industrial revolution' which began in the eighteenth century, and which – also in advanced Western countries – is not fully concluded. If we pass to a millenary historic scale, we have to say that the process of industrialization has been very rapid, because in two centuries it has changed the face of humanity, after a relatively stable multi-secular economy.

4. Thus, for example, some critics of the so-called 'neo- classical' school of economics, called by some 'orthodox' (amongst whom, for many reasons, but not by an act of faith, I would include myself), are not fair when they accuse this school of 'exogenizing' the technological conditions or preferences of the subjects (consumers and/or political decision-makers). There are many cases in which, for example, the available technology, on the one hand, or political preferences, on the other, must be considered *exogenous*, if there is an intention to give some shape to a set of technical-economic procedures to utilize. It will then be a matter of seeing *how much* the change of available technologies or the change of preferences (of the consumer and/or political decision-maker) – which moreover are the business of other subjects (the technologist or decision-maker/consumer or the decision-maker/political administrator) – *may imply change* in the technical-economic procedures: *but in the method rather than in the substance*.

The 'methodological' reasoning (which is not always to be discarded) needs to 'leave aside' the complexity. If we wish to 'analyze' the complexity, and if we wish, therefore, to identify its interlacing, it is necessary to separate the routes in order to know one from the other independently (without being so naive as to ignore the interdependency, but also not being so ingenuous to think that in each partial direction the same interdependencies – I would say 'temporarily' – cannot or must not be ignored). In other words, that the egg depends on the chicken and viceversa, does not mean that we cannot analyze how and with what causal mechanisms the chicken produces the egg, and viceversa how and with what causal mechanisms is the chicken born from the egg.

5. In a famous passage of an equally famous work in full depression (1930), Keynes interpreted it as

> not from the rheumatics of old age, but from the growing- pains of over-rapid changes, from the painfulness of readjustment between one economic period and another. The increase of technical efficiency has been taking place faster than we can deal with the problem of labor absorption; the improvement in the standard of life has been a little too quick; the banking and monetary system of the world has been preventing the rate of interest from falling as fast as equilibrium requires...(p. 321). The prevailing world depression, the enormous anomaly of unemployment in a world full of wants, the disastrous mistakes we have made, blind us to what is going on under the surface – to the true interpretation of the trends of things (p. 322). For the moment the very rapidity of these change is hurting us and bringing difficult problems to solve. Those countries are suffering relatively which are not in the vanguard of progress. We are being afflicted with a new disease of which they will hear a great deal in the years to come – namely, technological unemployment. This mean unemployment due to our discovery of means of economising the use of labor is outrunning the pace at which we can find new uses for labor. But this is only a temporarary phase of maladjustment. All this means in the long run is that *mankind is solving its economic problem*.   (Keynes's emphasis)

He was certainly right as compared with the prophets of doom of his times, unless we want to include also the Second World War which broke out some years later as an effect of the crisis. But of what was the war an effect? Of the depression itself, or of the inability to interpret it correctly? (See Keynes's writing of 1930 on 'the economic possibilities for our grandchildren', republished by himself in *Essays in Persuasion*, 1932, p. 359.)

6. From the first edition of Pigou's *Economics of Welfare* of 1920.

7. Some have applied to this behaviour Engel's old nineteenth-century law on the 'elasticity' of food and non-food consumption in relation to income: see, for instance, Bell (1973: pp. 127–8 of the 1976 edn); Gershuny and Miles (1983, pp. 25, 96, 246, 249). But the statistical evidence of 'tertiarization' has been provided since the 1950s: see, for instance, the background works by Minkes (1955); Fabricant (1954); and above all, Kuznets (1953, 1955, 1959).

8. We are referring, obviously, to the works of A.G.B. Fisher (1935, 1945, 1953 and 1954), and that of Colin Clark (1940), the classification of which has become a common paradigm for any other work on the structural division of economic activities.

    There is somebody (Rostow, 1990, p. 173) who wishes to rightly remember that 'in dealing with the dynamics of industrial progress, Marshall analyses with considerable subtlety, anticipating the later conclusions of Colin Clark and Simon Kuznets, the proportionate shift of labor force out of agriculture, the relative constancy (since 1851) of the proportions in manufactures and the relative rise of service employment, due primarily to the comparative lack of the technological progress in the latter'. Reference to Marshall's *Principles* (1890) (8th edn, Macmillan, 1920, pp. 274–7).

    A later pamphlet (of 1961) by Colin Clark is also to be recommended on the 'mystification' of investment growth. For the concept of 'quaternary' also developed, see in particular the works by Lengellé (1966), Gottman (1975), and others.

9. On this subject, see my essay of 1977, *Critique of the Tertiary* (Archibugi, 1977) from where I draw some arguments for this chapter. The many works of Fourastié have all been inspired by a unique basic conception of productivity; among others I suggest one of the first where that conception has been expressed, the book of 1950, *Le grand espoir du XX siècle; progrès technique, progrès économique, progrès sociale*. See also by Jean Fourastié a small treatment on the productivity (1952).

10. For example, J. Gershuny (1978). By the same author there is the more complete analysis in collaboration with I. Miles (already quoted) carried out in the framework of the 'Fast' studies mentioned above (Gershuny and Miles, 1983).

11. See a work by Peter Holmos on 'personal society' (1970). Other visions of the 'service society' are in Gartner and Riesmann (1978) and Stanback *et al.* (1981).

12. The term 'Fordism' today is increasingly used to indicate the technology of mass-production and of factory labour organization. Clearly, I prefer to remain consistent, using this term to express 'high wages policy'. This policy aims to replace financial equilibrium and connected profits in the short term, in order to project the equilibrium in a longer term to a higher level, with widespread economies and gains of dimension. We can best understand 'Fordian' logic by reading Ford himself (Ford, 1924, p.124):

> I have learned through the years a good deal about wages. I believe in the first place that, all other considerations aside, our own sales depend in a measure upon the wages we pay. If we can distribute high wages, then the money is going to be spent and it will serve to make storekeepers and distributors and manufacturers and workers in other lines more prosperous and their prosperity will be reflected in our sales. Country-wide high wages spell country-wide prosperity, provided, however, the higher wages are paid for higher production. Paying high wages and lowering production is starting down the incline toward dull business.

13. In the essay on the industrial processes of automation and their social and economic impact which I wrote in 1956 (Archibugi 1956, already quoted), I began to argue the above thesis that the shift to a service economy and the decline of opportunities to extend mass consumption could diminish the effectiveness of 'Fordist' and 'Keynesian' policies.

14. On this point see the scheme of the economic schools, named 'post-Keynesian', proposed by P. Davidson (1981). I am fully conscious of a certain 'simplification' of a debate very rich in hues. But it is always advisable to counterbalance complexity when it tends towards the elusive or chaotic (Davidson speaks of a Babel) with some 'reduced form'. I remember this kind of simplification in some masterly observations by Ragnar Frisch (in his lecture for the Nobel Prize (1969) republished posthumously among his writings on economic planning (1976). See also Wassily Leontief (1976). In this context it is impossible to forget an old witty remark of Keynes: 'Economics is a science of thinking in terms of models joined to the art of choosing models which are relevant to the contemporary world...Good economists are scarce because the gift for using "vigilant observation" to choose good models, although it does not require a highly specialized intellectual technique, appears to be a very rare one.' (Keynes, *Collected Works*, Vol. IV, quoted in Davidson, 1981).

I would like to recall also the lapidar phrase by Sylos Labini: 'The social reality which theoretical models seek to interpret change over time. All models are historically conditioned, but some are more so than others; those which express little more than logical schemes are least of all...For the weakness of these models, often and at least in part do not lie in the field of logic, but in the degree of realism of the initial hypothesis, and this realism, even when it originally exists, does not remain constant over time' (Sylos Labini, 1993, p 152).

The core of our reflection in this book is just that:

1. First of all, the initial hypotheses of industrial society are changing (some already have changed, others have not yet changed but are in the process of said change), in respect of the eventual hypothesis of the actual post-industrial society. This is the point that obliges us to rediscuss, in the transition from industrial to post-industrial society, almost all economic models with which we are accustomed to dealing and using.

2. Last but not least, we can transform our hypothesis (of a positivist flavour) in 'programmatic' hypothesis, and consequently, our models from interpretative to decisional models (in terms masterly defined by Frisch, 1976).

Other interesting considerations are in a essay by Daniel Bell (1981), 'Models and Reality in Economic Discourse'. On post-Keynesian economics, see also a beautiful essay by John Kenneth Galbraith (1978).

15. How can one be amazed if, in these circumstances, the general productivity level and – by unavoidable connection – even that of profitability (at least in the conventional economic sense) tend in the long term to decline? To this point we will return more specifically in Chapter 7, section 3. A large statistical and evaluation base is given by the studies on the matter by the National Bureau of Economic Research (NBER) of New York (see the works by V.R.Fuchs, 1964, 1965; 1966a and b; 1968; 1970). An overview on the 'tertiary revolution', even if this book has gone beyond the border of its real meaning, is that by Lengellé (1996), already cited.

16.   A sign of this phenomenon is the proliferation of different types of bread – which is a primitive and prime necessity good *par excellence* – such as to provide a range of typologies never known before. The same can be said for all alimentary consumption, which has attained frenetic levels of sophistication. See some interesting remarks in J. Williams *et al.* (1987).

17.   All the analysis of the consumerism by Fred Hirsch (1976) is founded on this psychological phenomenon. Other views in Kenny and Florida (1988).

18.   For want of serious programmatic-type quantitative analysis (see Chapters 10 and 12). We can only be amazed by the schizophrenia which seems also to affect many authoritative economists – maybe only as a result of mental laziness – who, on the one hand have been stating for many decades that the indicator of industrial production is no longer an appropriate indicator of true economic progress or of social welfare (in mature Western countries), but on the other hand are dismayed when the indexes of the industrial production decline, or become excited when these indexes increase. Always for want of more appropriate programmatic evaluations on a sufficiently desegregated and cognitive accounting frame of reference, I personally would assess a positive trend of the indexes of industrial production (in the mature post-industrial countries) as a signal of regress, of resources wasted, of damage to nature without improvement in social welfare, of artificial conservation of production levels, useless and detrimental, and of conservation of obsolete production structures. And when for intellectual honesty, people have to express these feelings (I insist this is always in absence of more appropriate and direct methods of evaluation which are named 'social and economic planning'), in the circles of 'right-thinking' economists (which today include many former radicals nowadays sensitive to the views of the powerful) one is thought an eccentric, or lover of the paradox.

19.   See the wide enquiry on the USA in Bluestone and Harrison (1982). See also the essays collected by Blackaby (1979).

20.   The book which has provided the most ideas for the concept of post-industrial society is the previously cited work by Daniel Bell (1973).

21.   I cannot but admire the essentiality of the Marxian expression (already quoted in Chapter 2, section 3):

> A social formation never dies before all the productive forces which it can contain are developed, and new and superior production relations are able to replace it before the material conditions of existence are matured in the bosom of the old society. Therefore, mankind always assumes only those tasks which it is able to accomplish, as, with a closer look, it will always be clear that these tasks arise only where the material conditions for its realisation are already present – or at least about to become so.
>
> (Marx, *Critique, etc.*, 1856, preface)

22.   This is today commonly defined as the 'globalization process'. At this point, however, it is impossible not to remark that in this process (of globalization) we do not have any evidence that global integration is largely taking the form of conversion of non-industrial countries to service economies dependent on the industrialization of the advanced countries (American Coca-Cola bought by developing countries that become or remain service economies); but more frequently takes the form of transfer of the industrialization process from countries which have experienced it to ones which have not yet experienced it (Coca-Cola which transferred its production plant to third world countries),

quickening the pace of transformation of 'industrial society' (in the developed countries) to 'service society'. But all this process (on a global scale) – which is very complex and would deserve a more systematic analysis – falls totally outside the field of our analysis. (A good starting point is a recent work by Bruno Amoroso, 1998).

5.   The Change in the Structure of Production

1.   Such a notion or definition of tertiary thus refers to the content of the technical progress incorporated in the activities to be classified, rather than their typological nature. Therefore it approaches J. Fourastié's concept (already evoked in Chapter 4, section 2), which led to a classification subsequently described as 'moving' (by Lengellé, 1966 and Malkin *et al.*, 1973) since each sector may have its classification changed over time according to its productivity rate. As for the definition of theory, consult Fisher's reply (1953) to Fourastié, and the more recent works of Dhrymes (1963), Katouzian (1970) and Archibugi (1977).
2.   See Lengellé, 1966.
3.   See the set of evaluation papers on the production of services edited by Stanback *et al.* (1981).
4.   We cannot forget, on this subject, the wise teaching of Joseph Schumpeter (very topical still after about sixty years) who navigated with skill between Scylla and Charybdis opposing visions of 'survival' and 'collapse', of 'optimism' and 'pessimism', concerning the capitalist system and its transformation. He said as conclusion to his remarks on the question 'Can capitalism survive?':

> We have rediscovered what from different standpoints and, so I believe, on inadequate grounds has often been discovered before: there is inherent in the capitalist system a tendency toward self-destructions which, in its earlier stages, may assert itself in the form of a tendency toward retardation of progress. I shall not stay to repeat how objective and subjective, economic and extraeconomic factors, reinforcing each other n imposing accord, contribute to that result. Nor shall I show what should be obvious that those factors make not only for a destruction of the capitalist but for the emergence of a socialist civilization. They all point in that direction. The capitalist process not only destroys its own institutional framework but it also creates the conditions for another. Destruction may not be the right word after all. Perhaps I should have spoken of transformation...
>
> But our answer to the question that heads this part ["Can capitalism survive?"] posits far more problems than it solves...
>
> First, that so far we have not learned anything about the kind of socialism that may be looming in the future... For Marx and for most of his followers – and this was and is one of the most serious shortcomings of their doctrine – socialism meant just one definite thing. But definiteness really goes no further than nationalization of industry would carry us and with this an indefinite variety of economic and cultural possibilities will be seen to be compatible.
>
> Second, that similarly we know nothing as yet about the precise way by which socialism may be expected to come except that there must be a great many possibilities ranging from a gradual bureaucratization to the most picturesque revolution...
>
> Third, that the various components of the tendency we have been trying to describe, while everywhere discernible, have as yet nowhere fully revealed

themselves. Things have gone to different lengths in different countries but in no country far enough to allow us to say with any confidence precisely how far they will go, or to assert that their 'underlying trends' have grown too strong to be subject to anything more serious than temporary reverses...

From the standpoint of immediate practice as well as for the purpose of shortrun forecasting – and in these things, a century is a 'short run' – all this surface may be more important than the tendency toward another civilization that slowly works deep down below.

(Schumpeter, *Capitalism, Socialism and Democracy*, 1956, pp. 162–3)

For a criticism of 'collapse' theory applied to the Welfare State, see F. Caffé (1981). For other well-known treatments of the 'Capitalism's collapse' literature, see: Daniel Bell (1979); Peter Drucker (1993); R. Dahrendorf (1957); C. Napoleoni (1970). An interesting Japanese viewpoint is in K. Eiichi (1989).

5. As principal references to the different approaches, we can mention the report by a group of OECD experts (1977) best known through the name of its president as the McCracken Report, a report by a European Commission group of experts (1976) similarly known as the Maldague Report, and a report by the European Trade Unions Institute (ETUI, 1979) best known by the title *Keynes Plus*. The Maldague Report found better and more homogenous expression as the concluding essay of a collective work (Holland, ed. 1978), where it appeared carrying the signatures of F. Archibugi, J. Delors and S. Holland, (1978) all members of said European Commission group. We should also point out the works of the Forum for International Political and Social Economy (IPSE Forum, 1983), a body created by S. Holland, who in the language of the Maldague Group had pursued and deepened work on the intepretation of the crisis, suggesting long-term policies and envisaging a new model for society. One should also recall another recent report by a group of more traditional economists, under the Institute for International Economics (IIE, 1982).

6. For example, the last chapter of the book *The New Industrial State* (Galbraith, 1967) is devoted to the 'future of the industrial state', yet still nowhere an argument for the decline of industrial society is made, just for its deep change.

7. It is interesting that much of the reasoning in more recent economic theory seems to have lost the critique of the development paradigm and the 'dependency effect', as formulated simply and clearly by Galbraith. The dependency effect instead was largely discussed at the beginning of the 1960s in a volume of essays coordinated by Edmund S. Phelps (1962), to which the following participated: Alvin H. Hansen, F.A. Hayek, Lionel Robbins, Walter Heller, George J. Stigler and many others.

8. Among the great number of analyses (of course only those seen by the present author), that by Piore and Sabel – which offers also a useful summary of the literature we mentioned – seems to be among the most acute and wide-ranging (Piore and Sabel, 1984). For example, they classify the modes of analysis of the crisis of industrial production in two main groups: (a) those which focus on shocks external to the economic system, and on the 'mistakes' that the macro-regulatory institutions made in responding to these shocks, conceiving thus the crisis as a 'chain of accidents compounded by accidents'; (b) those which consider the limits of development of the post-war economic system, and the incapacity of the institutional structures to conform to the diffusion of mass production technology. The authors examine in the first group those that aim at analyzing certain episodes (five, to be exact), that is: (1) social upheavals (student and civil rights protests in the late 1960s, especially in the USA), trade union

protests on behalf of the equality of immigrant workers and other disadvantaged groups, especially in Europe, and regional claims for equality; (2) fluctuating exchange rates (after the abandonment of the rigid ones); (3) the oil shock, the agrarian stocks surplus and the new deal of Russian wheat; (4) the second oil shock (Iranian Revolution) and the ensuing inflation; (5) the high interest rates, the global recession and the debt crisis of the Third World. In the second group of analyses they put those with a 'more fundamental explanation', based on 'long-term trends at work'; and these more fundamental explanations are identified in: (1) the saturation of industrial markets; (2) the Third World's development strategies; (3) the trends towards 'diversification' of consumption and the exhaustion of raw materials. From the analyses on the whole Piore and Sabel draw some conclusions that aim at a more structural, more fundamental evaluation of the change (of the industrial divide they regard historically as the 'second' after the success of mass production, and that seems to them to be characterized by the decline of mass production).

9.   See especially, about this theory, Berger and Piore (1980). See also the essay by Cutler *et al.* (1987).

10. In fact, however accurate the industrial dualism theory may draw the current economic structure, it does no justice – according to Piore and Sabel – to the most notorious districts of the last century, described by Alfred Marshall (1923) in his *Industry and Trade*, where small firms developed and exploited *new* technologies without becoming larger; and large firms which from the beginning used complex technologies without producing standardized goods. The technological dynamism of this kind of firm, both small and large, challenges the idea that craft can be both a traditional and a subordinate form of economic activity (Piore and Sabel, 1984, pp. 226–7).

11. One has the impression that the Italian case has been somewhat overestimated by the authors.

12. I would like to mention some not so recent research. For example, that carried out at MIT in Boston for the US Federal Department of Commerce (Birch, 1979) on small enterprises with less than twenty employees showed that between 1969 and 1976 these had created 66% of all new net jobs in the private sector. Furthermore, 80% of new employees come from enterprises less than five years old. The same study indicated that 87% of all new net jobs were created by companies with less than 500 employees (see also, Birch, 1981). In 1979 the US Congress gathered a series of documentation on and testimonies to the active role of small enterprise in the promotion of economic growth (US Congress, 1979). All this led to the creation in the USA of a special Federal agency for small business (SBA).

And a study by the Canadian Federation of Independent Business showed that in Canada small enterprises with less than twenty employees had created 72% of all new jobs between 1969 and 1977, and that in the period they had created 317,000 jobs in manufacturing industry, whilst enterprises with more than twenty employees had lost 124,000 jobs over the same period (cited by Van Buiren, 1981). Documentation on the role of new technology in this development can be found in a report by the US Department of Commerce (1967). See also analyses by Flender and Morse (1975) and Piore (1983) already quoted.

13. The works of G. Fuà (1978) and, with C. Zacchia (eds) (1983) are among the more elaborate analyses of this phenomenon, which have provided the base for many other territorial analyses in Italy on the evolution of the so-called 'Adriatic Model' of industrial development (for instance, Bagnasco and Pini, 1981; Brusco, 1982) Much of this has been utilized and recalled by Piore and Sabel (see above).

14. As far as the Italian experience is concerned, consult the ISPE study on decentralized production models which have been developed strongly in several of the country's regions (ISPE, 1981) and a study by CENSIS (1981) on the same subject. Still in Italy, the division of labour between large and small enterprise has been analyzed in a study by Gros-Pietro (1980).

15. On the productivity 'slope' of the economy a wide statistical documentation has existed for many years, especially for the USA: we refer especially to the studies of NBER of New York (for instance, Kendrick, 1961). More recent documentation and analysis can be found in: Denison, (1979), Norsworthy, Harper and Kunze (1979), Maital and Meltz (1980), Filer (1980), Kendrick and Vaccard (eds) (1980), and finally again Kendrick (1984).

16. For many years people have discussed, forecast and hypothesized the decline of enterprise, and also entrepreneurship. We can again recall Joseph Schumpeter and what he wrote in 1942 on the decline of the entrepreneurial function (in his book *Capitalism, Socialism and Democracy*). One of the authors who has dedicated major attention to the phenomenon of the decline of entrepreneurship in recent decades is Robert L. Heilbroner, to whose work we send the reader wishing to go deep into the subject (1985a, 1976, and overall the book by him and others, in 1972, and last essay on the future of capitalism, 1993). On the crisis of profitability, see a quantitative analysis by Heap *et al.* (1980/81), and essays on the phenomena of de-industrialization collected by Blackaby (1979) and Bluestone and Harrison (1982), already cited.

17. For an appraisal of the historical evolution of public expenditure – to which we will return in Chapter 9 – see the even less recent survey from the OECD, *Public Expenditure Trends* (1978, pp. 12–13) which includes an interesting discussion of the problem of the historical growth of public expenditure. This discussion has arrived at a point to even formulate a law ('Wagner's law'), which Wagner formulated some time ago, and which indeed seems to fall into epistimological ridicule, as many statistical laws often do. (See Bird, 1971.) For more recent data, see OECD (1985a). On the subject, however, the literature is endless. We mention, for instance, the analyses of Cameron (1978), and Boltho (1979). More recently wide-ranging discussion has developed aimed at 'explaining' such enormous expansion of the public sector (a good classification of the debate is in a work by Greve (1991). We may wonder, however, not only if such an explanation is 'possible' (as does Greve, in fact, reaching a negative conclusion), but also if it is 'useful'. In fact the combination of factors, or linked causes, of the expansion of the public sector is so strong that an analysis (inevitably 'theoretical', such as that, for example, in the framework of the 'theory of public choice') appears to a certain extent pointless.

18. Considerations on the breadth of the non-market and informal economy can be found in Schiray and Vivaner (1980). Bénard (1974) and Dupuis and Greffe (1979) have worked extensively on quantification of this sector. See also Archambault and Greffe (1984). Recently work in this area has been carried out in France by the Laboratoire d'Economie Sociale of the University of Paris I, Pantheon-Sorbonne, under the guidance of Edith Archambault (1990, 1992), and on the international scale a parallel and comparative investigation has been carried out under the auspices of the Johns Hopkins University (Anheier and Seibel, 1990; Salamon and Anheier, 1994, 1996). It should be emphasized that these reflections led to a definition of the 'informal' economy, which is not 'formal' since it is not subject to accounting. More on this below in Chapters 11 and 12.

19. Behavioural change in the supply of labour and analysis of how this affects labour markets has been the subject of an astonishing amount of work (see the next chapter, Chapter 6). Some time ago I found interesting Best's anthology (1973), a volume by Parker (1971), and the reflections of Giroud, d'Arvisenet and Sallois (1980). See also the essays of Bernard-Bécharies and Pinson (1981) and Berger (1974).

20. In terms of economic accounting, the works collected for an NBER conference in New York (Terleckyj, ed. 1975) are of great interest. For a more general view of the role of the family in the contemporary economy, see the works of the 'Vanier Institute of the Family', Ottawa (e.g.: VIF, 1976 and 1979) and the stimulating works by Burns (1975 and 1977). See also an interesting essay by Cammaille (1989) on the theme of the relation between Welfare State and Household, on 'the issues involved by a redefinition of the relation between public and private expenditure'.

21. In the United States, where a vast alternative communitarian movement has developed, one can find a series of general works that bear witness to this, such as Harman (1979), Hess (1979), McRobie (1981), Wismer and Pell (1981) and Zwerdling (1980). There is also official documentation on this subject by the federal government from the US Office of Consumer Affairs (1980). An up-to-date survey of the non-market sector can be found in the numerous works of the Independent Sector (1992); and, on an international scale, in the comparative research promoted by Johns Hopkins University, already quoted (Salamon and Anheier, 1994 and 1996).

22. See Nordhaus and Tobin (1973); see also Gronau (1973), Land and Juster (1981) and Fox (1974 and 1985b).

23. For more general considerations on this changing relations, see Sachs (1982). We will come back to this point and its policy implications in Chapter 11, section 4, and in Chapter 13.

24. Very likely, many 'paradoxes' that economic theory has discovered recently must be ascribed to this kind of 'schizophrenia' of the economists, who are unable to evaluate the crisis of parameters on which their separate theorems are based in an whole and integrated way.

25. This productivistic dichotomy, while commonly recognized, is afterwards neglected in a good deal of the quantitative macroeconomic analysis of the relationship between per capita output, investment, income, employment, etc. And this considerably impoverishes analyses, when it does not lead them toward misleading conclusions.

26. See, on the subject, Dhrymes (1963).

27. See, for example, just to quote two extremes: on the one hand, Ernest Mandel's analysis (1978), especially chapters 1 and 2, and, on the other, the above-mentioned McCracken Report (OECD, 1977), in particular paragraphs 224–9.

28. See more considerations included in the chapter on the grammar of the industrial revolution, in the early writing by the present author (Archibugi, 1956), recently republished, in a complete previously unpublished version (1995).

29. J. Stuart Mill (1848), *Principles*, etc., book 4, chap.6.

30. Daly (1973, p.19).

31. See Colin Clark (1961).

32. Among many 'indefinitenesses' read on the realm of the knowledge in our contemporary world, the least trivial seems to be that by Peter Drucker in the work on the 'post-capitalist society' (1993) (especially chapter 1: 'From Capitalism to the Knowledge').

33. Nijkamp *et al.* (1985).

34. The measure of the acquisition of human capital (knowledge) and of its effects has been a theme much debated in the past decades. We recall for instance a well-known and influential contribution by Hector Correa (1963), a follower of Jan Tinbergen, and his other further researches on integrated accounting (1977). A more recent treatment of the matter is in a study by OECD, targeted at accounting 'acquired knowledge' (1996c).

35. As far as the pleaders of 'zero growth' or stationary economies are concerned, see certain works that have since become classics, such as those of Colin Clark (1961), Scitovsky (1964 and 1976), Boulding (1966), and Mishan (1967). See also the contributions of H.E. Daly (1971 and 1973). For the relativity of indicators, we indicate the works (already quoted) of Nordhaus and Tobin (1973) and J. Bénard (1974).

36. Needless to say, the non-sense is evident in talking about unemployment in general in countries where the annual rate of immigrant workers (registered or not) remains always very high. Moreover, it is also useful to recall that the constant increase of social welfare provided by the state, which thus offers big shares of this welfare free of charge (or rather charging the tax-payers), decreases the marginal utility for 'income' for a growing strata of citizens, and thus reduces the latter's willingness to offer labour for income, fostering the lack of concern for work we are considering.

37. More extended reflections on the shrinking of the labour market as an important area of solution of social problems are in an interesting work by Offe and Heinze (1990, Engl. trans. 1992), translated into English with the title *Beyond Employment*, that is more significant than the German original one.

38. But to some extent this happened during the whole historical development of capitalist production.

39. For wider considerations, see Matzner (1991) and Kregel, Matzner and Roncaglia (1988).

40. In this respect the state is the non-market, and the market is the non-state. If one of the two institutions were to disappear, the nature of the remaining one would not be radically altered.

41. Except for what refers, in its beginnings, to the entrepreneurial *coté*.

42. On this point it is impossible not to refer to the many reflections made in another best-selling book of our time, *The End of Work*, by Rifkin (1995).

43. And the measurement tools for this are everywhere still non-existent or very incomplete. For further, particular considerations, see other works by Claus Offe (1992, 1995a).

44. And for measuring it, new measurement criteria and methods are emerging, which yet are still far from influencing the paradigms of traditional economic theory and its reflections on economic policy. (See further considerations in Schettkat, 1990).

45. Which could be available to the usual observers of economic evolution to the same extent as the current statistics on employment, product and income.

46. It is impossible to ignore the fact that, when it is advancing towards a broader evaluation of the 'value' upon which the the concept of social welfare is founded, the 'utilitaristic' paradigm, upon which most of the theoretical reasoning in political economy is founded and which has represented a categorial model of thought and judgement, probably will need to be revised *strongly* as well.

47. See for this the first results of the international survey promoted by Johns Hopkins University (Salamon and Anheier, 1992).

6 The Change in the Labour Market

1. We could perhaps call it a 'labour market policy', since it would be difficult to still speak of a true 'market', unless imposing the logic of the survival of an ancient schematism, unsuitable to the new reality.

2. This seems to be the obsession – for several decades – in dozens of empirical and theoretical studies of 'labour economics' and of analyses of the labour market. Among the best, and recommendable for its clarity and completeness, I mention that by a group from the University of Glasgow (Mackay *et al.*, 1971), which approached this problem but was somewhat rather defeated by it.

3. I would persist with the basic evolutive (or transitional) concept, concerning the existence of two forms of production in which a *traditional* sector and a *changing* or *innovative* sector always co-exist. The reasoning here developed concerns only the changing sector, and in the size assumed by it in each historical society, or country, in evolution; while the traditional sector may remain large. Thus the traditional sector can provide a place for manifestations of the traditional labour market (an extreme case is that of economies which register a high rate of immigration, which – with unimportant exceptions – concerns activities belonging to the traditional sector). What I would like to insist on is that in current academic analyses of the labour market, the situations, behaviours, even the changes, in the labour market are analyzed according to paradigms that belong to the traditional forms of production. This means that people still use a reading mode which does not allow them to see or understand fully what is really occurring. (On this subject, see many of the papers included in Darity (1992). See also Wilkinson (1981); Zwerdling (1980); and Boje (1992). See also the Handbook by Anshenfelter and Layard (1986).)

4. And not only *in* the market, because they all work in the market, including the public sector.

5. The analysis of the negative effect that the transformation of the labour demand structure has had, and still has, on the employment level has been pompously called by someone 'demand structuralism'. In reality, it is important to note (as we have tried to do) that the increase in unemployment, registered in recent decades, has something to do with the new technologies and with the changes in the structure of consumption in a mass-consumption society arrived at its full maturity (see, for instance, Driehuis, 1979, p.100). (However in regard to the problems raised by 'demand structuralism' it would be necessary to say much more, but this goes beyond the aims of this book).

6. Policies usually all aimed – with a great effort of energy and means – at reactivating the labour market, with simple expedients either in training or financial or fiscal incentives, and a 'labour demand' of the classic entrepreneurial type.

7. In this distinction I leave out of consideration the older split between the individual entrepreneur and the manager of the big company, which has become irrelevant to the present evolution of the labour market and the demand we are discussing. Here as 'entrepreneur' we mean both.

8. Attention to the motivational aspects of labour supply is a 'classic' of labour economics, especially of an institutional approach, in relation to the theorems and reasonings of neo-classical economics. With irony, Lloyd G.Reynolds, an authoritative father of 'labour economics', in a well-known book on the 'structure of the labour market' in 1951 stated (as I recall it): 'The fact that a worker does not jump permanently from one job to another, in conformity with the

labour gain that he can achieve, does not say anything about the 'rationality' of that worker (while one can say something about the rationality of whoever would claim that he should act in such way)' (Reynolds, 1951). Such irony would be fitting for many other academic 'theories' of neo-classical economics.

9. Many arguments in this direction can be found in numerous works that Eli Ginzberg has dedicated to the development of human resources for economic progress. See overall, Ginzberg (1985); Ginzberg (1988; and other less recent: 1976, 1965). See also Berger (1974).

10. See a European survey on stress at work, by Kompier and Levi (1994). See also another survey at plant level performed in eight European countries by the European Foundation for the Improvement of Living and Working Conditions (Bielenski, *et al.*, 1994)

11. Among many comments on the meaning of 'new employment', see Guttmann (1978 and 1979).

12. See also on this subject again Ginzberg *et al.* (1989).

13. As evidence of this situation I would cite a researcher engaged in the metal-workers' union in Italy, a country where unemployment always existed for structural reasons in the 1960s and 1970s:

> The reach of protected (unionized) labour, to which not all people, youth, women, etc. in search of work belonged, tended to diminish increasingly, above all in the industrial and agricultural sectors...In contrast one saw the growth of a supply of labour geared towards activities beyond the reach of unions, which offered substantial gains, and were concentrated in brief periods of time such as seasonal or part-time workers. This supply of labour came above all from students, beginning at the level of higher eduction, and youth in search of work, preferring irregular, intermediary and unprotected activities which left much free time for studies, family, and other matters, rather than taking up a job in the industrial sector where the only counter-part is stability, but not income or utility of training received.
>
> (Capecchi *et al.*, 1978, p. 31. See also 1989)

The same author indicates that in the province of Bologna, where he carried out his union activities, about 80 per cent of registered unemployed youth declined offers of work in various sectors based on accords worked out by employers and union. Moreover it is well known that such astonishing situations occur all over Italy, especially within the case of the Italian law on aid to work-training contracts. Many references for other countries are in Piore (1984) especially chapter 3.

14. See the arguments of Gerd Vonderach (1980, 1981 and 1982).

15. See the OECD report on perspectives of employment (1983, p.47). See, on the subject, also the set of papers edited by R.S. Belous (1989), under the title of *The Contingent Economy*, especially the paper by himself on 'the growth of temporary, part-time and subcontracter workers'. See also the interesting arguments by McCarthy and McGaughey (1989); Taddei (1989); Tilly *et al.* (1990); and Kleinknecht and Van Veen (1986).

16. On flexible working time, see an OECD report (1995a).

17. See the OECD report mentioned above (1983, p. 53).

18. Further appropriate considerations on these points are to be found in a challenging essay by Hinrichs, Offe and Wiesenthal (1986).

19. See Sylos Labini (1993), especially chapter 8, 'The theory of unemployment, too, is historically conditioned' (p. 154 ff), and chapter 9, 'Technical progress,

unemployment and economic dynamics' (p. 202 ff). The analysis of the labour market by Sylos Labini is peculiarly reliable for it is developed to the frontier of the assumption of the traditional economic theories.

20. Here we want to acknowledge that Sylos Labini is among the rare economists introducing this last dichotomy in the interpratative model of the change (see the importance that we confer to such dichotomy in Chapter 5, section 2).

21. Notwithstanding the effort made for the conceptual (not based on data) disaggregation, we are neglecting a dichotomy which should locate the selected phenomena in different socio- economic or socio-anthropological areas: for instance, in Europe between the North Sea and Mediterranean Sea areas; or in Italy, between north and south. Does this neglect oblige us to the same heroic assumptions?

22. This is the basic reason because some econometric modelling makes sense only in the short, I would say very short, period; and also because the long-term models can only be 'decisional', that is not directed to replicate the past but directed only to test some consistencies for the future.

23. In the presumption that, having modelled *ex post* the behaviour of a set of variables (even identified in their diachronic identity) supposed as explicative of the past unemployment phenomenon, we are able to replicate the functional relations between the different variables of the model even to orient ourselves in policy decisions for the future.

24. Presently a wider consciousness is developing about all of this, starting from the reflections of one of the founders of modern econometrics, Ragnar Frisch (1976), whose last precepts reformulate on the right programmatic tracks all of econometrics (changing it into what I would like to call planometrics). These precepts have not had enough time to affect contemporary economic culture and have been rather ignored.

25. For the difference between the prescriptive modelling of the Neoclassical or 'positivist' approach and the 'decisional' or 'programmatic' one, I make reference always to the work of Frisch (1976) and to one of my specific essays (Archibugi, 1998).

26. On the other hand the personal reflection that is expressed by this book has itself had a long gestation (in decades), as is shown by the data in the writings on which the single chapter is based; it is probable that the objective maturation of the studied transformation renders the visions exposed here and the solutions proposed in the second part less premature and abortive than the approach could risk implicating by itself.

27. For a wider discussion of the shortcomings of the economic analysis of the labour market, see the acute observations by Sylos Labini (1992, p. 162 ff.).

28. Should all that push us to reflect more on the utility of so-called scientific or academic work, used to give sustance to this or that theory? And if not, would it not be preferable to know better through appropriate inquiries and surveys in the field of a quantitive/qualitative character, the divisions, motivations, expectations, and willingness of actual and present operators and decision-makers of any type, private and public?

29. As the demand of large populations in the Third World and Eastern European countries would be.

30. And as often happens, what is lacking is also the knowledge of the new phenomena and new situations necessary to move away from past platitudes.

31. See further considerations in Ginzberg *et al.* (1989)

32. This renders current 'unemployment' quite different from that which for decades has dominated the arguments of economic theory and analyses of

the labour market, to the point that we should be using two different words, just to assure an appropriate distinction of concepts in the employment/ unemployment debate. (More extended considerations in Bluestone, et al. 1994.)

33. See Leontief (1982). I have not only supported this position for many years, but have tried to examine what kind of income policy could be compatible with an effective reduction of the 'formal' working hours (and vice-versa) (Archibugi, 1969). I argued (and I still would argue) that the kind of income policy should be that of the 'architect' and not that of the 'fireman' (using a then current metaphor). In other words, a policy oriented to 'design' some equilibria among variables in play, and not solely to cancel out the inflationary tensions, as economic policy usually aimed to do, and still does. I was also in favour of a certain 'programmed' inflation if it was the only instrument – given the institutional and social structures – to achieve certain 'real' social equilibria in a planned future perspective.

Today it is more and more clearly emerging – in contrast with the paradigms of the macroeconomic ('fireman') approaches – that the reduction of working hours in connection to a 'programmed' income redistribution, could be the result of the 'informal' economy becoming more important than the 'formal' one; a change in relative importance which could also result in a transformation of the problem of the formal length of working hours. (We will come back on this in Chapters 11 and 12.)

34. Leontief and Duchin's *'The Future Impact of Automation on Workers'* (1986) deserves much more attention in the economic academy and in economic policy decision-making. Among the comparative analyses on the work length, see the very good one by Lucy Kok and Chris de Neuborg (1986).

35. In fact, in this chapter I have anticipated the analysis of the managerial problems of the change in the labour market, which formally were destined for Part II of this volume. But this is because, in the case of the labour market, the interconnections between analysis of the change and that of the possible management of this change are so strong as to lose clarity if separated.

7   The Service Society versus the Industrial Society

1. In this chapter, we will highlight the antagonism between the two ideal-type models premising with argument (*a*), which illustrates the typical characters of the industrial society, and argument (*b*), which illustrates that of the service society.

2. All economic tradition (classical and neo-classical) has been based on the postulate concerning the identity, conceptual and statistical, of profits = investment. Marx, as is well-known, took this identity as the basis for his conviction that the accumulation and agglomeration of capital would have an effect on the rate of profit and, through the profit rate, on investment opportunities to the point of creating ever less investment opportunities, because of the tendentially falling rate of profit (see Marx, *Capital*, 3rd vol., chapters 13 and following.).

Even Schumpeter – basing himself on the same postulate – adopted the Marxian concept, first in his *Business Cycles* (1939) (chap. XV), and later in his book *Capitalism, Socialism and Democracy* (1942). And focusing on the question 'Can capitalism survive?' he came back to the basic idea about the 'vanishing of investment opportunities' (chap. X), on the 'obsolescence of the entrepreneurial function' (chap. XII), and, from this, the 'decomposition of capitalism' (chap.. XIV), and stated that even considering:

the possibility that the economic wants of humanity might some day be so completely satisfied that little motive would be left to push productive effort still further ahead...for the calculable future this vision is of no importance ...all the greater importance attaches to the fact that many of the effects on the structure of society and on the organization of the productive process that we might expect from an approximately complete satisfaction of wants or from absolute technological perfection can also be expected from a development that is clearly observable already...thus economic progress tends to become depersonalized and automatized.　　　(ibid., ed. 1954, pp. 131–3)

3. See the considerations on the decline of the spirit of enterprise by Heilbroner (1976), a quantitative analysis on the crisis of profitability by Heap *et al.* (1980/ 81), and essays on the phenomena of de-industrialization collected by Blackaby (1979).

4. This is the reason why my personal belief is that 75 per cent of 'economic science' has been a 'useless science', because it has sought over and over, in different and contradictory ways, and in very obviously dissimilar historical circumstances, a *regularity* in behaviour (and thus of 'effects') which does not exist.

5. That of the great, more or less monopolistic, power concentrations, and that of the 'separation between property and control' in the large corporations.

6. See Schumpeter, (*Capitalism, Socialism and Democracy*) (ed. 1954), p. 143 and following.

7. Public debt, which is a form of forced saving, increases, creating a counterbalancing factor. (See, on this aspect, Arrow and Boskin (1988); and also an unconventional essay by Bell and Thurow (1985).)

8. A good description of the organizational and formal 'code' of industrial society is in chap. 4 of Toffler's cited work on the 'third wave' (Toffler, 1980). But it is impossible not to recommend the masterly chapter XI on 'capitalistic civilization' in the work by Schumpeter (1956, orig. 1942) quoted above.

9. Again in 1956, Peter Drucker, already mentioned as theorizer of the evolution of industrial society, described with great acumen, the characteristics and sociological implications of this 'employee society', in an important essay in the *American Journal of Sociology* (Drucker, 1956).

10. See above, Chapter 2, section 4.3. The other (already cited) well-known and much discussed book by Burnham (1941) gave popular form to a condensation of important researches and debates on industrial sociology and economics in the 1930s, especially in the USA.

11. One of the best summaries of the development of what has been called 'Neo-Capitalism' is in the work, already cited, by G. Ruffolo on the 'large corporation' in modern society (Ruffolo, 1967).

12. On this point I would refer to one work of mine, which *ex post*, we can say, was rather accurate in its foresight on 'industrial relations at the time of automation' (Archibugi, 1956).

13. George Friedmann (1947) in the work on 'the human consequences of industrial machinery'. See also the lessons by Raymond Aron (1962).

14. This is an old theorem of labour economics. For the first most recent references to the evolution of such a concept, see the cited essays edited by Darity (1992).

15. On the characteristics of a National Information System organized for use in an economic planning process, see a report by the present author, resulting from a teaching experience at the CSATA of Bari (Archibugi, 1978c).

16. We will come back on this point in Chapter 13. The author has devoted much of his academic life to the configuration of such a 'methodology' of planning, the results of which are in some works on the construction of an 'accounting frame for national planning' (Archibugi, 1973), and, I hope, will be concluded with the publication, in course, of a treatise on 'general planning'.

17. See, on this subject, the penetrating analyses already mentioned by G. Ruffolo (1984), and also by Rosanvallon (1988 and 1995) and Görz (1992).

18. We live in a epoch in which the emerging of this non-profit sector has stimulated an endless literature. In Chapter 12, which is the core of the book, we shall present much information and many observations. For those who have concerned themselves with the emergence of a third sector since the 1960s and 1970s, like Archibugi (1956, 1978a, 1985a), Etzioni (1973), Levitt (1973), Weisbrod (1977 a and b, 1988), Archibugi, Delors and Holland (1978), and the European Commission (Ruffolo Report) (1977), the present explosion of interest in research and evaluation, if it represents – as I think it does – a corroboration of certain approaches and visions, also creates some anxiety (in the turmoil of the actual approach) about the risk of impeding the perception of the substantial value of the historic phenomenon.

19. It is what Toffler, always the inventor of conceptual slogans, has called *'prosumerism'*, the spread of self- consumption identified in self-production (Toffler, 1980, chapter 20). See also the considerations on this subject by Weisbrod (1989).

8   The Process of Redistribution in the Two Models of Society

1. In the remainder of this chapter, developing the reasoning on the same characteristics of the redistribution and transfer process in the evolution of industrial society and on the changing of this process in the model of the service society, I drop the form of an antagonistic comparison of the two models, used in the preceding chapter, since it is not particularly useful for the present purposes. This discussion as well, included in this chapter, is drawn from the previously mentioned report by the author prepared for the OECD (Archibugi, 1985a) on the relationship between structural change and employment.

2. For wider knowledge of the income distribution theory, a milestone in the history of economic thinking, I refer the reader to an old collection of 'readings' edited by Fellner and Haley (1950); and, closer to the subject of this chapter, a set of papers by Sylos Labini (1974).

3. Naturally here we are taking for granted that this will happen through a balanced relationship of input and output between the various sectors, from primary goods to intermediate production until the final consumer. The possible disequilibria in the repercussion of productivity effects on prices in all the various passages in play, are for the moment excluded from the analysis and hypothesis.

4. A beautiful analysis of the cost and benefit of redistribution policies, especially in connection with regulatory policies of the inflation process from one end, and with the occupational effect of the monetary planning policies at the other end, is that by Edmund S. Phelps (1972). From the same author, see also the more recent consideration on the subsidies policies in the occupational process (1997). Such policies, anyway, could be much more effective if framed in an evaluation of their total effect to be appreciated within a general planning policy.

5. Today it is largely evident that the price 'regime' is far from being a 'market price' regime, such as we might have experienced at the beginning of the nineteenth century (and even this is doubtful if we consider what Sismondo de Sismondi, Pellegrino Rossi, Friedrich List and many other 'liberal' but not 'laissez faire' economists were saying at that time. This makes yet more amazing the survival of economists who persist in dreaming of the utopia of a regime of prices determined by a mythical or irrecoverable 'market'. For an extended critical survey of this literature, I would suggest to the reader to refer to the work of Geoffrey M. Hodgson, that presents itself as a very useful *summa* of the methodological objections to these kind of approach (Hodgson, 1988).

6. I would like to emphasize here the schematic value of the argument which does include more articulated and specialized cases which obviously enhance and render less plausible a good part of the argument itself; but it is not exactly necessary to examine these cases because our intention is far from trying to develop here a sort of 'treatise' on inflation. For an extended treatment of the subject in relation to the globalization process, I suggest a very recent volume of papers by Davidson and Kregel (1999). See also the essays edited by Kregel (1989) and the works by Modigliani (1987) and Modigliani and Tarantelli (1975).

7. It is not difficult to see that in this rough analysis of the distributive process we overturn the conventional approach which theoretical economics is used to adopting for analysis of the market: here we consider the 'normal' theoretical model (of industrial society), that of the rigidity of prices, and the imperfection (or anomaly), that of non-rigidity. Perhaps we could say that here lies the difference between 'classical' economics and 'institutionalist' economics.

8. It is a question of the behaviour that, according to theses of academic economics, is considered obvious and normal behaviour see Modigliani (1987).

9. In this note we would like to point out how interesting it would be to develop suitable statistical enquiries, more or less samples, in order to know the real personal and 'family' conditions of many of those 'unemployed by productivity', and on the strength of what monetary income they continue to live. It is a shame that enquiries of this type are, in almost all countries, seldom developed by social scholars, less than the expenditure in material means and intellectual energy in the *theorization* of social behaviour, i.e. in the search for and possible formulation of behaviour regularities which do not exist (see Modigliani, 1987).

10. See again the cited work by E. S. Phelps (1997).

9 The Expansion and Decline of Public Services

1. The literature is full of tautological definitions; for instance: 'Public goods is any economic mean with which a public need is satisfied'; 'public service is...an activity developed...for the satisfaction of public needs'. Among the less tautological there is that from Greffe: 'A public good is a good indivisible, mixed or divisible, the allocation of which is taken charge of by the state or by the local collectivities' (Greffe, 1994).

2. In his milestone essay of 1954 on the 'pure theory of public expenditure' (Samuelson, 1954), he states in this way: 'It is convenient to distinguish two categories of goods: On one side there are the private and ordinary consumption goods which may be divided between different individuals; on the other side are the collective consumption goods from which all individuals benefit in common, in the sense that the consumption of such a good does not implicate any diminuation of the consumption of the same good on behalf of other individuals' (Samuelson, 1954).

3. See, for instance, Oakland (1985).
4. From the first modern textbook (like Musgrave's *Theory of Public Finance* (1959) with which the author became the acknowledged 'guru' of public economics) probably to the last, every textbook of public economics opens the description of the state role indicating the three taxonomic roles: (1) resource allocation (goods and services, just 'public'); (2) the distribution, of incomes or also of the assets, represented mainly by the transfer of income, for many purposes; (3) a stabilization policy, in order to guarantee the macro-economic equilibria.
5. All difference would be reduced to that between a public good and the good of the public: a difference a little too small to sustain such taxonomy!
6. I found an excellent compendium of these debates in Jan-Erik Lane, *The Public Sector: Concepts, Models and Approaches* (1995), and Xavier Greffe, *Economics of Public Policies* (1994).
7. Phenomena present – more or less – in all advanced Western countries (or similar).
8. For a rapid appraisal of the modern normative theory of public finance I have consulted – I think with profit – Musgrave (1959), chs. 1 to 6); McKean (1968, ch. 5); Bénard (1985); Greffe (1994); and some papers in the Handbook edited by Auerbach and Feldstein (1991).
9. See Chapter 5, section 3.
10. Musgrave (1985, p.53).
11. To be honest, analysis of the growth factors of public expenditure has been the subject of a good deal of academic debate. See for this topic: Greve (1991); Alber (1988). But the 'effects' of this phenomenon have been analyzed less than its 'causes'. See also Peacock (1979) and Tarschys (1975).
12. In 'general government', the standardized SNA (System of National Accounts) includes: (1) any public authority with its administration at all levels: central or federal, regional (state or provincial) local and social security funds; (2) public services provided by governments (at all levels) on a non-market basis (e.g. public schools, hospitals, welfare services); (c) non-profit institutions providing services on a non-market basis which are controlled and mainly financed by the public authority; (4) social security funds imposed, controlled or financed by the public authorities for purposes of providing social security benefits for the community, which are separately organized from the other activities of the public authorities and hold their assets and liabilities from them. General Government does not include public enterprises. Therefore the General Government sector is not equivalent to the concept of the larger public sector, which includes public enterprises, often used in the context of evaluating public sector borrowing requirements.
13. By 'total outlay' is meant all expenditure (current disbursement and capital expenditure). It includes (1) the *final consumption expenditure*: current (excluding capital) government operating outlays, net of sales of goods and services and of fixed capital formation for their own account; which encompasses compensation of employees (payments of wages and salaries, contributions in respect of social security, pension, income maintenance and similar schemes); (2) *transfers* (current and capital transfers) of which 'social security' (i.e. benefits paid to individuals under social security schemes, usually out of a special fund), 'subsidies' (i.e. current government transfers or grants to private or public enterprises, mainly to offset operating losses) and other transfers (like current transfers, intangible assets and net capital transfers); (3) *investments*, i.e. gross fixed capital formation plus increase in stocks (gross investment); (4) *debt interest payments*.

14. General government receipts is a broader concept than revenues, which encompasses only tax receipts. It is made up of the sum of the operating surplus, property and entrepreneurial income, indirect taxes, direct taxes, social security contributions, fees, fines and penalties, and current transfers received.

15. The thresholds of this non-tolerability have been defined in the past and met with noisy denials. Leroy-Beaulieu, the famous economist of public finance at the College of France at the end of the last century (1887, 1898), claimed that it would not be possible to go beyond 12–13%. In the 1920s authoritative economists such as Keynes or Colin Clark claimed it would be impossible to go beyond 25% (see Cazes, 1981). I wonder if the role of public expenditure and 'deficit spending', which are the pivot of Keynesian logic, would be seen today by Keynes himself in the same way, in light of the present change of weight of the pressures of the state on the economy as a whole. And moreover I wonder if this fact has been kept in mind by the participants in the theoretical debate on 'Keynesism' in the post-war years up to now, and by people who studied the reason for the 'dissolution of the Keynesian consensus' (see, on the subject, Dean, 1981).

16. For example, for the OECD as a whole it passed from 1.20 in the period 1967–76 to 1.28 in the period 1972–6 (OECD, 1978). For more ample reasoning on the ways of financing of the public sector and on the distributional consequences, see some essays by Greve (1992 and 1996).

17. Reprinted in *International Economic Papers*, no. 4, 1954. On the 'collapse' of the Welfare State, see F. Caffé (1981) (already quoted).

18. Further considerations on fiscal burdens can be found in King (1975), Beck (1979), Glennerster (1979) and Pedone (1981). For the fallacy of the monetary equilibrium of the public budget, see the masterly consideration by Arrow (Arrow and Boskin, 1988), which I warmly recommend to read to all wise, haughty and conventional consultants of governments and central banks, in their role as inspirers and commentators of the 'official' economic policies in most of the Western countries.

19. We have dwelt on this crucial point for the discussion developed here in the preceding chapters. See, in particular, section 3 of Chapter 4.

20. See also other contributions on this problem by the same author (Klein, 1977, 1980a and 1980b, and an edited book on the future of welfare, Klein and O'Higgins, 1985). The essays collected by Rose (1980) elaborated remarkably on the topic of a necessary 're-socialization' of the Welfare State. See also the essays from the Fabian environment also in the early 1980s on the future of the Welfare State and the necessity of reforming it (Glennerster, 1983).

21. A short selection of this literature brings us to indicate works such as Mercer (1991), Bryson (1995); Steiner (1997) and Newcomer and Wholey (1989). A textbook on Strategic Planning for Public Administrations is at press, prepared by the present author (with the help of a team of scholars) which has been the didactic base of a course at the Post-graduate School of Public Administration in Italy (an institution belonging to the Prime Minister's office).

22. On this matter, see the very striking arguments of Fred Hirsch (1976); and also Scitovsky (1976) on the 'joyless economy'.

23. See, for example, the well-known reasoning of Lipsey (1967), and Killingsworth's analyses (1966 and 1970). (Alas! rapidly ignored by new, less informed and less accurate generations of scholars.)

24. See some of my writings on the 'evolution of industrial relations in the age of automation' (Archibugi, 1956), on 'basic trends in collective bargaining' (1957), on the 'relationship between economic planning and collective bargaining (1958); an essay on the 'reference criteria for an incomes policy in conformity

with planning goals' (1969), and an essay 'on the nature, causes and consequences of the current transformations in the social structure' (1966).

25. Cf. the debates of the OECD conference of experts, March 1977 (OECD, 1977–79), and particularly Malinvaud's résumé of some of the debates (Malinvaud, 1977–79), and Driehuis's report (1979).

26. It is not by chance that the exceptions, which have always been associated with the dominant tendencies for the marketed supply of required social services, occur when the said supply is not purely mercantile, but is also associated with a high professional interest on the part of the operator (especially in the educational and cultural fields).

27. On the modalities and problems connected to this genesis of a new form of business, and of a new type of economy deriving from it, we will devote in general Chapter 11 (sections 3 and 4), and more specifically Chapter 12 (which constitutes a more in-depth examination of Chapter 11).

10 Beyond the Welfare State

1. This semantic distinction has old and noble origins which deserve to be recalled. William Robson, an active promoter of Fabian studies, scholar of the public economics, and esteemed patriarch of the London School of Economics, said in one of his last works, *Welfare State and Welfare Society* (1976):

    The welfare state is what the government does. The welfare society is what people do, feel and think about the general welfare. Unless people generally reflect the policies and assumptions of the welfare state in their attitudes and in their actions, it is impossible to attain the objectives of the welfare state ... - When an industrial nation becomes a welfare state, the need for a strong sense of individual, group and institutional responsibility, the need for social discipline, become very much greater. (pp. 7, 11)

2. This dream is inherent with many scholars of the Welfare State's future. See for instance: Heclo (1981), Amoroso (ed.) (1991), Barr (1987 and 1992), Evers *et al.* (eds) (1987), Glennerster (ed.) (1983), Guillotin (1886), Himmelstrand *et al.* (1981), Hirst (1994), Therborn and Roebroek (1986), Albeda (ed.) (1986), Johnson (1987), Walzer (1988), Abrahamson (1988). I must thank, especially in this field, Mathias Konig-Archibugi for helping me (with photocopying) to be aware (and be a reader) of a vast contribution on the issues and future of the Welfare State, otherwise of difficult access.

3. This seems to me the gist of the most recent works (which have attracted many enthusiast neophytes) of A.O. Hirschman (see 1991, 1995).

4. This theme has distant origins. For example, it prevails in the position – in all times – of the 'liberal' and moderate political thinking. Tocqueville, a fervent democrat, as is known, made it the focal point of his whole analysis of the burgeoning American 'democracy': 'When the conditions are equal, everyone isolates themselves voluntarily and forgets the public' (Tocqueville, 'Democracy in America', 1835–40, p. 284, Italian edn, 1953).

5. Ragnar Frisch has set up the most clear system of definitions of equilibrium and disequilibrium (Frisch, 1936). And Schumpeter, later, in his *History of Economic Analysis*, posthumously published (1954), related to Frisch's definitions some further, very important annotations. Even though it is not particularly relevant to our discussion on the dynamic relation between

Welfare State and Welfare Society, here it is interesting to bear in mind how Schumpeter recommends making the due distinctions when dealing with the subject of equilibrium:

> The reader will please observe that, in logical principle at least, 'statics' and 'dynamics' on the one hand, and 'stationary' and 'evolutionary' states, on the other hand, are independent of one another. We may describe a stationary process by a dynamic model: this will be the case whenever we make the conditions for stationarity of a process in any given period depend upon what happened to the process in preceding periods. We may also describe an evolutionary process by a succession of static models: this will be the case whenever we deal with disturbances of a given state by trying to indicate the static relations obtaining a given disturbance impinged upon the system and after it had time to work itself out....
> ...Whether static or dynamic, equilibrium may be stable, neutral, or unstable...
> ...Thus we may consider stationary and evolutionary processes and we may analyze both of them by either a static or dynamic method. We shall now introduce the concept of equilibrium. Suppose we have settled the question, what elements in an economic universe we wish to determine and what are the data and the relations by which to determine them. Then the question arises whether these relations that are supposed to hold simultaneously (simultaneous equations) are just sufficient to determine sets of values for those elements (variables) that will satisfy the relations. There may be no such set, one such set, or more than one such set, and it does not follow that our system is valueless if there exist several. But the most favorable case and the one every theorist prays for is of course uniqueness of the set. Such a set or such sets we call equilibrium sets and we say that the system is in equilibrium if its variables take on the values thus determined. It goes without saying that these values are very much more useful for us if they are stable than if they are neutral or unstable. A stable equilibrium value is an equilibrium value that, if changed by a small amount, calls into action forces that will tend to reproduce the old value; neutral equilibrium is an equilibrium value that does not know any such forces; an unstable equilibrium is an equilibrium value, change in which calls forth forces which tend to move the system farther away from equilibrium values. A ball that rests at the bottom of a bowl illustrates the first case; a ball that rests on a billiard table, the second; and a ball that is perched on the top of an inverted bowl, the third case. Naturally, the conditions which insure stability and the absence of which produces instability are of particular interest in order to understand the logic of the economic system. In this sense it has been said that it is stability conditions that yield our theorems.
>
> (Schumpeter, 1954, pp. 963–71)

6.   Those mechanisms on which there has been exercised, from its birth, the thoughts of economic 'science', which has always fundamentally been a 'theory' of general equilibrium.
7.   Some have claimed that Adam Smith was the father of the theory of general equilibrium, which, as known, is normally attributed – with some precursors – to Leon Walras. On this point, see the work of Ingrao and Israel (1987) on 'economic equilibrium in the history of science', to which work the allusive but not singular title 'The invisible hand' was given. For other interesting contributions, see also Hahn (1973 and 1981) and Kregel (1983).

8. See, for instance, also M. Moran (1988) and Alber (1988 and 1995).
9. This is what was recommended by an influential Italian economist, Federico Caffé (especially the already quoted book (1986) on the 'defense of the Welfare State') with whom I had a friendly intellectual relationship. Further considerations in Amoroso (ed.) (1996), Habermas (1985), Rosanvallon (1981).
10. This is a point on which I have dissented strongly, in a long diatribe, with the positions of many faithful upholders of the Welfare State (for example, see Caffé quoted in previous note (1986)).
11. Who probably are much more responsible for the expansion for the Welfare State than the left-wing streams. See the book by Crouch and Streeck (1996).
12. A useful reference to the topic which we will deal with here is in a paper by A.O. Hirschman (1980). See also an interesting paper by Flora (1989).
13. On the importance of the shortening of working hours as a factor of social integration, and therefore as an expression of the passage from the mere Welfare State to a Welfare Society, the reader is referred to another writing of mine (Archibugi, 1976). More recently the argument has been treated under many aspects by the contributors to a book from the European Centre for Work and Society at Maastricht, edited by Kleinknecht and Van Veen (1986), entitled *Working Time Reduction and the Crisis in the Welfare State*. See also a special view by Freeman and Soete (1994).
14. We have chosen here the word 'societal' to designate the entire set of conditions and aspirations of a society, or community, overall, without regard to the distinction between conditions or aspirations of the 'economic' type and those of the 'social' type. This last word is now usually used to describe the reductive character of something which is placed in contrast to all that is 'economic'. 'Societal', moreover, serves to designate all those objectives of a society, or community, *globally*, without regard to the distinction between the objectives to be achieved through the action of *public* bodies (the state, in its multiple expressions) and those to be achieved by other bodies normally considered *private* (family, groups, enterprises, associations, trade-unions and even single individuals).
15. More development in Frisch (1971). Stimulating views also can be found in some recent books by Galbraith (1996 and 1998).

11 Beyond Capitalism?

1. For example, the reader is referred once again to the contributions gathered for the OECD Conference on 'social policies in the 80s' (Paris, October 1980) and published by the OECD itself under the title *The Welfare State in Crisis* (OECD, 1981).
2. Here I am referring to almost all the literature 'defending' the Welfare State on the one hand, and also to a large part of the more critical type, which has studied new ways of development: from the Welfare State to Welfare Society. See, on this subject, the vast review of ideas contained in the book by C. Pierson (1991) who, adopting the same title as the famous book by Myrdal (*Beyond the Welfare State*), and adding a sorry question mark, completely ignores its existence: just as – on the other hand – in this type of literature on the Welfare State, on its crisis and future prospects, any hint of the need for planning for its management, which represented the core of Myrdal's analysis (as said in the preface to this book), is ignored.
3. Even those essays which are the closest to the type of analyses made by us (such as those of Bernard Cazes (1981 and 1985) and Rudolf Klein (1981), included in the above-mentioned OECD volume (1981), do not indicate, as the natural

outcome of a revitalization of the Welfare State, a more pronounced coordination of the choice in expenditure, and therefore a greater degree of societal programming. Other works which have tackled the topic of crisis and the future of the Welfare State are even less sensitive to being able to reconnect the evident and recognized manifestations of crisis of the Welfare State itself, to the criticisms of the type advanced in his time by Myrdal (quoted) which seem particularly applicable today. In this regard, we refer the reader to the collection of essays on the general theme of the future of the Welfare State, by Howard Glennerster for the Fabian Society (1983); and by Wil Albeda (1986) for the European Centre for Work and Society in Maastricht. Not a single one of the authors involved in these collections mentions the now classic criticism made by Myrdal.

An exception is a less recent collection of English essays by Timothy A. Booth (1979), dedicated to examining exactly how the *Welfare Budget* is considered by central government and by local authorities, and how decisions are taken on how to allocate the resources available for Welfare needs between different claims. But this type of study has left few traces on the debate about the crisis and the future of the Welfare State.

4. One cannot ignore the fact that a very important role in the relaunch of planning has been played, especially in the United States, by efforts at 'rationalization' of public expenditure (decreasing the total and making it more efficient and effective), and also the role played by the state apparatus itself (in particular the federal one). These efforts were initiated chiefly by the famous ordinances of Reagan and Bush. Then, too, the 1993 Government Performance and Result Act (GPRA), signed by Clinton (and which I believe to be of epoch-making importance in the reform of public sector governability), is the result of a long gestation in Congress promoted by the Republican senator Roth (and commonly known as the 'Roth Law'). More generally, it can be said that the banner of 'rationality' in public expenditure (or decision-making) has passed from the hands of the political left to those of the more moderate part of opinion and of the political right. It is incredible but true. What is only lacking is for the policy analyst to work out the reasons why. The advent of the moderates is welcome if it serves to make such progressive and radical steps forward in managing public affairs and to introduce a requirement for rationality and programming in those affairs, overcoming their traditional scepticism and contrasting faith in the natural adjustment and spontaneous optimization of events.

5. Many have introduced alternative expressions, in order to avoid linguistic exorcisms: for example, some French scholars use the word 'regulation', trying to link the word to some specific concepts (see Boyer, 1986). See also Jessop (1990) for more general considerations.

6. The volume by Jon Elster (the prolific and versatile author of influential essays) and Karl Ove Moene, entitled *Alternatives to Capitalism*, is an interesting anthology of essays, which they edited in the same year of the collapse of the Communist empire (Elster and Moene, 1989). I will come back to it later. But there are dozens of works which asked the same question in earlier years and well before that collapse. For instance, see the essays edited by Bell and Kristol (1971) and, more recently, the book of M. Albert (1992).

7. This is the subject that divides general scholars and historians. Karl Polanyi (1944) should be mentioned among the former, and Henri Pirenne (1913–14) and Henri Sée (1951) among the latter – all well-known examples.

8. See some works and studies developed above all in the 1970s which were influenced by the 'feeling of the time'; see, for example the very title of the edited book by S. Holland: *Beyond Capitalist Planning* (1978). Also see Stephens (1979).

9.   To use expressions strongly defended in the cited Report of a Committee created by the President of the United States and the US Congress in 1976 (see US Advisory Committee on National Growth Policy Processes, 1977).

10. With regard to debates about the 'planning crisis', which are in reality very numerous but of poor quality, the reader will find exhaustive and complete considerations in the works of a 1971 meeting organized at the Institute of Development Studies in Sussex (Faber and Seers, 1972) and, more recently, in the complex work by J. Friedmann (1987). For a deeper analysis of the implementation problem in the planning process, I am obliged to refer to a wide debate on methods, experiences and perspectives, that have been held in the past two decades among the scholars of urban and regional planning, having a general validity. I limit the references among the most important works to that by Faludi (1973) and Alexander (1986). For an economic point of view connected with the national economic programming experience in the 1960s, see Meade (1970) and Fuà and Sylos Labini (1963).

11. For all this, the reader is referred to the considerations of Ragnar Frisch, in one of his essays, 'Cooperation between Politicians and Econometricians on the Formalization of Political Preferences' (1971, republished in Frisch, 1976). Some years ago, on the initiative of the Planning Studies Centre in Rome, a movement on an international scale for the recovery and relaunch of a technology suitable for planning took place. Under the auspices of the United Nations University, UNESCO and the University Institute of Florence, a first 'World-Wide Conference on Planning Science' was held in Palermo in September 1992. A large group of scholars from all over the world participated, and from it arose the will to permanently pursue a multi-disciplinary action of cooperation for the advancement of *Planning Science* (or *'Planology'*), as the advanced technical solution to offer to political applications of coordinated management of socio-economic development. In that conference an International Academy for the Progress of Planning Science was initiated, and Jan Tinbergen and Wassily Leontief accepted the honorary chairmanship (alas, both now deceased).

For this, see two pamphlets produced by the Planning Studies Centre (1993a and b) about the initiative of the above-mentioned Academy for Planning Sciences, and some of the recent contributions of mine that conceptually support this movement: 'Towards A New Discipline of Planning' (Archibugi, 1992c), and 'The Resetting of Planning Studies' (Archibugi, 1992b). An overall evaluation of the new trends towards planning and their cultural roots can be found in one of my studies published by The Planning Studies Centre (Rome) in 1992 under the title *Introduction to Planology: Toward a Multidisciplinary Convergence of the Planning Sciences* (Archibugi, 1992a).

12. An analysis of the causes of the 'crisis' of economic planning experiences in Europe in four countries (Great Britain, France, the Federal Republic of West Germany and Italy), with contributions by Thomas Balogh, Jacques Delors, Karl Georg Zinn and Giorgio Ruffolo and myself, may be found in the cited book edited by Stuart Holland (1978), *Beyond Capitalist Planning*. See also the collection of essays edited by Amoroso and Jespersen (1992).

13. On this point, particularly significant is the masterly contribution of W. Leontief, 'National Economic Planning: Methods and Problems' (Leontief, 1976). This essay was written at a time when the main ephemeral economic planning experiences in the world (from that of the West to those of the developing countries) had already entered a stage of scepticism and decline.

14. See, in this regard, the essays contained in the collective work edited by Mark D. Ten Hove (1986), *The Institutions of a Changing Welfare State* (in particular

those of Frederik Hegner, Theo Berben and Leo van Snippenburg). See also the essays collected in Booth (ed.) (1979).

15. For further considerations on the crisis and the future of planning after the experience of the 1960s and the crisis of the 1970s, the reader is referred to the collection of essays in the volume (above quoted) *Beyond Capitalist Planning* (edited by Stuart Holland) (1978); and in particular the essay with which the volume concludes, entitled 'Development Planning' (bearing the joint signatures of F. Archibugi, J. Delors and S. Holland).

16. I would like to refer to the basic work of Frisch, Tinbergen, Leontief, and Johansen as milestones of a starting point for a developing planning discipline (or Planology). In my opinion, it is scandalous, the way in which the last, often posthumous, works of these authors (works that can be considered the authentic products of their scientific maturity) have been completely ignored by the conventional economic and academic literature of the last three decades.

17. On this point see an essay by J. K. Galbraith (1976). The limits of an incomes policy in a context of absence of planning procedure have been analyzed in essays collected by Archibugi and Forte (1969). There is also a good biography for the vast literature on this point in the late 1960s and early 1970s, and which is still up-to-date.

18. The reader is referred to the collection of my contributions on the argument of the relationships between planning and collective bargaining, under the title *Verso la contrattazione collettiva di piano* [Towards Planning Collective Bargaining] (Archibugi, 1979), which recalls essays extending over a period of time which ranges from 1957 to 1978.

19. On this point see a masterly essay by Bob Solow (1966).

20. In Italy this proposal has often been put forward by G. Ruffolo, former Secretary General of the Economic Programming of Italian Government (1965–73) and former Minister of Environment (1988–92). Currently, Ruffolo is a European MP. There is a presentation of the proposal in his book *La qualità sociale* (Ruffolo, 1984).

21. Even if it is only a pun, the 'instinctively negative reaction to the word "planning" when it is applied to government activities' (US Advisory Committee, 1976), justifies it, in the intention of clarifying the actual meaning of the words adopted. The American report quoted expresses very well – under the title of 'An American Approach to Planning' – the characteristics of the system of planning that is advisable for Europe too. Allow us to reproduce some further passages:

> To them [the Americans] it has a connotation alien to this country's way of doing things.
> Much of this anxiety stems from the fact that people envisage a small group of technocrats, insulated from criticism, who will achieve centralized power and impose a rigid program on an unwilling electorate, while destroying all private-sector freedom and market mechanisms in the process. Obviously, no one who cares about American liberties could possibly relish such an outcome. Fortunately, there is nothing in the nature of planning that requires such an undemocratic process. The problem is rather that proponents of planning have failed to make clear how the dangers that frighten so many people are to be avoided.
> The Committee does not advocate a planned society. We urge that America become a planning society... [see the continuation of this in the quotation in Chapter 1]

Ideological critics who think of planning as 'totalitarian' seem to forget that no program will go forward until the duly elected and democratically accountable representatives of the people want it to go forward. Any planning will be conducted within the Constitutional framework.... One widely shared fear about planning is that it will lead to more offensive forms of Federal intervention than we have known in the past. It might, however, have just been most severe in times of unforeseen emergency...

If we look ahead and identify problems down the road, perhaps we will be spared the need to act precipitously in ways that jeopardize our freedom.... If intervention is more conscious and coherent, it can be more easily controlled.   (US Advisory Committee, pp. 111–13)

22. An appropriate system of a decisonal planning process at national govermental scale is designed by Giorgio Ruffolo in the quoted book on 'social quality' (1984).

23. For further indications on these institutional aspects of planning, the reader is referred to my contribution at a conference (Sousse, Tunisia, 1978) of the Institut Internationale des Sciences Administratives, on the theme '*Accounting and Institutional Instruments of a True Social Planning*' (Archibugi, 1978b).

24. The operational distinction between the two phases, which constitutes a pillar of the 'planological' approach, was argued by Ragnar Frisch, in recurrent and subsequent periods of his scientific production: in a 1962 essay on decision models; in another from 1964 on the system of implementation of optimal national planning; in one on the tasks of econometrics from 1969; and finally one from 1971 on cooperation between econometricians and political decision-makers 'for the formalization of political preferences'. All these are published in the posthumous volume *Economic Planning Studies* (1976).

25. Ragnar Frisch 1960, (1962 and 1964) (republished in Frisch, 1976, on pages 105–6). This problem was revisited by Leif Johansen in vol. 1 of his *Lectures on Macro-Economic Planning* (Johansen, 1977–78).

26. The changes to which we allude are moreover changes which are widely studied and discussed. It is those changes which have for a long time now caused talk of a so-called post-industrial revolution (mentioned briefly in Chapter 2 and also in other chapters). However, we consider it essential to observe that, in the last two decades, the 'political' implications have not been sufficiently drawn (or at least with sufficient clarity or energy) from the analyses of the evolution of contemporary society. In fact the panorama of instruments, be they institutional or technico-operational, has not been discussed and described sufficiently, for a new type of cooperation between technicians ('policy scientists') and politicians ('policy makers') at the new levels and the new forms of operation that the changes about which we are talking demand.

In any case, we would like to remind the reader of the attempt made to give an answer to this pressure by a group of European economists and technicians ('policy scientists') gathered together at the 'Forum for International Political and Social Economy' in a 'Project for European Reconstruction' – see the mentioned publication edited by S. Holland, coordinator of the Group (IPSE Forum, 1983). In particular, the third part of the collective document of that Forum (in which the author was very involved) was dedicated to the 'goals and the instruments: new priorities for policies', and in it an attempt was made to indicate a repertoire of new instruments to be employed in the face of the structural changes of contemporary society. These goals and instruments will be looked at again in Chapter 13.

27.   The social effects of the new technologies have been widely studied by a vast sociological (Bell, Touraine), economic Galbraith, Leontief), managerial (Drucker), and futurological literature (Toffler), to name only some of the representative authors. I gave my own contribution to this reflection through a cited essay (published by the Italian National Research Council), 'Industrial Relations in the Age of Automatism', in which I consider the theme of professionalization of work and its economic and social consequences (Archibugi, 1956).

28.   In this connection, it has already been pointed out that in all OECD countries, but more systematically and generally in the United States, these closing years of the century are seeing an epoch-making revolution with the large-scale introduction of methods of *strategic planning* and *result-based management* into the public sector (and into non-profit organizations). A major role is being played by the GPRA law passed by Congress in 1993. I am convinced that if this law is not supplemented as quickly as possible with an initiative of economic programming on a societal scale (of the type suggested by the quoted US Advisory Committee on National Growth Policy Processes (1977)), implementation of the GPRA could encounter many difficulties. However, the US Congress, which currently has a Republican majority, seems to have a firm intention of moving in that direction, as can be deduced from this declaration from the Congressional Institute (an institution providing technical support, chiefly to the Republican wing) registered in Chapter 1.

29.   One of the first American authors to use the term 'third sector', Amitai Etzioni, expressed the reasons for this conceptual approach thus, as early as 1973:

> Whereas the debate on how to satisfy our needs is focused on the public–private alternative, in effect a third sector has grown up between that of the state and that of the market. In reality, this third sector could very well be the most important alternative for the coming decades, not replacing the other two but uniting and balancing their important roles...We find ever more missions – such as control of pollution – where the profit motive is not great enough and/or the costs necessary to make the mission profitable seem too high. At the same time we are ever more tired of depending on state bureaucracies that multiply and expand. A method must be developed for combining the best of the two worlds – the efficiency and skill of the business world with the pubic interest, the responsibility and the wider planning of the state.   (Etzioni, 1973, p. 315)

Amitai Etzioni is an author who has sufficiently anticipated the concept of an 'active' society and of a 'voluntarist' economics. An early work of his (1968) had already outlined the same process requirement of the economic theory, but successive works by him have made more precise the voluntarist and problematic character of the economic reflection itself, on which the associative economy is based. We indicate only some principal works by Etzioni: on the moral dimension of the economic value assessment (1988), on the task of a society tended to a deliberate social change (1991a), and on the implications of a communitarian spirit (1993). In 1991 Etzioni edited with P.R. Lawrence a volume of essays by various authors for a new synthesis of a 'socio-economic' theory. See also another of his 'anti-utilitarist' essays, in cooperation with Weimer (1991b).

Furthermore, I consider very significant the attention that P.F. Drucker came to pay to the third sector, or non-profit sector; he is the person that (paraphrasing Marx in the 27th chapter of the third volume of *Capital*) we could call the Pindar of American management. In fact, Drucker not only wrote an important book on the subject (Drucker, 1990), but has also established a foundation for the non-profit organization ('the Drucker Foundation for Non-Profit Management'); and being the theorist perhaps more famous for capitalist managerialism, all this can sounds like a significant acknowledgement of a trend toward the post-capitalism. We have, incidentally, already mentioned Drucker's book on the post-capitalist society: Drucker (1993).

Another author who has developed the theme of transformation of the social fabric of the post-industrial society and the urgent challenges to the traditional border between public and private, in a sort of disorganized capitalism which put in crisis the welfare state and led it towards a new type of society, is Claus Offe, with a set of books of great interest (1985–1986, 1985 and 1987a).

30. In the USA the term 'Independent Sector' has become consolidated. The most important Confederation organization in this sector in the USA (which has approximately 800 associations of the operational sector affiliated) is called in fact the 'Independent Sector' (IS). See Independent Sector (1992), Hodgkinson *et al.* (1989). The emergence of this sector has been the subject of numerous analyses from various points of view for several years now. On this, see the economic analyses by Weisbrod (1977b) and Weisbrod (1988); Young (1983); Gassler (1986) and Powell ed. (1987). See also the analyses, from a more legal-institutional point of view, by James and Rose-Ackerman (1986) and Anheier and Seibel (1990). There has recently been an exploratory investigation of the third sector with an international character coordinated by Johns Hopkins University (Salamon and Anheier, 1996). See also Rose-Ackerman (ed.) (1986).

31. This sector has long been called the 'social economy' in France; and 'social sector' is the societal three-way graphical division of the socio-economic world offered by the Republicans' Congressional Institute mentioned earlier.

32. This is the name I most commonly gave it in the 1950s (e.g.Archibugi, 1957).

33. The literature on 'Economic Systems' is enormous, and it has developed in the wake of the 'institutionalist' school. Many reorganizations of the Faculties of Economics in the various European and American Universities have introduced special courses on 'economic systems'. At its base there lies the thesis that economic theory (with its relative 'rules' of behaviour) is not unique: the economic theories are as many as there are economic 'systems' to which they apply. Eckstein (1971) can be considered the father of this kind of 'discipline'. A work, among the many, which I hold particularly significant, of this school of thought is that of Reynolds (1971). The taxonomy of 'economic systems' is not however easy. There is a certain amount of discussion on the criteria on which to base a typology of economic systems; whether, for example, upon the systems which have followed each other historically (which evokes primarily the classic approach of Sombart, and before him that of Marx), or upon economic or legal criteria. (On this aspect, the work of Karl Polanyi and Conrad Arensberg (1975) is recommendable.) An up-to-date evaluation of the debate on the 'theory of economic systems' (unfortunately only in italian) are in the papers edited by B. Jossa (1989).

What is perhaps worth mentionly is that this type of literature has given little attention to the objective characteristics of the 'coexistence' of economic systems. Here we do not intend the classical coexistence on this planet (for example the well-known question of the peaceful coexistence between the Western capitalist system and the collectivist system of the countries of Eastern Europe, with the relative thesis of 'convergence' dear to Tinbergen, 1961, and others), but rather it dealt primarily with the *co-presence* in the same economic structure of a country or of a set of countries. From the historical point of view, the question is posed in terms of a transitional co-presence from a historically preceding system, supposed to be on the decline, in the face of another which is rising up. Certainly every taxonomic attempt always proves inadequate in terms of the rich and sometimes not understandable multiplicity provided by the real world, but it is the only way through which it is possible to develop, in a critical (and not chaotic, and therefore misleading) way, an understanding of such a reality. I believe that this current epoch, highly pluralistic as it is, in which we live and, above all, towards which we are venturing, is the most suitable for developing the research project on the forms of the 'co-presence' of different economic systems, no longer seen as competitive or incompatible, but rather as cooperative and complementary. On this point there are interesting observations in a not very recent work of Ginzberg and others (1965). For a more recent and updated treatment of the matter within the sphere of the Welfare States, see Esping-Andersen (1990 and 1994).

Concerning a very extended and very 'complex' treatment in itself of the 'pluralism in economics' ('methodological pluralism') as a response to, or an instrument for, the analysis of the 'complexity' of the economic systems (the theme which, standably, goes far beyond the purposes of this book), the reader can consult the contributions to a very important and interesting conference (promoted by EAEPE and University of Bergamo) in 1994 (Salanti and Screpanti, eds, 1997).

34.   The most emblematic case is that of the oligopoly on an international and world-wide scale (that is the multinational and transnational enterprises), which have often rendered powerless and useless all public bodies on the national scale. This has occurred to such an extent that it has required a revision of the very economic theory of the behaviour of the operators (multinational enterprises on the one hand, and the state on the other) in as much as the 'rules' of the market for the former, and the identification of a 'function of collective welfare' for the second, are no longer taking shape according to the well-known formulas: in this way the new theory of 'meso-economics' was born (as developed principally by Holland, 1987). The implications of the meso-economic power manifest themselves overall in the field of financial powers concentrations, but have small impact on the 'associative economy'.

35.   Like Mandel (1975) cited earlier. On 'Welfare Capitalism' and its different models, see Esping-Andersen (1990). See also Crouch and Streeck (1994).

36.   'Liberal Socialism' has been widely described, discussed and theorized in the 1950s and 1960s, and also in terms more important than in the present times (i.e. with a stronger futurist intuition), by two Italian authors of exceptional value: Carlo Rosselli (1994) and Guido Calogero (1944 and 1945). In Italy, a large group of scholars of political science (among whom I am honoured to belong) have followed and developed their doctrine. The work of Carlo Rosselli has been finally made available in the English language (i.e. for a real international readership) only recently (Rosselli, 1994) and I look forward to this work being revisited not only by scholars, but even by political operators, because of its great topicality. (See also Urbinati, 1994.) The work of Guido Calogero, which equally deserves to be accessible to an international readership, has not yet been translated into English.

37.   See L.G. Reynolds (1971).

38.   As has been said, the word economic 'systems' evokes taxonomic problems not entirely resolved, even if it would be preferable for designating the 'third sector'. We will therefore use the word 'sector' because, even if it is highly ambiguous and lends itself to misunderstandings, it still remains the most direct.

12   A New Social Model: The Associative Economy

1. In the American world, albeit with different traditions and motivations, linked more to an academic than an operational approach, the social economy has been recognized, on the one hand, and promoted, on the other, for a very long time. Among the scholars, the social economy took the form of social economics. To the reality of the business for profit, theorized by classical economics, people discovered and theorized the non-profit activities, operating as outside the paradigms of economic theory, therefore subject to other principles, other behaviour, other paradigms, to investigate and to define (social economy). The non-profit activities went very slowly at this stage. Only recently, after the economic crisis of the 1970s, did the role emerge of the non-governmental non-profit organizations. Some of the first studies of the third sector appeared in the USA with the roots in Austrian (von Wieser) and Swedish (Cassel) authors from the beginning of the century, and reinvigorated by the solitary study of John M. Clark and by a group of American 'institutionalists' (Veblen, Commons, Ely, Mitchell, etc.). A recent collective book (ed. Mark A. Lutz), *Social Economics: Retrospect and Prospect* (1990), makes a wide survey of the intellectual and operative experiences which take the name of social economy. Among the best work of such scholars, see Etzioni (1973); Levitt (1973). Some more recent essays that can be recommended on the non-profit economy and its principles, and which have already been cited in the previous chapters, are those of Young (1983), Gassler (1986) Weisbrod (1988); Hodgkinson (1989) and Hodgkinson, Lyman and Associates (1989). See also O'Neill (1989).
2. See Van Buiren (1981).
3. For which, consult particularly the works of Coates (1981) and Lipnack and Stamps (1982).
4. Documented by Stokes (1981) and the already-mentioned Lipnack and Stamps (1982).
5. On this, see the works of Schaaf (1977), and the Institute of Local Self-Reliance's guide (1979) which contains impressive documentation. See also Lobell's guide (1981) with a larger horizon. The cases of employee ownership have been studied and evaluated by researchers such as William White (1978, and – with J. R. Blasi – 1982) and Joseph R. Blasi (1981; *et al.*, 1982). It may also be useful to consult F. Heller's yearbook (published in the UK, 1982) and the publications by the National Centre for Employee Ownership in Arlington, Va., notably that of Rosen (1981).
6. In fact it is assumed generally that those organizations are part of the sector, which are indicated by section 501(c) of the Internal Revenue Code (IRC), characterized by the fact that their revenues are not used for the private benefit of shareholders, directors, or other persons with an interest in the company, and thus enjoy tax exemption. Within the overall 'non-profit' scenario, the 'independent sector' includes those organizations indicated by sections 501(c)(3) (organizations with exclusively religious, charitable, scientific, literary, educational or similar objectives) and 501(c)(4) (civic leagues, social welfare associations, local employees' associations), who are considered 'public serving' and thus may receive tax-deductible donations. An update on the American (and non-American) legislation, on this subject, is included in the work of Salamon and Toepler (1997).
7. For the history of the concept, see Desroche (1983). There were studies on the 'économie sociale' in the last century, by authors like Charles Dunoyer, Frederic

Le Play, and Constantin Pecquenz; and (between the end of the century and the beginning of the twentieth century) Benoit Malon, Marcel Mauss, Charles Gide and also Jean Jaures. In more-recent years (between the 1970s and 1980s) this movement, in France, has been, further, updated involving authors like the above-quoted Delors, and then Bloch-Lainé (1977, 1980), Rocard (1981), Gaudin (1980), and many others.

8. Moreau (1982). See also the works of Delors and Gaudin (1978 and 1979).
9. Archambault (1997) and Archambault and Boumendil (1995).
10. Greffe *et al.* (1983) pp. 38–9.
11. In any case, see the writings of Jeantet (1982a,b and c), of Chomel (1982), Moreau (1982), Gaudin (1982a and b), and finally the research-enquiry of Greffe, Dupuis and Pflieger (1983) oriented toward the fundamental problem of financing.
12. We note that in Germany the concept of 'social economy' is viewed with much distrust. See the references in Bauer (1992, pp. 172–4).
13. See the accounts of two meetings, one in Lille in 1979 and the second in Nantes in 1981, published in the journal *Autrement* (1980 and 1982). The first of these was on 'the new entrepreneurs', the second on 'another model of work and enterprise'.
14. See the texts, in the journal *Futuribles*, of Benoun and Senicourt (1981 and 1982), and of Eme and Laplume (1981 a and b)
15. See in the same journal, Chancel and Tixier (1981). On local initiatives in France of collective utility, one may consult the reports of Gaudin (1982a) and Gaudin and Pflieger (1982).
16. Bauer (1995), p. 63. The same thing is true for Austria (Badelt, 1990; Shaurer, 1995) and Switzerland (Purtschert, 1995; Schnyder, 1995).
17. According to Reichard the organizations in this sector may be disposed in a decreasing order of 'officialness' (*Amtlichkeit*), according to their closeness to or distance from the state, to form four sub-sectors: (i) public institutions which have a certain amount of autonomy from state administration (universities, radio, television, theatres, hospitals, social security organs); (ii) private institutions to which public functions are delegated (professional chambers, research institutes, political foundations); (iii) private institutions which carry out activities of general interest, without depending prevalently on state transfers (the Red Cross, Automobile Club, cooperatives which are not active in the market); (iv) 'alternative' initiatives which arise in the wake of 'new social movements', which range from self-help groups to self-managed enterprises. National peculiarity resides in the fact that subjects are found in this list which, because of their public status, in other national contexts (in particular the American one) would not have been included in the third sector.
18. See Olk and Heinze (1985); and Backhaus-Maul and Olk (1994).
19. The proposed typology divides the projects into four types:

   – the first concerns *collective and individual production and consumption and services* in support of, and pertaining to, the project (auto-supply);
   – the second type concerns *reciprocal exchange of goods and services* in support of the project (exchange);
   – the third concerns *benevolent services to others* (assistance);
   – the fourth and final type concerns the *production of goods and services remunerated* in the private and economic sector and public sector (social).

See Maier (1981); and the several works of, and collected by, J. Huber (1979, 1980a and b; Huber *et al.*, 1982); see also Vonderach (1980, 1982).

20. However there are some studies which have to be recalled. For Great Britain, for instance, an important activity has been developed by the foundation of the International Institute for Social Economics, which includes authors such as George F. Rohrlich (1977) and Barrie O. Pettman (1977).

It seems that the British scene is being influenced and activated by recent exchanges with the 'social economy' pattern from France: see the report by Simon Wilson of a Seminar held by the Franco-British Council in 1995 (Wilson, 1995).

For Italy, there has been a great attention, especially by Catholic authors, to the evolution and importance of the 'voluntary' sector: for instance Ardigò (1981), Donati (1978), and Tarozzi and Bernfeld (1981). Many works, more recently, have been produced on the third sector: (Barbetta, 1995), Bassanini and Ranci (1990), Vanoli and Ranci (1994) Ferrera (1993); and the collection of experiences by the 'Lunaria Association' (1997); and the book edited by Iovene and Viezzoli (1999), with recent news of Italian experiences.

21. European Commission (1989) p. 4.
22. European Commission (1994a).
23. See TEN (1979).
24. This means, on the other hand, that the comparison field is contained to the evolution of the Western industrialized countries (even if signs of such evolution can also be detected in some developing countries). This also means that many of our conclusions on the evolutive charactersitics of the third sector cannot be well applied to the experiences of the third sector which we record in the nations not belonging to the group of the advanced countries (like the so-called Third World countries, and, maybe, to the ex-socialist countries).
25. Salamon and Anheier (1994); Barbetta (1995).
26. For practical reasons, the project excluded from its field of enquiry the religious communities and the political associations, which however belong to the non-profit sector as it has been defined.
27. Occasional surveys of the third sector are numerous in all countries, but have the defect that each uses its own taxonomy. They are therefore unusable for comparisons between times and countries.
28. European Commission (1994b). According to this study, the social economy in the EU countries employs almost 2.9 million people, and has a turnover of 1,550 billion ECU. The largest component is the cooperatives, with 61% of jobs and 79% of turnover; then come the associations, with 31% of jobs and 16% of turnover; last come the mutuals, with 8% of jobs and 5% of turnover. Mutuals have 96.6 million members (almost all pension scheme members), cooperatives have 53.7 million members (53% of these being cooperative bank depositors) and associations have 32.1 million members. However, the Social Economy Unit warns that this first survey excluded a large proportion of the voluntary sector and, awaiting the results of a more complete research, estimates that the social economy in EU countries employs over 5 million people and that it makes up between 4% and 7% of the total economy.
29. The data cited in the following are taken from other tables in Salamon and Anheier (1996). For further data, see also Salamon and Anheier (1992), Barbetta (1995), Archambault (1997), Anheier and Priller (1995).
30. They list the following impressionistic data. In Germany 40% of all hospital patient days are spent in non-profit institutions, 50% of all nursing-home residents stay in non-profit homes, 60% of all residential care facilities are

non-profit, 33% of all children in day care attend non-profit institutions. In France 55% of all residential care residents stay in non-profit facilities, 20% of all primary and secondary students attend non-profit schools. In Italy 41% of residential care facilities and 21% of kindergartens are non-profit. In the United Kingdom non-profit primary and secondary schools are attended by 22% of all students, and 10% of dwelling units are built or rehabilitated by non-profit organizations. In the United States 51% of all hospital beds are provided by non-profit institutions, and non-profit are also 49% of all colleges and universitites, 95% of all orchestras, 60% of all social service agencies. In Japan 77% of all university students attend non-profit universities, 40% of all hospital patient days are spent in non-profit institutions.

31. As can be seen from the following table, employment in the non-profit sector as percentage of total employment is, in the single countries (1990): USA 6.8%, France 4.2%, UK 4%, Germany 3.7%, Japan 2.5%, Italy 1.8% and Hungary 0.8%. The analogous data, limited to service employment, are: USA 15.4%, Germany 10.4%, France 10%, UK 9.4%, Japan 8.6%, Italy 5.5% and Hungary 3%.

Employment in the non-profit sector as the percentage of overall employment and in services, and current spending of the non-profit sector as a percentage of GNP, in seven countries (1990)

	Employment in the non-profit sector as the percentage of total employment	*Employment in the non-profit sector as the percentage of employment in services*	*Current spending in the non-profit sector as the percentage of GNP*
United States	6.8	15.4	6.3
France	4.2	10.0	3.3
United Kingdom	4.0	9.4	4.8
Germany	3.7	10.4	3.6
Japan	2.5	8.6	3.2
Italy	1.8	5.5	1.9
Hungary	0.8	3.0	1.2

Source: Salamon and Anheier (1994).

We can also see the operating expenditures of the non-profit sector as the percentage of GNP of each country (1990). These are: USA 6.3%, UK 4.8%, Germany 3.6%, France 3.3%, Japan 3.2%, Italy 1.3% and Hungary 1.2%.

32. See the 'International Classification of Nonprofit Organizations' (IC-NPO) developed by the Johns Hopkins research group.

33. As seen in another table included in the cited report, in the field of education and research, for example, which in the seven countries (France, Germany, Hungary, Italy, Japan, United Kingdom, United States) as a whole is the most developed, the non-profit sector is very present in the United Kingdom (43% of total expenses of the sector), but relatively little in Germany (12%) (France 25%, USA 23%, Italy 22%).

In the second most important field, health (towards which in the seven countries taken together a fifth of the total expenses of the non-profit sector is directed), most of third sector resources flow in this field in the USA (53%), but only a small part in the United Kingdom (4%) (Germany 35%, Italy 17%, France 14%).

In the field of social services the proportion of resources that converges on this field is 29% in France, but only 10% in the USA and 12% in the UK (Italy 25%, Germany 23%).

On the field of culture and recreation are concentrated 21% of total expenses of the British third sector, but only 4% of the American one (France 18%, Italy 9%, Germany 8%). (Salamon and Anheier, 1994, table 4.2)

34. In Italy and in the United Kingdom the financing by fees prevails over that by public payments (Italy: 53% fees, 43% state, 4% charitable giving; United Kingdom: 48% fees, 40% state, 12% charitable giving). In Germany and France public transfers prevail over private payments for services (Germany: 68% state, 28% fees, 4% charitable giving; France: 59% state, 34% fees, 7% charitable giving) (ibid., table 5.2).

35. The most useful data for the USA are found in the commendable *Nonprofit Almanac 1992–93* (Dimension of the Independent Sector), published by the 'Independent Sector', Washington DC (Independent Sector, 1992).

36. The German data are featured in the study on Germany by the 'Johns Hopkins Comparative Nonprofit Sector Project', edited by H. K. Anheier and E. Priller (1995).

37. Archambault (1997) reports some approximate data on employment trends in the French third sector between 1981 and 1991, from which emerges an evolution similar to the American and German experience. Whilst between the ten years of reference overall employment increased from 21.7 to 22.2 million units, thus 2.2%, employment in the third sector increased from 711,000 to 993,000 units, thus recording an increase of 39.6%. The result is that between 1981 and 1991 the share of employment in the third sector for total employment passed from 3.3% to 4.5%.

38. On the employment potential of the Italian third sector, see especially the recent research promoted by the Lunaria Association (1996), which arrived at the conclusion that 'by adopting a series of institutional, economic and tax measures, in the next two years the third sector could create up to 200,000 jobs in the fields of welfare, culture, environment, training and multimedia'.

39. Badelt (1990). See also Gassler (1986), and an interesting interpretation by R. Dahrendotf (1983).

40. James and Rose-Ackermann (1986), James (1990).

41. See also the interesting development of Weisbrod's hypothesis made by Achille Ardigò (1981), who at the same time points to some of its weaknesses. Ardigò has for some time insisted on the contemporary trend toward a

> cultural revolution of expectations, for objectives of substantial and even radical correction or alteration of the dual system on behalf of a division of labour and life styles, in which – in each country – the importance of the market and of family consumption that can be satisfied only through liquidity in the purchase of commodities will be reduced, but the importance of the state will be reduced as well. (Ardigò, 1981)

42. Ben-Ner (1986) and Ben-Ner and Gui (1993); Easley and O'Hara (1983, 1986); Krashinsky (1986); Nelson and Krashinsky (1973).

43. By 'consumer' Hansmann means also the donor or volunteer who wishes to benefit third parties, and who is interested in particular in seeing that his gift or labour actually reaches its destination.

44. See the above cited James and Rose-Ackerman (1986), pp. 50–62.
45. L.M. Salamon (1989, 1990, 1995).See also the collection of papers edited by Salamon, Gidron and Kramer (1992).
46. See Seibel (1990, 1992)
47. For this, among the vast literature on the subject, the volume edited by Anheier and Seibel (1990) may be usefully consulted.
48. A more complete exposition may be found in Archibugi (1985a, 1985b, 1996). For a comment, see Shirley Williams (1984).
49. More details on this subject in Chapter 4.
50. More details on this subject in Chapter 8.
51. More details on this subject in Chapters 5 and 6.
52. Delors and Gaudin (1978, 1979).
53. In the Commission – and certainly on impulse of President Delors – a document was already drawn up in 1989 on '*Les entreprises de l'Economie Sociale et la réalization du marché européen sans frontières*', and it should have been used as an attachment to a 'Communication' of the Commission to the Council (European, Commission, 1989). In any case, the initiative of the Commission has followed some of the resolutions of Parliament, having quite immmediate goals: for example, a Resolution on the 'Non-Profit Associations in the EC' (Fontaine Report of 13 March 1987); a Resolution of Parliament for inviting the member states to ratify the Convention of the Council of Europe on the reciprocal acknowledgement of the associations and non-governmental organizations (of 3 March 1988); and lastly a Working Document of a mixed group (presided by Ms Eyraud on '*Un Projet de Statut de Association Européenne*' (April 1989). Also important, on this topic, is the Conference promoted by the economic and social Committee of the EEC of October 1986 on 'Cooperative, mutualistic and associative activities within the Community'.
54. In English: European Confederation of Workers' Cooperatives, Social Cooperatives and Participative Enterprises.
55. CECOP, *Déclaration d'engagement*, Brussels, 17 November 1996.
56. See also the 'Cecop political programme 1997–2000', a document approved by its General Assembly on 12 May 1997.
57. More documentation on relations between trade unions and third sector can be found in the already quoted Report and book (Archibugi and Koenig-Archibugi, 1998) which is drawn from a report prepared for the European Commission, on an indication from Jacques Delors. See also Archibugi and Koenig-Archibugi (1997).
58. The reader is referred to a vast documentation in the works of Greffe, Dupuis and Pflieger (1983) on the 'financing of the social economy'. See also Meunier (1992) and Moore (1995).
59. The changes in the behaviour of the employment market, above all on the part of the supply, in post-industrial society, have been the subject of the above Chapter 6. We recall again anyway the good analyses by Gershuny (1978), Gershuny and Miles (1983), the essays collected by Henry (1980), and a rich bibliography in South (1980).
60. See consideration and bibliography referred in Chapter 6. On the fallacy of unemployment statistics,see the works of Gutmann (1978 and 1979), Clarkson and Meiners (1977), Foudi *et al.* (1982).
61. Further considerations may be found in the lucid essay by W. Leontief (1982), and the work in cooperation with Faye Duchin on the 'social impact of new technologies' (Leontief and Duchin, 1986).

62. In this regard the reader is referred to the well-known proposal of the Swedish trade-unions (Meidner, 1978). For several objections, see also Brems, (1975).
63. One of the most important documents of the International Confederation of Trade Unions tackles this theme without giving it much interest. This document is the well-known *Keynes Plus*, drawn up to oppose the restrictive economic policies of the European governments in the 1970s (ETUI, 1979).
64. Also in this sense, the presence of a European Trade Union Fund, nurtured by collective negotiation and by other forms of collective trade-union savings, would be another powerful factor of social and economic cohesion in a Europe with a single monetary and capitals market; and as such it constitutes a beautiful vision of the development of the twenty-first century.
65. On this point the reader is referred to the very interesting and little known work of Sinden and Worrel (1979).
66. See, Bryson, (1995) and S.P. Osborne, ed. (1996), Moore (1995) and Meunier (1992). For the evaluation systems see the basic works of Lichfield (1996) and Fauldi and Voogd (1985).

13   New Policies and Instruments

1. In fact some doubts should be admitted to here since, given the current state of growth and expansion of the public sector, one may still speak about a 'visible hand' on the basis of the traditional consideration of the formal explanation of public intervention (decisions of the representative organs, and manifest rigidity in the decisions themselves and connected management). The agents which in a complex modern society operate in the public name, and which may have general economic relevance, are so numerous that the public sector has become almost as 'pluralistic' as the private sector. And the coordination of decisions in this sector is as difficult as a 'visible' hypothetical coordination of the private sector. It is therefore very probable that the recourse to the concept of 'invisible' hand of the market, in order to realize a sort of spontaneous coordination between the operators, may be applied today with as much plausibility to the set of operations undertaken in the public name.
2. Wider reflections on the subject are in the book by Fred Hirsch (1976) on the 'social limits to development'.
3. Leontief (1976) on the one hand, and Frisch (1976) on the other, have written memorable pages on this argument.
4. On this argument, the reader is referred to Stuart Holland's considerations in the paper included in the already quoted collective volume *Beyond Capitalist Planning* (Holland, 1978) and reconsidered in the book *The Global Economy* (Holland, 1987).
5. Jan Tinbergen's fundamental and, at the same time, simple booklet on 'central planning' (1964) is exhaustive on the subject.
6. This was an attempt which was made in the 1960s in all Western countries, and which was killed by the (petrol) crisis of the 1970s. That attempt, of which there have been timid and uncertain 'renewals' a little everywhere, has not yet found the correct way of consolidating the practice. And yet I consider inevitable even only a slow (as in all 'organic processes') evolution towards central and systemic (multi-level) planning, if we wish to lead the way to a more efficient political organization of the community.

   I have been personally connected with the Italian experience of 'Progetto 80' (1968–9) which configured a 'central system of programming' (see Ministero del

Bilancio e della Programmazione Economica, 1969). This system has been further described by Giorgio Ruffolo, the inventor and coordinator of Progetto 80, in a more recent book (unfortunately available only in Italian) on the 'social quality and the new ways of development' (Ruffolo, 1984). Some of the inspiring principles of the Project 80 have been resumed and updated politically by Jacques Delors (1997) and Giorgio Ruffolo (1997) in a common booklet entitled *Left at the End of the Century*.

7. The thesis that lack of planning obliges the state to a more pressing presence in economic activities and heavier interventions in them, is amply and unceasingly developed by the report, already cited, of the US Joint Advisory Committee (Congress – White House) on 'National Growth Policy Process; Forging America's Future', etc. (1977).

8. On the inappropriateness of instruments founded on aggregate models, the reader is referred to the important works developed within the Economic Commission for Europe of the United Nations (UNECE, 1967, 1970, 1975). But also the models of Frisch (1976) and of Leontief (1976) are motivated along these same lines.

9. On this argument I would refer the reader to one of my writings, presented at the UNECE Conference (Moscow, 1974) mentioned above, on a 'system of models for planning' (Archibugi, 1974), and reproposed – in a corrected and updated version – at the XII International Input–Output Conference (March 1993, Seville).

10. An interesting matrix of the different degrees of centralization in the expression of preferences on the one hand, and in the allocations of resources on the other, in which one can find a cross-section of 9 typologies of systems of planning, is a work executed within the framework of utilization of advanced technology for planning in the UNECE, mentioned above (in particular, see Margolis and Trzeciakowski, 1970). As appetizer, see Figure 13.1.

11. See Shonfield and Shaw (1972).

12. The existence of such a 'market' has, for a long time, and repeatedly, been placed in doubt by the theory found in the literature. One of the most recent and complete studies is found in Holland (1987).

13. We have already given (Chapter 5, section 3.2) an appraisal of the wide debate and discussion on new 'integrated' socio-economic accounting, which is useful both for the concrete implementation of planning choices and decisions, and, at the same time, for the concrete measuring of socio-economic development (and, consequently, cohesion). Many exercises in the socio-economic extension of the SNA (System of National Accounting) have been proposed in the past two decades. (See UN, 1993a and b; see also Kendrick, 1996). For more information on the entire spectrum of initiatives and approaches toward new socio-economic accounting, see an essay of mine (Archibugi, 1992d); a symposium by Chicago's Social Research Institute (Land and Juster, 1981), and, more recently, Archibugi and Nijkamp (1989) and a recent bibliographical survey by the Planning Studies Centre on 'indicators and accounting for planning' (Cicerchia, 1993). More insights in an old work by Gambling (1974).

14. I am taking up here some old concepts expressed from as far back as the 1950s, but which the immobilism of the trade unions on the one hand, and the absurd mental 'closure' of the pseudo socialist states (and the satellite political 'cultures') on the other, for over thirty years, now render even more highly topical (see a paper of mine given at a seminar of the International Confederation of Free Trade Unions (ICFTU), 1958 on 'The Trade Union and the State', Archibugi, 1958; see also Archibugi, 1981).

15. See on this subject the consideration by R. Taylor (1994) in a book on the future of the Trade Unions, promoted and published by the British Trade Unions.

16. On the role of the consumers' movement in post-industrial society, see the more detailed considerations in one of my writings (Archibugi, 1987).

17. The interested reader can find a deeper description and discussion of the working of strategic planning in and for the goverance of the advanced and post-industrial societies, and in emergent 'associative economy' in other works of mine, more technical and more didatic, particularily in my course on 'strategic planning and economic programming' (already announced in note 6 of the preface). About the evalutation methods at the disposal for a strategic planning, in all aspects – sectorial and spatial – in which it is developed (matter that is outside the scope of this book), I recommend the works of Greffe (1997 and 1999), Faludi and Voogd (1985), Lichfield (1996), Lichfield *et al.* (1998), Nijkamp *et al.* (1985), Sinden and Worrel (1979) and Voogd (1985).

Bibliography

ABRAHAMSON, P. (1988). *Welfare State in Crisis: The Crumbling of the Scandinavian Model?* Roskilde: Institute of Economics and Planning Roskilde University Centre.

ABRAHAMSON, P. (1989). 'Social Science Discussing Present Modern Society: Post-Something', in Abrahamson, P. (ed.), *Postmodern Welfares: Market, State, and Civil Society Towards Year 2000.* Roskilde: Institute of Economics and Planning.

ALBEDA, W. (ed.) (1986). *The Future of the Welfare State.* Maastricht: Presses Interuniversitaires Européennes.

ALBER, J. (1988). 'Is There a Crisis of the Welfare State? Crossnational Evidence from Europe, North America and Japan', *European Sociological Review*, vol. 4, no. 3, pp. 181–207.

ALBER, J. (1995). 'Soziale Dienstleistungen: Die vernachlässigte Dimension vergleichender Wohlfahrtsstaat-Forschung', in Benstele, K., Reissert, B. and Schettkat, R. (eds), *Die Reformfähigkeit von Industriegesellschaften.* Frankfurt: Campus.

ALBERT, M. (1992). *Capitalism Against Capitalism.* London: Whur.

ALEXANDER, E. R. (1986). *Approaches to Planning: Introducing Current Planning Theories, Concepts and Issues.* New York: Gordon & Breach.

AMOROSO, B. (ed.) (1991). *The Theory and Future of Welfare Societies.* Roskilde: Department of Economics and Planning, Roskilde University.

AMOROSO, B. (1996). 'Welfare State and Development Models', in Greve, B. (ed.), *Comparative Welfare Systems.* London: Macmillan.

AMOROSO, Bruno (1998). *On Globalization: Capitalism in the 21st Century.* New York: St. Martins Press.

AMOROSO, B. and JESPERSEN, J. (eds) (1992). *Macroeconomic Theories and Policies: A Scandinavian Perspective.* London: Macmillan.

ANDERSON, M., BECHOFER, F. and GERSHUNY, J. (eds) (1994). *The Social and Political Economy of the Household.* Oxford: Oxford University Press.

ANHEIER, H. K. and PRILLER, E. (1995). *Der Nonprofit-Sektor in Deutschland: Eine sozial-oekonomische Struckturbeschreibung. Zusammenfassung Darstellung* (The Johns Hopkins Comparative Studies of Nonprofit Organisations).

ANHEIER, H. K. and SEIBEL, W. (eds) (1990). *The Third Sector: Comparative Studies of Nonprofit Organizations.* Berlin and New York: De Gruyter.

ANSHENFELTER, C. O. and LAYARD, R. (eds) (1986). *Handbook of Labor Economics.* Amsterdam: North-Holland.

ANTONI, C. (1939). *Dallo storicismo alla sociologia.* Firenze: Sansoni.

ANTONI, C. (1941). *La lotta contro la ragione.* Firenze: Sansoni.

ARCHAMBAULT, E. (1990). 'Public Authorities and the Nonprofit Sector in France', in Anheier, H. K. and Seibel, W. (eds), *The Third Sector: Comparative Studies of Nonprofit Organisations.* New York and Berlin: Walter de Gruyter.

ARCHAMBAULT, E. (1992). 'Definition of the Nonprofit Sector in France', in ANHEIER, H. K. (ed.), *Defining the Nonprofit Sector in Twelve Countries.* Baltimore, Md.: The Johns Hopkins University Press.

ARCHAMBAULT, E. (1997). *The Nonprofit Sector in France.* Manchester: Manchester University Press.

ARCHAMBAULT, E. and BOUMENDIL, J. (1995). *Le secteur sans but lucratif en France.* Paris: Fondation de France.

ARCHAMBAULT. E. and GREFFE, X. (1984). *Les economies non officielles.* Paris: La Decouverte.

ARCHIBUGI, D. (1985). 'Paradigmi e rivoluzioni: dalla scienza alla tecnologia', *Prometheus,* no. 2.

ARCHIBUGI, D. and MICHIE, J. (eds) (1997). *Technology, Globalisation and Economic Performance.* Cambridge: Cambridge University Press.

ARCHIBUGI, D. and MICHIE, J. (eds) (1998). *Trade, Growth and Technical Change.* Cambridge: Cambridge University Press.

ARCHIBUGI, D. and SANTARELLI, E. (eds) (1990). *Cambiamento tecnologico e sviluppo industriale.* Milan: Franco Angeli.

ARCHIBUGI, F. (1956). 'Panorama delle relazioni industriali nell'epoca dell'automatismo', in CNR (ed.), *Atti della Conferenza del Consiglio Nazionale delle Ricerche su Problemi dell'Automatizazione, Milano 8–13 Aprile 1957.* Roma: CNR.

ARCHIBUGI, F. (1957). *Basic Trends in Collective Bargaining,* General Report of the 'International Seminar on the Problems of Collective Bargaining' sponsored by the OECD in Berlin (West), June (mimeo). Berlin.

ARCHIBUGI, F. (1958a). 'Les Syndicats et l'Etat', in Confederation International des Syndicats Libres (ed.), *Les Syndicats dans la Societé Moderne* (Cours Syndical Européen, Florence, 22 Sept.–4 Oct.1958). Brussels.

ARCHIBUGI, F. (1958b). 'Pianificazione economica e contrattazione collettiva. Appunti per una definizione teorico-pratica del loro rapporto con riferimento all'Italia'. *Studi Economici,* vol. XIII, no. 6.

ARCHIBUGI, F. (1960). 'Recent Trends in Women's Work in Italy', *International Labor Review,* vol. LXXXI, no. 4.

ARCHIBUGI, F. (1966). *Appunti per una trattazione dei caratteri, cause e conseguenze delle trasformazioni in atto nella struttura sociale* (Communicazione al Colloquio internazionale su 'I Gruppi Dirigenti in Europa Occidentale fra Dimensioni Sopranazionali', 25–26 Nov. 1966. Rome: CIRD.

ARCHIBUGI, F. (1969). 'Alcuni criteri di riferimenti per una politica dei redditi conforme agli obiettivi della programmazione', in Archibugi, F. and Forte, F. (eds), *Politica dei redditi e pianificazione.* Milan: Etas Kompass.

ARCHIBUGI, F. (1973). *La costruzione del Quadro contabile per la pianificazione nazionale: metodologia, sistema di ricerche, processi iterativi e primi risultati.* (Rapporto no. 1 del Progetto Quadro). Rome: Ministero del Bilancio e della Programmazione Economica/ISPE.

ARCHIBUGI, F. (1974). *A System of Models for the National Long-Term Planning Process* (Report to a UN Economic Commission for Europe Seminar on the theme 'On the Use of a System of Models in Planning'). Moscow: Planning Studies Centre.

ARCHIBUGI, F. (1975). *Le controle cognitif de l'inflation.* Brussels: DGII, CEE.

ARCHIBUGI, F. (1976). 'L'integrazione sociale degli emarginati fra il passato e l'avvenire', *Economia e Lavoro,* no. 1.

ARCHIBUGI, F. (1977). *Critica del terziario. Saggio su un nuovo metodo di analisi delle attività terziarie.* Rome: Centro di studi e piani economici, 1979.

ARCHIBUGI, F. (1978a) 'Capitalist Planning in Question', in Holland, S. (ed.), *Beyond Capitalist Planning.* Oxford: Basil Blackwell.

ARCHIBUGI, F. (1978b). *Les instruments comptables et institutionnels d'une veritable planification sociale (Rapport presenté au Colloque du Comité 'Planification et Prospettive', Institut Internationale des Sciences Administratives, Sousse, Tunisie, mai 1978).* Rome: Centro di studi e piani economici.

ARCHIBUGI, F. (1978c). 'Progetto di un sistema informatico per la programmazione', *Rivista italiana di Economia, Demografia e Statistica,* vol. XXXII, no. 1.

ARCHIBUGI, F. (1978d). 'Sulla programmazione dell'occupazione: nota metodologica', *Economia e Lavoro*.

ARCHIBUGI, F. (1979). *Verso la contrattazione collettiva di piano: aspetti evolutivi nelle relazioni fra il movimento sindacale e la pianificazione (Saggi dal 1957 al 1979)*. Rome: Centro di studi e piani economici.

ARCHIBUGI, F. (1981). 'Sindacato e programmazione: dalla contrattazione di mercato alla contrattazione di piano'. *Il Progetto*, no. 3.

ARCHIBUGI, F. (1985a). 'The Possibilities for Employment Creation in the "Third Sector"', in OECD (ed.), *Employment Growth and Structural Change*. Paris: OECD.

ARCHIBUGI, F. (1985b). 'Un nuovo modello di occupazione: l'economia associativa', *Quaderni di Rassegna Sindacale*, vol. Anno XXII, pp. 15–18.

ARCHIBUGI, F. (1987). *Consumatorismo: perchè e come*. Rome: Centro di studi e piani economici.

ARCHIBUGI, F. (1991). *Insight into European Cohesion. A Contribution to a Study of a Policy for the Strengthening of Socio-Economic Cohesion in the EC*. Rome: Planning Studies Centre.

ARCHIBUGI, F. (1992a). *Introduction to Planology: A Survey of Developments Toward the Integration of Planning Sciences*. Rome: Planning Studies Centre.

ARCHIBUGI, F. (1992b). 'The Resetting of Planning Studies', in Kuklinski, A. (ed.), *Society, Science, Government*. Warsaw: KBN.

ARCHIBUGI, F. (1992c). 'Towards a New Discipline of Planning' (The First Worldwide Conference on Planning Science). Palermo, 8–11 Sept. Planning Studies Centre 1992. (Republished in *Socio-Economic Planning Science*, vol. 30, no. 2, pp. 81–102, 1996, Elsevier Science Ltd).

ARCHIBUGI, F. (1992d). *Gli indicatori di programma degli impieghi sociali* (Series: Centro Piani, Reports, 92.4). Rome: Centro Piani.

ARCHIBUGI, F. (1996). 'Beyond the Welfare State: Planning for the Welfare Society', in GREVE, B. (ed.), *Comparative Welfare Systems*. London: Macmillan.

ARCHIBUGI, F. and FORTE, F. (eds) (1969). *Politica dei redditi e pianificazione. Criteri e modelli*. Milan: Etas-Kompass.

ARCHIBUGI, F. and KÖNIG-ARCHIBUGI, M. (1995). *Industrial Relations and the Social Economy: Forms and Methods of Negotiated Destatalization of the Social Welfare Systems in the European Union* (Report to the European Commission, Bruxelles, November 1995).

ARCHIBUGI, F. and KÖNIG-ARCHIBUGI, M. (1997). 'Il futuro dell'economia non-profit', *Lettera internazionale*, no. 53.

ARCHIBUGI, F. and KÖNIG-ARCHIBUGI, M. (1998). *L'arte dell'associazione. Saggio su una prospettiva sindacale per il terzo settore*. Roma: Edizioni Lavoro.

ARCHIBUGI, F. and NIJKAMP, P. (eds) (1989). *Economy and Ecology: Towards Sustainable Development*. Dordecht: Kluwer.

ARCHIBUGI, F., DELORS, J. and HOLLAND, S. (1978). 'International Crisis and Planning for Development', in Holland, S. (ed.), *Beyond Capitalist Planning*. Oxford: Basil Blackwell.

ARCHIBUGI F. *et al.* (1998). *La pianificazione strategica nella PA e la programmazione economica (manuale per la SSPA)*. Rome: Centro di studi e piani economici.

ARDIGÒ, A. (1976). 'Introduzione all'analisi sociologica del Welfare State e delle sue trasformazioni', in La Rosa, M. (ed.), *I servizi sociali tra programmazione e partecipazione*. Milan: Franco Angeli.

ARDIGÒ, A. (1981). 'Introduzione: volontariato, "Welfare State" e terza dimensione', in Tarozzi, A. and Bernfeld, D. (eds), *Il volontariato: un fenomeno internazionale*. Milan: Franco Angeli.

ARNDT, H. W. (1978). *The Rise and Fall of Economic Growth*. Sydney: Longman.
ARON, Raymond (1961). *Sociologie des sociétés industrielles: esquisse d'une theorie des regimes politiques*. Paris: Centre de documentation universitaire.
ARON, R. (1962). *Dix-huit leçons sur la société industrielle*. Paris: Gallimard.
ARON, Raymond (1965). *Trois essais sur l'age industriel....* Paris: Plon (English tr.: New York: Praeger, 1967)
ARROW, J. K. and BOSKIN, M. J. eds. (1988). *The Economics of Public Debt: Proceedings of a Conference Held by the International Economic Association*. Stanford, California: Macmillan Press.
ARROW, J. K. and RAYNAUD, H. (1986). *Social Choice and Multicriterion Decision-Making*. Cambridge, Mass.: MIT Press.
ASHFORD, D. E. (1986). *The Emergence of the Welfare State*. Oxford: Basil Blackwell.
ASHTON, T. S. (1937). *The Industrial Revolution: A Study in Bibliography*. (Bibliographies and Pamphlets, No. 3). Econ. History Society.
ASHTON, T. S. (1948). *The Industrial Revolution 1760–1830*. Oxford: Oxford University Press.
ASHTON, T. S. and SYKES, J. (1929). *The Coal Industry in the 18th Century*. Manchester: Manchester University Press.
ATKINSON, A. B. (1983). *Social Justice and Public Policy*. Brighton: Wheatsheaf Books.
ATKINSON, A. B. (ed.) (1989). *Poverty and Social Security*. London: Harvester Wheatsheaf.
ATKINSON, A. B. (1991a). 'Income Maintenance and Social Insurance', in Auerbach, A. J. and Feldstein, M. (eds), *Handbook of Public Economics*. Amsterdam: North-Holland.
ATKINSON, A. B. (1991b). 'Poverty, Economic Performance and Income Transfer Policy in OECD Countries', *World Bank Economic Review*, pp. 3–21.
ATKINSON, A. B. and ALTMANN, R. M. (1989). 'State Pensions, Taxation and Retirement Income, 1981–2001', in Atkinson, A. B. (ed.), *Poverty and Social Security*. London: Harvester Wheatsheaf.
AUERBACH, A. J. and FELDSTEIN, M. (1991). *Handbook of Public Economics*. Amsterdam: Elsevier Science Publishers.
Autrement (1980). 'Les nouveaux entrepreneurs' (roneo). (Rapport du Colloque de Lille). Paris.
Autrement (1982). 'Un autre modèle de travail, un autre modèle d'entreprise' (roneo).(Rapport du Colloque de Nancy, 1981). Paris.
BACKHAUS-MAUL, H. and OLK, T. (1994). 'Von Subsidiarität zu "outcontracting": Zum Wandel der Beziehungen von Staat und Wohlfahrtsverbänden in der Sozialpolitik', in STREECK, W. (ed.), *Staat und Verbände (Pvs-Sonderheft 25)*. Opladen: Westdeutscher Verlag.
BADELT, C. (1990). 'Institutional Choice and the Nonprofit Sector', in Anheier, H. and Seibel, W. (eds), *The Third Sector: Comparative Studies of Nonprofit Organisations*. New York and Berlin: Walter de Gruyter.
BAGNASCO, A. and PINI, R. (1981). 'Sviluppo economico e trasformazioni sociopolitiche dei sistemi territoriali a economia diffusa', *Quaderni fondazione Giangiacomo Feltrinelli*, no. 14.
BALDASSARI, M., PAGANETTO, L. and PHELPS, E. S. (eds) (1995). *Equity, Efficiency and Growth: The Future of the Welfare State* (CEIS Conference, Rome). New York: St Martins Press.
BALDASSARI, M., PAGANETTO, L. and PHELPS, E. S. (eds) (1998). *Institutions and Economic Organization in Advanced Economies: The Governance Perspective* (CEIS Conference, Rome). Basingstoke: Macmillan.

BALDWIN, T. (1996). 'Can We Define a European Welfare State Model?', in GREVE, B. (ed.), *Comparative Welfare Systems: The Scandinavian Model in a Period of Change*. London: Macmillan.

BARBETTA, G. P. (1995). *Senza scopo di lucro. Dimensioni economiche, storia, legislazione e politiche del settore nonprofit in Italia*. Bologna: Il Mulino.

BARNARD, C. (1938). *The Functions of the Executives*. Cambridge, Harvard University Press. Mass.

BARR, N. (1987). *The Economics of the Welfare State*. London: Weidenfeld & Nicolson.

BARR, N. (1992). 'Economic Theory and the Welfare State: A Survey and Interpretation', *Journal of Economic Literature*, vol. XXX.

BARRETT, M. (1980). *Women's Oppression Today: Problems in Marxist Feminist Analysis*. London: Verso.

BASSANINI, M. C. and RANCI, P. (eds) (1990). *Non per profitto. Il settore dei soggetti che erogano servizi di interesse collettivo senza fine di lucro*. Milan: Fondazione Adriano Olivetti s. l.

BAUER, R. (1992). 'Sozialstaat und Wohlfahrtsverbände zwischen EG-Binnenmarkt und Beitrittsländer', in Bauer, R. (ed.), *Sozialpolitik in der deutscher und europäischer Sicht*. Weinheim: Deutscher Studien Verlag.

BAUER, R. (1995). 'Nonprofit-Organisationen und NPO-Forschung in der Bundesrepublik Deutschland', in Schaurer, R. *et al.* (eds), *Nonprofit-Organisationen (NPO) – dritte kraft zwischen Markt und Staat?*. Linz: Universitätsverlag Rudolf Trauner.

BAUMOL, W. J. (1967). 'The Macroeconomics of Unbalanced Growth', *American Economic Review*, vol. 57, no. 3, pp. 415–26.

BECK, M. (1979). 'Public Sector Growth: A Real Perspective', *Public Finance*, no. 3.

BELL, D. (1960). *The End of the Ideology*. Glencoe, Ill.: Free Press.

BELL, D. (1966). 'Social Choice and Social Values: The Need for a New Calculus', in GROSS, B. (ed.), *A Great Society?*. New York: Basic Books.

BELL, D. (1973). *The Coming of the Post-Industrial Society*. New York: Basic Books.

BELL, D. (1979). *The Cultural Contradiction of Capitalism*. London: Heinemann.

BELL, D. (1981). 'Models and Reality in Economic Discourse', in Bell, D. and Kristol, I. (eds) (1981) *The Crisis in Economic Theory*. New York: Basic Books. (Italian ed. 1982, Milan: Comunità).

BELL, D. and KRISTOL, I. (eds) (1971). *Capitalism Today*. New York: Basic Books.

BELL, D. and THUROW, L. (1985). *The Deficits: How Big? How Long? How Dangerous?*. New York: New York University Press.

BELOUS, R. S. (1989). 'The Growth of the Temporary, Part-Time and Sub-contracted Worker', in Belous, R. S. (ed.), *The Contingent Economy*. Washington, DC: National Planning Association.

BÉNARD, J. (1974). 'The Proper Measurement of Economic Welfare', in Marois, M. (ed.), *Towards a Plan of Action for Mankind: Problems and Perspectives*. Amsterdam: North-Holland.

BÉNARD, J. (1985). *Economique publique*. Paris: Economica.

BEN-NER, A. (1986). 'Nonprofit Organizations: Why Do They Exist in Market Economics?', in Rose-Ackerman, S. (ed.), *The Economics of Nonprofit Institutions*. New York: Oxford University Press.

BEN-NER, A. and GUI, B. (eds) (1993). *The Non-Profit Sector in the Mixed Economy*. Ann Arbor: University of Michigan Press.

BENOUN, M. and SENICOURT, P. (1981). 'Creation d'entreprise: à la recherche d'une politique', *Futuribles*, no. 49.

BENOUN, M. and SENICOURT, P. (1982). 'Pour un systeme français d'aide à la creation d'entreprise', *Futuribles*, no. 51.

BERGER, B. (1974). 'People Work: The Youth Culture and the Labor Market', *The Public Interest*.

BERGER, S. and PIORE, J. M. (1980). *Dualism and Discontinuity in Industrial Societies*. Cambridge: Cambridge University Press.

BERLE, A. A. Jr. (1954). *The 20th Century Capitalist Revolution*. New York: Harcourt & Brace.

BERLE, A. A. Jr. (1959). *Power Without Property: A New Development in America Political Economy*. New York: Harcourt Brace.

BERLE, A. A. Jr. (1965). *If Marx Were to Return*. Washington: US Information Service.

BERLE, A. A. Jr. and HARBRECHT, P. P. (1960). *Toward a Paraproprietal Society*. New York: The Twentieth Century Fund.

BERLE, A. A. Jr. and MEANS, G. (1932). *The Modern Corporation and Private Property*: Harcourt, Brace & World.

BERLINER, J. S. (1972). *Community Planning for the Welfare of the Elderly: A Study in Social Economics*. New York: Praeger.

BERNARD-BÉCHARIES, J. F. and PINSON, C. (1981). 'Mode de vie et style de vie: quatre observations sur le fonctionnement des termes', *Consommation, Revue de Socio-Economie*, no. 3.

BEST, F. (ed.) (1973). *The Future of Work*. Englewood Cliffs, N.J.: Prentice-Hall.

BEZANSON, A. (1921–22). 'The Early Use of the Term Industrial Revolution', *Quarterly Journal of Economics*.

BIELENSKI, H. *et al.* (1994). *New Forms of Work and Activity. Survey of Experience at Establishment Level in Eight European Countries*. Dublin: European Foundation for the Improvement of Living and Working Conditions.

BIRCH, D. L. (1979). *The Job Generating Process* (MIT Study for the Department of Commerce).

BIRD, R. M. (1971). 'Wagner's Law of Expanding State Activities', *Public Finance*, vol. XXVI.

BIRCH, D. L. (1981). 'Who Creates Jobs?', *The Public Interest*, no. 65.

BLACKABY, F. (ed.) (1979). *De-industrialization*. London: Heinemann.

BLASI, J. R. (1981). *Employee Ownership and Self-Management in Legislation and Society Policy (Conference on 'Exploring the Frontiers of the Possible Social Inventions for Solving Human Problems')*. Toronto: American Sociological Association.

BLASI J. R. *et al.* (1982). 'The Politics of Workers Ownership in the USA', in HELLER, F. (ed.), *The International Yearbook of Organizational Democracy for the Study of Participation, Cooperation and Power*. Sussex: Wiley & Sons.

BLAUG. M. (1980). *A Methodological Appraisal of Marxian Economics*. Amsterdam: North-Holland.

BLAUG, M. (1990). *Economic Theories, True or False?: Essays in the History and Methodology of Economics*. Aldershot: Edward Elgar.

BLOCH-LAINÉ, F. (1977). 'Entre l'Administration et le Marché: les Associations gestionnaires', *Revue d'Economie Politique*.

BLOCH-LAINÉ, F. (1980). 'Pour les Progres des Associations', *Pour*, no. 4.

BLOCK, F. L. (1985). 'Postindustrial Development and the Obsolescence of Economic Categories', *Politics & Society*, vol. 14, no. 1, pp. 53–70.

BLOCK, F. L. (1990). *Postindustrial Possibilities: A Critique of Economic Discourse*. Berkeley: University of California Press.

BLOCK, F. L. and HIRSHORN, L. (1979). 'New Productive Forces and the Contradictions of Contemporary Capitalism', *Theory and Society*, no. 7, pp. 363–95.

BLUESTONE, B. and HARRISON, B. (1982). *The Deindustrialization of America: Plant Closing, Community Abandonment, and Dismantling of Basic Industry*. New York: Basic Books.

BLUESTONE, B., *et al.* (1994). *Public Policy Alternatives for Dealing with the Labor Market Problems of Central City Young Adult: Implications from Current Labor Market Research*. (Boston, Mass.: John W. McCormack Institute of Public Affairs, University of Massachusetts, Boston).

BOJE, T. P. (1992). 'Welfare State Systems and Labour Market Stratification', in Amoroso, B. and Jespersen, J. (eds), *Welfare Society in Transition, Annals 1992/93*. Roskilde: Department of Economics and Planning.

BOJE, T. P. (1996). 'Welfare State Models in Comparative Research: Do the Models Describe the Reality?', in Greve, B. (ed.), *Comparative Welfare Systems*. London: Macmillan.

BOLTHO, A. (1979). 'Courses and Causes of Collective Consumption Trends in the West' (Paper to the IEA Conference on 'Grants Economy and Collective Consumption', Sept.). Cambridge.

BOOTH, T. A. (ed.) (1979). *Planning for Welfare, Social Policy and the Expenditure Process*. Oxford: Basil Blackwell.

BOULDING, E. K. (1966). 'The Economics of the Coming Spaceship Earth', in E. H. DALY (ed.), *Toward a Steady-State Economy*. San Francisco: W. H. Freeman & Co.

BOYER, R. (1986). *La théorie de la régulation: une analyse critique*. Paris: Découverte.

BRAUDEL, F. (1982–84). *Civilization and Capitalism, 15th–18th Century*. New York: Harper & Row. (En. tr. 1981)

BREMS. H. (1975). *A Wage Earner's Investment Fund: Forms and Economic Effects*. Stockholm: Swedish Industrial Institute.

BRUSCO, S. (1982). 'The Emilian Model: Productive Decentralisation and Social Integration', *Cambridge Journal of Economics*, pp. 167–84.

BRYSON, M. J. (1995). *Strategic Planning for Public and Nonprofit Organizations: A Guide to Strengthening and Sustaining Organizational Achievement*. San Francisco: Jossey-Bass.

BURNHAM, J. (1941). *The Managerial Revolution*. New York: Day.

BURNS, S. (1975). *Home Inc.: The Hidden Wealth and Power of the American Household*. Garden City, NY: Doubleday.

BURNS, S. (1977). *The Household Economy: Its Shape, Origins and Future*. Boston: Beacon Press.

CAFFÉ, F. (1978). *Lezioni di politica economica*. Turin: Boringhieri.

CAFFÉ, F. (1981). 'La fine del "Welfare State" come riedizione del crollismo' (mimeo) (contributo al Convegno ISSOCO, Dic.). Turin.

CAFFÉ, F. (1986). *In difesa del 'Welfare State': saggi di politica economica*. Turin: Rosenberg & Sellier.

CALOGERO, G. (1944). *La critica dell'economia e il marxismo*. Florence: La Nuova Italia (4th edn, Bari: Laterza, 1967).

CALOGERO, G. (1945). *Difesa del Liberalsocialismo*. Rome: Atlantica (2nd edn, Milan: Marzorati, 1972).

CAMERON, D. (1978). 'The Expansion of the Political Economy: A Comparative Analysis', *American Political Science Review*, vol. 72, no. 4.

CAMMAILLE, J. (1989). 'The Welfare State and the Family: Problems Involved in Redefining the Relationship Between the Private and Public Spheres', in Institute of Social Science (ed.), *The Advanced Industrial Societies in Disarray: What are the Available Choices?*. Tokyo: Institute of Social Science.

CANTWELL, J. (1989). *Technological Innovation and Multinational Corporations*. Oxford: Blackwell.

CANTWELL, J. (ed.) (1993). *Transnational Corporations and Innovatory Activities*. London: Routledge.

CAPECCHI, V. (1989). 'The Informal Economy and the Development of Flexible Specialization in Emilia Romagna', in Portes, A., Castells, M. and Benton, L. A. (eds), *The Informal Economy: Studies in Advanced and Less Developed Countries*. Baltimore: The Johns Hopkins University Press.

CAPECCHI V. *et al*. (1978). *La piccola impresa nell'economia italiana*. Bari: De Donato.

CASSEL, G. (1932). *The Theory of Social Economy*. New York: Harcourt Brace.

CAZES, B. (1981). 'L'état protecteur contraint à une double manoeuvre', in OECD (ed.), *L'Etat protecteur en crise*. Paris: OECD.

CAZES, B. (1985). 'Planning Approaches to the Welfare State Crisis', *Government and Opposition*, no. 20.

CENSIS (1981). *Tra sommerso e vitale. Luci ed ombre dell'industria italiana*. Rome: CENSIS.

CHAMBERLIN, E. H. (1933). *The Theory of Monopolistic Competition*. Cambridge, Mass.: Harvard University Press.

CHANCEL, J. and TIXIER, P. E. (1981). 'La nouvelle enterprise, une aventure moderne et interessante', *Autrement*, no. 29.

CHANDLER, A. D. (1977). *The Invisible Hand: The Managerial Revolution in American Business*. Cambridge, Mass.: Belknap Press, Harvard University.

CHANDLER, A. D. (1990). *Scale and Scope: The Dynamics of Industrial Capitalism*. Cambridge, Mass.: Belknap Press, Harvard Univeristy.

CHENERY, H. B. (1979). *Structural Change and Development Policy*. New York: Oxford University Press.

CHENERY, H. B. and SRINIVASAN, N. T. (1988). *Handbook of Development Economics*. Amsterdam: North-Holland.

CHOMEL, A. (1982). 'L'économie sociale face à la crise dans le changement', *Economie et Humanisme*, no. 264.

CICERCHIA, A. (ed.) (1993). *Indicatori e contabilità per la programmazione sociale: rassegna critica della letteratura*. Roma: Centro di studi e piani economici.

CLARK, C. (1940). *The Conditions of Economics Progress*. London: Macmillan.

CLARK, C. (1961). *'Growthmanship'. A Study in the Mythology of Investment* (Hobart Paper no. 10). London: Institute of Economic Affairs.

CLARK, J. B. (1907). *Essentials of Economic Theory* (Reprints Kelley 1968).

CLARKSON, K. W. and MEINERS, R. E. (1977). 'Government Statistics as a Good Guide to Economic Policy: Food Stamps and the Spurious Increase in the Unemployment Rates', *Policy Review*.

COATES, G. J. (1981). *Resettling America. Energy, Ecology, Community*. Andover, Mass.: Brick House Publ.

COHEN, G. A. (1978). *Karl Marx's Theory of History: A Defence*. Oxford: Oxford University Press.

COLEMAN, D. C. (1956). 'Industrial Growth and Industrial Revolution', *Economica* February.

COLOMBO, A. (1978). *Le società del futuro. Saggio utopico sulle società post-industriali*. Bari: Dedalo.

COMTE, A. (1976). *Oeuvres Completes (1844–1895)* (12 vols). Paris and Geneva: Slatkine.

Congressional Institute (The) (1997). *The Planning Vision*. Washington, D.C.

CORREA, H. (1963). *The Economics of Human Resources*. Amsterdam: North-Holland.

CORREA, H. (1977). *Integrated Economic Accounting*. Lexington, Mass.: D.C. Heath.

CROUCH, C. and STREECK, W. (1996). *Les capitalismes en Europe*. Paris: La Decouverte.

CUTLER A. *et al*. (1987). 'The End of Mass Production?', *Economy and Society*, vol. 16, no. 3, pp. 405–39.

DAHRENDORF, R. (1957). *Soziale Klassen und Klassenkonflikt in der industriellen Gesellshaft*. Stuttgart: Enke.

DAHRENDORF, R. (1983). *The Voluntary Sector in a Changing Economic Climate*. London.

DAHRENDORF, R. (1987). *Fragmente eines neuen Liberalismus*. Stuttgart: Deutsche Verlag.

DAHRENDORF, R. *et al.* (1995). *Report on Wealth Creation and Social Cohesion in a Free Society*. London: Commission on Wealth Creation and Social Cohesion.

DALY, E. H. (1971). *The Stationary-State Economy: Toward a Political Economy of Biophysical Equilibrium and Moral Growth* (Distinguished Lecture Series no. 2). University of Alabama.

DALY, E. H. (1973). *Toward a Steady-State Economy: Introduction*. San Francisco: Freeman.

DARITY, W. A. J. (ed.) (1992). *Labor Economics: Problems in Analyzing Labor Markets*. Dordrecht: Kluwer.

DASGUPTA, P. and STONEMAN, P. (eds) (1987). *Economic Policy and Technological Progress*. Cambridge, UK: Cambridge University Press.

DAVIDSON, P. (1981). 'The Post-Keynesian Economics', in Bell, D. and Kristol, I. (eds), *The Crisis in Economic Theory*. New York: Basic Books.

DAVIDSON, P. and KREGEL, J. A. (eds) (1989). *Macroeconomic Problems and Policies of Income Distribution: Functional, Personal, International*. Aldershot, England: Edward ELGAR.

DAVIDSON, P. and KREGEL, J. A. (1999). *Full Employment and Price Stability in a Global Economy*. Northampton: Edward Elgar.

DEAN, W. J. (1981). 'The Dissolution of the Keynesian Consensus', in Bell, D. and Kristol, I. (eds), *The Crisis in Economic Theory*. New York: Basic Books.

DEANE, P. H. (1967). *The First Industrial Revolution*. Cambridge: Cambridge University Press.

DELORS, J. (1997). 'Per un nuovo modello di suiluppo', in Delors, J. and Ruffolo, G. (eds), *Sinistra di fine secolo*. Milan: Reset.

DELORS, J. and GAUDIN, J. (1978). 'La création d'emploi dans le secteur tertiare: le troisième secteur en France' (mimeo) (Programme de recherche et d'action sur l'évolution du marché de l'emploi). Bruxelles: Commission CEE.

DELORS, J. and GAUDIN, J. (1979) 'Pour le création d'un troisième secteur', *Comment créer des emploi, Dossier Travail et Societé*. Paris: Club Echange et Projects.

DE MASI, D. (1985). *L'avvento post-industriale*. Milan: Franco Angeli.

DENISON, F. E. (1979). *Accounting for Slower Growth*. Washington, DC: Brookings.

DESROCHE, H. (1983). *Pour un traité d'économie sociale*. Paris: Coopérative d'Information et d'Édition Mutualiste.

DE SWAAN, A. (1988). *In Care of the State: Health Care, Education and Welfare in Europe and the USA in the Modern Era*. Cambridge: Polity.

DE VROEY, M. (undated). *The Separation of Ownership and Control in large Corporations: The Marxist View* (Working Paper No. 7419). Louvain: Institut des Sciences Économiques, Université catholique de Louvain.

DHRYMES, P. J. (1963). 'A Comparison of Productivity Behaviour in Manufacturing and Service Industry', *Review of Economics Studies*.

DI MATTEO, M. and VERCELLI, A. (1992). 'Onde lunghe e teoria economica', *Rassegna di lavori dell'ISCO*, no. 16.

DI MATTEO, M. *et al.* (eds) (1989). *Technological and Social Factors in Long Term Fluctuations*. Berlin: Springer.

DIXON, J. and SCHEURELL, R. P. (eds) (1989). *Social Welfare in Developed Market Countries*. London: Routledge & Kegan Paul.

DOBB, M. (1945). *Studies in the Development of Capitalism*. London: Routledge.
DONATI, P. (1978). *Pubblico e privato: Fine di una alternativa?*. Bologna: Cappelli.
DOSI, G. (1984). *Technical Change and Industrial Transformation*. London: Macmillan.
DOSI, G. (1985). 'Paradigmi tecnologici e traiettorie tecnologiche', *Prometheus*, no. 2.
DOSI G. *et al.* (eds) (1988). *Technical Change and Economic Theory*. London: Pinter.
DRIEHUIS, W. (1979). 'Substitution capital-travail et autres determinants structurels de l'emploi et du chomage', in OECD (ed.), *Les determinants structurels de l'emploi et du chomage*. Paris: OECD.
DRUCKER, P. F. (1946). *Concept of the Corporation*. New York: Day.
DRUCKER, P. F. (1954). *The Practice of Management*. New York: Harper.
DRUCKER, P. F. (1956). 'The Employee Society', *American Journal of Sociology*, no. 58.
DRUCKER, P. F. (1964). *Managing for Result: Economic Tasks and Risk-Taking Decisions*. New York: Harper.
DRUCKER, P. F. (1967). *The Effective Executive*. New York: Harper.
DRUCKER, P. F. (1973). *Technology Management and Society*. London: Heinemann.
DRUCKER, P. F. (1981). 'Toward the Next Economics', in Bell, D. and Kristel, I. (eds), *The Crisis in Economic Theory*. New York: Basic Books.
DRUCKER, P. F. (1990). *Managing the Non-Profit Organization: Practices and Principles*. Oxford: Butterworth-Heinemann.
DRUCKER, P. F. (1993). *Post-Capitalist Society*. New York: HarperCollins.
DUMENIL, G. (1978). *Le concept de loi economique dans 'le Capital'*. Paris: Maspero.
DUPUIS, X. and GREFFE, X. (1979). *Rapport technique sur les methodes de quantification du non-marchand, avec une application au cas des associations d'environnement*. Paris: Centre de Recherche 'Travail et Societé'.
EASLEY, D. and O'HARA, M. (1983). 'The Economic Role of Nonprofit Firms', *Bell Journal of Economics*, vol. 14, pp. 531–8.
EASLEY, D. and O'HARA, M. (1986). 'Optimal Nonprofit Firms', in Rose-Ackerman, S. (ed.), *The Economics of Nonprofit Institutions*. New York: Oxford University Press.
ECKSTEIN, A. (1971). *Comparision of Economic Systems: Theoretical and Methodological Approaches*. Berkeley: University of California Press.
EIICHI, K. (1989). 'The Historical Context of Contemporary Capitalism', in Institute of Social Science (ed.), *The Advanced Industrial Societies in Disarray: What Are the Available Choices?*. Tokyo: Institute of Social Science.
ELSTER, J. (1985). *Making Sense of Marx*. Cambridge: Cambridge University Press.
ELSTER, J. and MOENE, K. O .(eds) (1989). *Alternatives to Capitalism*. Cambridge: Cambridge University Press.
EME, B. and LAPLUME, Y. (1981a). 'Les nouveaux entrepreneurs en France', *Futuribles*, no. 49.
EME, B. and LAPLUME, Y. (1981b). 'Les réseaux d'entraide et de solidarité en France', *Futuribles*, no. 40.
ENGELS, F. (1845). *Die Lage der Arbeitenden Klasse in England*. Leipzig.
ESPING-ANDERSEN, G. (1990). *The Three Worlds of Welfare Capitalism*. Cambridge: Polity.
ESPING-ANDERSEN, G. (1994). 'Welfare States and the Economy', in Smelser, J. N. and Swedberg, R. (eds), *The Handbook of Economic Sociology*. Chichester, UK: Princeton University Press.
ETUI (European Trade Union Institute) (1979). *Keynes Plus: A Participatory Economy*. ETUI (European Trade Union Institute).
ETZIONI, A. (1968). *The Active Society: A Theory on Societal and Political Process*. New York: Free Press.

ETZIONI, A. (1973). 'The Third Sector and Domestic Missions', *Public Administration Review*.

ETZIONI, A. (1988). *The Moral Dimension: Toward a New Economics*. New York: The Free Press.

ETZIONI, A. (1991a). *A Responsive Society: Collected Essays on Guiding Deliberate Social Change*. San Francisco: Jossey-Bass Publishers.

ETZIONI, A. (1991b). 'Beyond Self-Interest', in Weimer, D. (ed.), *Policy Analysis and Economics: Developments, Tensions, Prospects*. London: Kluwer.

ETZIONI, A. (1993). *The Spirit of Community: Rights, Responsibilities, and the Communitarian Agenda*. New York: Crown Publishers.

ETZIONI, A. and LAWRENCE, P. R. (eds) (1991). *Socio-economics: Toward a New Synthesis*. New York: M. E. Sharpe.

European Commission (1976). *Rapport du Groupe d'Etudes 'Problemes de l'Inflation'* ('Maldague Report'). Brussels: European Commission.

European Commission (1977). *Rapport du groupe de reflection 'Nouvelles caractéristiques du developpment socio-économique: Un Project pour l'Europe'* ('Ruffolo Report'). Brussels: European Commission.

European Commission (1989). *Les entreprises de l'économie sociale et la réalisation du marché européen sans frontières* (Communication de la Commission au Conseil), SEC(89) 2187 final. Bruxelles, 18.12.1989. Brussels: European Commission.

European Commission (1991). *Europe 2000: Outlook for the Development of Community Territory (Directorate-General for Regional Policy, Communication from the Commission to the Council and the European Parliament)*. Brussels: European Commission.

European Commission (1994a). *Presenting the Social Economy Unit of the European Commission, DG XXIII/A/4, leaflet*. Brussels: European Commission.

European Commission (1994b). *Proposition de decision du Conseil relative au programme phrianmuel (1994–1966) d'actions communautaries en feveur des coopératives, des mutualités, des associations et des fondations la Communauté, COM(93) 650 final, Bruxelles 16.2.1994*. Brussels: European Commission.

EVANS, A. A. (1973). *Flexibility in Working Life: Opportunities for Individual Choice*. Paris: OECD.

EVERS A. *et al.* (eds) (1987). *The Changing Face of Welfare (Studies in Social Policy and Welfare, No. XXVII)*. Aldershot: Gower.

FABER, M. and SEERS, D. (1972). *The Crisis in Planning (Vol.1: The Issues, Vol.2: The Experiences)*. London: Chatto & Windus for Sussex University Press.

FABRICANT, S. (1954). *Economic Progress and Economic Change*. New York: National Bureau of Economic Research, NBER.

FALUDI, A. (1973). *Planning Theory*. Oxford: Pergamon.

FALUDI Andreas and VOOGD Henk (eds) (1985). *Evaluation of Complex Policy Problems*. Delft, Netherlands: Delftsche Uitgevers Maatschappij.

FELLNER, W. and HALEY, F. B. (1950). *Readings in the Theory of Income Distribution*. London: Allen & Unwin.

FERRAROTTI, F. (1985). *Max Weber and the Destiny of Reason*. New York: M. E. Sharpe.

FERRAROTTI, F. (1989). *Max Weber and the Crisis of Western Civilization*. New York: Academic Faculty Press.

FERRERA, M. (1993). *Modelli di solidarietà. Politica e riforme sociali nelle democrazie*. Bologna: Il Mulino.

FILER, K. R. (1980). 'The Downturn in Productivity Growth: A New Look at its Nature and Causes', in Maital, S. and Meltz, M. N. (eds), *Lagging Productivity Growth: Causes and Remedies*. Cambridge, Mass.: Ballinger.

FISHER, A. G. B. (1935). *The Clash of Progress and Security*. London Macmillan.

FISHER, A. G. B. (1945). *Economic Progress and Social Security*. London: Macmillan.

FISHER, A. G. B. (1953). 'A Note on Tertiary Production', *Economic Journal*, vol. LXII, no. 248.

FISHER, A. G. B. (1954). 'Marketing Structure and Economic Development', *Quarterly Journal of Economics*, vol. LXVII, no. 1.

FLENDER, J. O. and MORSE, R. S. (1975). *The Role of New Technical Enterprise in the US Economy*. MIT Development Foundation Study.

FLORA, P. (1986). 'Introduction', in FLORA, P. (ed.), *Growth to Limits. The European Welfare States Since World War II*. Berlin and New York: De Gruyter.

FLORA, P. (1989). 'From Industrial to Postindustrial Welfare State?', in Institute of Social Science (ed.), *The Advanced Industrial Societies in Disarray: What are the Available Choices?*. Tokyo: Institute of Social Science.

FLORA, P. and HEIDENHEIMER, A. J. (1981a). *The Development of Welfare States in Europe and America*. London: Transaction Books.

FLORA, P. and HEIDENHEIMER, A. J. (1981b). 'The Historical Core and Changing Boundaries of the Welfare State', in Flora, P. and Heidenheimer, A. (eds), *The Development of Welfare States in Europe and in America*. New Brunswick: Transaction Books.

FLORENCE, P. S. (1961). *Ownership, Control and Success of Large Companies*. London: Sweet & Maxwell.

FORBES, R. J. (1960). *Man the Maker*. New York: H. Schuman.

FORD, H. (1924). *My Life and Work (in collaboration with Samuel Crowther)*. London: Heinemann.

FOREY, D. and FREEMAN, C. (eds) (1993). *Technology and the Wealth of Nations*. London: Pinter.

FOUDI R. *et al.* (1982) 'Les chomeurs et l'economie informelle' *Travail noir, productions domestiques et entraide*. Lille: CNRS.

FOURASTIÉ, J. (1950). *Le grand espoir du XX siècle: progrès économique, progrès social*. Paris: PUF.

FOURASTIÉ, J. (1952). *La productivité*. Paris: PUF.

FOURIER, C. (1971). *Oevres Completes (1841–1845). Completées par tous les textes tardifs, dispersés et inédits, publies de 1845 à 1858 (12 vols)*. Paris and Geneva: Slatkine.

FOX, K. A. (1974). *Social Indicators and Social Theory: Elements of an Operational System*. New York: Wiley Interscience.

FOX, K. A. (1985a). 'Behavior Settings and Objective Social Indicators', in Fox, K. A. (ed.), *Social System Accounts: Linking Social and Economic Indicators Through Tangible Behaviour Settings*. Dordrecht: Reidel.

FOX, K. A. (1985b). *Social System Accounts: Linking Social and Economic Indicators Through Tangible Behaviour Settings*. Dordrecht: Reidel.

FREEMAN, C. (1974). *The Economics of Industrial Innovation*. Harmondsworth: Penguin.

FREEMAN, C. (1984). *Long Waves in the World Economy*. London: Pinter.

FREEMAN, C. (1998). 'The Economics of Technical Change', in Archibugi, D. and Michie, J. (eds), *Trade, Growth and Technical Change*. Cambridge, UK: Cambridge University Press.

FREEMAN, C., CLARK, J. and SOETE, L. (1982). *Unemployment and Technical Innovation: A Study of Long Waves in Economic Development*. London: Pinter.

FREEMAN, C. and SOETE, L. (eds) (1990) *New Explorations in the Economics of Technological Change*. London: Pinter.

FREEMAN, C. and SOETE, L. (1994). *Work for All or Mass Unemployment? Computerised Technical Change into the Twenty-First Century*. London: Pinter.

FREEMAN, C. and SOETE, L. (1997). *The Economics of Industrial Innovation and Technological Change*. London: Pinter.

FRIEDMANN, G. (1947). *Problèmes humaines du machinisme industriel*. Paris: Gallimard.

FRIEDMANN, J. (1987). *Planning in the Public Domain: From Knowledge to Action*. Princeton, NJ: Princeton University Press.

FRISCH, R. (1936). 'On the Notion of Equilibrium and Disequilibrium', *Review of Economic Studies*.

FRISCH, R. (1960). 'Generalities on Planning', *L'industria*.

FRISCH, R. (1962). 'Preface to the Oslo Channel Model: A Survey of Types of Economic Forecasting and Programming', in Long, F. (ed.), *Economic Planning Studies (by Ragnar Frisch)*. Dordrecht: Reidel. 1976.

FRISCH, R. (1964). 'An Implementation System for Optimal National Economic Planning Without Detailed Quantity Fixation from a Central Authority', in LONG, F. (ed.), *Economic Planning Studies (by Ragnar Frisch)*. Dordrecht: Reidel. 1976.

FRISCH, R. (1969). 'From Utopian Theory to Practical Applications: The Case of Econometrics', in Long, F. (ed.), *Economic Planning Studies (by Ragnar Frisch)*. Dordrecht: Reidel. 1976.

FRISCH, R. (1971). 'Cooperation between Politicians and Econometricians on the Formalization of Political Preferences', in Long, F. (ed.), *Economic Planning Studies (by Ragnar Frisch)*. Dordrecht: Reidel.

FRISCH, R. (1976). *Economic Planning Studies*. Dordrecht: Reidel.

FUÀ, G. (1978). *Problemi dello sviluppo tardivo in Europa*. Bologna: Il Mulino.

FUÀ, G. and SYLOS LABINI, P. (1963). *Idee per la programmazione economica*. Bari: Laterza.

FUÀ, G. and ZACCHIA C. (eds) (1983). *Industrializzazione senza fratture*. Bologna: Il Mulino.

FUCHS, R. V. (1964). *Productivity Trends in Goods and Services Sectors 1929–1961: A Preliminary Survey (Occasional Paper No. 89)*. New York: National Bureau of Economic Research.

FUCHS, R. V. (1965). *The Growing Importance of the Service Industries*. New York: National Bureau of Economic Research.

FUCHS, R. V. (1966a). 'The Growth of Services Industries in the US: A Model for the Other Countries', *Manpower Problems in the Service Sector (suppl. 1966–2)*.

FUCHS, R. V. (1966b). *Productivity Differences within the Service Sector*. New York: National Bureau of Economic Research.

FUCHS, R. V. (1968). *The Service Economy*. New York: National Bureau of Economic Research.

FUCHS, R. V. (ed.) (1970). *Production and Productivity in the Services Industries*. New York: National Bureau of Economic Research.

GALBRAITH, J. K. (1952). *American Capitalism*. Boston: Houghton Mifflin.

GALBRAITH, J. K. (1958). *The Affluent Society*. Boston: Houghton Mifflin.

GALBRAITH, J. K. (1967). *The New Industrial State*. Boston: Houghton Mifflin.

GALBRAITH, J. K. (1976). 'L'imperatif de la politique des revenus', *L'Expansion*, October.

GALBRAITH, J. K. (1978). *On Post Keynesian Economics*. Cambridge: Cambridge University Press.

GALBRAITH, J. K. (1996). *The Good Society: The Human Agenda*. Boston: Houghton Mifflin.

GALBRAITH, J. K. (1998). *The Socially Concerned Today*. Toronto: Buffalo, in association with Victoria University by University of Toronto.

GAMBLING, T. (1974). *Societal Accounting*. London: Allen & Unwin.

GARTNER, A. and RIESMANN, F. (1978). *The Service Society and the Consumer Vanguard*. New York: Harper & Row.

GASSLER, R. S. (1986). *The Economics of Nonprofit Enterprise – a Study in Applied Economic Theory*. Lanham: University Press of America.

GAUDIN, J. (1980). *Interrogation et incertitudes liées au developpement du secteur associatif*. Paris: Centre de recherche 'Travail et Societé'.

GAUDIN, J. (1982a). *Initiatives locales et création d'emploi. Les emplois d'utilité collective*. Paris: La documentation française.

GAUDIN, J. (1982b). *L'économie sociale, specificité et perspective d'emploi des cadres*. Paris: Centres de recherche 'Travail et Societé'.

GAUDIN, J. and PFLIEGER, S. (1982). *Les emploi d'initiative locale: une mise en application decentralisée d'objectifs nationaux (Rapport realisé à la demande de la Delegation à l'Emploi, Centre de recherche 'Travail et Societé')*. Paris: Centre de recherche 'Travail et Societé'.

GERSHUNY, J. (1978). *After Industrial Society? The Emerging Self-Service Economy*. London: Macmillan.

GERSHUNY, J. (1983). *Social Innovation and the Division of Labour*. Oxford: Oxford University Press.

GERSHUNY, J. and MILES, I. (1983). *The New Service Economy (The Transformation of Employment in Industrial Societies)*. London: Francis Pinter.

GIDDENS, A. (1976). *New Rules of Sociological Method: A Positive Critique of Interpretative Sociologies*. London: Hutchinson.

GIDDENS, A. (1981). *A Contemporary Critique of Historical Materialism*. Ben Kelley, Calif.: California University Press.

GIDDENS, A. (1984). *The Constitution of Society: Outline of the Theory of Structuration*. Cambridge: Polity Press.

GIDDENS, A. (1990) *The Consequences of Modernity*. Cambridge, UK: Polity Press.

GIDDENS, A. (1991). *Modernity and Self-Identity in the Late Modern Age*. Stanford, Calif.: Stanford Univeristy Press.

GIDDENS, A. (1994). *Beyond Left and Right: The Future of Radical Politics*. Stanford, Calif.: Stanford University Press.

GIDDENS, A. (1995). *Politics, Sociology and Social Theory: Encounters with Classical and Contemporary Social Thought*, Stanford, Calif.: Stanford University Press.

GIDDENS, A. (1996). *In Defense of Sociology: Essays, Interpretations, and Rejoinders*. Cambridge, UK: Polity Press.

GIDDENS, A. (ed.) (1974). *Positivism and Sociology*. London: Hutchinson.

GINZBERG, E. (1976). *The Human Economy*. New York: McGraw-Hill.

GINZBERG, E. (1985). *Understanding Human Resources: Perspectives, People, and Policy*. Lanham, MD: University Press of America.

GINZBERG, E. (ed.) (1988). *Executive Talent: Developing and Keeping the Best People*. New York: Wiley.

GINZBERG E. *et al.* (1965). *The Pluralistic Economy*. New York: McGraw-Hill.

GINZBERG, E., WILLIAMS, T. and DUTKA, A. (1989). *Does Job Training Work?: The Clients Speak Out*. Boulder: Westview Press.

GIROUD, F. et al. (1980). *Reflexions sur l'Avenir du Travail*. Paris: Commissariat au Plan, La Documentation Français.

GLENNERSTER, H. (1979). 'The Determinants of Public Expenditure', in Booth, T. A. (ed.), *Planning for Welfare, Social Policy and the Expenditure Process*. Oxford: Blackwell.

GLENNERSTER, H. (ed). (1983). *The Future of the Welfare State: Re-making Social Policy*. London: Heinemann.

GORDON, R. A. (1945). *Business Leadership in the Large Corporations*. Washington, DC.

GÖRZ, A. (1992). *Capitalisme, socialisme, ecologie*. Paris: Galilée.

GOTTMANN, J. (1975). 'The Interweaving of Quaternary Activities', *Ekistics*, vol. 39, no. 233.

GREEN, C. (1967). *Negative Taxes and the Poverty Problem*. Washington, DC: Brookings Institution.

GREFFE, X. (1992). *Sociétés postindustrielles et redéveloppement*. Paris: Hachette.

GREFFE, X. (1994). *Économie des politiques publiques*. Paris: Dalloz.

GREFFE, Xavier (1998). *L'evaluation des politiques publiques*. Paris: Anthropos.

GREFFE, Xavier (1999). *Gestion publique*. Paris: Dalloz.

GREFFE, X., DUPUIS, X. and PFLIEGER, S. (1983). *Financer l'économie sociale*. Paris: Economica.

GREVE, B. (1991). 'Is It Possible to Explain the Growth of the Public Sector?', in AMOROSO, B. (ed.), *The Theory and Future of Welfare Societies; Annals 1991*. Roskilde, DK: Department of Economics and Planning, Roskilde University.

GREVE, B. (1992). 'Financing the Public Sector: New Ways in the Nineties?', in Amoroso, B. and Jespersen, J. (eds), *Welfare Society in Transition* Annals 1992/93. Roskilde, DK: Department of Economics and Planning, Roskilde Univeristy.

GREVE, B. (1996). 'Ways of Financing the Welfare State and their Distributional Consequences', in Greve, B. (ed.), *Comparative Welfare Systems*: The Scandinavian model in a period of change. London: Macmillan.

GREVE, B. (ed.) (1996). *Comparative Welfare Systems*. London: Macmillan.

GRONAU, R. (1973). 'The Measurement of Output of the Non Market Sector: The Evaluation of Housewives' Time', in Moss, M. (ed.), *The Measurment of Economic and Social Performance*. New York: National Bureau of Economic Research, Columbia University Press.

GROS-PIETRO, G. M. (1980). 'Cambiamenti nella divisione del lavoro tra grandi e piccole imprese', *Economia e Politica Industriale*, no. 28.

GROSS, B. M. (1966). *A Great Society?* New York: Basic Books.

GROSS, B. M. (1967). 'Space-Time and Post-Industrial Society' (Paper presented to 1965 Seminars of Comparative Administration Group of the American Society for Public Administration, Syracuse University, 1966).

GUILLOTIN, Y. (1986). 'A New Democratic Method of Decision for Social Protection', in Ten Hove Mark, D. (ed.), *The Institutions of a Changing Welfare State: The Future of the Welfare State, Vol. II*. Maastricht: Presses Interuniversitaires Européennes.

GUSTAFSSON, B. (ed.) (1979). *Post-industrial Society*. London: Croom Helm.

GUTMANN, P. (1978). 'Are the Unemployed, Unemployment?', *Financial Analysts Journal*.

GUTMANN, P. (1979). 'The Grand Unemployment Illusion', *Journal of the Institute of Socio-Economic Studies*.

HABERMAS, J. (1985). 'Die Krise des Wohlfahrtsstaates und die Erschöpfung utopisher Energien', in Habermas, J. (ed.), *Die Neue Unübersichtlichkeit: Klein Politische Schriften V.* Frankfurt: Suhrkamp.

HAGEMANN, R. (1989). 'Aging Population and the Pressure on Pensions', *OECD Observer*, no. 160, pp. 12–15.

HAHN, F. H. (1973). *On the Notion of Equilibrium in Economics*. Cambridge: Cambridge University Press.

HAHN, F. H. (1981). 'General Equilibrium Theory', in Bell, D. and Kristol, I. (eds), *The Crisis in Economic Theory*. New York: Basic Books.

HANSMANN, H. B. (1980). 'The Role of Nonprofit Enterprise', *Yale Law Journal*, no. 89, pp. 835–98.

HANSMANN, H. B. (1986). 'Economic Theories of Non-Profit Organizations', in POWELL, W. (ed.), *Handbook of Non-Profit Organizations*. New Haven: Yale University Press.

HANSMANN, H. B. (1989). 'The Two Nonprofit Sectors: Fee for Service Versus Donative Organizations', in Hodgkinson, V., Lyman, W. R. and Associates (eds), *The Future of the Nonprofit Sector*. San Francisco: Jossey-Bass Publishers.

HARMAN, W. W. (1979). *An Incomplete Guide to the Future*. New York: Norton.

HAY, J. (1978). *The Development of the British Welfare State, 1880–1975*. London: Arnold.

HEAP H. S. *et al*. (1980–1). 'World Profitability Crisis in the 1970's: Some Empirical Evidence', *Capital and Class*, no. 12.

HECLO, H. (1981). 'Toward a New Welfare State?', in Flora, P. and Heidenheimer, A. (eds), *The Development of Welfare States in Europe and in America*. New Brunswick: Transaction Books.

HEERTJE, A. (1977). *Economic and Technical Change*. London: Weidenfeld & Nicolson.

HEERTJE, A. (ed.) (1988). *Innovation, Technology and Finance*. Oxford: Blackwell.

HEERTJE, A. and PERLMAN, M. (eds) (1990). *Evolving Technology and Market Structure*. Ann Arbor: University of Michigan Press.

HEILBRONER, R. L. (1976). *Business Civilisation in Decline*. New York: Boyars.

HEILBRONER, R. L. (1985a). *The Nature and Logic of Capitalism*. New York: Norton.

HEILBRONER, R. L. (1985b). *The Act of Work*. Washington: Library of Congress.

HEILBRONER, R. L. (1993). *21st Century Capitalism*. New York: Norton.

HEILBRONER, R. L. (1995). *Visions of the Future: The Distant Past, Yesterday, Today, Tomorrow*. New York: Oxford University Press.

HEILBRONER, R. L. *et al*. (1972). *In the Name of Profit*. New York: Doubleday.

HELLER, F. (1982). *The International Yearbook of Organizational Democracy for the Study of Participation, Cooperation and Power*. Sussex: Wiley & Sons.

HENRY, S. (ed.) (1980). *Informal Institutions in Post-Industrial Society*. London: Architectural Press.

HESS, K. (1979). *Community Technology*. Scranton, Pa.: Harper.

HIMMELSTRAND, U. *et al*. (1981). *Beyond Welfare Capitalism: Issues, Actors and Forces in Societal Change*. London: Heinemann.

HINRICHS, K., OFFE, C. and WIESENTHAL, H. (1986). 'The Crisis of the Welfare State and Alternative Modes of Work Redistribution', in Van Veen, T. and Kleinknecht, A. (eds), *Working Time Reduction and the Crisis in the Welfare State*. Maastricht: Presses Interuniversitaires Européennes.

HIRSCH, F. (1976). *Social Limits to Growth*. Cambridge, Mass.: Harvard University Press.

HIRSCHMAN, A. O. (1970). *Exit, Voice and Loyalty: Responses to Decline in Firms, Organisations and States*. Cambridge, Mass.: Harvard University Press.

HIRSCHMAN, A. O. (1980). 'The Welfare State in Trouble: Systemic Crisis or Growing Pains?', *American Economic Review May*.

HIRSCHMAN, A. O. (1981). 'The Rise and Decline of Development Economics', in Hirschman, A., *Essays in Trespassing: Economics in Politics and Beyond*. Cambridge: Cambridge University Press.

HIRSCHMAN, A. O. (1991). *The Rhetoric of Reaction: Perversity, Futility, Jeopardy*. Cambridge, Mass.: Belknap Press.

HIRSCHMAN, A. O. (1995). *A Propensity to Self-Subversion*. Cambridge, Mass.: Harvard University Press.

HIRST, P. (1994). 'An Associational and Confederal Welfare State', in Hirst, P. (ed.), *Associative Democracy: New Forms of Economic and Social Governance*. Cambridge: Polity Press.

HOBSBAWM, E. J. (1968). *Industry and Empire; The Making of Modern English Society, 1750 to the Present Day*. New York: Pantheon Books.

HODGKINSON, V. A. (1989). 'Key Challenges Facing the Nonprofit Sector', in HODGKINSON, V. A., LYMAN, W. R. and Associates (eds), *The Future of the Nonprofit Sector*. San Francisco: Jossey-Bass Publishers.

HODGKINSON, V. A., LYMAN, W. R. and Associates (1989). *The Future of the Nonprofit Sector*. San Francisco: Jossey-Bass Publishers.

HODGSON, Geoffrey M. (1988). *Economics and Institutions: A Manifesto for a Modern Institutional Economics*. Oxford: Polity Press.

HOLLAND, S. (ed.) (1978). *Beyond Capitalist Planning*. Oxford: Basil Blackwell.

HOLLAND, S. (1987). *The Global Economy: From Micro to Mesoeconomics, Vol. 2 of Toward a New Political Economy*. London: Weidenfeld & Nicolson.

HOLMOS, P. (1970). *The Personal Society*. London: Constable.

HUBER, J. (1979). *Anders arbeiten, anders wirtschaften*. Frankfurt: Wirtschaft.

HUBER, J. (1980a). 'Jenseits von Markt und Staat Netzwerke der Selbsthilfe und Eigen arbeit', *L'80 Zeitschrift fur Literatur und Politik*, no. 17.

HUBER, J. (1980b). *Wer soll das alles aendern. Die Alternativen der Alternativsbewegung*. Berlin: Rotbuch.

HUBER J. *et al.* (1982). 'Development of the Informal Sector in the Federal Republic of Germany'. (The Informal Economy. Social Conflicts and the Future of Industrial Societies, by the 'Consiglio Italiano per le Scienze Sociali'), Rome, 25–28 November.

HURFF, G. (1950). *Social Aspects of Enterprise in Large Corporations*. Philadelphia: University of Pennsylvania Press.

IIE (Institute for International Economics) (1982). *Promoting World Recovery: A Statement on Global Economic Strategy*. Washington, DC: IIE (Institute for International Economics).

ILLICH, I. (1971). *Deschooling Society*. New York: Harper & Row.

Independent Sector (1992). *The Nonprofit Almanac 1992–1993: Dimensions of the Independent Sector*. Washington, DC: Independent Sector.

INGLEHART, R. (1971). 'The Silent Revolution in Europe: International Change in Post-Industrial Society', *American Political Science Review*, pp. 991–1017.

INGLEHART, R. (1977). *The Silent Revolution, Changing Values and Political Styles Among Western Publics*. Princeton NJ: Princeton University Press.

INGRAO, B. and ISRAEL, G. (1987). *La mano invisibile. L'equilibrio economico nella storia della scienza*. Rome and Bari: Laterza.

INOSE, H. and PIERCE, R. J. (1984). *Information Technology and Civilization*. New York: W. H. Freeman.

Institute of Local Self-Reliance (1979). *A Guide to Cooperative Alternatives*. New Haven.

IOVENE, N. and VIEZZOLI M. (1999). *Il libro del terzo settore: l'universo del nonprofit tra impresa e solidarietà sociale*. Rome: Adn-Kronos.

Ipse Forum (Forum for International Political and Social Economy) (1983). *Out of Crisis: A Project for European Recovery* (ed. S. Holland). Nottingham.

Ispe (1981). 'Vitalità e vulnerabilità dell'industria italiana: il sistema decentrato di produzione', *Ispe-Quaderni*, no. 21.

JAMES, E. (1990). 'Economic Theories of the Nonprofit Sector: A Comparative Perspective', in Anheier, H. and Seibel, W. (eds), *The Third Sector: Comparative Studies of Nonprofit Organisations*. New York and Berlin: Walter de Gruyter.

JAMES, E. and ROSE-ACKERMAN, S. (1986). *The Nonprofit Enterprise in Market Economics*. Chur, Switzerland: Harwood Academic Publishers.

JEANTET, Th. (1982a). *Economie Sociale et Secteur Marchand* (Conference Université de Paris IX). Paris: Université de Paris IX.

JEANTET, Th. (1982b). *Epargne et Economie Sociale* (Rapport (roneo) à la Delegation a l'Economie Sociale).

JEANTET, Th. (1982c). 'L'économie sociale trouve-t-elle sa source dans l'économie cachée?'. (Conference Internationale sur 'L'Economie Cachée Conflits Sociaux et Avenir des Sociétés Industrielles'), Rome-Frascati, November 1982.

JESSOP, B. (1990). 'Regulation Theories in Retrospect and Prospect', *Economy and Society*, vol. 19, no. 2, pp. 153–216.

JOHANSEN, L. (1977–8). *Lectures on Macroeconomic Planning. Vol.1: General Aspects. Vol. 2: Centralisation, Decentralisation, under Uncertainty Planning*. Amsterdam: North-Holland.

JOHNSON, N. (1987). *The Welfare State in Transition: The Theory and Practice of Welfare Pluralism*. Brigton, Sussex: Wheatsheaf Books.

JOSSA, B. (1989). 'Socioalismo e autogestione', in Jossa, B. (a cura di), *Teoria dei Sistemi Economici* ('Biblioteca dell'Economista', Serie ottava). Turin: UTET.

JOSSA, B. (a cura di) (1989). *Teoria dei Sistemi Economici* ('Biblioteca dell'Economista, Serie ottava). Turin: UTET.

JUNGK, R. (1954). *Tomorrow is Already Here; Scenes from a Man-made Wold*. London: R. Hart-Davis.

JUNGK, R. and GALTUNG, J. (eds) (1969). *Mankind 2000*. London: Allen & Unwin.

KAHN, H. and WIENER, A. J. (1967a). *The Year 2000: A Framework for Speculation on the Next Thirty-three Years*. New York: Macmillan.

KAHN, H. and WIENER, A. J. (1967b). 'Post-Industrial Society in the Standard World', in Kahn, H. and Wiener, A. J. (eds), *The Year 2000: A Framework for Speculation on the Next Thirty-three Years*. New York: Macmillan.

KATOUZIAN, M. A. (1970). 'The Development of the Service Sector: A New Approach', *Oxford Economic Papers*, no. 3.

KENDRICK, J. W. (1961). *Productivity Trends in the US*. New York: Princeton University Press.

KENDRICK, J. W. and VACCARA N. (eds) (1980). *New Development in Productivity Measurement and Analysis*. Chicago: University of Chicago Press.

KENDRICK, J. W. (ed.) (1984). *International Comparison of Productivity and Causes of the Slowdown*. Cambridge, Mass.: Ballinger & Co.

KENDRICK, J. W. (ed.) (1996). *The New System of National Accounts*. Boston: Kluwer Academic.

KENNY, M. and FLORIDA, R. (1988). 'Beyond Mass Production: Production and the Labor Process in Japan', *Politics and Society*, vol. 16, no. 1.

KERR, C. *et al.* (1960). *Industrialism and Industrial Man. The Problem of Labor and Management in Economic Growth*. Cambridge, Mass.: Harvard University Press.

KEYNES, J. M. (1930). 'The Economic Possibilities for Our Grandchildren', *Essays in Persuasion*, 1932.

KILLINGSWORTH, M. R. (1966). 'Structural Unemployment in the US', in Stieber, J. (ed.), *Employment Problems of Automation and Advanced Technology: An International Perspective*. London: Macmillan.

KILLINGSWORTH, M. R. (1970). 'A Critical Survey of Neoclassical Models of Labour', *Bulletin of the Oxford University Institute of Economics and Statistics*, vol. 32, no. 2.

KING, A. (1975). 'Overload: Problems of Government in the 1970's', *Political Studies*, vol. 23, no. 2–3.

KLEIN, R. (1977). 'Democracy, the Welfare State and Social Policy', *Political Quarterly*, vol. 48, no. 4.

KLEIN, R. (1980a). 'Costs and Benefits of Complexity: The Case of the British National Health Service', in Rose, R. (ed.), *Challenge the Governance*. London: Sage.

KLEIN, R. (1980b). 'The Welfare State: A Self-Inflicted Crisis', *Political Quarterly*, vol. 51, no. 1.

KLEIN, R. (1981). 'La Politique Sociale des année 80: valeurs, rapport de force politique', in OECD (ed.), *L'état protecteur en crise*. Paris: OECD (see OECD, 1981, English ed.).

KLEIN, R. and O'HIGGINS, M. (eds.) (1985). *The Future of Welfare*. Oxford: Blackwell.

KLEINKNECHT, A. and VAN VEEN, T. (1986). *Working Time Reduction and the Crisis in the Welfare State (The Future of the Welfare State, Vol. III)*. Maastricht: Presses Interuniversitaires Européenes.

KLEINKNECHT, A., MANDEL, E. and WALLERSTEIN, I. (eds.) (1992). *New Findings in Long-wave Research*. New York: St Martin's Press.

KOK, L. and DE NEUBORG, C. (1986). 'Working Time: Length, Past and Future. An International Comparison', in Kleinknecht, A. and Van Veen, T. (eds), *Working Time Reduction and the Crisis in the Welfare State*. Maastricht: Presses Interuniversitaires Européennes.

KOMPIER, M. and LEVI, L. (1994). *Stress sul lavoro: cause, effetti e prevenzione*. Dublin: Fondazione europea per il miglioramento delle condizioni di vita e di lavoro.

KONDRATIEF, N. D. (1935). 'Long Cycle Theory' (translation by W. F. Stolper), *Review of Economic and Statistics*, November 1935.

KRAMER, R. M. (1981). *Voluntary Agencies in the Welfare State*. Berkeley, Calif.: University of California Press.

KRASHINSKY, M. (1986). 'Transaction Costs and a Theory of the Nonprofit Organisations', in Rose-Ackerman, S. (ed.), *The Economics of Nonprofit Institutions*. New York: Oxford University Press.

KREGEL J. A. (1983). 'Conceptions of Equilibrium, Conceptions of Time and Conceptions of Economic Interaction', in Caravale, G. (ed.), *La crisi delle teorie economiche*. Milan: Franco Angeli.

KREGEL, J. A. (ed.) (1989). *Inflation and Income Distribution in Capitalist Crisis: Essays in Memory of Sidney Weintraub*. New York: New York University Press.

KREGEL, J. A., MATZNER, E. and RONCAGLIA, A. (1988). *Barriers to Full Employment*. London: Macmillan.

KUZNETS, S. (1953). *Economic Change*. New York: Norton.

KUZNETS, S. (1955). 'Toward a Theory of Economic Growth', in Leckachman, R. (ed.), *National Policy for Economic Welfare at Home and Abroad*. New York: Doubleday.

KUZNETS, S. (1959). 'On Comparative Study of Economic Structure and Growth of Nations', in National Bureau of Economic Research (ed.), *The Comparative Study of Economic Growth and Structure*. New York: National Bureau of Economic Research.

KUZNETS, S. (1961). 'Quantitative Aspects of the Economic Growth of the Nations: IV. Long Term Trends in Capital Formation Proportions', *Economic Development Change*, no. 9, pp. 1–124.

KUZNETS, S. (1962), 'Inventive Acitvity: Problems of Definition and Measurement', in NBER, *The Rate and Direction of Inventive Activity: Economic and Social Factors*. Princeton: Princeton University Press.

KUZNETS, S. (1966). *Modern Economic Growth: Rate, Structure and Spread*. New Haven: Yale University Press.

KUZNETS, S. (1973a). 'Modern Economic Growth: Findings and Reflections', *American Economic Review*, no. 63, pp. 247–58.

KUZNETS, S. (1973b). *Population, Capital, and Growth*. New York: Norton.

LAL, D. (1985). *The Poverty of Development Economics*. Cambridge, Mass.: Harvard University Press.

LAND, K. and JUSTER, F. T. (1981). *Social Accounting Systems: Essays on the State of the Art*. London: Academic Press.

LANDES, D. S. (1969). *The Unbound Prometheus: Technological Change and Industrial Development in Western Europe from 1750 to the Present*. Cambridge: Cambridge University Press.

LANDES, D. S. (1998). *The Wealth and Poverty of Nations: Why Some Are So Rich and Some So Poor*. New York: Norton.

LANE, F. C. and RIEMERSMA, J. C. (eds) (1953). *Enterprise and Secular Change: Readings in Economic History*. London: Allen & Unwin.

LANE, J. E. (1995). *The Public Sector: Concepts, Models and Approaches*. London: Sage Publications.

LANGAM, M. and OSTNER, I. (1991). 'Gender and Welfare. Towards a Comparative Perspective', in Room, G. (ed.), *Towards a European Welfare State*. Bristol: Saus Publications.

LE GRAND, J. (1982). *The Strategy of Equality*. London: Allen & Unwin.

LE GRAND, J. (1983). 'Making Redistribution Work: The Social Services', in Glennerster, H. (ed.), *The Future of the Welfare State: Remaking Social Policy*. London: Heinemann.

LENGELLÉ, M. (1966). *La Révolution Tertiaire*. Paris: Genin.

LEON, P. (1967). *Structural Change and Growth in Capitalism: A Set of Hypotheses*. Baltimore: Johns Hopkins Press.

LEONTIEF, W. (1976). 'National Economic Planning: Methods and Problems', in *The Economic System in an Age of Discontinuity*. New York: New York University Press.

LEONTIEF, W. (1982). 'Labor and Income Sharing', *Scientific American*, no. 171.

LEONTIEF, W. and DUCHIN, F. (1986). *The Future Impact of Automation on Workers*. New York: Oxford University Press.

LEROY-BEAULIEU, P., (1887). [orig. ed.1876] *Trattato della scienza delle finanze*. ('Biblioteca degli Economisti', Serie III, Vol. X, Parte I). Turin: UTET, 1887.

LEROY-BEAULIEU, P., (1897–8), *Trattato teorico-pratico di economia politica* (trad.: Ludovico Eusebio). ('Biblioteca degli Economisti'), Serie IV, Vol. IX, Parti I e II. Turin: UTET.

LEVITT, T. (1973). *The Third Sector: New Tactics for a Responsive Society*. New York: AMACOM, A Division of American Management Associations.

LEWIS, W. A. (1961). *The Theory of Economic Growth*. London: Allen & Unwin.

LICHFIELD, Nathaniel (1996). *Community Impact Evaluation*. London: UCL Press.

LICHFIELD, et al. (1998). *Evaluation in Planning: Facing the Challenge of Complexity*. Dordrecht: Kluwer.

LILIENTHAL, D. E. (1952). *Big Business: A New Era*. New York: Harper.

LIPNACK, J. and STAMPS, J. (1982). *Networking: The First Report and Directory*. Garden City, NY: Doubleday.

LIPSEY, R. G. (1967). 'Structural and Deficient-Demand Unemployment Reconsidered', in ROSS, A. M. (ed.), *Employment Policy and the Labour Market*. Berkeley: University of California Press.

LITTLE, I. M. D. (1982). *Economic Development: Theory, Policy, and International Relations*. New York: Basic Books.

LOBELL, J. (1981). *The Little Green Book. A Guide to Self-Reliant Living in the 80's*. Boulder, Colorado: Shambhala.

LUNARIA Association (1997). *Lavori scelti. Come creare occupazione nel terzo settore.* Turin: Edizioni Gruppo Abele.

LUTZ, A. M. (ed.) (1990). *Social Economics: Retrospect and Prospect.* London: Kluwer.

MACHLUP, F. (1962). 'The Supply of Inventors and Inventions', in NBER, *The Rate and Direction of Inventive Activity: Economic and Social Factors.* Princeton: Princeton University Press.

MACKAY D. I. *et al.* (1971). *Labour Markets: Under Different Employment Conditions.* London: Allen & Unwin.

MAIER, H. E. (1981). 'Les nouveaux entrepreneurs en RFA', *Futuribles November.*

MAITAL, S. and MELTZ, M. N. (1980). *Lagging Productivity Growth: Causes and Remedies.* Cambridge, Mass.: Ballinger.

MALINVAUD, E. (1977–9). 'Substitution du capital au travail, évolution technologique et effects sur l'emploi (Resumé des discussions sur le thème 2 de la réunion d'expert OECD à Paris, mars 1977)', *Le déterminants structurels de l'emploi et du chomage* (Vol. 1, 1977; Vol. 2, 1979). Paris.

MALKIN D. *et al.* (1973). 'Le Tertiarisation de la Societé', in *Questions à la Societé Tertiaire.* Paris: Datar.

MANDEL, E. (1962). *Marxist Economic Theory.* (English trans. New York: Monthly Review Press, 1968).

MANDEL, E. (1967). *La formation de la pensée économique de Karl Marx.* Paris: F. Maspero.

MANDEL, E. (1971). 'La storia e le leggi di movimento del capitalismo', in Mandel E. *et al.* (eds), *Il capitalismo negli anni '70.* Milan: Mazzotta.

MANDEL, E. (1975). *Late Capitalism.* Atlantic Highlands, NJ: Humanities Press.

MANDEL, E. (1976). *La troisième âge du capitalisme.* Paris: Union générale d'éditions.

MANDEL, E. (1978). *The Second Slump: A Marxist Analysis of Recession in the Seventies.* London: NLB.

MANDEL, E. (1980). *Long Waves of Capitalism Development: The Marxist Interpretation.* Cambridge: Cambridge University Press.

MANDEL, E. (1981). 'Explaining Long Waves of Capitalist Development', *Futures,* vol. 13, no. 4, pp. 332–8.

MANDEL, E. (1993). *The Place of Marxism in History.* Atlantic Highlands, NJ: Humanities Press.

MANSFIELD, E. (1968). *The Economics of Technological Change.* New York: Norton.

MANTOUX, P. (1928). *Industrial Revolution in the 18th Century.* London: Jonathan Cape.

MARGOLIS, I. and TRZECIAKOWSKI, W. (1970). 'Multi-Level Planning and Decision-Making (Background Paper presented at the VI Meeting of the 'Senior Economic Advisers' of UN-ECE, Ginevra, Nov. 1968)', in United Nations (ed.), *Multi-Level Planning and Decision-Making.* New York: UNO.

MARIEN, M. (1976). *Societal Directions and Alternatives: A Critical Guide to the Literature.* LaFayette, NY: Information for Policy Design.

MARIEN, M. (1977). 'The Two Visions of Post-Industrial Society', *Futures,* no. 5.

MARIEN, M. (1996). *Environmental Issues and Sustainable Futures.* Bethesda, Md.: World Future Society.

MARRIS, R. (1964). *The Economic Theory of Managerial Capitalism.* London: Macmillan.

MARSHALL, A. (1890) (8th edn, 1920). *Principles of Economics.* London: Macmillan.

MARSHALL, A. (1923). *Industry and Trade.* London: Macmillan.

MARX, K. and ENGELS, F. (undated). *Collected Works.* London: Lawrence & Wishart.

MARX, K. and ENGELS, F. (1846). *The German Ideology* (Edn, Moscow, 1956).
MARX, K. (1967). *Capital I, Capital II, Capital III*. New York: International Publishers.
MATZNER, E. (1991). 'Policies, Institutions and Employment Performance', in Matzner, E. and Streeck, W. (eds), *Beyond Keynesianism: The Socio-Economics of Production and Full Employment*. Aldershot: Edward Elgar.
McCARTHY, E. and McGAUGHEY, W. (1989). *Non-Financial Economics: The Case for Shorter Hours of Work*. New York: Praeger.
McKEAN, R. N. (1968). *Public Spending*. New York: McGraw-Hill.
McROBIE, G. (1981). *Small is Possible*. New York: Harper.
MEADE, J. E. (1970). *The Theory of Indicative Planning*. Manchester: Manchester University Press.
MEADE, J. F. (1989). *Agathopia: The Economics of Partnership*. Aberdeen: Aberdeen University Press.
MEANS, G. C. (1962). *The Corporate Revolution in America: Economic Reality vs. Economic Theory*. New York: Crowell-Collier.
MEIDNER, R. (1978). *Employee Investment Funds (An Approach to Collective Capital Formation)*. London: Allen & Unwin.
MEIER, G. M. and SEERS, D. (eds) (1984). *Pioneers in Development*. New York and Oxford: Oxford University Press for the World Bank.
MERCER, J. L. (1991). *Strategic Planning for Public Managers*. New York: Quorum Books.
MEUNIER, B. (1992). *Le management du non-marchand*. Paris: Economica.
MILL, J. S. (1848). *Principles of Political Economy, With Some of Their Applications to Social Philosophy*. London.
Ministero del Bilancio e della Programmazione Economica (1969). *Progetto 80– Rapporto preliminare al Programma Economico Nazionale 1971–1975*.
MINKES, A. L. (1955). 'Statistical Evidence and the Concept of Tertiary Industry', *Economic Development and Cultural Change*, no. 4, pp. 366–73.
MISHAN, E. J. (1967). *The Costs of Economics Growth*. New York: Praeger.
MODIGLIANI, Franco (1987). *Reddito, interesse, inflazione: scritti scientifici*. Torin: Einaudi.
MODIGLIANI, Franco and Tarantelli, Ezio (1975). *Mercato del lavoro, distribuzione del reddito e consumi privati*. Bologna: Il Mulino.
MOMMSEN, W. J. (ed.) (1981). *The Emergence of the Welfare State in Britain and Germany*. London: Croom Helm.
MOORE, M. H. (1995). *Creating Public Value: Strategic Management in Government*. Cambridge, Mass.: Harvard University Press.
MORAN, M. (1988). 'Review Article: Crises of the Welfare State', *British Journal of Policy Science*, 18, pp. 397–414.
MORAN, R. (1993). *The Electronic Home: Social Aspect* (A scoping Report by EKOS). Dublin: European Foundation for the Improvement of Living and Working Conditions.
MOREAU, J. (1982). *Essai sur une politique de l'Economie Sociale*. Paris: Ciem.
MORGAN, J. N. *et al.* (1966). *Productive Americans*. Ann Arbor: University of Michigan Press.
MUSGRAVE, R. A. (1959). *The Theory of Public Finance*. New York: McGraw-Hill.
MUSGRAVE, R. A. (1985). 'A Brief History of Fiscal Doctrine', in Auerbach, A. J. and Feldstein, M. (eds), *Handbook of Public Economics*. Amsterdam: North-Holland.
MUSSON, A. E. and ROBINSON, E. (1969). *Science and Technology in the Industrial Revolution*. Manchester: Manchester University Press.

MYRDAL, G. (1960). *Beyond the Welfare State: Economic Planning in the Welfare State and Its International Implications*. New Haven: Yale University Press.

MYRDAL, G. (1962). *Challenge to Affluence*. New York: Pantheon Books.

NAISBITT, J. (1984). *Megatrends. Ten New Directions in Transforming Our Lives*. New York: Warner Books.

NAISBITT, J. and ABURDENE, P. (1985). *Re-inventing the Corporation: Transforming Your Job and Your Company for the New Information Society*. New York.: Warner Books.

NAPOLEONI, C. (ed.) (1970). *Il futuro del capitalismo. Crollo o sviluppo?*. Rome and Bari: Laterza.

NBER (1962). *The Rate and Direction of Inventive Activity: Economic and Social Factor*. Princeton: Princeton University Press.

NELSON, R. R. (1959). 'The Economics of Invention: A Survey of Literature', *Journal of Business*, vol. 32.

NELSON, R. R. (1962). 'Introduction' to *The Rate and Direction of Inventive Activity: Economic and Social Factor*. Princeton: Princeton Unversity Press.

NELSON, R. R. (1987). *Understanding Technical Change as an Evolutionary Process*. Amsterdam: North-Holland.

NELSON, R. R. and KRASHINSKY, M. (1973). 'Two Major Issues of Public Policy: Public Subsidy and the Organization of Supply', in Young, D. and Nelson, R. (eds), *Public Policy for Day Care for Young Children*. Lexington, Mass.: Lexington Books.

NELSON, R. R., PECK, M. J. and KALACHEK, E. D. (1967). *Technology, Economic Growth and Public Policy*. London: Allen & Unwin.

NELSON, R. R. and WINTER, S. G. (1982). *An Evolutionary Theory of Economic Change*. Cambridge, Mass.: Harvard University Press.

NEWCOMER, E. K. and WHOLEY, S. J. (1989). *Improving Government Performance: Evaluation Strategies for Strengthening Public Agencies and Programs*. San Francisco: Jossey-Bass.

NIAUDET, P. (1973). 'Pauvreté et repartition des revenus dans la societé industrielle avancée', *Futuribles* April.

NICHOLAS, B. (1992). 'Economic Theory and the Welfare State: A Survey and Interpretation', *Journal of Economic Literature*, vol. 30, pp. 741–803.

NIELSEN, K. (1994) April. 'From Paternalistic Workfare States to Discount Welfare States – Eastern European Welfare Systems in Comparative Perspective'. (Conference on 'Comparative Welfare Studies'), Roskilde University, 5–6 May, Department of Economics and Planning.

NIJKAMP, P., LEITNER, H. and WRIGLEY, N. (eds) (1985). *Measuring the Unmeasurable*. Dordrecht: Martinus Nijhoff Publishers.

NIJKAMP, P., RIETVEL P. and VOOGD H. (1990). *Multicriteria Evaluation in Physical Planning*. New York: North-Holland.

NORDHAUS, W. (1969). *Invention, Growth and Welfare: A Theoretical Treatment of Technological Change*. Cambridge, Mass.: MIT Press.

NORDHAUS, W. D. and TOBIN, J. (1973). 'Is Growth Obsolete?', in Moss, M. (ed.), *The Measurement of Economic and Social Performance*. New York: Columbia University Press.

NORSWORTHY, J. R., HARPER, J. M. and KUNZE, K. (1979). 'The Slowdown in Productivity Growth: Analysis of Some Contributing Factors', *Brookings Papers on Economic Activity*, no. 2, pp. 387–421.

OAKLAND, W. H. (1985). 'Theory of Public Goods', in Auerbach, A. J. and Feldstein, M. (eds), *Handbook of Public Economics*. Amsterdam: North-Holland.

O'CONNOR, J. (1973). *The Fiscal Crisis of the State*. New York: St. Martin's Press.

O'CONNOR, J. (1987). *The Meaning of Crisis*. Oxford: Blackwell.

OECD (1971). *Flexibility de l'âge de la retraite*. Paris: OECD.

OECD (1976). *Mésure du bien-etre social: un rapport sur les progrès d'élaboration des indicateurs sociaux*. Paris: OECD.

OECD (1977). *Toward Full Employment and Prince Stability* (McCracken Report). Paris: OECD.

OECD (1977–79). *Les déterminants structurels de l'emploi et du choumage*, 2 vols. Paris: OECD.

OECD (1978). *Public Expenditure Trends*. Paris: OECD.

OECD (1981). *The Welfare State in Crisis*. Paris: OECD.

OECD (1983). *Employment Outlook*. Paris: OECD.

OECD (1985a). *Social Expenditure 1960–1990: Problems of Growth and Control*. Paris: OECD.

OECD (1985b). *Employment Growth and Structural Change*. Paris: OECD.

OECD (1985c). *The Integration of Women into the Economy*. Paris: OECD.

OECD (1987). *The Future of Migration*. Paris: OECD.

OECD (1988a). *Ageing Population: The Social Policy Implications*. Paris: OECD.

OECD (1988b). 'The Future of Social Protection', *Series OECD Social Policy Studies*, no. 6.

OECD (1988c). 'Reforming Public Pensions', *Series OECD Social Policy Studies*, no. 5.

OECD (1989a). *Environmental Policy Benefits: Monetary Valutation* (by D. W. Pearce and A. Marhandya). Paris: OECD.

OECD (1989b). *Labour Market Flexibility: Trends in Enterprises* (by B. Bruhnes, J. Rojot and W. Wassermann). Paris: OECD.

OECD (1990). *Labour Market Policies of 1990s*. Paris: OECD.

OECD (1991). *Evaluating Labour Market and Social Programmes: The State of a Complex Art*. Paris: OECD.

OECD (1992). 'Private Pensions and Public Policy', *Series OECD Social Policy Studies*, no. 9.

OECD (1993). *The Changing Course of International Migration*. Paris: OECD.

OECD (1994a). *Disabled Youth and Employment*. Paris: OECD.

OECD (1994b). *Etude sur l'emploi et le chomage*. Paris: OECD.

OECD (1994c). *Evidence and Explanation: Part, I – Labour Market Trends and Underlying Forces of Change; Part. II – The Adjustment Potential of the Labour Market*. Paris: OECD.

OECD (1994d). 'Technologie, innovation et emploi', *Etude sur l'emploi et le chomage*. Paris: OECD.

OECD (1995a). *Flexible Working Time: Collective Bargaining and Government Intervention*. Paris: OECD.

OECD (1995b). *Household Production in OECD Countries: Data Sources and Measurement Methods*. Paris: OECD.

OECD (1995c). *Investment, Productivity and Employment*. Paris: OECD.

OECD (1995d). *The Labour Market and the Older Workers*. Paris: OECD.

OECD (1995e). *Trends in International Migration: Continuous Reporting System on Migration (Sopemi)*. Paris: OECD.

OECD (1996a). *Ageing in OECD Countries: A Critical Policy Challenge, No. 20*. Paris: OECD.

OECD (1996b). *Enhancing the Effectiveness of Active Labour Market Policies*. Paris: OECD.

OECD (1996c). *Job Creation and Loss: Analysis, Policy and Data Development*. Paris: OECD.

OECD (1996d). *Technology, Productivity and Job Creation: Vol. 1: Highlights; Vol. 2: Analytical Report*. Paris: OECD.

OFFE, C. (1985). *Disorganized Capitalism: Contemporary Transformations of Work and Politics* (edited by J. Keane). Cambridge, Mass.: MIT Press.

OFFE, C. (1985–86). 'New Social Movements: Challenging the Boundaries of Institutional Politics', in Maier, C. S. (ed.), *Changing Boundaries of the Political: Essays on the Evolving Balance between the State and Society, Public and Private in Europe.* Cambridge: Cambridge University Press.

OFFE, C. (1987). *Contradictions of the Welfare State*. London: Hutchinson Education.

OFFE, C. (1992). 'A Non-Productivist Design for Social Policies', in Van Parijs, P. (ed.), *Arguing for Basic Income: Ethical Foundations for a Radical Reform*. London: Verso.

OFFE, C. (1995). 'Full Employment: Asking the Wrong Question', *Dissent Winter.*

OFFE, C. and HEINZE, R. G. (1990). *Organisierte Eigenarbeit. Das Modell Kooperationsring*. Frankfurt/New York: Campus.

OFFE, C. and HEINZE, R. G. (1992). *Beyond Employment: Time, Work and the Informal Economy.* Cambridge: Polity Press.

OLK, T. and HEINZE, R. G. (1985). 'Selbsthilfe im Sozialsektor-Perspektiven der Informellen und Freiwilligen Produktion sozialer Dienstleistungen', in Olk, T. and Otto, H.-U. (eds), *Gesellschaftliche Perspektiven der Sozialarbeit 4: Lokale Sozialpolitik und Selbsthilfe*. Neuwied e Darmstadt: Luchterhand.

O'NEILL, M. (1989). *The Third America: The Emergence of the Nonprofit Sector in the United States*. San Francisco: Jossey-Bass.

ORLOFF, A. S. (1993). 'Gender and the Social Rights of Citizenship', *American Sociological Review*, vol. 58, no. 3, pp. 303–28.

OSBORNE, S. P. (1996). *Managing in the Voluntary Sector: A Handbook for Managers in Charitable and Non-profit Organizations*. London: International Thomson.

PAMPEL, F. C. and WILLIAMSON, J. B. (1989). *Age, Class, Politics and the Welfare State.* Cambridge: Cambridge University Press.

PAPANDREOU, A. (1972). *Paternalist Capitalism*. Minneapolis: University of Minnesota Press.

PARETO, V. (1896–7). *Cours d'économie politique*. Lausanne: Rouge.

PARETO, V. (1906). *Manuale di economia politica*. Milan: Società Editrice Libraria.

PARETO, V. (1913). 'Alcune relazioni tra lo stato sociale e le variazioni della prosperità economica', *Rivista italiana di sociologia*.

PARETO, V. (1916). *Trattato di sociologia generale*. Florence: Barbera.

PARETO, V. (1918). 'Economia sperimentale', *Il Giornale degli Economisti.*

PARKER, S. (1971). *The Future of Work and Leisure*. New York: Praeger.

PASCALL, G. (1986). *Social Policy – A Feminist Analysis*. London: Tavistock.

PASDERMADJAN, H. (1959). *La deuxième Révolution Industrielle*. Paris: Presses Universitaires de France.

PASINETTI, L. (1981). *Structural Change and Economic Growth: A Theoretical Essay on the Dynamics of the Wealth of Nations*. Cambridge, UK: Cambridge University Press.

PATEMAN, C. (1988). 'The Patriarchal Welfare State', in Guttman, A. (ed.), *Democracy and the Welfare State*. Princeton, NJ: Princeton University Press.

PAVITT, K. (1971). *The Conditions for Success in Technological Innovations*. Paris: OECD.

PAVITT, K. (1979). 'Technical Innovation and Industrial Development: The New Causalities', *Future*, no. 6.

PEACOCK, A. (1979). 'Public Expenditures Growth in Post-Industrial society', in Gustafsson, B. (ed.), *Post-Industrial Society*. London: Croom Helm.

PEDONE, A. (1981). *Some Notes on Public Expenditure Growth and Financing in Post-War Europe* (Report to the Meeting 'The Transformations of the Welfare State, Between History and Future Prospects') (roneo). Turin.

PENROSE, E. (1959). *The Theory of the Growth of the Firm*. New York: Wiley.

PETTMAN, B. O. (1977). 'Socio-Economic Systems', in Pettman, B. O. (ed.), *Social Economics: Concepts and Perspectives*. Hull: MCB.

PHELPS, E. S. (ed.) (1962). *Private Wants and Public Needs: Issues Surroundings the Size and Scope of Government Expenditure*. New York: Norton

PHELPS, E. S. (1972). *Inflation Policy and Unemployment Theory: The Cost–Benefit Approach to Monetary Planning*. New York: Norton.

PHELPS, E. S. (1997). *Rewarding Work: How to Restore Participation and Self-Support to Free Enterprise*. Cambridge, Mass.: Harvard University Press.

PIERSON, C. (1990). 'The "Exceptional" United States: First New Nation or Last Welfare State?', *Social Policy and Administration*, vol. 24, no. 3, pp. 186–98.

PIERSON, G. (1991). *Beyond the Welfare State? The New Political Economy of Welfare*. Cambridge: Polity Press.

PIGOU, A. C. (1920). *The Economics of Welfare:* London: Macmillan.

PIORE, M. J. (1983). 'Computer Technologies, Market Structure, and Strategic Union Choice' (MIT-Union Conference on 'Industrial Relations in Transition') mimeo, June 1983.

PIORE, M. J. and SABEL, F. C. (1984). *The Second Industrial Divide: Possibilities for Prosperity*. New York: Basic Books.

PIRENNE, H. (1913/14). 'The Stages in the Social History of Capitalism', *American Historical Review*, vol. XIX.

Planning Studies Centre (1993a). *Post Conference Notes. The First World-Wide Conference on Planning Science*, Palermo, Italy, 8–12 Sept.1992. Rome: Planning Studies Centre.

Planning Studies Centre (1993b). *Towards an International Organisation for the Advancement of Planning Science*. Rome: Planning Studies Centre.

POLANYI, K. (1944). *The Great Transformation*. New York and Toronto: Farrarand & Rinehart.

POLANYI, K. and ARENSBERG, C. M. (1975). *Les systèmes économiques dans l'histoire et dans le théorie*. Paris: Larousse.

POWELL, W. W. (ed.) (1987). *The Nonprofit Sector: A Research Handbook*. New Haven: Yale University Press.

PREBISH, R. (1984). 'Five Stages in My Thinking on Development', in Meier, G. M. (ed.), *Pioneers in Development*. New York and Oxford: Oxford University Press for World Bank.

PURTSCHERT, R. (1995). 'NPO-Forschung in der Schweiz', in Schaurer, R. *et al.* (eds), *Nonprofit-Organisationen (NPO) – drite Kraft zwischen Markt und Stat?* Linz: Universitätsverlag Rudolf Trauner.

REICHARD, C. (1988). 'Der Dritte Sektor-Entstehung, Funktion und Problematik von Nonprofit-Organisationen aus verwaltung- wissenschaftlicher Sicht', *Die Oeffentliche Verwaltung*, no. 9.

REIN, M. (1985). 'Women, Employment and Social Welfare', in Klein, R. and O'Higgins, M. (eds), *The Future of Welfare*. Oxford: Blackwell.

REYNOLDS, L. G. (1951). *The Structure of Labor Markets: Wages and Labor Mobility in Theory and Practice*. New York: Harper & Brothers.

REYNOLDS, L. G. (1971). *The Three Worlds of Economics*. New Haven: Yale University Press.

RIFKIN, J. (1995). *The End of Work: The Decline of the Global Labor Force and the Dawn of the Post-Market Era*. London: Putnam.

RIMLINGER, G. V. (1974). *Welfare Policy and Industrialization in Europe, America and Russia*. New York: Wiley.

RITTER, G. A. (1991). *Der Sozialstaat. Enstehung und Entwicklung im internationalen Vergleich*. Munich: Oldenburg Verlag.

ROBINSON, J. (1933). *Economics of Imperfect Competition*. London: Macmillan.

ROBSON, W. A. (1976). *Welfare State and Welfare Society*. London: Allen & Unwin.

ROCARD, M. (1981). 'Le tiers secteur, c'est la primaute de l'individu sur l'argent', *Autrement*.

ROHRLICH, G. F. (1977). 'Social Economics: Concepts and Perspectives', in PETTMAN, B. O. (ed.), *Social Economics: Concepts and Perspectives*. Hull: MCB Books.

ROSANVALLON, P. (1981). *La crise de l'Etat Providence*. Paris: Seuil.

ROSANVALLON, P. (1988). 'Beyond the Welfare State', *Politics and Society*, vol. 16, no. 4, pp. 533–44.

ROSANVALLON, P. (1995). *La nouvelle question sociale: repenser l'Etat-providence*. Paris: Editions du Seuil.

ROSE, R. (ed.) (1980). *The Challenge the Governance: Studies in Overloaded Policies*. London: Sage.

ROSE-ACKERMAN, S. (ed.) (1986). *The Economics of Nonprofit Institutions: Studies in Structure and Policy*. New York: Oxford University Press.

ROSEN, C. (1981). *Employee Ownership: Issues, Resources and Legislation*. Arlington, Va.: National Center for Employee Ownership.

ROSENBERG, N. (1976). *Perspective on Technology*. Cambridge: Cambridge University Press.

ROSENBERG, N. (1982). *Inside the Black Box: Technology and Economics*. Cambridge, UK: Cambridge University Press.

ROSENBERG, N. (1994). *Exploring the Black Box: Technology, Economics and History*, Cambridge, UK: Cambridge University Press.

ROSENSTEIN-RODAN, P. N. (1961). 'Programming in the Theory and in Italian Practice', in TINBERGEN J. *et al*. (eds), *Investment Criteria and Economic Growth*. New York: Asia.

ROSENSTEIN-RODAN, P. N. (1984). 'Natura Facit Saltum', in Meier, M. G. and Seers, D. (eds), *Pioneers in Development*. New York: Oxford University Press for the World Bank.

ROSSELLI, C. (1994, orig. 1937). *Liberal Socialism*. Princeton: Princeton University Press.

ROSTOW, W. W. (1952). *The Process of Economic Growth*. Oxford: Clarendon.

ROSTOW, W. W. (1960). *The Stages of Economic Growth*. Cambridge: Cambridge University Press.

ROSTOW, W. W. (1971). *Politics and the Stages of Growth*. Cambridge: Cambridge University Press.

ROSTOW, W. W. (1978). *The World Economy: History and Prospect*. Austin: University of Texas Press.

ROSTOW, W. W. (1990). *Theorists of Economic Growth from David Hume to the Present, with a Perspective on the Next Century*. New York and Oxford: Oxford University Press.

RUFFOLO, G. (1967). *La grande impresa nella società moderna*. Turin: Einaudi.

RUFFOLO, G. (1984). *La qualità sociale. Le vie dello sviluppo*. Rome and Bari: Laterza.

RUFFOLO, G. (1988). *Potenza e Potere*. Rome and Bari: Laterza.

RUFFOLO, G. (1996). 'Immaginiamo un varco tra economia e società', *Politica ed economia*, no. 1/2.

RUFFOLO, G. (1997). 'Europa senza soggetto, sinistra senza progetto', in Delors, J. and Ruffolo, G. (eds), *Sinistra di fine secolo*. Milan: Reset.

SACHS, I. (1982). *La crise, le progrès technique et l'économie caché*. Paris: Ecole des Hautes Etudes en Sciences Sociales.

SACHS, I. (1987). *Development and Planning*. Cambridge: Cambridge University Press.

SAINT-SIMON, H. C. de (1965). *La physiologie sociale*. Paris.

SAINT-SIMON, H. C. de (1975). *Oeuvres Completes (1868–1878)*. *Completées par tous les textes tardifs, dispersés et inedits, publiés ou manuscrits*. *(6 vols)*. Paris and Geneva: Slatkine.

SALAMON, L. M. (1989). 'The Changing Partnership Between the Voluntary Sector and the State', in Hodgkinson, V. A., Lyman, W. R. and Associates (eds), *The Future of the Nonprofit Sector*. San Francisco: Jossey-Bass Publishers.

SALAMON, L. M. (1990). 'The Nonprofit Sector and Government: The American Experience in Theory and Practice', in Anheiel, H. and Seibel, W. (eds.), *The Third Sector: Comparative Studies of Nonprofit Organisations*. New York and Berlin: Walter de Gruyter.

SALAMON, L. M. (1995). *Partners in Public Service: Government–Nonprofit Relations in the Modern Welfare State*. Baltimore, Md.: Johns Hopkins University Press.

SALAMON, L. M. and ANHEIER, H. K. (eds) (1992). *Defining the Nonprofit Sector in Twelve Countries*. Baltimore: The Johns Hopkins University Press.

SALAMON, L. M. and ANHEIER H. K. (1994). *The Emerging Nonprofit Sector: An Overview*. Baltimore: The Johns Hopkins University, Institute for Policy Studies.

SALAMON, L. M. and ANHEIER, H. K. (1996). *In Search of the Non Profit Sector: A Cross-National Analysis*. New York: Manchester University Press.

SALAMON, L. M. and TOEPLER, S. (1997). *The International Guide to Nonprofit Law*. New York: Wiley.

SALAMON, L. M., GIDRON, B. and KRAMER, R. M. (eds) (1992). *Government and the Third Sector: Emerging Relationship in Welfare States*. San Francisco: Jossey-Bass.

SALANTI, A. and SCREPANTI, E. (eds) (1997). *Pluralism in Economics: New Perspectives in History and Methodology*. Cheltenham, UK: Edward Elgar.

SAMUELSON, P. A. (1954). 'The Pure Theory of Public Expenditure', *Review of Economics and Statistics*, vol. 36, pp. 387–9.

SAMUELSON, P. A. (1965). 'A Theory of Induced Innovations along Kennedy–Weisacker Lines', *Review of Economic and Statistics*, vol. 47.

SANTARELLI, E. and ARCHIBUGI, D. (1990). 'Teoria, storia e istituzioni nell'analisi economica del cambiamento tecnologico', in Archibugi, D. and Santarelli, E. (eds), *Cambiamento tecnologico e sviluppo industriale*. Milan: Franco Angeli.

SAUVY, A. (1956). *Théorie générale de la population. Volume 1: Economie et population*. Paris: PUF.

SCHAAF, M. (1977). *Cooperatives at the Crossroads: The Potential for a Major Economic and Social Role* (Explorating Project for Economic Alternatives). Washington.

SCHAURER, R. (1995). 'NPO-Foprschung in Österreich', in Schaurer, R. *et al.* (eds), *Nonprofit-Organisationen (NPO) – dritte Kraft zwischen Markt und Staat?*. Linz: Universitätsverlag Rudolf Trauner.

SCHAURER, R. *et al.* (eds) (1995). *Nonproft-Organisationen (NPO) – drite kraft zwischen Markt und Staat?*. Linz: Universitätsverlag Rudolf Trauner.

SCHERER, F. M. (1986). *Innovation and Growth: Schumpeterian Perspectives*. Cambridge, Mass.: MIT Press.

SCHETTKAT, R. (1990). 'Innovation and Labour Market Adjustment', in Matzner, E. and Wagner, M. (eds), *The Employment Impact of New Technology: The Case of West Germany*. Aldershot: Avebury.

SCHIRAY, M. and VIVANER, K. (1980). 'Consommation, Usage du Temps et Style de Vie. Vers un Economie Politique du Hors-Marché', *Futuribles*, no. 32.

SCHMID, T. (ed.) (1984). *Befreiung von falscher Arbeit. Thesen zum garantierten Mindesteinkommen*. Berlin.

SCHMOOKLER, J. (1962). 'Changes in Industry and in the State of Knowledge as Determinations of Industrial Invention', in NBER, *The Rate and Direction of Inventive Activity: Economic and Social Factors*. Princeton: Princeton University Press.

SCHNYDER, S. (1995). 'Dritte Sector oder die Nonprofit- Organisationen (NPO) in der Schweiz', in Schaurer, R. *et al.* (eds), *Nonprofit-Organisationen (NPO) – dritte Kraft zwischen Markt und Staat?*. Linz: Universitätatsverlag Rudolf Trauner.

SCHOTTLAND, C. (ed.) (1977). *The Welfare State in Historical Perspective*. London: Harper & Row.

SCHUMACHER, E. F. (1973). *Small is Beautiful: Economics As If People Mattered*. New York: Harper & Row.

SCHUMPETER, J. A. (1911). *Theorie der Wirtschaftlichen Entwicklung* (1st edn, 1911; English edn, 1934, Oxford University Press; Italian trans. 1971, Sansoni).

SCHUMPETER, J. A. (1918). 'The Crisis of the Tax State', *Reprinted International Economic Papers*, no. 4, 1954.

SCHUMPETER, J. A. (1928). 'Sulla instabilità del capitalismo (Trad. it. della seconda parte del saggio, in C. Napoleoni, Il futuro del capitalismo, Laterza, 1970)', *Economic Journal*, 1928.

SCHUMPETER, J. A. (1939). *Business Cycles: A Theoretical, Historical and Statistical Analysis of the Capitalist Process*. New York: McGraw-Hill.

SCHUMPETER, J. A. (1956) (orig. 1942). *Capitalism, Socialism, and Democracy*. London: Allen & Unwin.

SCHUMPETER, J. A. (1949). 'The Historical Approach to the Analysis of Business Cycles', in Schumpeter, J. A. (ed.), *Essays*. Cambridge, Mass.: Addison-Wesley.

SCHUMPETER, J. A. (1954). *History of Economic Analysis*. New York: Oxford University Press.

SCITOWSKY, T. (1964). 'What Price Economic Growth?', *Papers on Welfare and Growth*.

SCITOWSKY, T. (1976). *The Joyless Economy: An Enquiry into Human Satisfaction and Consumer Dissatisfaction*. New York: Oxford University Press.

SÉE, H. (1951). *Les origines du capitalisme moderne*. Paris: Colin.

SEERS, D. (1979). 'The Birth, Life and Death of Development Economics', *Development and Change*, vol. 10, no. 3, pp. 707–18.

SEIBEL, W. (1990). 'Organizational Behavior and Organizational Function: Toward a Micro-Macro Theory of the Third Sector', in Anheier, H. K. and Seibel, W. (eds), *The Third Sector: Comparative Studies of Nonprofit Organizations*. Berlin and New York: De Gruyter.

SEIBEL, W. (1992). *Funktionaler Dilettantimus. Erfolgreich scheiternde Organisationen im 'Dritten Sector' swischen Markt un Staat*. Baden-Baden: Nomos.

SEN, A. K. (1976). 'Poverty: An Ordinal Approach to Measurement', *Econometrica*, no. 44, pp. 219–31.

SEN, A. K. (1979). 'Issues in the Measurement of Poverty', *Scandinavian Journal of Economics*, no. 81, pp. 285–307.

SEN, A. K. (1983). 'Poor, Relatively Speaking', *Oxford Economic Papers*, no. 35, pp. 153–69.

SHILS, E. (1968). *Criteria for Scientific Development: Public Policy and National Goals*. Cambridge, Mass.: MIT Press.

SHONFIELD, A. and SHAW, S. (1972). *Social Indicators and Social Policy*. London: Heinemann Education Books.

SILVERBERG, G. and SOETE, L. (eds) (1994). *The Economics of Growth and Technical Change: Technologies, Nations, Agents*. Aldershot: Edward Elgar.

SIMIAND, F. (1903). 'Causal Interpretation and Historical Research', *Revue de synthese historique* (trans. in Lane, F. C. and J. C. Riemersma, *Enterprise and Secular Change: Readings in Economic History*, Allen, London 1953).

SINDEN, J. A. and WORRELL, A. C. (1979). *Unpriced Values: Decisions Without Market Prices*. New York: Wiley.

SINGER, C. (1952). *Technology and History*. London: Oxford University Press.

SINGER, C. *et al*. eds (1954–84). *A History of Technology*, 8 vols. London: Clarendon Press.

SIRAGELDIN, I. A. (1969). *Non-Market Components of National Income*. Ann Arbor: University of Michigan Press.

SKOCPOL, T. (1985). 'Bringing the State Back In: Strategies of Analysis in Current Research', in EVANS, P. B. *et al*. (eds), *Bringing the State Back In*. Cambridge: Cambridge University Press.

SKOCPOL, T. (1987). 'America's Incomplete Welfare State', in Rein, M., Esping-Andersen, G. and Rainwater, M. (eds), *Stagnation and Renewal*. New York: M. E. Sharpe.

SKOCPOL, T. and IKENBERRY, J. (1983). 'The Political Formation of the American Welfare State: An Historical and Comparative Perspective', in Tomasson, R. F. (ed.), *The Welfare State, 1883–1983: Comparative Social Research*. London: Jai Press.

SOLOW, R. M. (1966). 'The Case Against the Guidepost', in Schultz, G. P. and Aliber, R. Z. (eds), *Guidelines, Informal Controls and the Market Place*. Chicago: University of Chicago Press.

SOMOGYI, S. (1979). *Introduzione alla demografia*. Palermo: Università di Palermo.

SOUTH, N. (1980). 'The Informal Economy and Local Labour Markets' (A Review of some of the Relevant Literature, Bibliographic References and some Suggestions for Future Research) (mimeo), Centre for Occupational & Community Research, Middlesex Polytechnic.

SPIETHOFF, A. (1948). 'Pure Theory and Economic Gestalt Theory: Ideal Type and Real Type', in Lane, F. C. and Riemersma, J. C. (eds), *Enterprise and Secular Change, Readings in Economic History*. London: Allen & Unwin, 1952.

STANBACK T. M. Jr. *et al*. (1981). *Services: The New Economy*. Columbia University.

STEINER, G. A. (1997). *Strategic Planning: What Every Manager Must Know*. New York: Free Press.

STEPHENS, J. (1979). *The Transition from Capitalism to Socialism*. London: Macmillan.

STOKES, B. (1981). *Helping Ourselves: Local Solutions to Global Problems*. New York: Norton.

STOLERU, L. (1973). 'Politique sociale et garantie de revenu', *Analyse et prevision*.

STONEMANN, P. (1983). *The Economic Analysis of Technological Change*. Oxford: Oxford University Press.

STONEMANN, P. (1987). *The Economic Analysis of Technology Policy*. Oxford: Oxford University Press.

STONEMANN, P. (ed.) (1995). *Handbook of the Economics of Innovation and Technological Change*. Oxford: Blackwell.

SYLOS LABINI, P. (1950). 'Le problème des cycles économiques de longue durée', *Economie appliquée*, no. 3–4, pp. 481–95.

SYLOS LABINI, P. (1956). *Oligopoly and Technical Progress* (English translation). Cambridge, Mass.: Harvard University Press, 1969.

SYLOS LABINI, P. (1970). *Problemi dello sviluppo economico*. Bari: Laterza.

SYLOS LABINI, P. (1974). *Trade Unions, Inflation, and Productivity*. Lexington, Mass.: Lexington Books.

SYLOS LABINI, P. (1984). *The Forces of Economic Growth and Decline*. Cambridge, Mass.: MIT Press.

SYLOS LABINI, P. (1989). *Nuove tecnologie e disoccupazione*. Bari and Rome: Laterza.

SYLOS LABINI, P. (1992). 'Capitalism, Socialism, Democracy and Large-Scale Firms', in Scherer, F. M. and Perlman, M. (eds), *Entrepreneurship, Technological Innovation and Economic Growth: Studies in the Schumpeterian Tradition*. Ann Arbor: The University of Michigan Press.

SYLOS LABINI, P. (1993). *Economic Growth and Business Cycles: Prices and the Process of Cyclical Development*. Aldershot, England: Edward Elgar.

SYRQUIN, M. (1988). 'Patterns of Structural Change', in Chenery, H. and Srinivasan, N. T. (eds), *Handbook of Development Economics (Vol. I)*. Amsterdam: North-Holland.

TADDEI, D. (1989). *Enjeux Economiques et Sociaux du Temps de Travail dans la Communauté* (Rapport pour la DGII, CEE – version roneo, Janvier 1989).

TAROZZI, A. and BERNFELD, D. (1981). *Il volontariato: un fenomeno internazionale*. Milan: Angeli.

TARSCHYS, D. (1975). 'The Growth of Public Expenditure: Nine Modes of Explanation', *Scandinavian Political Studies*, vol. 10.

TAYLOR, R. (1994). *The Future of the Trade Unions*. London: TUC.

TEN (Cooperative des Conseil, Paris) (1979). Les Services Collectifs, 3 vols (Enquete menée dans 3 villes en France, 3 villes en R-U, 3 villes en Rep. Fed. d'Allemagne: Programme de recherche et d'actions sur l'évolution du marché du travail) (mimeo). Bruxelles: Commission CEE.

TEN HOVE, M. D. (ed.) (1986). *The Institutions of a Changing Welfare State. The Future of the Welfare State, Vol. II. Work & Society*, N.2. Maastricht: Presses Interuniversitaires Européennes.

TERLECKYJ, N. E. (1974). *The Effect of R & D on Productivity Growth in Industry*. Washington: NPA.

TERLECKYJ, N. E. (ed.) (1975). *Household Production and Consumption*. New York: NBER (National Bureau of Economic Research).

THANE, P. (1982). *Foundations of the Welfare State*. London: Longman.

THANE, P. (1987). 'The Coming Burden of an Ageing Population?', *Journal of Social Policy*, vol. 7, no. 4.

THEOBALD, R. ed. (1965). *The Guaranteed Income: Next Step in Economic Evolution?*. New York: Doubleday.

THEOBALD, R. (1972). *Economize Abundance: A Non-Inflationary Future*. Chicago: Swallow Press.

THEOBALD, R. (1987). *The Rapid Change: Social Entrepreneurship in Turbulent Times*. Indianapolis: Knowledge Systems, Inc.

THEOBALD, R. (1992). *Turning the Century: Personal and Organizational Strategies for Your Changed World*. Indianapolis: Knowledge Systems, Inc.

THERBORN, G. and ROEBROEK, J. (1986). 'The Irreversible Welfare State: Its Recent Maturation, its Encounter with the Economics Crisis, its Future Prospects', in Albeda, W. (ed.), *The Future of the Welfare State*. Maastricht: Presses Interuniversitaires Européennes.

THUROW, L. C. (1981b). *The Zero-Sum Society: Distribution and the Possibilities for Economic Change*. New York: Penguin Books.

THUROW, L. C. (1996). *The Future of Capitalism: How Today's Economic Forces Shape Tomorrow's World*. New York: W. Morrow.

TILLY C. *et al.* (1990). *Causes and Consequences of Part-Time Work*. Washington, DC: Economic Policy Institute.

TINBERGEN, J. (1964). *Central Planning*. New Haven: Yale University Press.

TINBERGEN, J. (1981). 'Kondratiev Cycles and So-Called Long Waves. The Early Research', *Futures*, vol. 13, no. 4 pp. 258–63.

TINBERGEN, J. *et al.* (1967). 'Convergence of Economic Systems in East and West', in BENOIT E. (ed.), *Disarmament and World Economic Interdependence*. Oslo: Universitëtsforlaget.

TITMUSS, R. M. (1968). *Essays on 'The Welfare State'*. London: Allen & Unwin.

TITMUSS, R. M. (1979). *Commitment to Welfare*. London: Allen & Unwin.

TOCQUEVILLE DE, A. (1835–1840). 'De la democratie en Amerique', in Edition (1967) sous la direction de J. P. Mayer, *Oeuvres complètes*. Paris: Gallimard.

TOFFLER, A. (1980). *The Third Wave*. New York: Morrow.

TOMASSON, R. F. (ed.) (1983). *The Welfare State, 1883–1983: Comparative Social Research*. London: Jai Press.

TORTAROLO, E. (1989). *La ragione sulla Sprea. Coscienza storica e cultura politica nell'illuminismo berlinese*. Bologna: Il Mulino.

TOURAINE, A. (1969). *La societé post-industrielle*. Paris: Donoel-Gonthier.

TOURAINE, A. (1973). *Production de la societé*. Paris: Ed. du Seuil.

TOURAINE, A. (1992). *Critique de la modernité*. Paris: Fayarde.

TOYNBEE, A. (1884). *The Industrial Revolution* (Other edn, 1956, Boston: Beacon Press).

TSAKLOGLOU, P. (1996a). 'Elderly and non-elderly in the European Union: a comparison of living standard'. *Review of Income and Wealth*, No. 3, September 1996, pp. 271-91

TSAKLOGLOU, P. (1996b). 'On relative welfare position of older persons in the member-states of the European Union: evidence and policy implications', in T. Georgapoulos, R. Grinspun, C. Paraskevopoulos, *Economic integeration and public policy: NAFTA, EU and beyond*. London: Edward Elgar.

UN (1956). *Le viellissement des populations et ses consequences économiques et sociales*. New York: UN.

UN (1973). *Distribution Policies in Long-term Development Planning*. New York: UN.

UN (1975). *Towards a System of Social and Demographic Statistics*. New York: UN.

UN (1982). *Report of the World Assembly on Ageing (Vienna 6–26 August 1982)*. New York and Geneva: UN.

UN (1991). *Ageing and Urbanisation (A Collection of Reports and Recommendations of the Sendai Conference held in Japan in September 1988)*. Japan: UN.

UN (1992a). *Annuaire démographique. Edition speciale: Vieillissement de la population et situation des personnes âgées*. New York: UN.

UN (1992b). *Economic and Social Implications of Population Aging*. Geneva: UN.

UN (1993a). *System of National Accounts*, 1993. New York: UNO.

UN (1993b). *Integrated Environmental and Economic Accounting*. New York: UNO.

UN-ECE (1967). *Macro-Economic Models for Planning and Policy-Making* (Paper for the 4th Meeting of Senior Economic Advisors to ECE Governments, June 1966). Geneva: UN.

UN-ECE (1970). *Multi-Level Planning and Decision-Making* (Paper presented to the 6th Meeting of Senior Economic Advisers to ECE Governments, November 1968). New York: UN.

UN-ECE (1974). *Politiques de répartition dans la planification à long terme du développement*. New York: UN.

UN-ECE (1975). 'Use of Systems of Models in Planning'. (Seminar on the Use of Systems of Models in Planning), Moscow, 2–11 December 1974, UN 1975.

UN-ECE (1979). *Employment, Income Distribution and Consumption. Long-term Objectives and Structural Changes*. New York: UNO.

UNSO (1975). *A System of Demographic and Social Statistics*. New York: UNO.

URBINATI, N. (1994). 'The Liberal Socialism of Carlo Rosselli', *Dissent*, Winter 1994.

US Advisory Commitee on National Growth Policy Processes (1977). *Forging America's Future: Strategies for National Growth & Development (Report of the 'Advisory Committee on National Growth Policy Processes')*. Washington, DC: US Advisory Commitee on National Growth Policy Processes.

US Congress (Joint Economic Committee) (1979). *The Effective Utilization of Small Business to Promote Economic Growth*. Washington, DC: GPO.

US Department of Commerce (1967). *Technological Innovation: Its Environment and Management (Charpie Report)*. Washington, DC.

US Office of Consumer Affairs (1980). *People Power*. Washington, DC: US Office of Consumer Affairs.

UUSITALO, H. (1984). 'Comparative Research on the Determinants of the Welfare State', *European Journal of Political Research*, vol. 12, no. 1, pp. 21–33.

VAN BUIREN, S. (1981). 'New Information Technologies and Small Scale Job Creation (The Alternative Economy and Job Creation in the USA with Policy Recommendation Applicable to the European Context)', Study by Battelle Institut E. V. for the EEC Commission (mimeo). Brussels: European Commission.

VANOLI, A. and RANCI, C. (1994). *Beni pubblici e virtù private. Il terzo settore nelle politiche di welfare*. Milan: Fondazione Adriano Olivetti.

VEBLEN, T. (1923). *Absentee Ownership and Business Enterprise in Recent Times: The Case of America*. New York: Huebsh.

VERCELLI, A. (1989). 'Un riesame critico della teoria schumpeteriana della "transizione" al socialismo', in Jossa, B. (a cura di), *Teoria dei Sistemi Economici* ('Biblioteca dell'Economista', Serie VIII). Turin: UTET.

VIF (Vanier Institute of the Family) (1976). *Seeing Our Whole Economy: Families and Communities as the Economic Foundation of the Economy*. Ottawa.

VIF (Vanier Institute of the Family) (1979). *Exploring Work and Income Opportunities in the 1980's: Our Future in the Informal Economy*. Ottawa.

VOLPI, F. (1989). 'Sistema economico e modo di produzione', in Jossa, B. (a cura di), *Teoria dei Sistemi Economici*, ('Biblioteca dell'Economista', Serie VIII). Turin: UTET.

VONDERACH, G. (1980). 'Die neue Selbstandigen', *Mittel AB,*.

VONDERACH, G. (1981). 'Eigeninitiativen, Informelle Arbeit und Arbeitszeitflexibilität, Uberlegungen zu einer wunschbaren Umstrukturierung der Arbeitsgesellschaft', in Hinrichs, K., Offe, C. and Wiesenthal, H. (eds), *Arbeitzeitpolitik und Wandel*. Frankfurt and New York: Campus.

VONDERACH, G. (1982). 'New Self-Employed – New Working Life?', in Huber, J. *et al.* (eds), *Developments of the Informal Sector in the FRG* (Document prepared for the Conference on 'The Informal Economy, Social Conflicts and the Future of the Industrial Society', Nov. 1982). Rome-Frascati.

VOOGD, Henk (1983), *Multicriteria Evaluation for Urban and Regional Planning.* London: Pion.

WALZER, M. (1988). 'Socializing the Welfare State', *Dissent*, pp. 292–300.

WEBER, M. (1922). *Gesammelte Aufsätze sur Wissenschaftslehre* (ed. J. Winckelmam). Tübingen.

WEBER, M. (1968). *Economy and Society*, 3 vols. New York: Bedminster.

WEIR, M., ORLOFF, A. S. and SKOCPOL, T. (eds) (1988). *The Politics of Social Policy in the United States*. Princeton, NJ: Princeton University Press.

WEISBROD, A. B. (1977a). 'Toward a Theory of the Voluntary Nonprofit Sector in a Three Sector Economy', in Weisbrod, A. B. (ed.), *The Voluntary Nonprofit Sector*. Lexington: D. Heath.

WEISBROD, A. B. (ed.) (1977b). *The Voluntary Non-Profit Sector*. Lexington, Mass.: Lexington Books.

WEISBROD, A. B. (1988). *The Non-Profit Economy*. Cambridge, Mass.: Harvard University Press.

WEISBROD, A. B. (1989). 'The Complexities of Income Generation for Non-Profits', in Hodgkinson, V., Lyman, W. R. and Associates (eds), *The Future of the Nonprofit Sector*. San Francisco: Jossey-Bass Publishers.

WHITE, W. F. (1978). *In Support of the Voluntary Job Preservation and Community Stabilization Act*. Ithaca, USA: Cornell University Press.

WHITE, W. F. and BLASI, J. R. (1982). 'Worker Ownership, Participation and Control: Toward a Theoretical Model', *Policy Sciences*.

WHOLEY, S. J., HATRY, P. H. and NEWCOMER, E. K. (eds) (1994). *Handbook of Practical Program Evaluation*. San Francisco: Jossey-Bass Publishers.

WILKINSON, F. (1981). *The Dynamics of Labour Market Segmentation*. London: Academic Press.

WILLIAMS, J., WILLIAMS, K., CUTLER, A. and HASLAM, C. (1987). 'The End of Mass Production?', *Economy and Society*, vol. 16, no. 3, pp. 405–39.

WILLIAMS, S. *et al.* (1981). *Youth Without: Three Countries Approach the Problem: Report*. Paris: OECD.

WILLIAMS, S. (1984). *Employment Creation in the 'Third Sector'. A Commentary on Professor Archibugi's Paper*. Paris: OECD.

WILLIAMS, S. (1985). *A Job to Live: The Impact of Tomorrow's Technology on Work and Society*. Harmondsworth, Middlesex: Penguin Books.

WILSON, E. (1977). *Women and the Welfare State*. London: Tavistock.

WILSON, S. (1995). *New Challenges for Work and Society: Can the Social Economy Provide an Answer?* (Report of a Seminar 5–6 December 1995, held by the Franco-British Council).

WISMER, S. and PELL, D. (1981). *Community Profit: Community Based Economic Development in Canada*. Toronto: Is Five Press.

YOUNG, R. D. (1983). *If Not for Profit, for What? A Behavioural Theory of Non-Profit Sector Based on Entrepreneurship*. Lexington, Mass.: Lexington Books.

YOUNG, R. D. (1986). 'Entrepreneurship and the Behaviour of Nonprofit Organizations: Elements of a Theory', in Rose-Ackerman, S. (ed.), *The Economics of Non-profit Institutions*. New York: Oxford University Press.

ZANDVAKILI, S. (1994). 'International comparison of household inequalities based on microdata with decomposition', in D. P. papadimitriou (ed.) *Aspects of Distribution of Wealth and Income.* (The Jerome Levy Economic Institute Series). New York: St Martin's Press,

ZWERDLING, D. (1980). *Workplace Democracy*. New York: Harper.

Author Index

Subject Index